The
Motorcaravan
Manual

Choosing, using and maintaining your motorcaravan

Third Edition

John Wickersham

Author: John Wickersham
Project Manager: Sophie Blackman
Page build: James Robertson
Photographs: John Wickersham
Illustrations: Geoff Denney

© John Wickersham 2012

First published 1998
Reprinted 1999, 2001 (twice), 2002 (twice), and 2003
Revised 2nd Edition 2004
Reprinted 2007, 2008, 2009 and 2010
Revised 3rd Edition 2012

Published by: Haynes Publishing, Sparkford,
Yeovil, Somerset BA22 7JJ, UK

A catalogue record for this book is available
from the British Library

ISBN 978 0 85733 124 3

Printed in the USA by Odcombe Press LP,
1299 Bridgestone Parkway, LA Vergne, TN 37086

While every effort is taken to ensure the accuracy of the information given in this book, no liability can be accepted by the author or publishers for any loss, damage or injury caused by errors in, or omissions from, the information given.

Photograph above: The Matrix is one of the popular VW van conversions from Middlesex Motorcaravans.
Cover photograph: The Approach SE 760 from Bailey of Bristol was first launched in October 2011.

Gas Regulations

Gas Regulations and the way in which appliance manufacturers interpret them regarding the installation of their products are subject to continuing change. It is *strongly recommended* that anyone contemplating the installation of a gas appliance should consult the appliance manufacturer's customer service department before undertaking any work themselves. This may reveal different recommendations from those stated here, in which it is suggested that a competent amateur could consider tackling the preliminary carpentry and fitting work in accordance with the installation instructions. However, it is suggested in the chapters concerned with gas systems and appliances that work on the gas connection(s), flues and the final testing of an installation should always be entrusted to a competent and appropriately qualified gas engineer as defined on page 117.

Contents

Foreword

The Motorcaravan Manual is brim full of useful information and The Camping and Caravanning Club is delighted to be able to recommend this educational read. This highly regarded guide offers valuable motorcaravan knowledge across a breadth of topics in an informal style. It will undoubtedly become a firm favourite with our 60,000 club members who use motorcaravans, and in turn, we're certain it will generate interest across the motorcaravan industry.

Robert Louden
The Camping and Caravanning Club

Fourteen years after the initial conception of The Motorcarvan Manual, The Caravan Club welcomes the latest edition by Haynes. Written by a motorcaravanner, for motorcaravanners, the Manual addresses the questions that you have always wanted the answer to, and provides exclusive information that is unlikely to be found elsewhere. Approximately a quarter of Caravan Club members use a motorcaravan, and the value of knowing more about such a significant investment cannot be underestimated. With ever-evolving model designs, maintenance requirements and system updates, along with changing laws and regulations, an updated version of this must-have manual is invaluable for all motorcaravanners.

Nick Lomas
The Caravan Club

In the last seven years, motorcaravanning has grown faster than any other area of travel camping, and John Wickersham has fully revised this book to suit. John is well known for writing in great detail what he knows to be true, and using both description and photography, he shows you how it should be done. Motorcaravans now include more features and equipment than ever before, and there is a larger choice of layouts that may or may not suit your vehicle, so buying and maintaining a motorcaravan has become a challenge for us all. The Motor Caravanners' Club started in 1960 due to the enthusiasm of self-builders, and continues to grow today. Our club is proud to be associated with this work.

Rik Whittaker
The Motor Caravanners' Club

Introduction

Help given by industry specialists, advice from hundreds of motorcaravan owners, and experiences gained from practical projects have enabled me to compile this third edition of *The Motorcaravan Manual*. And haven't things changed since the first edition appeared in 1998!

Motorcaravans are remarkable vehicles and there is so much to learn about different types – and accessories, too. This is why I am grateful to Martin Spencer who agreed to write the appendix on Standard and Regulations. Frankly, I don't enjoy spending hours trawling through Government websites, whereas Martin, who is the Technical Manager of The Caravan Club, attends countless important committees as part of his job. Accordingly, he has kindly passed on information regarding ever-changing Codes of Practice and Legal Directives that underpin practical issues contained in the text.

Avoiding the job of compiling a compendium of European legislation left me time to conduct more motorcaravan tests for magazine reports. It also provided space in a busy schedule to tackle another self-building project. My first two DIY motorcaravans have been coachbuilt models and

I was eager to embark on a van conversion. So I purchased a pre-owned VW T5 van, and after 12 months of exacting work with a former teaching colleague, the project is now complete.

Hands-on jobs such as this contribute to knowledge about products and manufacturing techniques, and are a chance to see how they work. Some installation tasks have thus been included in the final chapter of this manual, which outlines several popular improvement projects. However, less space is devoted to self-build projects for one very good reason. After the previous manual was published in 2004, I was invited by Haynes Publishing to write *Build Your Own Motorcaravan,* and that is now the sourcebook for self-build advice.

By removing self-build case histories and then begging a further 20 pages over and above the publisher's limit, I can confidently claim that readers are now offered the most comprehensive *Motorcaravan Manual* ever produced. I hope you enjoy the pictorial presentations supporting all the technical content.

John Wickersham
January 2012

Although we use the word 'motorcaravan', the term encompasses a wide range of different leisure vehicles. In this opening chapter, we compare contrasting designs and draw attention to strengths and weaknesses of different models – both on the road and on-site.

Campervans, coachbuilts, recreational vehicles and van conversions are particular types of motorcaravan. Then there are dismountables, high-tops, low-lines, A-Class and more besides! It can all be a bit confusing so the aim of this introductory chapter is to explain what all these terms mean. Distinguishing features are highlighted and critical comments offered because the different vehicles all have their own strengths and weaknesses.

Driving characteristics

The 'perfect' motorcaravan would offer the driving characteristics of a car as well as providing spacious comfort in the living area. Some types of campervan *have* been designed in the past using car components, including the engine, transmission, instrumentation and suspension systems. For instance, the Rickman Rancher was based on

Mk1 or 2 Ford Escort parts. Similarly, the self-build Starcraft used a radically modified Ford Cortina. Notwithstanding the origin of their automotive elements, these unusual projects were not particularly renowned for good driving characteristics and are seldom seen on the roads today.

Another strategy successfully employed by some manufacturers, *eg* Wheelhome, involves the conversion of multi-purpose 'people carriers'. These types of vehicle are undoubtedly 'car-like' to drive and the constructor replaces some of the rear seats with a compact kitchen, a miniature refrigeration unit and a fold-out sleeping facility. However, a pre-converted base vehicle is usually costly and this is probably the main reason why few models are built this way.

In contrast, most medium-sized motorcaravans are based on light commercial vehicles, (LCVs) and today these are far easier to drive than the models of 20 years ago. Large motorcaravans are constructed using *heavy* commercial vehicles as their base unit and are more comfortable inside the cab than many people realise. Features such as power steering, sprung seating, and smooth transmission systems all help to make the driving experience a pleasant one. On the other hand, it would be quite wrong to imply that these are 'car-like' vehicles to manoeuvre. They are not, and if your touring holidays are likely to include places like the rural areas of the West Country or remote venues in the Scottish Highlands, large vehicles are not suitable on many of the roads. Irrespective of the grand interiors found in American Recreational Vehicles (RVs), this type of motorcaravan is more at home on interstate highways than on country lanes in Europe.

Engine options

A key element for any buyer to consider is a motorcaravan's engine. Many of the commercial base vehicles used by motorcaravan builders in the 1990s and earlier were slow off the mark, ponderous

The Rickman Rancher is one of the few motorcaravans that was built using car components.

on twisty roads and sluggish on hills. Moreover, a lot of models used diesel engines that were not equipped with turbo assistance. For example, some of the smaller coachbuilt motorcaravans built around this time used 1.9 non-turbo diesel power units, and with a fully laden habitation facility to contend with, their progress can be painfully slow. Of course, speed isn't everything, but an inability to keep up with today's flow of traffic on motorways is disconcerting, if not a little dangerous.

However, great strides have been made since the turn of the century. Engines are quieter, electronic systems help to achieve an improved performance, and they are notably economic on fuel too. No less important is the fact that their emission features are also much improved.

In addition to technical improvements, there appears to be a shift in preferences concerning petrol- and diesel-driven power units. For many years, motoring writers and motorcaravan testers often expressed a preference for petrol engines. Their lively performance played a part in the debate, coupled with the fact that diesel fuel is more expensive in the UK than it is in most of the other countries in mainland Europe. However, opinions have changed and if you like the low-rev pulling power of a diesel engine, the addition of a turbo undoubtedly adds more sparkle. Admittedly, it is sometimes claimed that turbo assistance is likely to shorten the life of a diesel engine, but since motorcaravans seldom cover the large mileage achieved by commercial drivers, this is less of a concern.

Choosing the best engine to meet your particular needs is certainly important and will be influenced, in part, by your normal driving style. It is unwise for anyone to purchase a motorcaravan without arranging a test drive on a variety of roads. 'Hire before you buy' schemes are discussed in the next chapter and this is a useful way to ensure that your choice of engine is the right one.

Chassis type

Another important element is the chassis, which is discussed under Motorcaravan Types, and also in Chapter 4.

Many potential purchasers overlook this element, but when buying a coachbuilt motorcaravan, it is a critical design feature. The type of chassis used on a 'coachbuilt' has implications for driving characteristics, the suspension, access to the living area and interior headroom.

Daily use

Another factor to consider is whether a motorcaravan has to be used for routine transport such as driving to work. Van conversions can fulfil this role quite well whereas coachbuilt models are far less versatile. Height is often a handicap and some public car parks have a barrier at the point of entry which restricts access.

Where funds permit, it is undoubtedly better to run a second vehicle for routine transport. At

the same time, a motorcaravan needs to be used regularly, so putting it into store for prolonged periods is best avoided. It is not just a battery that suffers when a vehicle is parked for a long spell; mechanical components can seize up, tyre sidewalls deteriorate and so on.

Motorcaravan types

Although there are many types of motorcaravan, they fall into one of two broad categories. These are:

- **CONVERSIONS** which use an existing road-going vehicle, such as a panel van with no windows rearwards of the cab; vans fitted throughout with single-glazed vehicle windows (often called 'window vans'); fully-upholstered multi-purpose vehicles (MPVs).
- **COACHBUILT MODELS** where a body shell is purpose-built and mounted on a suitable chassis. Some 'coachbuilts' retain a base vehicle's metal cab whereas other motorcaravan manufacturers construct a new, all-enclosing body shell.

This is a broad simplification but it distinguishes the two main routes in design and construction that characterise motorcaravans. Within these groups are a number of variations – including a few vehicles which defy classification.

Articulated units are a case in point. In the United States, 'fifth-wheel' recreational vehicles are relatively common and while their overall size is usually too large for Britain's smaller roads, the flexibility they offer is attractive. Smaller versions are now built in Britain but are not produced in large numbers.

Apart from special cases like fifth-wheelers, motorcaravans are typically sub-divided further using the following categories. Some are variations on the conversion theme described already: others are versions of coachbuilt models.

Small campervans can often gain access to public car parks; owners of larger motorcaravans are less likely to share this benefit.

Terminology

A growing number of manufacturers refer to their products as 'motorhomes' whereas others continue to call them 'motorcaravans'. Most people consider the terms to be synonymous and this book could easily have used either word in its title. In law-related publications and European Type Approval documents the two words 'motor caravan' are used.

Right: Original Volkswagen T2 window vans of the 1950s, complete with simple accommodation facilities, are still in use today.

How large?

When purchasing a motorcaravan, remember that size isn't everything! Decide what is the smallest living space that would provide you with comfort and convenience. Having compared models in the light of this decision, your chosen motorcaravan is likely to offer much more versatility than one which is unnecessarily large.

A. CONVERSIONS

FIXED ROOF

A panel van or a 'window' van is a good base vehicle for a motorcaravan builder. The construction process is often described as a 'conversion', although some manufacturers dislike this term. For the DIY builder, a 'van conversion' is certainly more straightforward than self-building a coachbuilt motorcaravan from scratch.

One problem with many fixed-roof base vehicles is that many are too low to permit full standing room, and later sections in the book describe how roofs can be altered to resolve this. Other vans give more height, although this cannot match the headroom found in many coachbuilt models. In effect, this introduces two variations on the theme: low fixed-roof conversions, which include 'micro campers', and high fixed-roof conversions.

LOW FIXED-ROOF CONVERSIONS

The idea of using a small van to provide simple accommodation became popular in the 1950s when Volkswagen (VW) T2 vans were converted into simple leisure vehicles. Cooking was carried out from a seated position and the interior could

be rearranged to create simple sleeping facilities. Even today, some of these vehicles are lovingly restored and used in this way. Similar arrangements are also created using modern vans and these are sometimes described as micro campers.

Other low fixed-roof vehicles are built using multi-purpose vehicles (MPVs) and in a few cases these are designed as mobile offices, used to meet clients, and they come complete with a tiny fridge and facility for preparing hot drinks. Some have surround seating instead of overnight sleeping provision.

Plus points
- Easy to drive and park
- Good fuel economy
- Suitable for daily commuting to work
- Can often be kept in a domestic garage
- Available in business form for mobile executives
- Few access problems through height restriction barriers

Minus points
- Storage facilities are minimal
- Not practical vehicles for long holidays
- Single-glazing means heat loss in winter and solar gain in summer

Right: This Peugeot Partner Origin micro-camper built by Young Conversions is easy to drive and should fit in a standard garage.

Far right: Although a small fixed-roof van has advantages, preparing and cooking meals in a seated position is not to everyone's taste.

- Impossible to stand up indoors to stretch your legs
- MPV models can be surprisingly costly

Recent examples
Several manufacturers build low fixed-roof, van-based motorcaravans including: Bilbo's, Murvi, and Young Conversions. Microcaravans based on MPVs are available from Wheelhome.

HIGH FIXED-ROOF CONVERSIONS
Some light commercial panel vans that are converted into motorcaravans have a much higher roof and a long wheelbase (LWB). For instance, an unconverted Fiat Ducato LWB Maxi offers internal headroom of around 1.88m (74in) and although this will be reduced when lined with insulation, it can still offer standing room for some owners. High roof vans like the Mercedes Sprinter, the Renault Master, and Peugeot/Fiat models have thus been chosen for conversion by several UK manufacturers. These are unlikely to appeal to taller users, but models like the Murvi Morello have won awards for their comfort and driving characteristics.

The fact that no alterations are carried out to improve the amount of headroom space inevitably means that money is saved. On the other hand, the business of working within an enclosed compartment when fitting-out the interior of a van is slow and builders have to install furniture to curving surfaces. Many of the manufacturing processes used for building a flat-sided coachbuilt model, which is assembled by a team of builders working with prefabricated structures, cannot be employed here. This explains why the finished price of relatively small van-based vehicles is always surprisingly high. On the plus side, be aware that a van's metal shell is far less likely to develop leaks in the later stages of its life, whereas the

joining seams on some coachbuilt constructions do develop leaks, as described in later chapters.

Plus points
- Easy to drive
- Reasonable fuel economy
- Good weather integrity
- More likely to fit into service centres than tall coachbuilt models
- Large rear and sliding side doors permit easy entry, especially for disabled users

Minus points
- Not suitable for tall occupants
- Limited inside floor area
- Finished models often seem costly
- Internal width restrictions limit the number of layout options inside

Recent examples
UK manufacturers include Autocruise, Auto-Sleepers, Devon Conversions, East Neuk, IHMotor Campers, Murvi, Romahome, Timberland, and Swift. Imported vehicles include models manufactured by Adria (Slovenia), Laika (Italy), Trigano (Italy), and la strada, (Germany).

Above: Manufactured in South Devon, the Morello has been one of Murvi's most successful models; it has won many awards since its launch in the 1990s.

Below: The Adria Twin was one of the first van conversions to feature a hinged double bed in the rear, which, when lowered for use, fits across the width of the vehicle.

VAN CONVERSIONS WITH REPLACEMENT ROOFS

Replacing the original factory-fitted steel roof on a van became a common practice when Volkswagen (VW) campervans gained popularity 50 years ago. All kinds of ingenuity has been shown in the quest to achieve greater indoor headroom. There's no doubt that the use of glass-reinforced plastic (GRP) mouldings has been prominent in most replacement structures. Two distinct types of roof have evolved: elevating roofs and fixed high-top mouldings.

Of course, removal of the original steel roof with its reinforcement struts is going to compromise the rigidity of a body shell unless replacement strengtheners are duly installed. Vehicle manufacturers provide guidance on how to firm up a structure after its roof panel is removed and it is critically important that all aspects of the specification are strictly followed.

Unfortunately, some unqualified rogue installers completely disregard the strengthening measures prescribed by vehicle manufacturers, and in a recent incident, a poorly-fabricated, cut-price roof structure came adrift from a vehicle when it was being driven on the M25 north of London. Increasing a van's headroom involves far more than removing a steel panel with cutting tools and sticking a flimsy lid in its place. Modification operations involve exacting procedures, the use of approved bonding agents and the installation of robust replacement structures. Reputable van converters take no short cuts, and inevitably there is a price to pay for a safe and good-quality installation.

ELEVATING (RISING) ROOF MODELS

The popularity of motorcaravans fitted with an elevating roof remains undiminished and reputable converters manufacture several models offering this feature. However, conversions based on the Mazda Bongo usually have an elevating roof that was installed in the vehicle factory at the time of manufacture. The same applies to the roof on the VW California, which is factory-built near Hannover.

In many instances, an installation can also be carried out retrospectively. For example, DIY builders often get this done by an experienced converter before commencing the fitting-out work inside.

Without doubt, a driver enjoys several benefits when a vehicle's elevating roof can be retracted. Road performance is certainly better on a low vehicle, particularly in strong wind; there is also a greater likelihood of being able to drive under the height barriers installed at car park entrances.

Although the main function of an elevating system is to improve headroom inside, many rising roof systems also incorporate a high-level bed. This may be little more than a stretcher-style structure to sleep a young child. On the other hand, some designers have cleverly incorporated an adult-sized double bed within their rising roof structures.

Not surprisingly, there are also disadvantages associated with this type of roof. For example, a fabric-sided product is not good at retaining heat in the winter; nor is it good if you want to keep the interior cool in summer, especially if you're parked on a pitch that has no shade. Also, a problem will occur if you need to lower a roof when it's raining and the fabric is wet. If you leave it stowed damp for more than a day, mould will start forming that cannot be removed.

From a constructional viewpoint, an elevating roof is also more elaborate than the fixed high-top roofs that will be described next. Consequently, the cost of an elevating roof is normally higher than the price of a permanent high-top structure. This often comes as a surprise to purchasers.

Also, be aware that there are several different designs. An elevating roof section usually deploys an attached fabric panel as it rises, whereas some assemblies are built with hinged, solid sides. There are also different hinging arrangements employed with fabric models, although most have a colour-matched GRP 'lid' that forms the roof.

Anyone who considers purchasing a motorcaravan fitted with one of these systems must look closely at its mechanism and practise lifting and lowering the assembly several times. Some designs require more strength than you might expect, and telescopic gas springs, which make elevation easy, will often make the closing operation surprisingly strenuous.

Plus points
- As with low fixed-roof conversions, easy to drive, park and garage
- Good fuel economy
- Suitable for commuting to work
- More comfortable indoors than a low fixed-roof van
- Most models have good access via the sliding side door

Minus points
- Not all lifting mechanisms are easy to operate
- Packing away a damp fabric roof can lead to damage
- High level storage is not available with the roof lowered
- The interior can get cold in winter and hot in summer

Below: Based on a Fiat Scudo Panorama, the MMM 2009 Award-Winning Wheelhome Panache has a slim rising roof. When lowered, the vehicle is still only 1.91m (75in) high.

Recent examples

Many converters include a model equipped with an elevating roof; others offer this as one of the options on their van conversion line-up. In total, there are too many models to give a complete list and the following are just a few examples: Auto-Sleepers, Bilbo's Design, Danbury, Devon Conversions, Middlesex Motorcaravans, Murvi, Reimo, Romahome, VW California, Westfalia, Wheelhome and Young Conversions.

HIGH-TOP ROOF MODELS

Some of the larger panel vans offer good headroom, as mentioned earlier, and it might be reasonable to describe them as 'high-top models'. However, in the motorcaravan industry, vehicles classified as 'high-tops' are usually smaller vans which have subsequently been fitted with a glass reinforced plastic (GRP) moulded roof in place of the original metal roof.

High-top motorcaravans are justifiably popular and the use of GRP helps to prevent the structure from being top-heavy. Road-holding characteristics when cornering are scarcely affected, although strong side-winds are not welcome.

When you step inside this type of motorcaravan, the generous headroom has the effect of making its interior seem surprisingly spacious. Roof-level double-glazed windows or glass panels play a prominent part in creating this impression and once you are inside, the overall effect helps to hide a vehicle's panel van parentage.

Many long-established converters include high-top models in their product range, but ownership opportunities don't stop there. Advertisements in motorcaravan magazines include independent roof section suppliers, such as Middlesex Motorcaravans, who will also install a GRP roof moulding on a van supplied by its owner. Young Conversions, for example, go one step further and this Company offers a complete roof installation service in which headlining and ventilation facilities are included as part of the project. With this modification work complete, many aspiring self-build enthusiasts are then able to fit-out the interior to meet their personal needs.

The cost of a high-top professionally-built motorcaravan is often surprisingly expensive. It has already been mentioned that this is because converting a small interior is more labour-intensive than constructing a larger coachbuilt model, which uses production line assembly strategies. Not surprisingly, this is one reason why many potential owners embark on their own fitting-out project. Some of the smaller converters are also willing to help with several of the more specialist tasks like installing a gas supply system. Regardless of how you choose your motorcaravan, high-top models fitted with a colour-matched roof moulding have much to offer. Although the internal space is small, there is a choice of several different layouts inside.

It should be noted that motor manufacturers offer short, medium and long wheelbase vehicles and this helps determine the internal facilities that can be included. Some professional conversions, like the Auto-Sleepers Symphony and the Romahome New Dimension, even include a generous-sized washroom and toilet.

Smaller models lack this provision and toilet facilities are rather rudimentary. In some instances,

Above: The Auto-Sleeper Trooper, based on a VW Transporter window van base vehicle, has been built for many years with a distinctive solid-sided elevating roof.

Far left: This Matrix conversion from Middlesex Motorcaravans was fitted with an extra tall high-top roof to suit a customer who required headroom in excess of 1.83m (72in).

Left: The Murvi Mallard shown here on a VW Transporter window van is fitted with a colour-coded high-top. The rear detailing takes account of a raised, hatchback door.

a portable toilet has to be retrieved from a locker located in the living space, and then discreetly shielded using a makeshift curtain. This 'back to basics' approach isn't everyone's cup of tea.

Plus points
- Driving characteristics are generally good
- Suitable for commuting to work
- More comfortable indoors than a low fixed-roof van
- Most models have good access via the sliding side-door
- Some long wheelbase vehicles have a toilet and shower cubicle
- Small-scale converters often accommodate special requests from customers

Minus points
- Strong side-winds can spoil the driving experience
- Some conversions are surprisingly expensive
- There isn't the storage space found in similarly-priced coachbuilt models
- Models based on window vans lose heat in winter and get hot in summer

Recent examples
This is a competitive market and most of the converters already listed in the section on Elevating (Rising) Roof models also offer fixed high-top roof vehicles. Some of the names listed are large-scale National Caravan Council (NCC) member-manufacturers *eg* Auto-Sleepers. However, there are also small-scale 'bespoke' converters producing vehicles with a high standard of workmanship.

DISMOUNTABLES
Sometimes called a 'demountable', this design is particularly popular in the United States where pick-up trucks are comparatively common. Crew cab pick-ups, which have a double line of seats, are especially suitable as base vehicles.

The concept is simple: a purpose-made living compartment is carried 'piggy-back' style on the pick-up vehicle and can be detached when necessary. This enables a site pitch to be secured, after which the vehicle can be driven around independently.

The same advantage is offered when you return home; detached 'living capsules' are a common sight in many American back yards, thereby releasing the truck to be used as a day-to-day load carrier.

The versatility of dismountable units is attractive and some models are imported directly from America. A few of these are also built in Britain. For instance, the Apollo range has been popular for several years and is often exhibited at outdoor shows. The Ranger dismountable has also been displayed at these events.

In theory the idea is sound, but in practice there are several shortcomings. Even supposing you own a suitable pick-up truck, the mounted compartment often produces a top-heavy configuration. Folding-roof models help to improve the weight distribution difficulty but these are uncommon. Driving a dismountable motorcaravan on twisty roads can undoubtedly be disconcerting, and components that extend well beyond the sides of a base vehicle may be illegal under European legislation.

Plus points
- A detached pick-up vehicle can be used independently
- Living accommodation can be surprisingly neatly arranged
- The over-cab pod is often used for a permanent double bed

Left: Products like this Ranger dismountable are seldom seen at large indoor exhibitions; they are more likely to be displayed at outdoor shows.

Below: Once detached from its pick-up truck, this dismountable unit offers generous living space and a canvas-sided 'extension' bedroom.

Minus points

- A suitable pick-up truck is needed
- The cab is not part of the living accommodation
- On the road, some dismountables roll badly when driven on twisty lanes
- It is not quite as quick to mount or dismount the living pad as might be expected

Recent examples

Not many UK manufacturers produce dismountable units, although products from Apollo and Ranger Motorhomes are sometimes exhibited at outdoor shows. Also, a few distributors in Britain import models from North America.

B. COACHBUILT MODELS

CHASSIS-CAB COACHBUILTS

When a base vehicle 'chassis cab' is used, a coachbuilt construction can offer spacious accommodation. Sometimes a vehicle manufacturer's original chassis is retained, as it is on many recent Auto-Trail motorcaravans. Alternatively, a replacement AL-KO Kober lightweight single chassis platform is grafted on to the cab (as it is on many Bessacarr models). More recently, AL-KO Kober has also been manufacturing a double chassis platform which permits water tanks and services to be mounted in a protected void below the floor panel. Other features relating to different types of chassis are discussed and evaluated in greater detail in Chapter 4.

A more prominent distinguishing feature of 'coachbuilt' models is the fact that a vehicle manufacturer's cab complete with its doors, windows, bonnet, road lights, instrumentation and so on are all retained in the finished motorcaravan. Often the original cab seats are retained, too, although on some of the higher specified coachbuilt models high-quality luxury seats might replace these.

Another feature is that the rear section of the cab structure is *not* retained, thereby permitting access between the living section and the driving area. In some interior designs, swiveling cab seats allow the cab area to yield additional floor space when the vehicle is parked on its pitch. Also, the living accommodation can incorporate a variety of facilities, layouts and bed provision depending on the size of the vehicle. However, driving performance in a large coachbuilt is less 'car-like', which should be taken into account. Large models wouldn't be suitable for day-to-day utility transport.

As regards the constructional strategies used when building coachbuilt models, these are explained in more detail in Chapter 3. All that needs mentioning here is the fact that it is far easier for a well-equipped manufacturing plant to produce coachbuilt models, quickly, efficiently and economically than it is to fit-out a camper van. In some instances, a team of installers work simultaneously installing furniture, appliances and supply systems on a bare floor panel. The vehicle's sidewalls and roof are often intentionally added much later so as not to limit the access opportunities available for the construction team. This efficient use of labour is one of the main reasons why some medium-sized coachbuilt models cost much the same as far smaller van conversions.

Of course, not everyone wants to drive or own larger vehicles like coachbuilt models. The use of this kind of motorcaravan is constrained by height barriers, problems of roadside parking, storage issues and so on. In fact this has led to a creation of several versions of coachbuilt motorcaravans, especially with regard to the issue of height.

OVER-CAB COACHBUILTS

For many years, almost all UK coachbuilt models had a large over-cab compartment; often referred

Left: The over-cab bed on this SEA New Life was spacious and conveniently left in a made-up state. Externally, though, the structure wouldn't help fuel economy.

to as a 'Luton'. Typically, this is either used for storage or sleeping accommodation. However, when viewed from outside, many over-cab compartments are a clumsy feature that affect the aerodynamic design of a vehicle, and this also has implications for fuel economy. In addition, there are some users who do not wish to climb a ladder to reach an over-cab bed. They prefer a less lofty venue for the night, coupled with the benefits of an adjacent toilet and a nearby kitchen.

Plus points
- Over-cab coachbuilt models offer plenty of storage space
- An over-cab bed can be left in its made-up state, all ready for bed-time
- When considering size and price, coachbuilt models are good value

Minus points
- Though easy to drive, a coachbuilt motorcaravan doesn't perform like a car
- The height of an over-cab model encourages high-level storage, which leads to body roll
- Not as easy to drive when negotiating narrow lanes as small van conversions
- Parking can be a problem, and it's all too easy to hit overhanging branches
- Not a good choice of vehicle for daily commuting to work

Recent examples
Over-cab coachbuilt manufacturers include: Auto-Sleepers, Auto-Trail, Bessacarr, Buccaneer, Dethleffs, Elddis, Granduca, Hymer, Knaus, Laika, Lunar, Mobilvetta, Pilote, Rimor, Roller Team, SEA, Swift and TEC. Others that are no longer in production or are no longer being imported include: Avondale, Compass, Autocruise CH, Benimar and many others.

Although there are benefits offered by models equipped with a large over-cab compartment, several designers in mainland Europe started to evolve 'low-profile' coachbuilts as well. Their ideas came to fruition in the late 1990s.

LOW-PROFILE COACHBUILTS
At first, many UK motorcaravanners didn't seem to share the enthusiasm of our Continental 'cousins' for low-profile models. However, attitudes soon started to change, especially when UK manufacturers also commenced the production of low-profile motorcaravans. Today it is even possible to find models that are available in both high- and low-profile versions, such as the 2011 Auto-Trail Tracker.

Plus points
- Low-profile models are likely to achieve better fuel economy
- The need to store equipment lower down helps reduce body roll when cornering
- Less likely to accidentally hit low-hanging branches

Minus points
- Interior headroom may be insufficient for taller users
- Typically there is a reduction in equipment storage facilities
- The convenience of having a made-up bed over the cab is lost
- Not a good choice of vehicle for daily commuting to work

Recent examples
Low-profile manufacturers include: Auto-Sleepers, Auto-Trail, Bessacarr, Dethleffs, Elddis, Hobby, Knaus, Laika, Pilote, Rapido, Swift and many others.

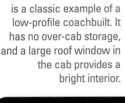

Below: The Knaus Sun Ti is a classic example of a low-profile coachbuilt. It has no over-cab storage, and a large roof window in the cab provides a bright interior.

A-CLASS

The construction of this kind of motorcaravan starts with a commercial chassis, running gear, power unit, seating, instrumentation – but no cab. This configuration is referred to as a 'chassis cowl', and an illustration of a typical base unit appears in Chapter 4. Without the benefit of a vehicle manufacturer's cab, the motorcaravan designer has to create an all-enclosing body structure in which the living area embraces the driver's section. The project would include the installation of a large windscreen, all the other windows, doors to access both the living and driving zones, and a multitude of other features.

Building an entire body from scratch is undoubtedly a major task and when it is done well, the finished vehicle will have an impressive presence on the road. However, mistakes can happen, and several A-Class models from reputable manufacturers have been fitted with bonnet lids that are too small to yield access to key items in the engine compartment. Even routine tasks like replacing an air filter are sometimes extremely difficult to accomplish.

Then there's the problem of cab access. The construction of steel automotive doors complete with electric windows is an exacting task, and one which many manufacturers avoid by mounting a conventional, lightweight, caravan-type door instead. In some models, this means that the only way for a driver to reach the cab is to enter via the same door that provides an entry to the living quarters. The arrangement on a chassis-cab type of motorcaravan is arguably much better.

There's also the matter of the windscreen. When driving, there is always the possibility that a stone could fly up and crack a screen. For this reason, anyone planning to purchase an A-Class model should check both the price of a new

screen and the availability of a replacement. In some instances, the designer has specified a standard commercial screen that might be installed on lorries or small buses. It shouldn't take too long to obtain a replacement for a screen such as this, but some owners do report dreadful delays.

Notwithstanding these potential difficulties, there are some magnificent A-class motorcaravans being manufactured in Europe. Many of the interiors, for example, feature a drop-down double bed in the cab area and this is normally ready-made-up for instant use. These fine models are costly, of course, and some are fitted-out to a very high standard.

British manufacturers, however, are disinclined to embark on such projects. Admittedly there was the rather 'boxy-looking' Autoking built by Elddis in the 1980s. Similarly, Machzone produced A-class models for several years but the Company is no longer trading. Several years later, the Bel-Air was

Above: The sumptuous interior of this 2007 model Auto-Trail Grande Frontiere A-7300 shows the space available when the drop-down bed is in the raised position in the cab.

Below: This 2010 Burstner model exhibits the clean lines and overall attractiveness of a modern A-class motorcaravan.

launched in 1998 by Swift Motorhomes. Then, in 2005, Auto-Trail launched the aptly named Grande Frontiere A-7300 with a Mercedes base vehicle. This was notable for its sturdy GRP doors that allowed proper access to the cab, and a styling as smart as you're likely to find. A great deal of time went into building these models, but none of the UK A-class motorcaravans were produced for very long. So if you want to consider a new A-class motorcaravan, you would have to look at models built in France, Germany, Italy or Slovenia.

Plus points
- The A-class body offers scope for clean attractive lines
- Storage capacity is extensive
- Many models have extremely well-finished interiors
- The installation of an elevating bed takes up no space by day

Minus points
- Access doors to the cab are often little more than lightweight caravan-type doors
- Replacement windscreens can be very expensive
- Hardly suitable vehicles for commuting or driving on narrow country lanes
- Some campsites are unable to accept large vehicles
- Fuel consumption is an issue to consider
- Repairing damage to large panels is usually a costly operation
- Some models offer poor access to the engine compartment

Recent examples
Many A-class motorcaravans are built by German manufacturers and Hymer has a wide range of

models. Models like the Pilote made in France, and Laika from Italy are often available through UK dealers. As for the more expensive brands, models like the Carthargo and ClouLINER are noteworthy. In Wales, models fitted-out to customer specifications are manufactured by MCL and these beautiful creations typically cost around £250,000.

AMERICAN MOTORHOMES
Calculated on price per square metre of living space, the American motorhome represents incredible value for money. *(Note: Often referred to using the North American term 'recreational vehicle' – RV).* For example, £95,000 could secure a huge nearly new vehicle fitted with an eight-litre engine. Typical examples offer a large number of robust external lockers, a built-in generator with dashboard control switch, a permanent double bed, a hip bath, a large over-cab TV set, a powerful turbo diesel engine with automatic transmission, and a multitude of extras. On the other hand, furniture inside is not to everyone's taste and sometimes the standard of cabinet-making craftsmanship is disappointing.

Without doubt, these substantial vehicles have a keen following and are ideal recreational vehicles in the US. Whether they are suited to Britain's roads is left for the reader to decide. And whilst there are hundreds of American camping grounds offering drive-on/drive-off hard standings equipped with purpose-made couplings for fresh water, waste ('grey') water and sewage ('black water'), facilities like these are seldom found on European sites.

Plus points
- Remarkable value for money when measured on floor space and fittings
- Ideal for large groups – some models sleep up to eight people

Left: The Celtic Rambler manufactured by the Fifth Wheel Company in Rhuallt, Denbighshire, is now one of the longest established examples of this type of vehicle made in the UK.

Minus points

- Maintenance costs are likely to be high and relatively few specialists are able to carry out servicing work
- Obtaining spare parts might present problems
- A number of camping sites are unable to take American motorhomes
- Fuel and general maintenance costs are high
- Parking and access problems limit use
- The furniture in some American motorhomes is poorly built
- Many non-standard parts are fitted
- Cleaning the body is a major operation

Recent examples

Imported models are subject to frequent changes. A good source of guidance is the publication *American RV Magazine* from ABP Leisure. See the Appendix for the address.

FIFTH-WHEELERS

Until recently, this type of motorcaravan was mainly sold and used in the USA. Occasionally a few UK specialists import fifth-wheelers, although the products are usually too large for normal travelling in Europe. In response to this, the Fifth Wheel Company, based in Denbighshire North Wales, developed a GRP model designed for European use. It is over 10 years since the Celtic Rambler was introduced. A smaller version, the DreamSeeker, has recently been added.

The design and finish of these British products is outstanding. The manufacturer attends indoor exhibitions and outdoor shows throughout the year. The products regularly receive awards in events run by organisations such as The Caravan Club, although they do not fit easily into the usual vehicle categories. Like the dismountable category mentioned earlier, these products also

rely on a robust pick-up truck, and products from Nissan are normally used in conjunction with the Fifth Wheel Company products.

Left: Although the trailer itself costs around the price of a medium coachbuilt motorcaravan, the finish inside is of an exceptionally high standard.

Below: A powerful pick-up truck has to be purchased as well, and the high quality fixtures and appliances call for a vehicle that is able to cope with the weight of this trailer.

2 Buying a Motorcaravan

Anyone thinking about buying a new or pre-owned motorcaravan will need to draw together as much information about different models as possible. Here are some points you might find helpful.

Manufacturers promote their products with vigour, so it helps to obtain impartial advice. Accordingly, this chapter looks at ways of building up a clearer picture about different models.

There are several ways of buying a motorcaravan, so purchasing procedures are discussed later. Equally, a prospective owner mustn't overlook considerations like insurance, licensing, seasonal storage, and breakdown schemes. However, topics like these – especially legal matters – are constantly changing. To keep up-to-date with ongoing issues, whether they are changes in road fund payments, emissions taxes, new accessories or vehicle developments, motorcaravan magazines are a good source of information.

Motorcaravan publications

Currently there are four monthly consumer magazines devoted specifically to motorcaravanning. In addition, there are three publications distributed to members of the national caravan and motorcaravan clubs, thereby giving an impressive total of seven magazines.

These publications contain helpful articles about accessories, services, places to visit, and include up-to-date information relating to all the latest models. Supplier and classified advertisements are useful as well.

DATA LISTINGS OF MODELS, SPECIFICATIONS AND PRICES

Consumer magazines often publish lists of current models, many of which include information on base vehicles, carrying capacity (payload), external dimensions, the number of beds, price and so on. Similar specification lists also appear on magazine websites.

Lists containing guide prices on older models are rather harder to find. However, the magazine *Motorcaravan Motorhome Monthly* (*MMM*) periodically publishes a six-part guide to the prices of pre-owned vehicles. These currently appear in successive issues under the following headings:

- Part One: Panel van conversions with fixed and rising roofs
- Part Two: Panel van conversions with high-tops
- Part Three: Low profile coachbuilts
- Part Four: Overcab coachbuilts
- Part Five: A-class models
- Part Six: American motorhomes.

Both *Practical Motorhome* (Haymarket Publishers) and *MMM* (Warners Publishers) publish buyers' guides and other supplements, and these are accessible via the internet. The Warner's guides can be found on www.outandaboutlive.co.uk and the website for *Practical Motorhome* is www.practicalmotorhome.com. Private owners who are selling a motorcaravan can place free advertisements on this website. This is linked to a search facility under the buy/sell button. To use the service, a purchaser enters his or her postcode, adds criteria relating to their proposed purchase, and is then given details about both private and dealer models on sale in their locality.

Without doubt, UK magazines and their associated websites provide an invaluable service to anyone wishing to buy or sell a motorcaravan.

Right: The pre-owned price guide groupings published in *MMM* magazine include vans with fixed and rising roofs.

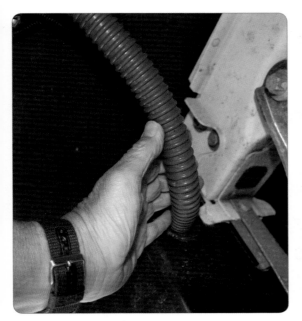

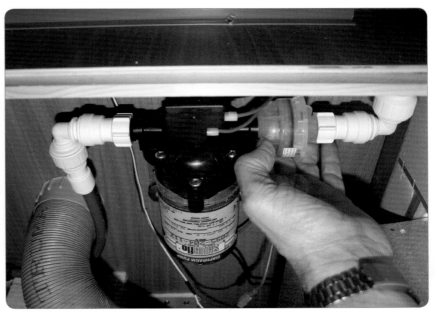

TEST REPORTS

Monthly magazines also run illustrated articles compiled by experienced motorcaravan testers, and these reports include helpful photographs showing a new vehicle in use. Especially informative are the comparative reports where two or three models of similar price and specification are tested alongside each other.

Older motorcaravans are occasionally tested too. Similarly you will find articles focussing on models that magazine writers have inspected on dealers' forecourts.

Most test reports tend to be thorough, although the content of critical appraisals varies a great deal. Some journalists are more focussed on 'liveability issues', whereas others pay greater attention to weaknesses in body construction, under-floor installations or incorrectly fitted appliances.

The point is made in Chapter 8, for example, that refrigerators have not always been installed in accordance with their manufacturers' instructions so then perform poorly. It's also true that technical deficiencies, flaws in body detailing, and access to service components might not become apparent during a test journalist's two week 'live-in' evaluation.

With regard to long-term performance, it is undoubtedly more revealing when the editorial department of a magazine is loaned a motorcaravan for an extended period. These opportunities allow a vehicle's performance to be assessed by a number of different journalists in a wide variety of conditions. A test that embraces both summer and winter weather undoubtedly provides a more accurate insight into the merits of a particular model. However, bespoke models and those manufactured in low volumes are unable to enjoy publicity of this kind.

Within the motorcaravan industry as a whole, there are many small-scale manufacturers, some of whom construct noteworthy products. However, their modest annual output seldom allows them the

Above left: Unlike the 'live-in' reports, technical tests look into the effectiveness of installations such as water systems.

Above: In this technical test, the easy removal of a grit filter on a Swift Sundance was pleasing to note.

Left: The Stimson Overlander embodies some exceptional design features but models like this seldom achieve the recognition they deserve.

Above: A cut-away version of a Bailey Approach motorcaravan was a revealing exhibit at a recent indoor exhibition.

Above right: Major indoor shows often have helpful presentations covering a wide range of motorcaravanning subjects.

Below: The huge, late-summer show at Dusseldorf is attended by many enthusiastic British motorcaravanners.

Below right: This outdoor show at Peterborough brings together hundreds of motorcaravanners who stay for a long weekend in April.

luxury of running a fleet of demonstrator vehicles to supply to journalists for testing. In consequence, the majority of magazine test reports focus on motorcaravans built by large scale manufacturers.

Recognising the usefulness of published tests to potential purchasers, motorcaravan publications sometimes operate a service whereby readers can obtain copies of past reports. In the case of *MMM*, the archive information includes every test that has been published since the magazine was first launched in 1966. Previous reports can be retrieved from websites, too.

CALENDAR OF EXHIBITIONS AND SHOWS

Most magazines include information about exhibitions and shows, both of which provide further opportunities to evaluate vehicles and accessories alike. Although manufacturer brochures and road test reports are informative, it is also important to see the products for yourself. One way to do this is to attend a national indoor exhibition such as The Motorhome & Caravan Show held in October at the National Exhibition Centre (NEC) in Birmingham.

This occupies a large site adjacent to Birmingham Airport and the NEC has excellent road links. The exhibition offers many services to visitors, including free driving tuition in the grounds, and stage presentations, where advice is given on a wide range of motorcaravanning products.

The event is also supported by one of the caravanning club's temporary 'campsites', and a free bus service is arranged to convey visitors to the nearby exhibition halls. Regional indoor exhibitions are similarly held in London, Manchester and Glasgow, although their venues occasionally change.

Further afield there is a late summer exhibition held in Düsseldorf, which is claimed to be the largest in Europe. It is certainly a big event and many British motorcaravanners drive the relatively short distance through the Netherlands to this German city adjacent to the River Rhine. It was the first exhibition of its type to introduce well-equipped, on-site car park camping facilities. The camp grounds are also supported by free bus services to the main entrances of the exhibition centre by day, and the historic 'old town' of Düsseldorf in the evenings.

Indoor exhibitions are large affairs, but also be aware of the many *outdoor* shows held around the UK, most of which are staged during the warmer months. These open-air events are typically held at agricultural showgrounds. Not only are local dealers in attendance with displays of new and pre-owned models, visitors are also able to seek advice from existing motorhome owners who bring their vehicles and stop overnight.

At outdoor shows there are small-scale

motorcaravan manufacturers, too, and many accessory suppliers that find it too costly to take stand space at the more formal indoor exhibitions.

Outdoor shows also offer on-site accommodation for motorcaravan owners. Typically, the camping fields are divided into areas for particular brands of motorcaravan, thereby making it easy for an observer to judge vehicles of particular types in a 'real-life' outdoor setting.

Note: *Both indoor exhibitions and outdoor shows have large areas hired by dealers who display new and pre-owned models for sale. The later section on **Buying New** (page 32) gives advice regarding the purchase of a motorcaravan at exhibitions.*

ADDRESS LISTS OF OWNERS' CLUBS

Some clubs for motorcaravanners are devoted to particular marques; other clubs focus on areas of special interest relating to motorcaravanning. The list currently published in *Motorcaravan Motorhome Monthly* (*MMM*) gives information on over 90 clubs, four of which cater for owners of American motorhomes. There is even an organisation for DIY enthusiasts called The Self-Build Motorcaravanners' Club. The addresses of club secretaries are occasionally published in motorcaravan magazines, and these organisations hold regular social events around the country.

Once you've established a shortlist of models that meet your requirements, talking to owners is a good way to find out what a product is really like. Admittedly, some members show great manufacturer loyalty and defend their choice of motorcaravan with eager enthusiasm. Others are more impartial and willingly divulge the problems they've encountered during ownership. These clubs are undoubtedly an important source of information – particularly if you're interested in a pre-owned model that is no longer in production.

National caravan and motorcaravan clubs

The two national clubs concerned with caravanning and motorcaravanning have over half a million members. The historical development of these two clubs has given them distinctive and individual characteristics. The Camping and Caravanning Club welcomes users of all kinds of units, including tents, and also features specialist hobby groups for canoeists, climbers, photographers and so on. The Caravan Club, however, is principally run for caravan and motorcaravan owners, although tents are accepted on a few club-managed sites.

Differences aside, both organisations provide members with holiday booking services, insurance schemes, instruction courses in driving skills, advisory services and technical help lines.

A third club, The Motor Caravanners' Club, is more specific, as its title indicates. This club has fewer members than the two major caravanning clubs, but again there is a members' magazine,

Left: Plenty of pre-owned models are sold by dealers attending outdoor shows and there are often good bargains.

Technical Literature

■ *The Motor Caravanners' Club* publishes a 36-page booklet entitled *Motor Caravans – Choosing and Using*, which is available to members.

■ *The Camping and Caravanning Club* publishes technical leaflets for members; one of its special interest groups – The Motor Caravan Section – has members with experience of owning a wide range of models.

■ *The Caravan Club* publishes a pamphlet, *Tips for Motorcaravanners*, available to members and non-members alike. In addition, members can request a free leaflet titled *Choice of Motor Caravan*, together with a number of related technical leaflets on topics such as TV reception and water systems. The free booklet; *Getting Started – A Beginner's Guide to Motor Caravanning* is helpful, too.

---

advice on technical issues, guidance on choosing a motorcaravan and so on.

A summary of the publications produced by the clubs, which offer advice on choosing and using a motorcaravan, is given in the adjacent box: Technical Literature.

Annual motorcaravan awards

Award schemes to evaluate good practice in design and construction are conducted by the national clubs, the trade magazine, Caravan Industry and Park Operator and consumer magazines. For instance, The Motorhome Awards is an annual collaborative venture involving *MMM* and *Which Motorhome*.

The Caravan Club also introduced the Motor Caravan Design Awards in 1996.

Left: In the 2011 motorcaravanning awards organised by Warners' Magazines, this Burstner Ixeo time it 585 was the overall winner.

The evaluations were conducted with notable thoroughness and the first overall winner was the Murvi Morello van conversion. In the years which followed, Murvi has continued to win awards with impressive regularity.

However, this contest only evaluated motorcaravans in a static position, thereby omitting a crucial element: the driving experience. Bearing in mind that performance on the road is an important aspect of ownership, the format and title of the award was amended, and from 2000 onwards, driving qualities have been incorporated in the judging schedule. The Caravan Club Design & Drive event now takes place at a venue that gives access to varying types of public roads, and the judging process is even more thorough. Not surprisingly, both manufacturers and members of the public take the results seriously.

Notwithstanding the value of these events for potential purchasers, it must be recognised that many small-scale manufacturers have such a limited output that they are unable to supply a vehicle for these competitions. The fact that Murvi, a small van conversion specialist from Devon, has won so many of The Caravan Club's annual awards is evidence indeed that products from small builders are sometimes better than their mass-produced rivals. However, some van converters have an even smaller annual output of vehicles than Murvi – a few of whom build vehicles that incorporate elements particularly requested by their clients. Naturally, these would not meet the entry criteria for design competitions, yet their build quality can be second to none.

Despite being informative, award schemes shouldn't be regarded as the only way to identify high quality products.

Quality and reliability surveys

In 2001, The Caravan Club commissioned Sewell Information and Research to conduct the first ever survey of motorcaravan quality and reliability. Over 2,000 owners of motorcaravans up to six years old were asked a wide range of questions on topics including delivery condition, long-term quality and reliability, experience of dealers, servicing, repair and warranties. The results were published in a 159-page document in 2002, and a summary of the findings appeared in the August 2002 *Members' Magazine*. A second survey was conducted in 2008. Research of this kind certainly highlights week spots in the motorcaravan industry as a whole. For example, it is frequently reported that obtaining spare parts for some types of repair work could involve a wait of many weeks. This can be very inconvenient, especially when a motorcaravan is off the road during the height of a summer season.

Some manufacturers undoubtedly operate better after-sales services than others, and existing owners, and members of owners' clubs, will be well placed to advise on this. Clearly, The Caravan Club's Quality & Reliability Surveys produce a deep insight into the realities of buying and running particular makes of motorcaravans, drawing on the experiences of owners.

Note: *In the 2002 survey, owners of 59 different makes of motorcaravan provided information on the quality and reliability of the models they owned.*

Choices of a base vehicle

In Chapter 1, reference was made to different engine options and the importance of choosing a vehicle with the power and economy to meet your requirements. Other elements you will need to consider include the fuel choice, emission levels, ride quality, and options like automatic transmission to name a few. Also, look at the cab. In truth, most Light Commercial Vehicles (LCVs) now offer car-like comfort. On the other hand, heavier vehicles such as IVEKO commercial products tend to retain the more rugged character of a lorry cab.

This is only a short overview and vehicle manufacturers regularly release new models and different specification options. If you would like to find more information, be aware that not only motorcaravan magazines publish reports on light commercial vans and other vehicles, trade magazines frequently run reports on light commercial vehicles whenever new ones are announced. These are predominantly addressed to building contractors, plumbers, electricians, roofing specialists and many others.

Starting with a general driving element, most British-built motorcaravans are fitted with a manual gearbox; automatic transmission is seldom needed on what is essentially a commercial vehicle. But there are exceptions. For example, the Tiptronic automatic six-speed gearbox has been available as an option on some models in the Volkswagen Transporter range. Similarly, some Ford Transits have been specified with a Durashift system that links a conventional manual gearbox with an

Below: The Renault dC140 used on the 2006 Mobilvetta Kimu 122 offered car-like comfort in the cab.

automatic clutch and electronic gear change; this means there's neither a gear stick nor a clutch pedal. The Mercedes Sprinter has offered the optional Sprintshift system, which is an automated gearbox as opposed to a torque converter automatic transmission. However, the Sprintshift system did not win universal approval and some journalists preparing test reports have referred to it as 'an acquired taste'. This again underlines why motorcaravan purchasers *must* undertake test drives in order to make personal judgements.

In 2011, developments in the Fiat Ducato ranges included the option of a Comfort-Matic auto gearbox, but it was initially available only on the biggest 180bhp engine. Constraints like this are disappointing for those who would like an auto box but don't want to pay the significantly higher price for a big engine. For anyone preferring a manual gearbox, Fiats have five gear transmissions (at the time of writing) whereas some Ford Transits offer six gear transmissions. Naturally, these specifications are constantly changing, and to obtain details of the latest options, definitive information can be found on manufacturers' websites.

Another concern is the subject of emissions, especially with the establishment of London's Low Emission Zone (LEZ). In broad terms, the LEZ includes nearly all of London inside the M25. Since 3 January 2012, drivers of diesel motorcaravans exceeding 2.5 tonnes gross weight that do not meet LEZ standards are required to pay a daily three-figure sum if they want to drive in this zone. This fee has been heavily criticised by motorcaravan visitors. Moreover, residents within this zone who currently own non-compliant vehicles are deeply aggrieved by the cost of taking their motorcaravan onto the road where they live.

Vehicles with emissions exceeding the accepted level have engines that were fitted in 2005 or earlier. (**Note:** *This is only a rough date; more specific advice appears later.*) Of course, it is technically possible to carry out modifications on non-compliant vehicles, but alterations are expensive. Work includes the installation of an approved filter, which needs periodic testing, and a full modification operation costs a four-figure sum. Although the date given above is only a rough guide, anyone who owns a motorcaravan or is about to purchase a pre-owned model can establish if the vehicle is subject to the LEZ daily fee by visiting www.tfl.gov.uk/lez or by telephoning 0845 607 0009. Entering a vehicle's registration number on the website produces a definitive answer.

Emission penalties are harsh, and it has been hinted in the national Press that other UK cities may follow the lead taken by Transport for London. Needless to say, new models avoid these problems and at the time of writing, base vehicles are being fitted with Euro V emission-compliant engines. Base vehicles from Mercedes, Volkswagen and Renault achieved Euro V compliance in 2010; Fiat Ducato vehicles – and Peugeot badged versions – achieved this in 2011.

EXAMPLES OF BASE VEHICLES

In recent years, five makes of base vehicle have been commonly used for the majority of European motorcaravans. These are the Fiat Ducato, Ford Transit, Mercedes-Benz Sprinter, Peugeot Boxer, VW Transporter T4 and now the T5.

Be aware that the Fiat Ducato and Peugeot Boxer were collaboratively developed and are constructed at the same factory in northern Italy. Apart from very small differences, the vehicles are virtually identical; sales of these products, however, are conducted independently and competitively. The Citroën Relay is also a 'badge-engineered' Ducato, although motorcaravan manufacturers use it less often.

Others makes, models and badge-engineered varients appear in lesser numbers. Examples include the Citroën Berlingo, Dispatch (re-badged Fiat Scudo) and Synergie; Daihatsu Hijet; Fiat Scudo; IVEKO Daily and Eurocargo; LDV Convoy, Pilot and Cub (re-badged Nissan Vanette); MAN 4.6TD; Mazda SGL5; Mercedes-Benz Vito; Nissan Vanette; Renault Master, Kangoo and Trafic; Suzuki Carry; Toyota HiAce; and VW LT.

Up-to-date lists of base vehicles are frequently published in motorcaravan magazines and occasionally form the subject of special supplements. Volkswagen UK has also published

Above: Thousands of comfortable campervans have been built using the VW Transporter as their base vehicle.

Below: The 2006 Knaus Sun Ti coachbuilt motorcaravan won several awards and its Renault engine is remarkably lively.

leaflets listing British-built motorcaravans constructed on the company's base vehicles.

If you're are interested in older pre-owned motorcaravans, *eg* built before 1994, their base vehicles include the Talbot Express/Fiat Ducato (forerunner of the Fiat Ducato/Peugeot Boxer launched in 1994), earlier models of Ford Transit, Renault Trafic, Volkswagen Transporter (T2, T3, and T4), Bedford CF and Leyland Sherpa.

Recognising the options available and acknowledging the differences between models, it is strongly recommended once again that a prospective purchaser arranges a test drive. It is only when you take a vehicle on the road that more subtle aspects of performance and the driving experience as a whole become evident.

Conversion elements

When comparing motorcaravans, reference is often made to their chassis. However, van conversions are not built on a traditional chassis. which is principally an assembly of heavy steel members. Instead, they employ what is known as a floor pan, which is strengthened with steel box sections welded to the base panel.

A few coachbuilt motorcaravans use a GRP (fibreglass) shell such as the CI Carioca 15 and Romahome Duo Outlook. These models are built on a structure called a 'platform cab'. This is rather like a van without its steel side panels and roof; an example is shown in Chapter 4. Platform cabs are also used in the construction of French-built Chausson and Challenger low-line coachbuilts, but this building method is not adopted often. Most

coachbuilt motorcaravans are constructed on what is known as a 'chassis cab'.

Types of chassis, together with their fitted running gear, suspension and brakes are considered in more detail in Chapter 4. For the moment, bear in mind that some chassis are fairly high above the ground and this gives their users a pronounced 'step-up' when they're climbing aboard. Other motorcaravans are built on a low-level chassis and are easier to enter; their lower centre of gravity is also an advantage when they are negotiating twisty roads.

One of the best-known low-level chassis is the purpose-designed AL-KO AMC unit. These galvanised structures, discussed in Chapter 4, are light and often fitted on front-wheel-drive vehicles. Curiously, chassis and suspension details are sometimes omitted from motorcaravan magazine data listings – in spite of their obvious importance.

When comparing more general features in a conversion, look at the following elements:

LAYOUT AND SLEEPING ARRANGEMENTS

This is largely a matter of personal taste, but check that bed making is straightforward. If there is a high-level bed, check both the access and provision for bedside items and clothing storage. If a bed has to be made using seating cushions, look to see if it's a complicated jigsaw. Also be aware that a knee roll (discussed in Chapter 9) is fine when a cushion is used as a seat, but it forms an inconvenient hump when the cushion is used to form a bed. Fixed beds avoid the need to convert seats every evening but they take up a lot of daytime living space. Finally, check if awkwardly shaped seat sections can be stowed away at night.

TRAVEL SAFETY

Check how many rear seats have a safety belt and relate this to the number of berths. Several motorcaravans have more berths than belted 'travel seats' and manufacturers now state how many travel seats are provided in the models they are selling. More information on this subject is given in the Appendix *Standards and Regulations* section.

KITCHEN

Look at the usable worktop space. Is there adequate food storage? Is there an oven? Some imported models have neither an oven nor a grill,

Right: An island bed was an option in this 2007 CI Mizar Elite, which means that space is sacrificed by day for a good sleep at night.

Far right: Fully belted travel seats are now expected in family motorcaravans, although child seats are less stable on a soft foam base.

and many British motorcaravanners regard this as a serious omission. Is there provision for rubbish? Many British motorcaravan kitchen designers used to overlook this matter, whereas imported models were generally fitted with a bin as standard. In recent UK models, this has largely been resolved.

STORAGE

Look for storage potential, including inside and outside lockers. A tall locker for skis or fishing rods is useful, as are lockers in the side skirts, but check their weight limits. Some purchasers require roof racks and rear ladders, but the roofs on some vehicles are not robust enough to carry heavy loads.

BIKE AND SCOOTER RACKS

Many owners would like to carry bikes on the back of their van, but adding a racking system retrospectively often poses problems. To create a safe and sturdy structure, steel plates and fixing bolts usually need to go right through the rear wall. In the past, poorly fastened racks *have* fallen off and landed on the road. Using a robust installation is even more important if you plan to transport a motorcycle. In that case, you also need to confirm that its addition would not exceed the weight-carrying limits of the motorcaravan's rear axle.

It is pleasing, then, to report that some motorcaravan manufacturers include a pre-formed internal structure to make the later addition of a rack a quick-fit operation. For instance, Auto-Sleepers vans have fitted plywood blocks at key points in the rear walls of coachbuilt models, and many dealer-suppliers hold drawings showing their

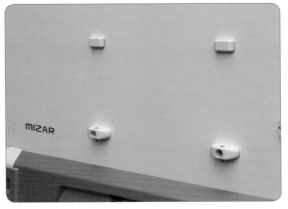

location. Complete structures terminated by cover caps on the rear were factory fitted on AutoRoller models in the 1990s. This strategy was also adopted in 2008 on the Mizar Elite, and by Bailey in 2011 when the Approach range of motorcaravans was launched. In view of the large number of motorcaravanners who use racks, it is a pity that more manufacturers do not adopt this practice.

SPARE WHEEL

Check how easy it is to remove a vehicle's spare wheel. Some locations are easy to reach; others are truly dreadful, especially when the back of a vehicle is sagging as a result of a rear puncture.

In some recent models, such as the 2009 Excel coachbuilt models, a spare has not been fitted at all, and purchasers are merely supplied with a 'Fix and Go' injection kit to deal with straightforward punctures.

Above left: Rear storage compartments provide valuable space for family holiday gear, but when used for heavy items they can lead to rear axle overloading.

Above: A short overhang at the back and a weighbridge check proved that this light motorbike was fine to carry on a well-fitted rack.

Left: It is a pity that more motorcaravans are not fitted with pre-installed fixing points for racks at the time of manufacture.

Far left: For spare wheel accessibility, few models beat the 2011 Auto-Trail Tracker; its wheel is released in minutes.

Left: There may be advantages of a Fix and Go kit, but injecting a sealant into the tyre will fail to safely repair certain types of puncture.

Right: Romahome is not a large manufacturer, but this owner's manual was far more helpful than many of the others supplied with motorcaravans.

Loading terms and user responsibilities

Weight is currently expressed in kilograms (1kg = 2.2lbs). Whereas an imperial ton is 20cwt, *ie* 2.240lb, a 'metric' ton, properly called a 'tonne', is 1,000kg, or 2,204.62lb. For more information, including the ton in the USA, see the Technical Tip on 'Tons and Tonnes' in Chapter 4.

Maximum technically permissible laden mass (MTPLM): This refers to a vehicle's total allowable legal weight, as defined by the base vehicle manufacturer. It has previously been called 'Maximum Laden Weight' (MLW), 'Maximum Authorised Mass' (MAM), Gross Vehicle Weight (GVW) and Maximum Authorised Weight (MAW). Unhelpfully, the DVLA uses the term MAM whereas the touring caravan and motorcaravan industries refer to it as MTPLM.

Actual laden weight (ALW): This is the total weight of a motorcaravan and includes the driver and passengers, all personal effects, fuel and all other items including fixed accessories. The ALW should be checked on a weighbridge to confirm that it doesn't exceed the vehicle's MTPLM.

Mass in running order (MIRO): This is the unladen ('ex-works') weight of a vehicle. It normally takes into account a full fuel tank, essential liquids, and in some manufacturers' literature, an estimated weight allowance for a driver (usually 75kg).

Maximum user payload (MUP): The payload is a vehicle's maximum carrying capacity and is calculated by deducting a vehicle's mass in running order (MIRO) from its maximum technically permissible laden mass (MTPLM).The lack of consistency relating to the inclusion (or omission) of a 75kg driver in a MIRO figure can lead to irregularities when published payload information is compared.

Maximum axle weights (MAW): Front and rear axles have maximum weight limits too, and these figures must not be exceeded. On vehicles with front and rear axles, their individual loading can be checked on a weighbridge by driving one axle at a time on to the weighing plate.

Gross train weight (GTW): This refers to the maximum weight permitted for a vehicle together with a trailer and the combined loads being carried. It is important to note this weight limit when towing heavy items such as a support car. GTW is sometimes referred to as the 'Combined Weight'.

Information plates: Data relating to weights is displayed on an information plate permanently fixed in the engine bay or mounted on a door surround.

Left: This data sticker was affixed to a 'door-shut' surround on the 2005 Renault-based Knaus Sun Ti low line coachbuilt model.

HANDBOOKS

When purchasing a motorcaravan, (especially a pre-owned model), ask to see the handbooks. A handbook is usually called an 'owner's manual'. There should be one for the base vehicle and another for the living faciliteis. Many owner's manuals relating to the motorcaravan itself are surprisingly poor; some converters include no documentation material, apart from leaflets from the manufacturers of individual appliances.

PRICE AND HIDDEN COSTS

Check the total price, ensuring that delivery charges and all 'hidden costs' are included. Most new models are supplied without any accessories. On the other hand, a model like the Murvi Morello is sold with a complete on-the-road package including gas, cutlery, crockery and leisure battery – but this is quite unusual.

LOADING GUIDANCE

When comparing models, look at their quoted user payload and relate this to the number of people you intend taking on holiday. A rough rule of thumb is to allow 75kg for each passenger's personal weight, 100kg for the personal effects of two people, which takes into account cutlery, crockery and cooking utensils, and then 25kg for the personal effects of each subsequent passenger. Then there is the weight of accessories that you might want to install on your motorcaravan, some of which are surprisingly heavy. Inevitably, this is only a rough starting point, so check the accompanying advice about loading terminology and the use of a weighbridge.

Since 1999, new motorcaravans have been covered by BS EN 1646-2, which specifies the way that weights and payload should be expressed.

Unfortunately, manufacturers often express the weight of ex-works vehicles (*ie* mass in running order or MIRO) in different ways. Some include a hypothetical 75kg driver, fuel tank filled to 90%, tools and a spare wheel. Also confusing is the fact that some models are sold with a 'deluxe' package that might include a rollout sunblind, a TV set, and alloy wheels. The addition of accessories like these inevitably means that a published MIRO figure applicable to the *standard* model is not applicable to the deluxe version with its package of extras. In consequence, the payload figure for these otherwise identical models will be different.

However, there can be no argument about a vehicle's maximum weight limit, which is shown on its data plate. Not only could it be dangerous to exceed this limit, it is also a serious offence. The problems arise when it comes to manufacturers' claims relating to payload. The information published in some brochures is pleasingly accurate; on other occasions it's wide of the mark. In consequence, when the author conducts tests for magazine reports, an empty vehicle is always filled to the brim with fuel and then checked on a public weighbridge. A calculation duly reveals if a claimed payload figure is accurate or optimistically exaggerated.

Inaccurate claims are not unusual. This problem

has also been noted by The Caravan Club when vehicles are entered for the annual Design and Drive competition. As a matter of routine, each model is taken to a weighbridge for checking before the judges commence their searching evaluations. Extraordinary and unexpected figures are often found during weight checks.

Roadside inspections conducted by the police have similarly revealed examples of gross overloading, and whilst towed caravans used to gain more scrutiny, attention is now also turning to motorhomes.

Of course a driver and other passengers logically represent part of a vehicle's payload. Other items can be classified in separate categories, namely:

- Essential equipment – such as gas cylinders and toilet chemicals.
- Optional equipment – such as solar panels, a cycle rack and an air conditioning system.
- Personal effects – such as clothing, food and holiday gear.

Unfortunately, the motorcaravan industry's classification system is periodically amended, which can lead to unwanted misunderstandings. In reality, the essential issues are delightfully simple:

Firstly, a motorcaravan has a stated maximum weight limit (MTPLM) together with maximum weight limits for each of its axles.

Secondly, a motorcaravan has an actual laden weight (ALW), which can be made up of various elements, including the weight of its occupants, fixed accessory items and everything else that is taken on trips. As long as the Actual Laden Weight (normally checked on a weighbridge), added to the weight of its occupants (usually checked on some scales), doesn't exceed the stated MTPLM limit, the vehicle is both safe and legal.

In view of the importance of being safe and legal, it is helpful that motorcaravan manufacturers are now publishing weights of optional extra items offered in their sales brochures. There is only so much that your vehicle is permitted to carry and if you insist on transporting something like a large motorbike, or fitting a heavy air conditioning appliance, you may have to cut down on something else in order to stay within your vehicle's weight limit. And let's face it; the weight of a motorbike equates with a mammoth pile of shoes, shirts, blouses, socks, pants and knickers.

USING A WEIGHBRIDGE

To confirm a vehicle doesn't exceed its MTPLM, it is necessary to put a fully-laden motorcaravan with a full petrol tank on a weighbridge. Passenger weight can then be calculated separately using scales and added to the weighbridge total later. Even if this check reveals that the MTPLM has not been exceeded, you also need to establish that the weight being borne by the individual axles does not exceed their loading limits either.

Another strategy is to weigh your motorcaravan when it's empty. Subtracting its empty weight from the MTPLM gives you a clear indication of how much equipment can now be loaded, and what extra accessories can be installed, not forgetting to include its occupants in the calculations, too. Let's check what is actually involved when using a weighbridge.

1. Start by locating the addresses of nearby weighbridges that can be used by members of the public. As a rule, phoning your Local Authority and asking for the Weights and Measures Department is a good place to start. However, in some authorities, this information is now held by the Council Trading Standards Service. In some instances you may find that the council's addresses include *private* industrial weighbridges, which cannot offer a service to members of the public.

2. Contact your preferred weighbridge and check whether it would be possible for your motorcaravan to be weighed. Enquire about the fee, bearing in mind that there is usually a charge for each individual check. Unless there is a need for critical accuracy, most owners get: (1) the overall weight measured, and (2) a weight check on the rear axle. Subtracting the rear axle loading from the total weight indicates the weight being borne by the front axle. *(Owners insisting on scrupulous accuracy weigh the front axle as a third weight check.)*

3. Confirm that a dated printout including the vehicle's registration number is issued as part of the service. Enquire if there are times during the opening period that are better avoided. Truck movements into and out of depots sometimes cause busy spells.

4. Establish if there is a fuel station in the vicinity of the weighbridge. Before recording a vehicle's weight it is preferable to have the fuel tank as near brimful as possible. Then you know that this particular imposition of weight cannot be exceeded. Also note down all the items that are left in the vehicle if it is being weighed *before* holiday possessions are added. For instance, record if there is any water in the fresh-water tank or in the toilet flush tank (if that is separate). How many gas cylinders are on board and what is their state of fill? Obviously the cylinders can be weighed individually on some bathroom scales back at home. Whether you decide to leave bikes on a rack or not is your decision – but make a note of these details.

5. Weighbridges differ and the one shown here is owned by agricultural engineers. It isn't spick and span, but it *is* subject to obligatory accuracy checks by local Weights and Measures officials. Some weighbridges have an adjacent office, supervisors in uniform, and an appearance of clinical efficiency. Prices vary, too, and at the time of writing, the weighbridge shown here carries a charge of £12 (including VAT) for each weight check. Access to its weighing plate is

CASE HISTORY: AUTO-TRAIL TRACKER EKS 2011 MODEL

Submitted for weight check with full diesel tank, two 13kg gas cylinders and empty water tanks. **Note:** *The weight marked on a cylinder only refers to its gas content and doesn't include the container's weight.*

Maximum published weight limits and the weighbridge findings

- **Overall MTPLM:** 3,500kg
- **Mass in running order (MIRO) from weighbridge:** 3,160kg
- **Mass in running order in Auto-Trail's brochure:** 3,215kg
- **Actual payload (MTPLM, 3,500kg – MIRO, 3160kg):** 340kg
- **Max rear axle loading limit:** 2,000kg
- **Actual rear axle loading from weighbridge:** 1,780kg
- **Additional loading that could be borne by the rear axle:** 220kg
- **Max front axle loading limit:** 1,850kg
- **Actual front axle loading (calculated):** 1,720kg
- **Additional loading that could be borne by the front axle:** 130kg
- **Stated gross train weight limit:** 4,750kg

To calculate how heavy a trailer and its load could be:
- Take the total weight of the vehicle when it's fully laden for a trip.
- Add to this the approx 70kg trailer nose weight bearing down on the tow ball.
- Subtract this total sum from 4,750kg.

Comments on the Auto-Trail Tracker EKS 2011 model

It is very pleasing to find a motorcaravan with an actual MIRO *lighter* than the figure quoted by its manufacturer. Recognising that this is a vehicle with only two belted seats in the cab, a payload of 340kg is good. Too many motorcaravans offer far less payload than their owners would like, and it's little wonder that roadside checks are finding vehicles that are badly overweight. Also be aware that it is extremely misguided to have heavy accessories installed if you haven't been to a weighbridge first to check how much payload is available when your vehicle has been packed for a typical trip.

As regards the low payload potential of the Auto-Trail Tracker's front axle (130kg), that is normal. After all, very few personal possessions can be stowed right at the front of a motorcaravan. It's the back axle that often gets over-laden, especially on a vehicle with a pronounced rear overhang. That acts like a long lever that accentuates the weight of a rack laden with heavy bikes or a motor scooter. In the case of the Tracker, an opportunity to add a further 220kg to the rear axle is reasonable – but not particularly generous. However, that is partly because the spare wheel is mounted in a splendidly accessible position on the rear wall. This was shown earlier in this chapter (page 25). If pressed, you could always remove this wheel temporarily and place it on the floor indoors and nearer the front. That would be useful on one of those special occasions when you wanted to carry a heavier-than-normal load at the back.

Right: The vehicle is driven onto the weighing plate; the driver gets out and stands to the side.

Far right: The vehicle is taken completely off the plate; the rear wheels are then reversed onto it again.

Right: Information is checked in the weighing booth, payment is made and the information is printed out.

Far right: Data on both the Fiat plate and the Auto-Trail conversion plate, mounted under the bonnet, are checked.

AUTO – TRAIL 'VR' LIMITED		
e13*2007/46*1088*		
SECOND STAGE CONVERSION		
*ZFA250000*01792084*		
		3500 kg
		4750 kg
1–		1850 kg
2–		2000 kg
3–		0000 kg

easily achieved, although the access road is dusty, rough but free of industrial debris. Since truck checks are carried out for scrap metal merchants, agricultural grain suppliers and general industrial purposes, the staff are always intrigued to see motorcaravans being weighed. That's partly because a disappointingly small number of touring and motorcaravan owners check their outfits on a weighbridge.

After gathering the all-important figures, be prepared for some surprises, especially when comparing weighbridge information with data published in advertising literature and owner's manuals. Also, keep a copy of the printout in your glovebox. Should you ever be stopped for a police road check, you can then show that you are not only mindful of the importance of safe loading; you also make an effort to stay within your vehicle's limits.

Incidentally, when purchasing a pre-owned model, it is worth asking a dealer or private vendor if there is a weighbridge certificate accompanying the papers that come with the vehicle. If there isn't, some buyers request that a weight check is carried out (at their expense) before conducting a purchase transaction. Let's look at a real life situation. See the 'Case History' panel on the facing page.

UP-RATING THE MTPLM

If checking a motorcaravan on a weighbridge subsequently reveals that it would be more versatile if its MTPLM were to be increased, this is sometimes possible. For instance it is mentioned in Chapter 4 that commercial vehicle consultants like SvTech in Leyland, Lancashire, are able to calculate whether the MTPLM of a vehicle can be increased. For example, it might be possible to upgrade and re-plate a light commercial vehicle from 3,500kg to 3,850kg. In practice, this could turn out costly because it might necessitate fitting up-rated tyres, strengthening the rear axle tube, altering the suspension, improving brake specification and so on.

Also be aware that there are some disadvantages when running a vehicle plated with an MTPLM greater than 3,500kg:

- Since January 1997, new driving licence holders in the UK are limited to driving vehicles up to 3,500kg – or 4,250kg when towing a trailer.
- Many motoring organisations in the UK will not recover motorhomes weighing over 3,500kg.
- In the UK, the minimum age to drive a vehicle over 3,500kg is 18; for vehicles weighing less than 3,500kg the age is 17.
- When a driver over 70 years of age applies to renew a licence, additional eyesight and health tests are required if the applicant wishes to drive a vehicle in the UK with an MTPLM over 3,500kg.
- Drivers with certain medical conditions are not permitted to drive vehicles plated at more than 3,500kg. This includes diabetics who have to control the condition using insulin injections.

- In some countries, particularly Germany, a vehicle over 3,500kg is classified as a goods vehicle and is subject to lower speed limits, different overtaking rules and restrictions of vehicle use at weekends.
- In Switzerland, a motorhome exceeding 3,500kg has to pay a heavy goods vehicle tax supplement at the border in order to use motorways.

There is no doubt that keeping the MTPLM at 3,500kg or lower has several points in its favour. In fact, some owners of motorcaravans with an MTPLM of 3,850kg arrange to have this limit officially reduced and the vehicle re-plated accordingly.

DOWN-RATING THE MTPLM

There are several approved specialists that are able to reduce the MTPLM of a motorcaravan and fit an official replacement plate. Once again, SvTech can provide advice.

It is not a difficult operation and it avoids some of the constraints described in the list above. Of course, the lower MTPLM limit calls for a stricter approach when packing personal gear, but there are several benefits, particularly in respect of driving licence classifications, health and eyesight tests for drivers aged over 70, and speed limits.

NATIONAL CARAVAN COUNCIL APPROVED MODELS

Many models manufactured in the UK bear an NCC approval badge. The accompanying panel explains what has to be achieved to gain this accreditation.

Habitation codes

Two organisations representing motorcaravan manufacturers in the UK, The Society of Motor Manufacturers & Traders (SMMT) and The National Caravan Council (NCC), collaboratively produced the NCC/SMMT Habitation Code 201 concerning health and safety requirements in motorcaravans. After this had been in operation for several years, BS EN 1646-2 was published, which also sets out health and safety standards.

Today, all NCC member-manufacturers are required to submit a prototype of every new model for inspection by NCC engineers in order to verify its compliance with BS EN 1646-2. In practice, the NCC test exceeds minimum requirements specified by the British/European standards and involves around 600 further check items. It includes elements like emergency escape, electricity supply systems, fire precautions, gas, handbook, heating, insulation, security, ventilation, payloads, and safety notices. When full compliance is established, subsequent vehicles of the type inspected are permitted to display the NCC Approval badge.

Of course, a number of manufacturers – principally the smaller ones – are not members of the NCC, so their products are not submitted for testing and do not display an approval badge. It would be wrong to presume, however, that non-badged products would necessarily fail to meet the relevant standards. Some non-members manufacture motorhomes to very high standards – as achievements in The Caravan Club's Design Awards have confirmed.

National Caravan Council member manufacturers are required to build to British and European standards.

Nature of use

Some owners use a motorcaravan for day-to-day driving, some only for warm weather holidays, and others for year-round use, even when it's cold. Accordingly, different patterns of use *must* be taken into account when motorcaravans are compared.

WINTER USE

If a motorcaravan is going to be used in cold conditions, its design and specification need to be taken into account. For instance, if water tanks are mounted externally, sub-zero temperatures may cause fresh and waste water tanks to freeze. Some models are far more suitable for year-round use than others, and considerations relating to water supply systems are discussed in Chapter 7.

However, water isn't the only 'winterising' issue. Some motorcaravans intended for use in cold conditions feature blown-air heating systems with outlets directed under bed mattresses, such as in the 1988 Laika Ecovip range, or around a bed, as in the 2000 Mobilvetta Top Driver 52. There are also issues relating to insulation levels.

For instance, when Bailey was building its first motorcaravans in 2011, the company adopted the policy that they should be 'vans for all seasons'. To this end it was necessary to install thicker insulated wall panels than normal, a strategy that has also been adopted recently by Auto-Trail. Taking the policy further, rigid insulation was also installed over the rear wheel boxes and around the footwell at the entrance door. Thermal imaging cameras were then used to identify other unprotected weak spots. After careful appraisals of these prototypes, it was decided to submit the largest model in the *Approach* range for cold chamber testing at the internationally renowned Millbrook Proving ground in Bedfordshire.

The objective was to achieve a Grade III classification of Thermal Insulation (EN1646-1), which hitherto, very few UK motorcaravans have achieved. The test regime is summarised in the accompanying panel and the determined efforts of the Bailey design team were rewarded when Grade III accreditation was announced by Millbrook's specialist test team.

SUMMER USE

The importance of good thermal insulation is often considered in the context of winter temperatures. This is misguided. When a motorcaravan is parked

Thermal Insulation (EN1646-1)

It is no easy task to achieve a Grade III classification of Thermal Insulation (EN1646-1). To test thermal performance, it takes 10 hours to get a purpose-made building housing a vehicle down to -15ºC. Then the motorhome heating is switched on to raise its internal temperature to 20ºC, which it has to achieve within four hours. When sensors located throughout the vehicle identify that the temperature has stabilised, fresh water is connected and the supply should be operational even when the external temperature is still -15ºC. Not many UK motorcaravans achieve this accreditation, but for year-round users, a Grade III classification is a benchmark achievement.

in bright summer sunshine, its interior temperature can rise so much that it becomes excessively hot. In these circumstances the better the insulation used in its external structure, the more tolerable it becomes indoors. In other words, a vehicle that has achieved a Grade III classification of thermal insulation affords better comfort indoors in summer as well as in the winter.

MOTORHOMES FOR DISABLED USERS

Adaptations are possible on a number of models and motorcaravan magazines often publish articles and supplements that describe special products for elderly and disabled users.

In order to help purchasers with disabilities, HM Customs and Excise has operated a scheme for several years whereby some registered disabled people can purchase a motorcaravan with a VAT element at the zero rate. The scheme applies to new motorcaravans as well as to pre-owned models that have been specially adapted. To benefit from this concession, several conditions have to be met and the scheme is principally focussed on wheelchair users. The arrangement should be agreed prior to purchase; there is no facility for reclaiming VAT after payment has been made.

Further details are given in VAT Notice 701/59 *Motor vehicles for disabled people.* This is available from HM Customs and Excise, Charities and Healthcare, London SE1 9PJ Tel: 08450 109000 and www.hmce.gov.uk

Right: A prototype Bailey Approach SE 760 achieved Grade III classification of Thermal Insulation at the Millbrook cold chamber test facility.

Far right: Several of the low output van converters are experienced in building motorcaravans with facilities to suit wheelchair users.

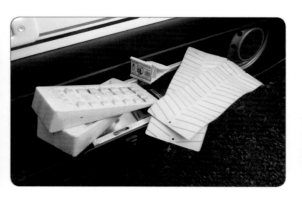

Purchasing considerations

Recognising the considerable cost of a new motorcaravan, a first-time purchaser might be advised to start with a pre-owned model in order to confirm that motorcaravanning lives up to expectations. Sometimes a pre-owned model will be sold with a full complement of items, such as a fitted external roller blind, cutlery, crockery, levelling devices and so on. In contrast, if you buy a *new* motorcaravan, many of these items are not included in the sale.

PRE-OWNED PURCHASES

Classified advertisements in motorcaravan magazines show that there are plenty of vehicles available for purchase. Vehicles with modest recorded mileages in immaculate condition are not unusual, and many motorcaravanners look after their vehicles very carefully.

Dealers also have stocks of pre-owned vehicles and more recent models might be sold with a warranty. Moreover, a full forecourt provides a good opportunity to compare models.

Lastly, there are auctions. Some are held at local level, often using a storage depot as the venue. On a national scale there is a caravan and motorcaravan division of British Car Auctions (BCA). Periodic sales are programmed around the country and the centres at Brighouse and Measham usually offer a good selection of models. Information on a motorcaravan's history is fixed to the screen of each lot in the sale and the process of buying is not the gamble that many people imagine. To assist a prospective bidder, buying and selling procedures are explained in a booklet available from BCA's head office.

Obviously anyone who plans to purchase a pre-owned vehicle from a private vendor will accept the meaning of *caveat emptor* – 'buyer beware'. A 'sold as seen' disclaimer emphasises the importance of thoroughly checking a product. This involves two elements – base vehicle and habitation provision. Regarding the base vehicle:

- Check for MoT and service vouchers – both of which help to verify the recorded mileage.
- Look at the tyres – irregular wear on the front may indicate steering misalignment.
- Look for worn foot pedals in the cab – a sure sign of a high mileage.
- Check for dirty oil on the dipstick.
- Look for damp under the cab carpets – which hints at a faulty screen seal or a leaking heater radiator matrix.
- Insist the owner takes you on a test drive. Better still; if all documents are in order, drive the vehicle yourself.
- Enquire if a weighbridge report is included in the paperwork.
- Check the owner's manual and service history book is included.

The list could go on and anyone with limited mechanical knowledge is advised to enlist the services of a motoring organisation or better still, a specialist company like Auto Van Services that

Right: In a pre-owned model, check the upholstery – replacements can be costly.

will issue a detailed report after an engineer's inspection has been completed.

Regarding the living area, further checks should be carried out. For example:

- Turn on the hob and other cooking appliances.
- Confirm the heating system is working.
- Try the fridge – but remember it takes time for cooling to commence.
- Look at cushions, seat backs and bases.
- Check carefully for signs of damp on the walls or inside internal lockers.
- Check documentation regarding habitation servicing.

A pre-owned motorcaravan being sold with the following documentation is likely to be a reliable purchase:

- Dated habitation servicing certificates.
- Dated refrigerator servicing certificates.
- Dated certificates from gas and electrical engineers confirming these supply systems are in safe working order.
- A recent, dated damp test report complete with a diagram showing the 50 or so checking points.
- The owner's manual regarding the conversion element.

Unfortunately, some of these important documents are often missing and you would be unwise to put systems (eg the gas supply) into commission until a qualified service specialist has carried out inspections and service work. Also be aware that some motorcaravans will have had no habitation work servicing carried out since the day they left the factory.

Right: Models from Middlesex Motorcaravans are purchased directly from the manufacturer; some are new *conversions* built on *nearly new* base vehicles at truly competitive prices.

BUYING NEW

Buying a new motorcaravan doesn't involve the uncertainty that surrounds the purchase of a used model. However, check the scope of any warranties and establish the procedure in the event of an early problem. For instance, if you visit an exhibition and accept an attractive sales offer from a dealer whose base is situated a long way from your home, ask what procedures have to be followed if there are warranty problems relating to the conversion (as opposed to the base vehicle). As a rule, you'll probably have to drive all the way back to the dealer to get faults rectified. Similarly, enquire what procedure has to be followed if there's a problem with the base vehicle; that is usually *less* problematic because mechanical faults can normally be carried out under warranty at any base vehicle franchise dealership in the UK.

You can buy a motorcaravan in a number of ways:

- An order can be placed at a major exhibition. For instance, a manufacturer's stand is usually staffed by sales representatives from approved dealers around the country as well as by personnel from the factory (or importing agency).
- Alternatively you can make the purchase at the premises of a dealer; there are a number of long-established UK specialists.
- Buying direct from a manufacturer is normally only possible in the case of low-volume specialists, many of whom attend outdoor shows.

Note: *Some potential owners contemplate buying directly from other countries. This isn't always a straightforward matter, especially if you want a right-hand drive vehicle. Other specification features differ on direct imports, too. Letters published in magazines show that the exercise can range from 'plain sailing' to a 'frustrating experience' fraught with delays and difficulties. Getting warranty work done on habitation elements may be a problem, too, and a lower-than-normal trade-in price is another issue to consider. Nevertheless, as methods of construction, codes of practice and choice of components become increasingly standardised, this purchasing strategy will probably become easier.*

Whichever route you take when making a purchase, insist on a road test. Sometimes there is diffidence on the part of sellers to sanction this. However, parting with a large sum of money without confirming a vehicle's driving characteristics and ride quality is clearly not advised.

BESPOKE MODELS

A rather different route to ownership is to buy a 'made-to-order' motorcaravan. Small-scale manufacturers like Young Conversions pride themselves on the fact that no two motorcaravans leave their factory the same. Even though the company lists fixed roof, rising roof and high-top models, in practice most clients make amendments to the standard specification. Some customers even arrange to supply a new or second-hand base vehicle themselves; others get Mike Young, the proprietor, to locate a suitable pre-owned van on their behalf. A number of clients submit drawings of what they require; one purchaser even supplied a balsa wood model showing the layout he wanted. Finally, some customers only want part of the fitting-out work completed professionally because they intend applying the finishing touches themselves.

Other manufacturers offering this flexibility include Middlesex Motorcaravans in Edgware, Nu Venture Campers in Wigan, and Rainbow Conversions in Wisbech, Cambridgeshire. The accommodation of individual requirements certainly cannot be done by large-scale manufacturers, but make an appointment before travelling to these factories to see examples of their products. Young Conversions also runs a series of open days.

SELF-BUILDING AND RENOVATING

Other strategies adopted by motorcaravan enthusiasts are:

- Renovating a second-hand vehicle.
- Converting a van themselves.
- Building a motorcaravan from scratch.

Many would-be constructors join the Self Build Motor Caravanners' Club (SBMCC) and attend one of the numerous rallies that are held around the country. People from all walks of life attend, and there is an unexpected array of converted vehicles to compare. Some are well-appointed vans: others are less conventional vehicles and even army trucks or former buses can yield luxury living accommodation.

After their accomplishments, some self-builders have gone into business (Elddis was originally set up after the late Siddle Cook built himself a DIY caravan. Auto-Sleepers was started after the late Calverly Trevelyan converted a panel van and took his family on holiday.)

Much can be learnt from the self-build approach, and even an 'armchair builder' who ultimately buys a new motorcaravan can be helpfully informed by seeing what is involved. A brief reference to self-build case studies is included in Chapter 10, although for more advice on self-building, see the Haynes publication, *Build Your Own Motorcaravan*.

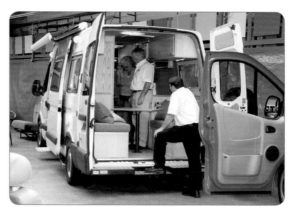

Left: During an open day at the Bletchley factory of Young Conversions, a customer discusses ideas for a one-off van.

Above: This is the fourth DIY van from Peter Anson of Night Owl Conversions and its quality compares well with professionally built models.

Left: All sorts of vehicles are built or converted by members of the SBMCC, as the pictures reveal on the club's website.

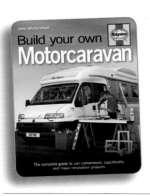

Left: If you want guidance on building a DIY motorcaravan, this book discusses a wide range of issues that you need to consider when taking the plunge.

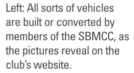

Left: This might be an Army vehicle on the outside but its interior is a sumptuous home-built conversion.

HIRING PRIOR TO BUYING

Hiring as a prelude to buying has much to commend it. Around 40 companies nationwide run hiring schemes; hirers often place advertisements in motorcaravan magazines.

Some hirers are independent specialists whereas others form part of a dealership whose vehicles are usually sold after a year of hiring. Sometimes, there are offers linked with purchasing and if a client who hires a vehicle subsequently purchases one of the dealer's motorcaravans, part of the original hire fee is reimbursed.

The majority of hire fleet vehicles are coachbuilt models, but you will also find van conversions – even historic VW campervans are sometimes available for hire.

Hiring before buying makes good sense and most vehicles are equipped with most of the items that a user is going to need. However, bear in mind that fees are considerably higher in peak summer periods than during the winter months.

Ownership issues

Choosing and buying is one thing: owning is another. Here are some issues to bear in mind.

MOT TESTING

When a motorcaravan is due for an MoT, the inspection is referred to as a Class IV test. Although goods vehicles classified between 3,000 and 3,500kg have to be submitted for a Class VII test, this is not the case for motorcaravans. In this instance they fall under the same classification and test procedures as a normal car, irrespective of their weight.

This is fine, except for the fact that many MoT Stations that conduct Class IV tests for car owners simply don't have good enough access or height to accommodate a large coachbuilt motorcaravan. Equipment like an elevating ramp might not have the lifting capacity to cope with a very large model either and the rolling road for brake testing might not be suitable.

For these reasons many owners take their vehicle to a goods vehicle test station, which is fine – provided the management is familiar with car/motorcaravan testing protocols.

Matters relating to MoT testing are dealt with by the Vehicle & Operator Services Agency (VOSA) and further information can be obtained from www.vosa.gov.uk. Moreover, if you want to check the MoT status of a vehicle, this can be done by visiting www.motinfo.gov.uk or by telephoning 0870 33 00 444. You will need the vehicle's registration mark and either the reference number on the V5C Registration Certificate or the test number from a new style VT20 MoT Test Certificate.

Nowadays, an MoT Test pass result is recorded on VOSA's database, and for legal purposes this is used, rather than a VT20 paper certificate, to verify that your vehicle has indeed achieved the necessary pass.

DRIVING LICENCES FOR MOTORCARAVAN DRIVING AND TOWING

■ Drivers under the age of 70:

If you passed your test prior to 1 January 1997:
A Category B Driving Licence obtained before 1 January 1997 permits you to drive a motorcaravan without a trailer as long as its MTPLM doesn't exceed 7,500kg. Alternatively, if you want to tow a trailer, you are permitted to do this as long as the GTW of the laden trailer *and* the laden motorcaravan doesn't exceed 8,250kg.

If you gained your Category B licence on or after 1 January 1997:
You are permitted to drive vehicles with an MTPLM up to 3,500kg. If you want to tow a small trailer behind your motorcaravan, no further test has

to be passed as long as the laden trailer doesn't exceed 750kg and the combined MTPLM of the motorcaravan and trailer doesn't exceed 4,250kg. However, if you successfully pass an LGV test, you are then qualified to drive a motorcaravan with an MTPLM up to 7,500kg.

To tow a trailer that weighs more than 750kg but less than the motorcaravan, and provided the MTPLM of the motorcaravan doesn't exceed 3,500kg, you are required to pass a further E Test. So if you want to tow a support car on a trailer, be aware that a Smart for Two exceeds 750kg even before the trailer weight is taken into account.

As regards owners wanting to tow a trailer heavier than 750kg behind a motorcaravan whose MTPLM exceeds 3,500kg, it is necessary to pass both an E Test and an LGV Test.

If you wish to drive a motorcaravan exceeding 7,500kg MTPLM you will have to pass a C Test.

■ Drivers exceeding the age of 70:

If you passed your test prior to 1 January 1997:
Provided the MTPLM of your motorcaravan is less than 3,500kg, the driving entitlement for both Category B and combined Category B+E is normally retained when you reapply for a licence, which will run for three years after reaching the age of 70. If the MTPLM of your motorcaravan is greater than 3,500kg, you will also have to submit a D4 medical form completed by your doctor. This involves an eyesight test to verify that your vision achieves the required standard at 20.5m (67ft). Further

information on medical requirements is given on the DVLA website: www.dvla.gov.uk.

If you passed your test on or after 1 January 1997:
As long as your medical condition is sound, you are permitted to drive a vehicle on your B licence provided its MTPLM is less than 3,500kg. However, if your motorcaravan's MTPLM exceeds this weight but is no greater than 7,500kg, you will have to take a further test to gain a C1 licence; this is the qualification needed by drivers of 'medium commercial vehicles'. Incidentally you can alternatively arrange for the MTPLM shown on the vehicle's plate to be down-rated as discussed earlier in this chapter.

If you wish to drive a motorcaravan exceeding 7,500kg MTPLM you will have to pass a C Test.

For further information, the DVLA Booklet D100 available from Post Offices is entitled: 'What you need to know about driving licences'. Unfortunately, some editions of the booklet appear not to give a great deal of advice on aspects relating to medical certification for the over 70s.

PARKING AT YOUR HOME
This is sometimes difficult and convenants might restrict the type of vehicle that can be parked at your house. So a prospective purchaser needs to decide if a motorcaravan would be better kept at a safe storage compound. Some storage centres even provide indoor accommodation for motorcaravans.

Above: The eligibility of drivers to tow sometimes depends on the weight of their loaded trailer and the date when they passed their test.

Body structure, maintenance and repair work

Looking after a motorcaravan amounts to more than keeping the engine tuned. The exterior bodywork should receive periodic maintenance and repairs are sometimes needed as well.

Understanding the way motorcaravans are built and being able to identify the materials used in construction have implications for routine issues like cleaning, as well as more involved issues like repairing accident damage.

Above: First introduced in the 1980s, the seam-free monocoque coachbuilts manufactured by Auto-Sleepers soon gained wide acclaim.

Below: Attractive designs and a noteworthy resistance to weather are a feature of recent Wingamm monocoque GRP models which are built in Italy.

Body construction

Since there are many different *types* of motorcaravan, it's hardly surprising that there are several different ways of building them. There are three distinctive areas of interest to note.

VAN CONVERSIONS, MONOCOQUES AND COACHBUILT STRUCTURES

The entire body of a van conversion is made up of steel panels, which can be cleaned using normal car-cleaning products. Similarly, repair procedures and re-painting can often be carried out by car body specialists. Problems from water ingress are uncommon, and leaks will usually only occur if components have been poorly installed, such as roof lights, ventilators and acrylic window units. As a rule, van conversions are very weather-resistant.

In contrast, the majority of coachbuilt motorcaravans are constructed in a wholly different way. The body is usually constructed with a greater variety of materials, which has implications for both repair and maintenance work. The only time this isn't the case is when a coachbuilt model is constructed using a monocoque (*ie* one piece) moulded GRP body shell. This shell material, commonly referred to as 'fibreglass', is frequently used for small boats, which shows that leaks are not expected to be a problem. Examples of monocoque coachbuilts include models from Auto-Sleepers, Esterel, Romahome and Wingamm, and their curving lines can be truly attractive. But this type of vehicle is costly.

Flat-sided coachbuilts are far more common, and the methods of assembling these have changed through the years. In the traditional approach to coachbuilding, work commenced with the fabrication of a skeleton framework using wooden struts. Decorative-faced plywood sheets were then fixed to this framework to form the ceiling and interior walls. Once these panels were

Thermal insulation

Anyone planning to purchase a motorcaravan for use in the winter months or in unusually hot places should seek manufacturers' advice concerning the use of insulating materials. Don't forget that a well-insulated living space not only retains the warmth generated by a heating appliance in cold weather: it also helps to prevent the interior becoming an oven when parked in direct sunshine.

Needless-to-say, the level of insulation varies from model to model and some coachbuilt motorcaravans only incorporate a 25mm layer of block foam in the side walls. The insulant is significantly thicker, however, in recent Auto-Trail coachbuilt models as you can see from the stepped portion in the wall around the entrance door.

NOTE: Information on tests of thermal performance and cold chamber testing was given in Chapter 2.

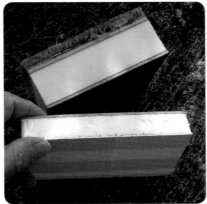

in place, a synthetic fibre quilt was usually placed between the struts to provide thermal insulation. Finally, a cladding material such as pre-painted sheet aluminium was added to the outside. This assembly technique was still being used in the 1990s by a few UK manufacturers. One of the last to use it was Buccaneer but its construction methods changed when the Company became part of The Explorer Group. Today, the majority of coachbuilt motorcaravans are constructed using pre-fabricated panels.

SANDWICH CONSTRUCTION

The use of prefabricated insulated boards is sometimes referred to as 'sandwich construction'. Components that make up the three-layer sandwich include:

- A 3mm decorative-faced plywood for the interior surfaces
- Block foam insulation such as Styrafoam or polystyrene in the middle
- Pre-painted aluminium sheet or a thin, flexible GRP sheet for the exterior

These components are not particularly strong when used individually, but when they are coated with a high specification adhesive and bonded together in an industrial press, the resulting composite panel is notably rigid. It is also remarkably light. Apertures

for the door and windows are prepared before the panel goes into the press and each opening has to be reinforced using a timber framework to improve rigidity. This wooden surround also provides sound fixing points for the hinges and catches, which will be added later. As a further innovation, Bailey of Bristol is now building 'sandwich construction' panels for its coachbuilt motorcaravans using plastic struts instead of softwood battens. In the event of water ingress, these will not deteriorate in the way that softwood supports will.

Above left: On some models a wall panel uses polystyrene for insulation; a floor panel is usually much thicker, and this example has blue Styrafoam instead.

Above: The remarkably well-insulated wall panels fitted on high specification Giotti Line models from Italy would be a great asset for discerning year-round users.

Left: This floor panel is assembled using timber battens and Styrafoam insulation. Once the top layer of ply and adhesive has been added it passes into a bonding press.

Left: Bailey of Bristol recently started using reinforcing struts made of a plastic compound instead of wooden battens. If these get damp there will be no depreciation.

Far left: Sandwich construction sides start with the internal ply; a timber framework is constructed around the perimeter and large apertures such as windows and doors.

Left: Most coachbuilt motorcaravans are constructed using pre-fabricated wall panels and these examples are ready for the assembly line.

Above: Some Bessacarr and Swift coachbuilt models have been clad with a thin glass-reinforced plastic (GRP) outer-skin, although aluminium sheeting is sometimes used instead.

Bonded sandwich construction offers several advantages, and coachbuilding specialists like Auto-Trail, Elddis and Swift have used prefabricated panels for over 20 years. However, a variation on the theme – growing in popularity – is to clad the exterior with a thin layer of pre-coloured glassfibre sheet instead of aluminium. The Swift Group has used this on some of its Bessacarr models, and on some Swift Royale and Kon-Tiki models. Sheet GRP cladding is also being used on the Bailey Approach SE models.

Other manufacturers who have used GRP sheet for exterior wall cladding include Auto-Sleepers (on models such as the Ravenna, Pescara and Pollensa) and Auto-Trail (all recent models). Before ceasing trading, Avondale also used GRP cladding on the Seascape and Seaspirit models.

As a rule, GRP sheet does not achieve the high-gloss finish that you see on painted aluminium. However, if minor accident damage occurs, it is possible for an experienced laminator to repair a GRP skin using polyester resin-based fillers. Dents in aluminium, especially if the cladding has a textured surface, are extremely hard to disguise using patch repairs. Not only does aluminium stretch when dented, it doesn't always adhere well to some automotive body-filler compounds. In consequence, damage to a side wall either necessitates bonding a complete new aluminium skin on top of the original cladding, or, as later photographs in this chapter show (see page 55), changing the entire wall panel. That, of course, is a major job.

Right: A completely new middle section of aluminium has been bonded on top of a damaged panel. Later the 'van will be parked closer to the wall and the black mattress will be inflated to apply consistent pressure to the entire area while the adhesive is setting.
(Photograph courtesy of Crossley Coachcraft)

(see page 55)

Localised repairs on aluminium cladding

Some skilled body specialists are able to create patch repairs on smooth aluminium cladding. The difficulty, however, is finding a filling compound that creates a permanent bond with aluminium, which is certainly not as easy as using 'filler' on a steel van panel. This is why larger areas of damage are usually dealt with by bonding a completely new sheet of cladding on top of the old one.

Even harder is patch-repairing a *textured* aluminium panel and most attempts to replicate its original surface are unsuccessful. In particular, pimpled aluminium surfaces are not easy to mend, and some purchasers avoid buying motorcaravans with a pimple finish for this reason. However,

several years ago a Danish system was introduced in which a flexible mould was created from a small section of a textured skin. This mould was then used to produce a replica for bonding and 'feathering-in' over the area of localised damage. The process requires several special tools and demands knowledge and skill. Although some body repairers might still use this patented system, adding a completely new panel is usually the preferred cure. Needless-to-say, that's a costly and time-consuming operation, which is annoying if the area of damage is merely a dent the size of a fist.

ASSEMBLY STRATEGIES

It was mentioned earlier that a few coachbuilt models are constructed using a monocoque glass-reinforced plastic (GRP) moulding. An enclosure made this way is usually strong, but it can be quite heavy. An attractively shaped 'pod' also takes more time to insulate than a flat, prefabricated sandwich panel. The internal plywood walls are not easy to assemble, so in effect, the operation is little different from the time-consuming lining work that has to be carried out in a van conversion. Inevitably, this is a labour-intensive way of building a coachbuilt motorcaravan, although a moulded monocoque often looks far more attractive than a 'slab-sided' box.

To improve the displeasing appearance of an angular, flat panel box, manufacturers often fit a moulded rear wall to improve the lines. In addition, ABS plastic mouldings are mounted around the rear wheels and a GRP-moulded roof panel adds further visual improvement. In fact Auto-Sleepers realised that the construction of their unique monocoque coachbuilt models, originally created by the revered car designer William Towns, had to be superseded by models that were less expensive to fit-out. So the search for more efficient construction methods led to a new range of models like the Pollensa and Ravenna. These employed flat-sided sandwich walls but continued the skilful use of GRP mouldings, including roof and over-cab assemblies similar in appearance to the shapely examples used in the monocoque models.

But how are all these different models assembled? In the case of fitting-out a panel van or a monocoque pod, the process is often described as an *'outside-in'* approach. Work starts with tasks such as adding a window or roof ventilator, and then focusses on the interior. When the interior walls have been insulated and lined, pre-assembled furniture units are installed. The diminishing space after this procedure strictly limits how many people can work inside the van simultaneously.

This disadvantage is less acute when prefabricated body panels are used. As the illustration above right shows, the rear of the vehicle was left completely open when these Elddis coachbuilt models were being assembled, which improved access dramatically. Pre-built furniture units could then be lifted inside and there was a wide entrance for the construction team. In this situation, installation of the rear panel is intentionally left until later.

Of course, construction strategies vary between manufacturers, and Auto-Trail employs a full *inside-out* strategy. Assembly of an Auto-Trail coachbuilt commences on a flat plinth. Using this as a datum

Left: In the former Explorer Group factory, roof, sides and floor are assembled, but the rear is left open until the furniture and appliances have been installed.

point, prefabricated furniture units and appliances are then positioned, mounted and coupled together. Progress is quick because the assembly team have open access from all sides. In addition, this technique allows for a high degree of accuracy and replication as each motorcaravan takes shape. When key elements of an interior are in place, the completed unit is then lifted by crane and lowered onto the chassis. Elements like Auto-Trail's robust GRP roof are subsequently lowered into place and external finishing work is carried out on high-level walkways. The accompanying illustrations show these stages in progress.

COUPLING PANELS TOGETHER

When a series of external panels are brought together to form an enclosure, the method of fixing has to be both strong and weather-resistant. In most instances, a sealant helps to provide a

Far left: An Auto-Trail coachbuilt is assembled on a wooden plinth, which ensures a totally flat base on which to build.

Left: Pre-assembled furniture units are coupled together and appliances are easily installed on account of the available space.

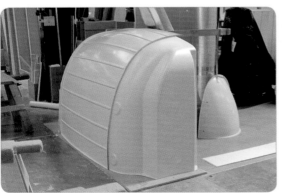

Far left: Prefabrication of key components allows replication. The item here is the internal skin of an over-cab pod.

Left: After an assembled interior has been mounted on the chassis, work on the roof can be easily carried out using high-level walkways.

water-resistant bond and the mechanical joining will usually involve the use of screws. In a similar way, screws are often used to secure ventilators, body trims, TV aerials, solar panels and so on. The trouble with this approach is that every screw forms a hole in an external panel. And holes in panels can often lead to leaks.

Without doubt, the use of sealants is extremely important, and a later section explains the types preferred by motorcaravan manufacturers. It helps if stainless steel screws are used throughout the construction, but some manufacturers use standard steel screws, which are cheaper. Inevitably these fixings soon start to rust and deteriorating threads quickly lose their ability to hold components firmly in place. A flexible sealant prevents this, but in time this will dry out, crack and lose its effectiveness. When cracked pieces of dried sealant become detached, gaps are left where the rain can get in.

THE ALU-TECH SYSTEM
In their determined attempt to improve resistance to poor weather, Bailey of Bristol developed the Alu-Tech system. This was first used on a new touring caravan launched in 2009. Products built in this way were immediately supported by a 10-year warranty against water ingress, which demonstrates the Company's confidence in this form of construction. When the Company developed prototypes of its first range of coachbuilt motorcaravans in 2010, it was no surprise to hear that the Alu-Tech system would be used.

Instead of linking panels together using screws, trim pieces and sealant, the Alu-Tech system uses a clamping arrangement as shown in the illustrations.

In an Alu-Tech enclosure, the external skin will only be punctured by screws in about 20 points, instead of the usual number, which could total around 250 depending on the size of the van. The integrity of Bailey's Alu-Tech assembly system in the context of motorcaravans should become increasingly apparent in the next few years.

EMBELLISHING MOULDINGS
Regardless of the way in which the main body of a motorcaravan is constructed, there are usually additional small mouldings manufactured in a plastic material such as ABS or GRP. These can include housings for rear lights, wheel spats, low-level fairings below floor level, small external locker lids, and a wind spoiler in front of a van conversion's elevating roof panel.

Both ABS and GRP can usually be repaired, although the products and processes are different. And whilst many repairers know how to mend fibreglass (GRP), few seem to attempt repairs on ABS mouldings. Guidance on how to go about these repairs is given later, but before embarking on this you need to be able to identify the two types of plastic. The accompanying panel shows you how.

SEALANTS AND MASTICS
One of the problems arising from a vehicle with a body built from many types of materials is the matter of differential movement. In hot conditions, some materials expand considerably more than others; in cold conditions, they contract at a different rate. Coupled with this is the fact that a motorcaravan is subjected to severe mechanical stresses when driven on poor road surfaces. The implication of this becomes evident where different materials fit closely together; gaps between these

Right: This mock-up supplied to dealers shows how three panels are held in close register using plates and threaded couplings.

Far right: Powder-coated, aluminium junction pieces are designed to hold panels in place and some have a channelling for awning attachment.

Right: Purpose-made plastic junctions are made for coupling-up lengths of the Alu-Tech channelling; other sections are made with gentle curves.

Far right: Insulation is inserted into the Alu-Tech sections to reduce heat loss; the completed enclosures achieve a high level of thermal efficiency.

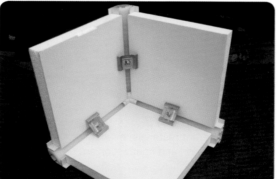

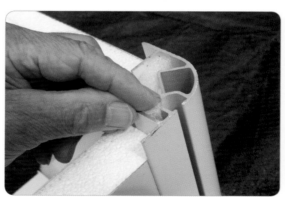

GRP stands for 'glass-reinforced plastic' – often called 'fibreglass'. Some GRP is self-coloured because it contains a pigment: other GRP mouldings are painted afterwards.

ABS stands for acrylonitrile-butadiene-styrene – and is almost always referred to as ABS!

Acrylic-capped ABS has a surface coating of acrylic in order to give it a high gloss finish.

These distinctive types of plastic used for moulded body panels are easy to identify. The rear face of a GRP moulding is normally rough and you will often be able to see the strands of glass used as the reinforcing binder in its laminated construction. In contrast, the rear face of an ABS moulding is smooth and this is often used for vehicle bumpers, albeit with a textured outer face. Acrylic-capped ABS is shiny on both faces and this is often used for fairings on race replica motorbikes, car bumpers made with a body-matching colour, or body panels such as the

wings on several recent models of cars. (The Ford Focus is an example).

When cracked or split, both GRP and ABS can be repaired but the chemicals required are very different. This is why you need to be quite clear which material has been used for the damaged component. Otherwise, the repair procedures have much in common, but there's a warning. Whereas many body specialists are familiar with GRP repairs, a lot are less willing to repair a damaged ABS panel and prefer to replace the entire section. This can be very costly.

Above left: The roughened rear face of this body skirt indicates it is made from GRP, which is easy to repair.

Above: A smooth finish on both surfaces of this wheel cover moulding shows that it is made from ABS plastic.

different materials may open or close due to the changing temperatures, or as a result of normal flexion. When this happens, the weatherproofing qualities of a motorcaravan's body are under threat.

As mentioned earlier, many coachbuilt models start to leak as a motorcaravan gets older. It was also pointed out that although van conversions are less likely to develop leaks, problems can occur if certain accessories have been poorly installed. The application of a sealant helps to fill gaps, as long as it permits flexion without a loss of adhesion.

There are several types of sealing products available, and these are classified according to their intended functions. For instance, some are described as 'non-setting sealants', whereas others are known as 'adhesive sealants'. The latter type could take as long as 24 hours to cure fully, but the bonding characteristics thereafter are remarkable. In fact, some adhesive sealants are also able to bond dissimilar materials together to great effect. This is demonstrated when a modern windscreen is installed on a vehicle. A purpose-made black adhesive is used to bond glass to its metal surround. However, it usually takes several hours for the bonding sealant to set properly, and this is why roadside replacements are carried out far less frequently than they used to be. Driving away shortly after the installation of a new screen was possible when screens were attached with rubber beadings. Screens were attached in this way in motorcaravans built into the late 1990s, but since then, screens have been fitted to light commercial vehicles using bonding sealant.

The remarkable bonding facility of adhesive sealants offers great benefits to motorcaravan builders and repairers. For instance, GRP over-cab structures, like the forward section of a moulded

roof, are normally attached to the steel top of a cab using an adhesive sealant rather than mechanical fixings such as screws. The only problem with this type of product is its permanence. The bond is so effective that it can be a tough job to remove a fitting or panel held in place with adhesive sealant.

Suffice it to say, sealants are made to perform widely different jobs, and the table overleaf provides guidance on product types and operations where they might be used.

As for external work on a motorcaravan, you would not normally use the types of silicone products employed indoors for jobs like sealing the rear of a washbasin. In contrast, *external* bedding sealants would be used for jobs like mounting an accessory such as a roof ventilator. This includes non-setting, butyl rubber-based sealants that retain their tackiness and flexibility for years. The aim of a bedding sealant (often called a 'mastic') is to retain a close register between different materials, even if their respective rates of expansion and contraction are dissimilar.

The DIY installer then has a decision to make. One option is to use a bedding sealant sold in

Left: When fitting this Remi roof window, a ribbon sealant was applied around the base.

Type	Example	Purpose	Form	Available from
Silicone sealant	Dow Corning 785 Sanitary Acetoxy mildew-resistant silicone sealant.	Sealing sanitary ware like shower trays, wash basins and non-porous surfaces.	Cartridge (310ml) to fit standard DIY dispenser gun.	Builders' merchants.
Bedding Sealant	Carafax Caraseal IDL 99 non-drying bedding sealant.	To provide a flexible bedding layer on which to mount external fittings like ventilators, awning rails, and trim strips.	Cartridge to fit standard DIY dispenser gun.	Caravan accessory shops.
Ribbon-type bedding sealant	W4 mastic sealing strip.	For the sealing and re-bedding of caravan and motorhome fittings.	Sold in 5m (approx.) rolls with a non-stick backing paper.	Caravan and motorhome accessory shops.
Adhesive sealant	Sikaflex-512 Caravan, Technique adhesive sealant systems.	For creating permanent bonds between dissimilar materials in order to attain a high level of adhesion and a barrier to the passage of moisture.	Cartridge to fit standard DIY dispenser guns.	Automotive specialists and selected caravan accessory suppliers – addresses from Sika Ltd.

Sold in several colours, silicone sealant is mainly used for sealing around sanitary ware like shower trays or wash basins.

A non-drying bedding sealant is used to weatherproof components which might need to be removed from the body at some future point.

A non-setting sealant sold in ribbon form is sometimes easier to position than a similar product applied from a cartridge gun.

Sikaflex-512 Caravan sealant is used here to seal a lamp fitting, but its adhesive properties also commend it for bonding body panels.

cartridge form and often used with enviable skill by professional repairers. The other option is to use a butyl bedding sealant sold on a roll in ribbon form. The advantage of the ribbon product is that it assures a consistent thickness when applied, which is especially helpful if you are positioning it on something like the flange of a component, or a length of aluminium trim-strip.

Ribbon sealant is usually easy to apply but you should be aware that some products are not like the ribbon sealant sold by W4 Accessories, which can be easily cut, lifted and re-positioned if applied with a slight inaccuracy. Others, such as Caraseal 303 are more 'sticky', and have greater 'grab' characteristic. Caraseal 303 is a good sealant, but this type of sticky ribbon is unlikely to be re-usable if you attempt to remove it or make adjustments. Either way, if you need to insert some screws through a flange to achieve a mechanical fixing, make small puncture holes through the sealant ribbon. Failing to do this means that when the

screws are inserted and tightened, they are likely to wind up sealant around their shaft.

Adhesive sealants such as Sikaflex-252 or Sikaflex-512 Caravan are not sold in many household DIY shops. Cartridges are available, however, from motorcaravan dealer accessory shops and mail order suppliers like Caravan Accessories Kenilworth (CAK). Adjoining surfaces should be free of contamination, so Sikaflex also supply a preparatory cleaner. A hand cleaner is necessary, too.

The Sikaflex products sold to the motorcaravan industry are either black or white. If you accidentally get these sealants on your hands, the black version has a habit of leaving marks all over the place. Its manufacturer also emphasises that at least a 4mm thickness of the product is needed in gaps between adjoining materials. In other words, if you cramp-up or screw down a fitting so tightly that sealant oozes out and leaves a gap smaller than 4mm, the bond strength will be greatly reduced.

Be aware that an adhesive sealant takes time to completely cure. For this reason, a product that you are mounting on a vertical surface needs to be held temporarily in place, perhaps with sticky tape or temporary screws. In practice, it is rare for light components to shift out of position an hour after installation, although it *does* take around 24 hours for most adhesive sealants to cure completely.

Whereas a product like Sikaflex-512 Caravan is mainly used for its adhesive merits, be aware that a small beading can be applied to achieve a weather-proofing function on components that have already been mounted on a non-setting mastic.

Right: Over a period of time a non-setting sealant often oozes out of installations; however, when Sikaflex adhesive sealant is applied, keep it to a minimum 4mm thickness.

MATERIAL SUMMARY

The different building strategies adopted by manufacturers, together with their wide choice of materials, underlines the point that body finishes on motorcaravans vary a great deal. Models might have painted steel panel bodies, moulded GRP sections, ABS plastic mouldings, pre-painted smooth-faced aluminium cladding, texture-faced aluminium cladding, or a pigmented (pre-coloured) layer of thin GRP sheet. When plastic ventilators, moulded bumpers, acrylic windows, and cab screens are taken into account, the sheer diversity of external materials becomes apparent. This has particular relevance when purchasing cleaning products. Without doubt, cleaning a motorcaravan is certainly more involved than cleaning a car.

Cleaning and protecting

Most owners like to keep their motorcaravan clean. This not only helps to protect a vehicle; it also helps when it's offered for sale. However, you must remember to apply the right products.

CLEANING PRODUCTS

Not surprisingly, some proprietary car cleaning products can also be used on motorcaravans; tyre dressing treatments and plastic bumper cleaners are much the same whatever you drive. But some cleaning chemicals used on cars can have serious damaging effects if used on certain motorcaravan components. For example, methylated spirits has been used for many years as an additive in windscreen washer reservoirs. 'Meths' is a good cleaner of automotive glass, and in winter a car's washer bottle freezes far less quickly if methylated spirits is mixed with the water. Sadly, however, some motorcaravanners have also used meths on their acrylic plastic windows. Initially the shine it produces is impressive, but a few weeks later, tiny hairline cracks appear all over the plastic. There is no cure for this and a set of replacement windows costs a king's ransom.

Recognising that motorcaravans are built using a formidable array of dissimilar materials, the chemists who formulate vehicle-cleaning products are faced with difficult challenges. Admittedly, some general-purpose treatments are surprisingly good, but it's impossible to produce an all-effective cleaning compound that deals with everything. You'll always need *some* additional material-specific treatments like rubber conditioners, bumper

cleaning products and tar removers. This was recognised when the author worked as an adviser to Auto Glym during the Company's development of *Caravan and Motorhome Cleaner.*

In fact, several cleaning specialists have recently addressed the particular needs of motorcaravanners. For instance, Farécla, a well-established supplier to boat owners, is now marketing 'Caravan Pride'. This compound is formulated for removing scratches from acrylic windows and then reviving their shine. The Company also sells a GRP surface renovator to revive dull, colour-faded body panels. In addition, Farécla recently took over the UK distribution of Mer vehicle cleaning products, which are imported from Germany.

Then there are long-established specialists like Fenwick's, whose caravanning products are well known. So, too, are the colour-specific bumper- and trim-restoration kits from CarPlan, manufacturer of the long-established T-Cut product. Bumpers on light commercial vehicles are large, and can be unpleasantly conspicuous if they become discoloured.

The company Arnchem also supplies a range of motorcaravan cleaning products, and operates schemes where teams of specialists clean your motorcaravan to save you the bother. The Arnchem valet service is also on offer at many of the outdoor motorcaravanning shows, which enables visitors to have their vehicle cleaned while they enjoy the event.

Without doubt, there are many other good cleaning products to consider. But how does a motorcaravanner decide what to use? Unfortunately it isn't easy to carry out exacting tests on cleaning compounds, and in many instances the owner only discovers which products produce the required results through recommendation and experience. Ease of application often influences choice; price plays a part, too. And don't forget that we are dealing with chemicals so avoid mixing different products together. Damage can occur unexpectedly, such as the methylated spirits issue mentioned earlier.

Left: This sliding roof window is bedded on a non-setting sealant but to enhance its weatherproofing, a thin bead of Sikaflex 512-Caravan was added around the edges.

Toilet cleaner

A special cleaning product, previously called Thetford Bathroom Cleaner, was re-launched in 2004 as Thetford Plastic Cleaner. It is specially formulated for cleaning bathroom and toilet components, including the rubber seal and opening blade on a cassette unit.

Far left: Although methylated spirits is sometimes used to clean glass windscreens, never let it come into contact with a motorcaravan's acrylic windows.

Left: Whereas Auto Glym *Caravan and Motorhome Cleaner* can be used on many surfaces, you will still need additional products for items like tyres.

Right: Used indiscriminately, high pressures hoses can damage components on motorcaravans; don't point one directly at a fridge vent, for example.

Far right: Professional polishing tools are made to run at slow speeds to prevent a build-up of heat. Ordinary DIY power drills sometimes cause damage.

Stain removal

The black carbon trickles that stain bodywork directly under ventilators, door stays and similar attachments can be effectively removed using Auto Glym Engine Cleaner. This is a versatile product which, in addition to engine cleaning, is good for removing grease from tyres, cleaning plastic covers, discoloured vents, fuel stains (especially diesel), exhaust marks, door shuts, ovens and even saucepans that are stained on the outside.

CLEANING TECHNIQUES

This guidance follows advice given by vehicle valet specialists and covers a full cleaning regime. However, valet-training courses are presented to professional operatives who work with an array of machine tools in various environments. Motorcaravan owners typically clean their vehicles at home or in a storage compound. So, firstly, let's start with a warning.

High-pressure hoses and polishing machines

In the hands of an experienced professional, a high-pressure hose can be a useful machine for cleaning a motorcaravan, especially a huge RV model. However, in the hands of an untrained person, a high-pressure hose can destroy and dislodge drying sealant, smash plastic badges, damage the operation of an absorption refrigerator via its vents, and cause other unexpected problems. There have been a number of instances where damp has unexpectedly been detected in owners' caravans and motorhomes soon after a high-pressure cleaning machine was used for the first time. This might be coincidental, of course, but there is no doubt that the sheer power of a water jet can dislodge sealant, especially when it's starting to lose its non-setting features.

Be aware of the differences between low-speed professional polishing tools and DIY drills fitted with a polishing mop. If you get the speed wrong on a drill, the heat that builds up will soon lead to damage. No one likes the hard graft associated with the application of vehicle polish, but in many cases this is the best way to achieve a notable shine.

Hand tools and accessories

Several products make the business of cleaning a motorcaravan both easier and more efficient. There's nothing wrong with a bucket, sponge, leather and stepladder but here are some items that make things easier.

Soft brushes mounted on telescopic alloy poles are sold at most caravan shows and are extremely useful when cleaning a large vehicle.

Wheel cleaning brushes sold at accessory shops are made to deal with intricate rim patterns and their stiff bristles don't distort easily.

Cranked brushes are sold by decorating specialists for painting the rear of household radiators but are very useful when cleaning a motorcaravan.

For years, window cleaners have used a squeegee blade to clear surface water. This super-flexible version is sold by Auto Glym to use on cars.

A chamois leather still takes some beating but imitation versions are now much-improved. Micro-fibre cloths have also become popular.

Cleaning cloths mustn't contain lint; use an open-weave 100% cotton cloth so that abrasive surface specks get picked up and lost in the fabric.

CLEANING PROCEDURE

In a full valet operation, the strategy is to start with really dirty jobs and then move to more refined tasks and finishing operations. The procedure here describes a full schedule – though you're unlikely to complete a routine like this on every cleaning operation.

Valet specialists recommend the following order of jobs:

1) Engine
2) Wheels and tyres
3) Door shuts
4) Body clean or shampoo
5) Interior cleaning
6) Tar spots
7) Body polishing
8) Glass/acrylic windows
9) Finishing jobs including tyre dressing

1. ENGINE If you like to keep an engine and its compartment clean, tackle this first. Note the instructions accompanying engine cleaners and remember to tie plastic bags over key electrical items, including an electronic alarm. With most products, the engine should be cold and switched off. The procedure involves applying the cleaner, agitating with a brush, and then gently and judiciously washing this off with clean water. Experts use high-pressure machines but an inexperienced owner is wiser to use a garden hose with a slow flow of water.

2. WHEELS/TYRES Make sure they are cold – hot brake discs react with some cleaning chemicals. Most cleaners should be removed promptly and not allowed to dry, so it is best to complete this one wheel at a time. After cleaning a wheel rim or cover, also clean the tyre. Grease should be removed and some engine cleaners are suitable for this. Agitate the cleaner with a brush and hose off. However, leave the final application of a tyre renovation treatment until the end of a cleaning operation.

3. DOOR SHUTS A grease remover should be used on door shuts and wheel arches – engine cleaners are effective here, too.

4. BODY CLEAN OR SHAMPOO Either use a purpose-designed product like Auto Glym Caravan and Motorhome Cleaner, or use a shampoo and conditioner. For really stubborn stains, streaks, algae marks or birdlime, some engine cleaners are able to shift these marks without inflicting damage. Check suitability of a product on the user instructions. Normally this type of cleaner is applied to the area of discolouration, agitated with a cranked radiator brush and then rinsed off with water. On the other hand, if you decide to use a shampoo, remember to rinse it off, but don't use a high-pressure hose. This can 'bounce off' the conditioning film that shampoos usually leave after application. Gentle flooding on a metal panel enables some conditioners to electro-statically bond to the surface, thus affording the best protection.

Left: After applying a general purpose cleaner, a soft brush or sponge should be used to agitate the product before hosing it off with clean water.

5. INTERIOR Now work inside. Several manufacturers sell treatments suitable on cushion fabrics as well as vehicle seats. Of course, it is always wise to try a product on a small test area first. As a rule, never use a scrubbing action, especially on fabrics like velour. It's better to employ a stippling action using a nylon brush with medium-strength bristles. When the surface is subsequently wiped with a clean, damp, white cotton cloth, the amount of dirt pulled away can be surprising. Where possible, it's best to carry out upholstery cleaning in warm weather so that cushions can be dried outside. You might also need to open a lot of windows when applying treatments as working in a confined space without airflow can lead to discomfort.

6. TAR REMOVAL Moving outside again, any remaining tar spots should be removed from the body before starting polishing work. Several proprietary products are specifically made to tackle tar deposits.

7. BODY POLISH The choice of body treatments is determined by the materials. If your motorcaravan is clad with patterned aluminium, such as a stucco or pimple surface finish, it's wise to leave this alone. Some of the paints used on aluminium sheet can be lifted by polishes so it is better to be content with the sheen left by a shampoo.

However, on painted steel, acrylic-capped ABS and GRP, a good coat of polish will provide a protective finish that may last six months or more. Take note of the product instructions and when applying the treatment, be careful to keep it from black plastic components like motorcaravan door handles and bumpers. These should be coated later with a purpose-made cleaner.

8. WINDOWS Remember that acrylic windows are easily scratched and in some instances a product formulated for use on a windscreen or cab-side window might not be suitable for use on a plastic unit. And whereas there are plenty of products available for cleaning safety glass, products intended for a motorcaravan's acrylic windows are harder to find. However, Seitz markets Acrylic Glass Cleaner, guaranteed not to cause tension cracks, and supplied to motorcaravan accessory shops by Dometic. Another product that can be used on

Right: In addition to cleaning plastic window surfaces, you are advised to apply a proprietary treatment to the rubber seals to prevent them sticking.

Far right: Most cleaning product ranges include a gel-type product which is applied to black plastic components. This is usually laid on gently with a small sponge.

Right: Finally adding a tyre dressing product completes the job. This example is sprayed on, left trickling down the tyre, and later it loses its white colour.

Far right: Dead insects often accumulate on the 'hard-to-reach' zone just above the windscreen. Now there are products designed to make them easy to remove.

a clean and dust-free window is Auto Glym Fast Glass. This has to be sprayed onto the window from its special container and promptly spread across the surface with a paper kitchen towel. With equal haste it should be removed using another piece of clean paper from a kitchen roll.

9. FINISHING JOBS Now to tackle the finishing jobs, such as the application of plastic treatments. Several products are made to deal with black fittings; bumper treatments, for example, can often be used to revive sheen on a door handle or the black housing enclosing a mirror.

Finally, an application of a tyre dressing treatment completes the valet in style. Note that rubber-based tyre paints are less popular nowadays. Products like Auto Glym Instant Tyre Dressing are much better – as long as you follow the application instructions. When this tyre conditioner is sprayed onto the rubber it forms white streaks that initially look unpleasant – but don't touch the tyre. Leave the dressing to dry for 10 to 15 minutes, after which the effect is most surprising. The milky streaks will have disappeared and the tyres look as good as new.

Note: *An irritating task for caravan and motorhome owners is the removal of a graveyard of squashed flies and other airborne insects that get stuck above a windscreen. These often look conspicuous on a light-coloured vehicle and are usually hard to reach. Recent spray-on products with names like Fly and Insect Remover have been introduced, and a soft brush mounted on a light pole allows the treatments to be agitated before they are then washed off.*

Bodywork sealing

Traditional cleaning techniques can produce superb results but anyone confronted with a jumbo jet, a line of railway carriages or a large motor launch would want to find an alternative cleaning strategy. This is partly why panel-sealing products were developed, and A-Glaze is one that is sold in the UK.

Paint-sealing products like A-Glaze have been used on large aircraft including the British Airways fleet. Similar treatments are also offered as an optional extra to purchasers of high-quality cars such as an Aston Martin, a Porsche or a Ferrari, so these products have provenance, and paint-sealing kits are sold by A-Glaze to owners of motorhomes. This product can be applied by the DIY person. A similar product is available from Paintseal Direct, although only Company staff can apply this.

Bear in mind that these treatments are neither polishes nor cleaning compounds. They are better described as paint protecting systems that also function effectively on pigmented GRP. This is a self-coloured GRP rather than one which has been painted. When a surface sealant has been applied, it protects the body from environmental hazards such as weather-induced fading, acid rain, birdlime, oxidation and loss of surface gloss.

If you own a large motorcaravan, the initial treatment operation may take a full day, but once the surface has been cleaned and coated, treatments can last for several years. All that is needed is an occasional wash, and even a shower of rain has a self-cleansing effect. In spite of initial scepticism, the author found from experience that sealants undoubtedly live-up to the claims, although

their effectiveness may be less impressive when applied for the first time to an older vehicle.

These treatments are expensive compared with traditional polishes, but the benefits can be pleasing, especially if you park a vehicle near trees during the winter. Green deposits and black streaks don't take such a firm hold as they usually do on unsealed surfaces.

The application of A-Glaze is shown alongside and it is claimed to achieve its objective on motorcaravans clad in dimpled aluminium panels, plain aluminium, GRP sheet or mouldings in GRP or ABS.

The first task is to wash the vehicle thoroughly. Then you treat all metal surfaces and smooth plastic mouldings with A-Prep Surface Cleaner. However, textured finishes like plastic bumpers and door handles must NOT be treated. Applying the cleaner is the 'hard graft' stage because all smears, black streaks and remnants of cleaning wax have to be removed. The motorcaravan will then look impressive, but the all-important coating of A-Glaze sealant is needed to achieve long-term protection.

The sealant is supplied in a surprisingly small container because it has to be applied very sparingly with a clean, soft cloth, used in tight circular motions. However, on large areas like the roof, A-Glaze is often applied using a telescopic-handled flat mop, as shown alongside.

Once a vehicle has been coated with sealant, you wipe all the surfaces using a damp, clean, soft cloth. On larger panels, an atomiser (sold at garden centres) is helpful for applying a fine mist of water; this enables the uncured sealant to flow over the surfaces. Finally, you go over everything using a soft, dry polishing cloth to create a pleasing shine.

In the following months a quick wash is all that is needed to re-create a gloss, and it isn't unusual for the product to maintain its effectiveness for 18 months or more. When the bodywork eventually loses its glossy surface, it's an indication that air-born deposits have settled on the surface, leaving a film. However, this can be removed with the Wash and Shine Shampoo included in an A-Glaze kit. The operation consists of a) a hose down, b) application of the non-foaming shampoo, c) rinse-off, and d) leather-off. It shouldn't take long and if it helps, a motorcaravan can be cleaned in two halves.

Suffice to say, using a sealing product is a very different way of keeping a motorhome looking smart. On the other hand it doesn't help items like texture-finish black plastic door handles and bumpers. To retain a dark satin finish on these components you still need to use a conventional plastic treatment product.

Reviving acrylic windows

Even the most careful driver will occasionally have to pull close to a hedgerow to avoid an oncoming vehicle when using a narrow lane. That is when brambles are likely to leave a deep scratch on an acrylic window.

Window manufacturers' instructions make it clear that abrasive compounds should NOT be used when cleaning an acrylic pane. However, this situation requires more than just cleaning, and

Handy tip – window scratch removal

■ When using wet-and-dry paper on an acrylic window, don't use a circular action until the final polish. Rub in straight lines instead; six to eight in one direction, followed by the same number at right angles. If you see a fresh scratch, this technique allows you to identify which piece of abrasive paper caused the fresh mark. There's no need to work solely across the original scratch mark.

■ If the 1200 grade wet-and-dry paper starts to remove the scratches, continue with 1500 grade which is even finer. If it proves too fine, try a 1000 or even 800 grade.

■ Remember to change the paper frequently or you will inflict new damage on the surface.

■ If a machine is used with a foam mop, water is critical and serves four functions:
  1) It keeps the cleaning compound out of the deep pores of the mop.
  2) It keeps the acrylic surface cooler.
  3) It acts as a lubricant.
  4) It prolongs the life of the mop.

■ Whether the scratch is removed manually or by machine, the work should be completed using a clean rag, buffing up the surface using circular motions.

Removing scratches in acrylic windows

1 Deep scratches are normally removed by starting with 1200 grade wet-and-dry paper mounted on a small block. The water acts as a lubricant.

2 Use an open-weave cloth made from 100% cotton stock and ensure it is wet. A garden spray bottle is useful for delivering a fine mist to the rag.

3 Apply scratch remover over the entire surface and be meticulous about regularly re-applying a fresh mist of water to the surface from a spray bottle.

4 A machine is quicker, but make sure you use only a purpose-made polisher. This revolves much more slowly than a drill fitted with a mop attachment.

to remove a deep scratch you will certainly need abrasive papers and a special cutting compound. Products for removing deep scratches are available from both Seitz and Farécla.

As an example, Caravan Pride scratch-remover from Farécla is a fine-grade rubbing compound that can be applied either with a slow-rotating buffing machine or by hand. To carry out the renovation work it isn't necessary to remove a window, although the accompanying sequence is shown using a unit which has been detached and transferred to a bench. Suffice to say, the product, originally packaged as 'Boat Pride', has been

used successfully for many years on boat windows, and the results on motorcaravans are equally impressive.

Replacing an acrylic unit

If an acrylic window pane needs to be replaced, this is usually a straightforward operation. Sometimes the most frustrating part is waiting several weeks for a replacement to be delivered.

Although some of the double-glazed acrylic panels are mounted in a frame (as in the case of Seitz S4 units) others are made without a frame and are top-hung using a retaining strip; this is mounted across the head of the aperture, providing the point of attachment. Either way, the first task is to remove support stays that are normally secured with screws. Retaining catches may also have to be detached, leaving the unit free to open and close while remaining hinged at the top. When the panel is lifted up towards its limit, you often find that it can be detached from its channelling. Failing that, some window units are released simply by sliding them to one side of their hinge rail. However, before that operation can be completed, a retaining end-stop on the rail has to be unscrewed and removed.

Right: Several manufacturers supply treatments for polishing-out the scratches in acrylic windows including Seitz (now part of Dometic), Fenwick's and Farécla.

Far left: Before a window pane can be removed, its retaining stays and catches have to be disconnected and removed.

Left: When this Seitz S4 window is raised towards its maximum opening position, the plastic pane can then be detached from its rail.

If you own an older motorcaravan, obtaining replacement windows can become an impossible task. Fortunately, a manufacturer called EECO runs a mail order operation making replicas in the size, shape and tint needed. Even at the height of the summer season, the manufacture and despatch of a new unit can be done in under four weeks. All the customer has to do is to send EECO the original plastic pane, or its remnants, so that material of the correct shade and specification can be identified before making the copy. The company's address is given in the Appendix. Cutting apertures in panel vans and coachbuilt models and the installation of windows is given in the Haynes publication *Build Your Own Motorcaravan.*

Leaks and damp problems

Earlier in this chapter, the issue of water ingress was described in detail. Deteriorating sealant was cited as one of many reasons why rain finds a way into the fabric of the body, but there are other weak spots too. Even components like lamp clusters can let in water, especially if a rubber mounting gasket loses its resilience. Moreover, one well-known monocoque coachbuilt had problems when rainwater started to penetrate through the mitred joints at the corners of rectangular window frames.

Earlier descriptions referred to traditional coachbuilt enclosures and compared them with today's models that are manufactured using prefabricated bonded panels. Logically, it might seem that walls constructed with prefabricated bonded panels wouldn't suffer from seepage as much as traditionally-built non-bonded sections.

But this isn't necessarily the case. Rainwater penetrates some types of insulating foam used in the core, whether or not the material is bonded. What's more, there may be unseen deterioration long before there are visible signs of damp on the interior wall ply.

As always, prevention is better than cure, and owners should get a dealer to carry out a damp test every year. If there *are* weak spots in the external envelope, these need to be identified at the earliest opportunity and repair work set in motion. The penalty of delaying this is clearly shown in the accompanying illustration.

If you arrange for a damp test to be carried out, make sure that all your lockers have been emptied out. All trainees preparing for the City & Guilds examination in Caravan Engineering (Touring Caravans and Motorhomes) are now taught to open all internal lockers and to leave them open so that the indoor temperature is stabilised throughout the vehicle.

Left: An annual damp check ensures that serious damage can be avoided.

Far left: This radio frequency damp meter leaves no marks when readings are taken.

Left: Prior to starting a test, all lockers should be opened and left for a while so that the caravan's internal temperature stabilises.

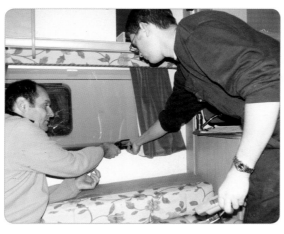

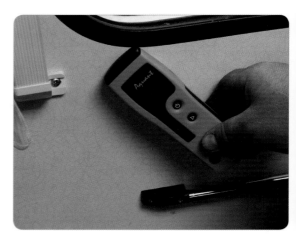

Far right: This radio frequency meter is methodically used all around window openings so that a dozen or so readings can be taken around each aperture.

Technical tip

Moisture test meters are fitted with a battery. They usually have two probes which are offered up to the interior ply of a caravan at key points – especially around windows, near light clusters, in the vicinity of an awning rail and so on. If there is a problem in the area being checked, a small current will track through the damp section from one probe to the other.

Below: This screw is badly rusted along its length, which means that rain water could be seeping into the structure here.

A checking instrument is then used, and some models emit an electric current that can detect zones of moisture. Typically these instruments have sharp metal probes which are gently pressed into the interior wall and ceiling ply of the living area. If used without due care, these can leave tiny pinholes on the interior plywood. More expensive meters operate using radio frequency detection instead.

Inexpensive damp testers are available from DIY stores but are unlikely to be as accurate as professional damp meters. For example, some cheap products use red, amber and green indicator lights to reveal any damp. However, this is too vague; professional devices express the level of damp as a percentage.

Skill and experience are also needed; a test meter must be used correctly and a competent checker will be constantly looking out for false readings. One cause of misleading information is the fact that some motorcaravans incorporate metal plates in a sandwich wall for the attachment of cupboards, seatbelt mountings and other components. If these are galvanised steel, a plate will often trigger an inaccurate reading. Similarly, condensation is sometimes present, especially if a motorcaravan has recently been in use, and this can also give misleading information.

There are usually around 40–50 places where readings are taken. For instance, the meter is used around the perimeter of windows, doors and roof-lights. It is also held at the junction points between walls and ceiling. These checking points are recorded on a line diagram and a copy of this should be given to a customer on completion of the test operation. Having one of these to hand, duly dated and signed by the tester, can be useful if you are intending to sell your motorcaravan in the near future.

Having carried out the checking operation, the test person then has to interpret the findings. Since timber has a natural moisture level it would be wrong to expect zero readings on a damp-test meter. Advice given to service specialists by The National Caravan Council offers the following guidelines when interpreting percentage readings:

0–15%	Acceptable moisture content.
16–20%	Further investigation is needed. Owners should have a repeat set of readings carried out three months or so after the test.
Over 20%	Indicates areas where remedial work is required at the earliest opportunity.
Over 30%	Damage to the structure of a motorcaravan may be taking place. Urgent remedial work is needed.

Note: *Visible evidence in the form of moisture stains or mildew sometimes supports the % reading but you cannot always rely on that.*

When an area of damp is identified, the next task is to ascertain where the moisture is coming from – which isn't always easy.

In a bad case of water ingress, major reconstruction work may be necessary immediately and most owners would entrust this to specialists. Companies like Crossley in Leyland, and Autovan Services at Wimborne, Dorset, are examples of experienced body repairers who undertake major rebuilding work. Most members of the Approved Workshop Scheme will also be equipped to undertake invasive investigations and carry out major repairs.

Re-bedding an awning rail

Once the screws are removed, the rail is removed as a unit.

The mastic shown here is still in reasonably good condition, but there are places with poor coverage.

Remains of the old mastic are removed with a cleaner; white spirit is often effective.

The aluminium seam is meticulously cleaned as well.

Photographs courtesy of Sika

Once all remnants of old sealant are removed, Sikaflex 221 or Sikaflex 512 Caravan is applied around the wall perimeter. Masking tape can be used to show the rail's position.

Sikaflex 221 or Sikaflex 512 Caravan is similarly injected on to the back of the rail; this will be temporarily held with tape or a few self-tapping screws while the sealant is curing.

A less demanding remedial measure that some owners tackle themselves involves the removal and reinstatement of decorative aluminium strips, wall ventilators, and components such as roof windows. Weather-resistance is greatly improved by re-fixing fittings like this on a fresh bed of flexible sealant.

Where decorative aluminium strips are concerned, the job necessitates removal of a plastic cover strip to reveal the screw heads. When the screws that hold the aluminium extrusion in place are removed, check to see if any of them are rusty. If the thread is in bad shape, this is a certain sign that water has crept behind the trim strip and has started to seep into the sub-structure via this particular screw. Replacement stainless steel screws, together with new flexible sealant, are urgently needed and a zealous repairer will seal up all the original holes and drill new ones.

But there is another approach to consider. It is also possible to attach a trim strip using a high bonding adhesive sealant instead of using screws. Reference was made earlier in the chapter to Sikaflex adhesive sealants and the way they are used. Although accompanying illustrations show the procedure being carried out on a caravan, the operation is no different when re-affixing a trim strip on a motorhome.

Moulding repairs and replacements

Before accident damage can be tackled, it is first necessary to establish the type of material in need of attention. Obviously, if you are dealing with the steel panels of a coachbuilt model's cab or the body of a van conversion, procedures and products are much the same as they are when repairing a car.

Guidance on body repairs and painting procedures are given in *The Classic Car Bodywork Restoration Manual* by Lindsay Porter, published by Haynes.

In addition to the cladding materials mentioned earlier in this chapter, coachbuilt motorcaravans usually have mouldings of GRP, ABS or acrylic-capped ABS. These materials are used for small items such as road-light housings and large items like roof panels. Since the repair strategies are not the same, your first task is to identify the material used in a damaged component; guidance was given in the earlier advice panel on page 41.

REPAIRING DAMAGE TO GRP

A notable feature of GRP is the fact that it is relatively easy to repair. Surface damage to the outer layer – called the 'gel coat' – can be remedied by applying fresh self-coloured gel coat, or even by using car

Repairing a damaged GRP surface using coloured gel coat

1. Loose remnants of the damaged, cracked gel coat are removed from this large body moulding using a steel disc or an old chisel.

2. Having cut back the damaged surface to the glass fibre reinforcing mat, a polyester filler paste is mixed with catalyst (*ie* 'hardener') and applied.

3. Once the filler has completely cured, the surface is rubbed over with either a sanding disc or a hand-held block covered with abrasive paper.

4. In this repair the service workshop was able to purchase some colour-matching gel coat from the caravan manufacturer. This eliminates the need to paint the damaged area.

Note: *Chips of brittle gel coat can fly into your face so it is recommended that eye protection is worn. This operator should also have used hand protection.*

Right: When mixing P40, a 'blob' the size of a golf ball is mixed with three 'blobs' the size of garden peas.

repair body filler (although this would need painting afterwards). The accompanying photo sequence shows how replacement gel coat is repaired.

If you would rather use DIY car repair products, be aware that there are two different versions.

Isopon P40 (Trade version U-Pol B)

This polyester paste contains a mixture of chopped glass fibre strands, which gives strength to a weak or damaged panel. It can be used to repair small splits in GRP as a first-stage operation, thereby giving strength to a fractured component before the finishing surface filler is added later. To repair a small split in a GRP moulding you need to access its reverse face, so you may need to remove the component. You would then:

i. Gouge deep scratches in the roughened *rear face* with an old chisel or wood rasp.

ii. Stabilise and support the splits by applying Sellotape or brown parcel tape on the *shiny face* of the component.

iii. apply a mix of catalysed Isopon P40 to the rough side of the moulding with a decorator's knife.

This type of repair product can be prepared on a scrap of plywood by adding a catalyst paste to the polyester/glass compound. Given temperatures around 16°C (60°F) the mix ratio is a 'blob' of P40 the size of a golf ball with three 'blobs' of catalyst paste the size of garden peas.

The two items have to be mixed thoroughly on the board and many people use a decorator's knife. The catalysed mix should be used promptly and applied with the knife to the reverse side of the component.

Acetone cleaner can be purchased at a modest cost from a GRP product supplier to clean the mixing knife; alternatively, and at risk of reprimand, you can use expensive acetone nail varnish remover obtainable from any well-equipped handbag.

Isopon P38 (Trade version U-Pol Extra)

This is a filler paste used to recreate a smooth surface on a damaged area of GRP. It lacks the strength of P40 but when applied to the outer side of a panel and rubbed-down, it produces a blemish-free finish.

Before commencing repair work, the damaged area must be cleared of chipped fragments and stray strands of glass. Next, the filler is prepared in much the same way as the P40 product, which you smear into place with a knife. When it has cured (a term meaning hardened), the filler is rubbed-down with abrasive wet-and-dry papers, progressively reducing the grades of coarseness. Once the surface is smooth and the edges have been neatly feathered into the surrounding area, the filler finally needs painting.

Polyester resins and chopped strand mat

More extensive damage is often repaired with the same products that were used to form an original GRP moulding. Structural damage, for example, usually involves the use of chopped strand glass fibre mat which has to be impregnated with polyester resin. The treated layer of mat then has to be stippled with a brush and pressed down with a laminating roller. Further guidance on GRP products and their use is available from Trylon, a specialist supplier of the materials that you would need.

Note: *Safety guidance, product descriptions, user information and necessary precautions and procedures are available from specialist suppliers like Trylon.*

Panels in GRP can also be repainted even if the original product was moulded with a polyester resin which contained a colouring pigment. Automotive paint suppliers will mix paint to the exact tint required and can supply the prepared product in an aerosol spray can. However, you would also need an etching primer to ensure the paint adheres to a GRP panel.

REPAIRING DAMAGE TO ABS

Body sections made from acrylic-capped ABS are also repairable and repair kits have been developed by firms such as Gramos and Bradleys. It is, therefore, rather disappointing to learn that many dealer workshop staff are unfamiliar with repair procedures. Some body specialists are all-too-eager to replace a completely new panel when the damage to the original one is only superficial. It doesn't help that obtaining a replacement body panel can take six weeks or more.

Similar issues occur when a vehicle's plastic bumper gets damaged. Costly replacements are often fitted when a repair could have easily been carried out at a fraction of the price. This is even more inexcusable when plastics specialists can also supply specially formulated 'textured' paint for use on vehicle bumpers. Illustrations overleaf show what is involved when ABS repairs are carried out.

Glass fibre reinforcement gives strength to a moulding and this product is known as 'Chopped strand mat' or CSM.

Catalyst is measured out and added to a resin to activate it. It can cause severe damage if it gets into your eyes so goggles must be worn.

An old set of scales is needed to measure the quantity of resin being used; the weight indicates how much catalyst is needed.

To impregnate a layer of CSM with catalysed resin, an operator uses brushes and then a roller to draw it through the strands.

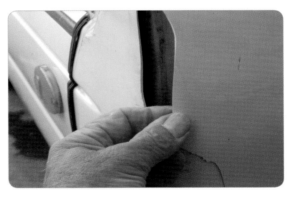

Above: The rear of this motorcaravan was damaged in a reversing manoeuvre and the skirt and lamp assembly were broken.

Matching paint

Specialist automotive paint suppliers will mix paint to the exact tint you require, and supply it in an aerosol spray can.

Left: No attempt was made to mend one of these rear lamp housings and this replacement was ordered instead; delivery times can take six weeks or more.

Repairing a split in an acrylic-capped ABS panel

1 Holes are drilled at the ends of the split to prevent further stress damage; the damaged area is also deepened in order to accommodate the repair compound and roughened with P80 grit paper to achieve a key.

2 Surface cleaner is applied to the damaged area, wiped over with a lint-free cloth, and left to dry. Primer Adhesion Promoter is sprayed on next and allowed to dry for 30 minutes.

3 Self-adhesive fibre reinforcing tape is cut to size and stuck to the rear of the damaged panel.

4 A two-part bonding filler is dispensed from a standard sealant gun through the spiral nozzle supplied so that the components are blended. This is applied to the split, to finish just below the surface.

5 When the bonding filler has fully cured, the area is rubbed down so that no filler appears above the surface.

6 Primer adhesion promoter is applied to the surface once again in readiness for the addition of a final top filler.

7 The filler paste is dispensed on to a board and a measured amount of red catalyst is mixed in thoroughly with a plastic applicator.

8 The filler is applied over the damaged area using the applicator and feathered off at the sides. This will be smoothed off when dry with abrasive paper; a matched etching paint suitable for this material will be applied and a colour-matched top coat added finally.

REPLACING A COMPLETE SIDE PANEL

Some incidents require more major repair operations; the large coachbuilt model shown here was caught in a severe hailstorm. This isn't uncommon in parts of mainland Europe and this vehicle had very large dents all over the roof panel and along one of the sides. This was an insurance repair that was carried out by V&G Caravan Repairs not far from Peterborough. It took many weeks to obtain a complete new side panel from the Hymer factory in Germany and the parts alone cost an eye-watering four-figure sum. The sandwich panel also had steel sections built into the sides to provide attachment points for passenger seatbelts. The sequence photographs give a brief insight into the demanding installation work.

TRACING SOURCES OF DAMP

Earlier mention was made of water ingress and the difficulties of tracing the source of a problem. It is unfortunate that soiled wall panels on the inside are often a long way from the point of failure. When rain finds a way into the fabric of a motorcaravan, it can follow a tortuous route inside its structure before leaving marks some distance away. Trim strips, external light fittings and window surrounds are just a few of the items to check. And have a close look at the roof.

If a motorcaravan roof is well designed, it should produce a gentle slope whenever the vehicle is parked on a level pitch. This prevents the 'ponding' of water whenever there's a shower of rain. There should also be planned points where the rain will discharge without causing problems to the fittings below. Frankly, this is common sense, and yet meeting this simple arrangement is beyond the ability of some European motorhome builders – both at home and abroad. It is one of the first areas of attention when the author tests new vehicles and some of the findings are shown alongside. What a pity that prospective purchasers don't borrow a set of steps to check what the roof is like.

Note: *In alphabetic order of countries, the manufacturers of vans shown in these illustrations are based in France, Germany, Italy and the United Kingdom. Evidence of disappointing roof designs can be seen throughout Europe.*

REPLICATING ABS AND GRP MOULDINGS

Sometimes, plastic mouldings are no longer available and this poses problems if you need a key item. Even well-known manufacturers cease production, and specialists like Avondale are no longer in business. If owners find that plastic components can't be traced, here are two sources of help. Both suppliers are able to take damaged ABS or GRP mouldings, repair them, and then create a mould in their workshops. Using a newly-produced mould enables the supplier to laminate replica mouldings in GRP.

Note: *The term 'mould' refers to the*

Replacing the side of an A-Class model

1 Many hours of repair work lay ahead when this A-Class Hymer motorcaravan was caught in a freak hail storm.

2 All exterior attachments on the damaged panel had to be removed first, including the rear garage door.

3 Many items had to be uncoupled inside including the passenger seatbelts which had mountings in the side panel.

4 The despatch and delivery of a replacement panel took several weeks and the cost of parts alone went into four figures.

Good and bad roof features

1 A well-designed roof will have a gentle slope when a vehicle is parked on the flat and outlets for discharging rainwater.

2 This model had outlet channels to release rainwater but these were filled with sealant and had uphill slopes as well.

3 It's ironic that the magnificent interior of this model won several awards. One suspects that the judges missed its dreadful roof design.

4 Prospective buyers seldom check roofs yet this is where leaks might start; this application of sealant on a nearly new model is an utter disgrace.

Replica mouldings

Starting with a damaged ABS plastic wheel spat, a GRP mould was painstakingly prepared at GFL Panels near Preston.

Once the wheel spat mould had been made, it was then possible to make replica mouldings in GRP.

When a bespoke motorcaravan wheel box was needed, staff at V&G created a mould in ply and then created the finished item.

The new wheel box was eased away from its plywood 'plug', which was then tidied-up in order to make a second box.

constructed assembly used to produce the components. Products which are subsequently made are then referred to as 'mouldings'.

Although this chapter is concerned with exterior components, both specialists mentioned here are also able to produce shower trays (in many shapes and sizes), washbasins and other interior items. Sometimes a completely new item is created using a wooden structure (referred-to as 'the plug') which is prepared in order to create a GRP mould. It's a long job, of course, and plastic lamination work is not the cleanest of crafts. However, GFL Panels based in a village not far from Preston, and V&G Caravans in a village several miles from Peterborough, have provided hitherto unavailable products for many caravan and motorhome owners. The accompanying illustrations give a brief insight into the services on offer.

Another manufacturer based in Essex, Elite Body Styling, also attends motorcaravan outdoor shows with examples of GRP replica plastic bumpers, vehicle cills, wheel spats and so on. Some of the items displayed on the stand are for recent vehicles: others are for vehicles that might have been built as long ago as the 1980s.

Delamination

Notwithstanding the merits of pre-fabricated floor and wall panels, it is a serious matter if the insulation foam loses its bond with either of the materials forming the outer part of the sandwich.

The condition is referred to as 'delamination' and a panel's strength is seriously affected when it happens. In practice, wall panels are seldom affected by delamination, whereas floors are more likely to give problems.

In a composite floor, both outer layers of the sandwich are formed using plywood; this is bonded to the insulation material forming the core. As a point of interest, the overall thickness of the three-part sandwich is usually greater than the thickness of bonded wall panels and there will also be more timber ribs in the core to add torsional strength. The weight of people and heavy appliances such as a full-size cooker impose a considerable loading. That's why the upper layer of plywood sometimes breaks away from the foam insulation, especially in areas which are frequently in use. Places where delamination often occurs are just inside the main entrance door and in the area near the kitchen sink.

A failing bond in a panel is easy to detect and a creaking floor is a common sign of problems. Sometimes there's a 'soggy' feeling to the floor, too, and occasionally the plywood section which has delaminated will bubble-up, creating a small rise around the problem zone. Needless to say, a failing floor needs urgent attention although a repair is sometimes fairly easy to carry out.

To begin with a repair kit has to be purchased, containing plastic syringes, wooden dowel pegs and a two-pack bonding agent in liquid form. One manufacturer of these kits is Apollo Chemicals Ltd, but the product has to be ordered through a caravan or motorcaravan accessory shop. Another supplier is Trade Grade Products (TGP) and addresses appear in the Appendix list. Aspects of the repair work are shown alongside. The task involves removal of the floor carpet or vinyl, drilling a matrix of holes, mixing the two-part chemicals in measured, workable batches, injecting the catalysed bonding agent, plugging the holes with a dowel peg cut to length to prevent adhesive oozing out of the holes, and finally holding the ply down around the treated area using bricks or a heavy object like a paving slab. As an alternative to dowel pegs, plastic caps are also available from TGP. As a rule, this isn't a difficult repair job, but some dealers are unwilling to sell repair kits to members of the public. This seems unhelpful, although it's true that if a DIY enthusiast were to make a mistake when injecting the bonding chemical into the core of the board, the process is irreversible.

You also have to mix up small quantities at a time because the reaction of the two chemicals happens fairly quickly. If there's a rush, it's not unknown for a repairer to forget to add the all-important 'Part 2' hardening compound in one of the mixes. Then the chemical action won't be activated and injecting the fluid into the floor panel will achieve nothing apart from a mess. So you need to work methodically, and let's face it – a floor panel is one component you wouldn't want to fail.

1 With the floor covering removed, sponginess in the floor panel adjacent to the kitchen units confirmed that delamination had taken place.

2 The straight edge of a spirit level sometimes reveals that there's a slight rise in the delaminating plywood.

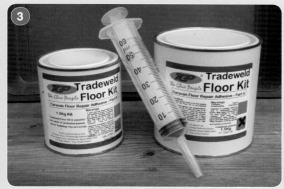

3 There are several repair products available and this two part repair kit from Trade Grade Products includes a syringe which has graduated markings.

4 You mustn't drill through the ply on the underside of the floor panel, so tape is used as a depth indicator on the twist drill.

5 On this repair, 42 holes were drilled in a measured block that completely covered the delaminating portion of the floor.

6 By temporarily inserting a dowel and pushing it down you establish how much the pegs need to be trimmed before injecting the chemical.

7 Mix in small batches at a time; the two chemicals are measured, mixed in the stated proportions, and then drawn into a syringe.

8 Inject the bonding agent. Hardly any is taken in by the sound areas, but where there's a zone of delamination, a large quantity disperses into the void.

9 When the agent leaks out of a hole, tap in a dowel peg. Wipe away any excess on the floor at once – it's hard to remove when it's dry.

10 Lay a sheet of brown paper over the area, followed by a sheet of thick boarding, then place something heavy such as bricks on top.

Driving characteristics, the comfort of passengers and the amount of equipment you can carry in your motorcaravan are determined by the chassis, suspension and tyres. In addition, fixtures under the floor determine whether it is possible to fit a tow-bar.

Very few potential purchasers of motorcaravans look underneath the models they are planning to buy. Of far greater interest to most people is the interior layout, items like appliances, storage facilities and the attractiveness of the soft furnishings. These features are important, of course, but it is a mistake to ignore what is often called the 'undergear'. This term usually includes items like the chassis, suspension components, brakes, axle tube, wheels and tyres.

When you've purchased a motorcaravan, the importance of its undergear soon becomes apparent. In fact, a number of new owners have been known to change their motorcaravan after a year or so because of features they failed to inspect before they bought it. For instance, many new owners presume that their vehicle could be used for towing. Take, for example, motorcaravans that are built using a Fiat Ducato base vehicle. If you check information in tow-bar manufacturers' catalogues you are likely to find brackets listed that have been designed to fit Fiat vans and chassis. However, these products are sold on the presumption that no alterations have been made to the original vehicle. This is certainly not the case with motorcaravans, which often have under-floor obstructions such as water tanks. If conversion components like these hide the all-important fixing points for a tow-bar, plans to tow a trailer may have to be abandoned.

On a similar note, there are owners who note with satisfaction that their vehicle's AL-KO Kober chassis – on which many coachbuilt motorhomes are constructed – can be matched with an AL-KO towing bracket, or even a purpose-designed scooter rack.

They then find to great dismay that neither of these items can be fitted after all, and this is because motorhome manufacturers often construct a body structure that extends *beyond* the rearmost extremities of AL-KO Kober's all-important chassis members. Needless to say, these are the structural elements on which AL-KO purpose-made tow-bars and racks have to be attached. The detrimental effect of an extended floor is evident on the Bessacar 2004 coachbuilt model shown alongside.

The extended overhang of its body meant that the added tow-ball didn't project far enough

Below: This purpose-made towing bracket can only be fitted to some of the motorcaravans built on an AL-KO chassis.

Below: Cutting away part of the rear skirt allowed a trailer to be coupled-up, but this tow-ball still didn't project far enough rearwards to provide adequate articulation.

rearwards. Cutting away parts of the rear skirt at least permitted a trailer to be coupled. However, the trailer's articulation was severely restricted, and it became perilously close to the rear corners of the towing vehicle on sharp bends.

The unsuitability of a vehicle for towing often comes as a shock as limitations such as this are seldom pointed out by salespersons. Even worse is the realisation that the model you've bought all too easily exceeds its maximum loading limit. This is potentially dangerous, and exceeding loading limits can lead to prosecution.

Quite often, the payload opportunities claimed by manufacturers give far less scope for carrying personal possessions than purchasers realise. This becomes particularly evident after accessories have been added like a bike rack, a roof box and a couple of large gas cylinders. It stands to reason that the weight of every accessory you fit represents a corresponding reduction in the personal items that you can carry within your permitted payload. Consequently, it's generally believed that many motorcaravan owners inadvertently break the law by exceeding their vehicle's Maximum Technically Permissible Laden Mass (MTPLM) limit as explained in Chapter 2. Moreover, surprisingly few owners check their laden vehicle on a weighbridge, and this is becoming increasingly necessary now that police roadside checks are starting to focus on motorhomes.

In recognition of this, some manufacturers offer payload upgrades which might take the MTPLM (see page 66) from 3,500kg to 3,850kg. Different MTPLM options have sometimes been offered at the time of purchase by manufacturers, such as Swift on some of its Kon Tiki models. Equally, Auto-Trail has built some models on a Fiat Maxi chassis instead of the standard Fiat 14, which meant that the MTPLM was raised from 3,500kg to 3,850kg. This option usually adds in excess of £1,000 to the price because a Maxi-base vehicle has bigger wheels, bigger brakes and a stronger suspension – and these are upgrading features that you cannot always add retrospectively.

Obviously it's better to purchase the right vehicle in the first place, but if you would like expert advice regarding your existing motorcaravan, SvTech in Leyland, Lancashire has long-standing expertise in both upgrading and downgrading modifications.

Be aware that the actual laden weight of a motorcaravan is also restricted by legal limitations. See Chapter 2 for more information.

Chassis variations

It was mentioned in Chapter 2 that a panel van does not have a chassis in the traditional sense. Like a car, its structure has strong box sections that form part of the steel floor, or 'floor pan'. In consequence, the following passage describing types of chassis does not include van conversions. However, the later sections on suspension systems and towing matters are relevant for all types of motorcaravan.

Having an understanding about types of traditional chassis is certainly useful for anyone intending to purchase a coachbuilt or A-Class model. The former is constructed using both the base vehicle's cab and an attached chassis (see photograph on page 60); the latter uses just a

Above: Specialists at SvTech run an advisory service for owners of commercial vehicles who want weight upgrades and downgrades.

Below: The Niesmann+Bischoff Flair 8000i is constructed on an Iveco Daily chassis.

Above: Light commercial vehicle (LCV) with cab and standard chassis.

Top right: Fiat's cab and purpose-made chassis for motorcaravan applications.

Right: Cab and platform chassis vehicle manufactured by Fiat.

Far right: Chassis cowl without a cab for A-Class motorcaravans.

Right: Fiat cab matched with AL-KO Kober AMC conversion..

Below: Heavy goods vehicle (HGV) with cab and heavy duty chassis.

chassis and an abbreviated cab, referred to as a chassis cowl. On a chassis cowl, the fascia and its instruments are supplied but there are no doors, no windscreen and no roof. That is because the A-Class builder will be creating these elements as part of the integrated construction.

In broad terms there are six different types of chassis used by motorcaravan manufacturers:

a) light commercial vehicle (LCV) with cab and standard chassis;
b) LCVs with cab and manufacturer-designed motor caravan chassis;
c) LCV with cab and platform chassis;
d) chassis cowl without a cab for A-Class manufacture;
e) the AL-KO Kober AMC conversion;
f) heavy goods vehicle (HGV) with cab and heavy duty chassis.

THE ORIGINAL COMMERCIAL CHASSIS

A large number of motorcaravans are constructed using a base vehicle whose chassis is principally designed for commercial applications rather than leisure use. In consequence, its design and accompanying suspension system is specified more for the carriage of goods than people.

Most types of chassis cab and chassis cowl are classified as light commercial vehicles (LCVs), examples of which are shown above. Only very large (and expensive) European motorhomes are constructed using the heavy goods vehicle (HGV) chassis used for large lorries. Models from

IVEKO and MAN are examples. Many American motorhomes are built on similar heavy structures.

The original LCV and HGV chassis are robustly built and have both advantages and disadvantages with regards to motorcaravan construction:

Advantages
- ▨ The structure is rigid.
- ▨ The chassis has been developed in conjunction with the cab and running gear as a whole.

Disadvantages
- ▨ Chassis sections are thoroughly painted but a galvanised construction might afford better protection.
- ▨ Outriggers that project outside the main longitudinal members are seldom provided, so a motorcaravan builder has to find a way to provide good support for the floor panel that serves the living area.
- ▨ The structure is usually quite high above the ground so steps have to be provided on the finished motorcaravan.
- ▨ The higher the finished vehicle, the greater the likelihood of body roll when cornering.

Irrespective of these features, many motorcaravans are built on a standard commercial base, which essentially has two longitudinal main members, but no side members to support a wider structure. If you look underneath a coachbuilt motorcaravan, some floors have little or no side support, whereas others have added outriggers that help to spread the load. If support is poor, it's hardly surprising that the composite floor panels used on most motorcaravans are able to flex, and this might hasten the delamination problems that sometimes occur. In recent crash testing experiments conducted during the design of Bailey motorcaravans, it was found that where outriggers were not used to support the outer extremities of floor panels, major floor breakages can occur at simulated speeds as low as 30mph.

This is an important issue for motorcaravan designers to resolve. A surprising number of motorcaravans are built without the addition of outriggers.

Since only a relatively small proportion of LCVs are used for conversion into motorcaravans, vehicle manufacturers have tended not to consider this purpose when their chassis are designed. In 2005, Fiat reconsidered the matter, and decided to introduce a chassis designed specifically for motorcaravan applications. An example of the modified low-line product was shown in the previous photographs. However, Fiat had not been the first to pursue this idea. Ford had recognised the needs of motorcaravan manufacturers more than 10 years earlier.

FORD-MODIFIED CHASSIS DESIGN
The commercial division of Ford announced its interest in motorcaravans at the Earl's Court Caravan and Leisure Show in autumn 1994. This led to chassis modifications to provide better

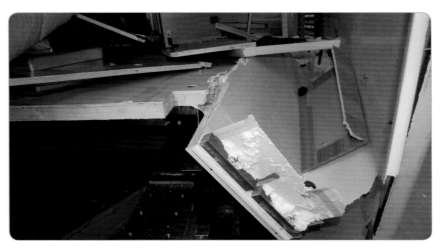

structural support for a living area on rear-wheel drive Transits.

The new product was duly used in the 1990s by Herald Motorcaravans, which were always built on a Ford base vehicle. (This manufacturer later became part of the Explorer Group). Auto-Sleepers similarly used these modified chassis on its Ford-based coachbuilt models built at this time.

To meet the needs of motorcaravanners, the main longitudinal chassis members on both medium and long wheelbase vehicles were lowered by 75mm (3in). In addition, these members incorporated a facility for the attachment of outriggers and side assemblies that would improve the support given to the floor panels normally installed in motorcaravans.

To assist motorcaravan manufacturers further, the rear-closing member of the chassis was also removable, thereby allowing a builder to extend the construction rearwards. With extension units bolted to the main chassis, the rear section of the living quarters was thus fully supported. However, since a rearward extension meant that the standard exhaust system wouldn't be long enough, an altered design took the pipe to one side. Ford's modified rear suspension also included an anti-roll bar and a higher specification of items fitted

Above: When crash testing this dummy vehicle, which had been built without chassis outrigger supports, the outer sections of its floor panel snapped.

Left: This floor panel extends outwards beyond the main chassis rails, but it has no outrigger supports.

in the cab. Overall, these alterations helped the Ford Transit become an appealing base vehicle in the later part of the 1990s. Since that period, the radically changed Transit range now includes front-wheel drive vehicles and the motorcaravan package launched in 1994 has been discontinued.

FIAT MOTORCARAVAN CHASSIS DESIGN

Light commercial vehicles manufactured by Fiat in Italy often bear Peugeot and Citroën badges, too. However, the marketing of these three products is conducted separately and competitively. And irrespective of the badge, a key feature of these products is the use of front-wheel drive, which eliminates the need for a central prop-shaft to drive the rear wheels. This offers considerable benefits to motorcaravan builders, including an opportunity to replace a commercial chassis with the lighter, low-line chassis designed by ALKO-Kober.

This increasingly popular practice may have prompted Fiat's decision to develop its own low-line lightweight chassis in the late 2000s. The photograph on page 60 shows Fiat's LWB 'Camper Chassis' being exhibited in 2009 with its wider rear track (1,980mm), 'Camper' specification tyres, and pre-cut cab roof and rear panel. In recognition of the interests of motorcaravanners, optional extras included equipment such as Automatic MTA transmission, air conditioning, special wheel trims, a painted front bumper and an integrated aerial in the door mirror.

Suffice to say, a front-wheel drive system makes chassis replacement work considerably easier to carry out. Furthermore, when Fiat introduced a fascia gear selector in 1994 instead of an intrusive floor-mounted gear-stick, both the Fiat Ducato and re-badged Peugeot Boxer became popular base vehicles with users and manufacturers alike.

AL-KO KOBER AMC CONVERSION

Another type of chassis designed specifically for motorcaravans is manufactured by AL-KO Kober, and these products can be installed on a number of front-wheel drive vehicles before the body assembly commences. Replacements can also be fitted on rear-wheel drive Mercedes Sprinter base vehicles, although this option has mainly been carried out by German motorcaravan manufacturers.

The AL-KO AMC conversion involves a radical alteration to the base vehicle but this modification is fully approved by manufacturers like Fiat. When these conversions were first carried out in the 1980s, the original commercial chassis was removed, scrapped and replaced with an AL-KO product.

This was undoubtedly a wasteful operation, so Fiat started to supply back-to-back 'chassis-less' units, as shown below.

Without question, the AL-KO product has proved successful on a large number of vehicles, including small buses, mobile libraries and motorcaravans. In fact, over 150,000 conversions have been completed worldwide since original development commenced in 1979.

However, the alteration involves more than just the installation of a purpose-built chassis; it also includes the installation of a replacement rear axle tube fitted with a different suspension system as described in the later section. Only the brake drums, bearing assemblies and wheels are retained from the original chassis cab.

The illustrations here show a brief synopsis of earlier conversions being carried out at AL-KO's factory in 1999. Minor features are not illustrated, such as rearranging the road light system and altering brake hydraulics. However, if you purchase an AL-KO-based vehicle of this period, this is how its chassis is coupled-up to the cab.

Note: *When brake assemblies and operating mechanisms are installed, the chassis is loaded with concrete blocks to simulate a typical load. The vehicle is then put onto a 'rolling road' to check and adjust the brake mechanisms.*

More recent developments coincided with the introduction of Fiat's redesigned vehicles, which

Right: Fiat back-to-back cabs are now supplied when AL-KO chassis are specified by motorcaravan manufacturers.

Replacing an original commercial chassis with an AL-KO AMC product

1. With the vehicle supported and a guiding jig in place, the original chassis is sawn away from the cab.

2. The original chassis is severed. Some of its components will be reused; the rest will be scrapped.

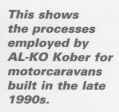

This shows the processes employed by AL-KO Kober for motorcaravans built in the late 1990s.

3. The junction point to the rear of the cab is cleaned and prepared for welding.

4. Using a jig to achieve accuracy, connecting flanges are welded to the stub chassis behind the cab.

5. An AL-KO Kober chassis is constructed using hot dip galvanised sections that are bolted together.

6. The cab flanges, coated with protective brown wax, are coupled to the new chassis; eight bolts are inserted.

appeared in January 2002. A key alteration was the introduction of a new connecting assembly for linking an AL-KO chassis to the cab. Another variation on this theme was the introduction of a chassis that permits the installation of a double floor. Between the two floor panels a motorcaravan manufacturer creates a capacious low-level storage compartment for personal equipment that can also house heating appliances, water tanks and heavy items like leisure batteries.

Many people now use their motorcaravans in winter and will need to prevent their water tanks from freezing, so models with double-layer floors have become popular. The enclosed (but accessible) compartments are used for cable runs, gas pipes, and central-heating ducting. In some vehicles, motorcaravan manufacturers also redirect one of the warm air heating outlets into the under-floor void for activation when temperatures drop below freezing.

Many of the motorhomes built with a double floor, such as the Swift Gazelle F63 High, have appealed to outdoor enthusiasts who need large lockers to stow equipment such as snow skis in the under-floor space. This places weight in the best place for driving: low down. Other motorcaravanners, however, are less enthusiastic about double-floor designs because the floor inside the living area is higher than it is on a stepped-down, low-level AL-KO chassis. This necessitates the installation of robust access steps. On a technical note, it is also important that all service pipes and cables mounted within an under-floor void are easy to access when repairs are needed.

That aside, an AL-KO chassis deserves close evaluation, whether it is a low-line or a double-floor design. The illustrations above and on page 64 show AL-KO AMC installations.

More recent features of AL-KO AMC conversions

1 Instead of employing the flange couplings employed in the 1990s, this connecting bracket was introduced in 2002.

2 If a low-level floor is preferred, the latest coupling system can achieve a considerable reduction in height

3 If underfloor storage is required, this chassis design enables a manufacturer to construct a motorcaravan with a double floor.

4 An AL-KO chassis is made to suit motorcaravanners' requirements and all the bolted members are assembled on a jig.

5 The damage sustained during Bailey crash tests confirmed that the addition of outriggers gives much better support to a floor panel.

6 Coupling accuracy is critically important and the bolts' recessed seatings on the coupling sections of the cab and the chassis help to achieve this objective.

7 Highly specified bolts are used to complete the coupling between this temporarily supported cab and the new ALKO chassis.

8 On all safety-critical couplings formed in the AL-KO caravan and motorhome chassis, tamper-proof identification paint is applied.

9 When the brake system has been coupled-up, concrete blocks of an appropriate weight are loaded onto the chassis and braking is calibrated on a rolling road.

Advantages

- Computer-designed chassis members produce a light structure without compromising rigidity.
- The installation of hot-dip zinc galvanised sections ensures longevity.
- Where requested by a motorcaravan manufacturer, AL-KO Kober can fit a 'stepped-down' chassis that is 225mm (9in) lower than the original. A lower floor height provides easier access to the living quarters and a lower centre of gravity helps reduce body roll when acute bends are negotiated.
- Single or tandem axle units can be fitted irrespective of the original back axle configuration.
- A suspension system offering increased load potential can be installed if requested by a motorcaravan manufacturer.
- Since the chassis sections are bolted together, replacement of a damaged unit may be possible, although it would be an involved operation.
- AL-KO Kober-designed towing brackets and motorcycle racks are available for attachment to this manufacturer's chassis if required (but see the earlier comments at the start of this chapter on page 58).
- Until back-to-back cabs were built, the least expensive vehicle could be converted to a long wheelbase unit with a minimum wastage of original chassis material.

Note: *Further advantages in respect of the suspension system are detailed later.*

Disadvantages
■ Additional items must not be welded to an AL-KO Kober chassis – this would invalidate the warranty.

Note: *Great reliance is placed on the bolts, flanges and fabrication which connect the new chassis to the donor cab. This is not a method of conversion that should be tackled by a self-builder.*

Clearly there is much to be gained by this constructional approach and AL-KO AMC assemblies are used on ambulance conversions, mobile chip shops, buses, travelling libraries and removal vans, as well as motorcaravans. The UK manufacturers who have used AL-KO Kober chassis on selected models in their ranges include Autocruise, Bailey, Bentley, Auto-Trail, Buccaneer, Compass, Elddis, Lunar, Machzone and Swift.

REAR OVERHANG AND CHASSIS EXTENSIONS

When a coachbuilt motorcaravan is built on an original chassis, a common practice is to extend the rearmost part of the structure using additional steel rails or a complete bolt-on framework. Remarkably, a few manufacturers achieve this by merely using timber struts to reinforce the rear floor-panel.

Arguably, a steel structure would provide a more rigid support when a floor is extended rearwards from a back axle to form the 'rear overhang'.

Type Approval Regulations together with Construction and Use guidelines state that this must not extend rearwards of the back axle by more than 60% of the wheelbase dimension.

Note: *A second calculation is given in the guidelines to verify the acceptability of a rear overhang but this involves turning circle data, and the measuring process is considerably more complex.*

When you check a wheelbase dimension (the distance between the centre of the front and the centre of the rear wheels) and then calculate the maximum permitted overhang, you soon realise that some models take full advantage of the 60% limit. Obviously this helps to create a larger living space on a relatively short chassis, but there are several issues to bear in mind.

Basic geometry, a rudimentary knowledge of the principles of leverage and simple common sense indicate that loading a heavy item at the very back of a prominent rear overhang will magnify the loading on the rear axle. Furthermore, there are strict loading limits on all rear axles and it is an offence – as well as dangerous – to exceed the limit stated on a vehicle's plate details. The longer the overhang, the greater the effect of the weight. But it is not just the rear axle loading that suffers.

Where there is a single rear axle, this can act as the pivot point on what is effectively a kind of see-saw. The heavier the load bearing down at the

Left: Galvanised extension members are bolted to this Fiat chassis to support the rear overhang on a Swift 2006 Sundance.

back, the more the front end of the vehicle wants to lift upwards. In extreme cases, the front tyres can have less positive contact with the road. This might affect the steering, braking, and in the case of front-wheel driven vehicles, the traction.

Bearing this in mind, you can appreciate the problems that might arise if you intend to carry a motorcycle or an electric mobility scooter on a rear-mounted carrier – especially if the overhang on your motorcaravan is near the 60% limit.

A similar situation can arise if you want to tow a trailer. To achieve good towing stability, a substantial nose-weight is needed, which is then born by the tow-ball. Inevitably, this down-force not only affects rear axle loading: it also tends to lighten the front of the vehicle. Some owners wrongly believe that upgrading the rear springs will solve this, but it won't. The load carried by the rear axle, and related issues like braking effectiveness, are not changed simply by firming-up the suspension. If you're planning on carrying scooters or similar heavy items on a rack at the back it would be wise to purchase a vehicle with the shortest rear-overhang you can find. In addition, carrying substantial loads is better managed on a base vehicle with an upgraded rear axle, larger wheels, brakes, and in some cases, a tandem axle configuration. The advantages of having a full air suspension system installed with reactive height-adjusting facilities are also very clear, but the designers of British motorcaravans seem slow to recognise the merits of these products.

A further way in which a motorcaravan manufacturer can overcome the problems caused by a large overhang is to have the base vehicle's

Left: Carrying a heavy mobility scooter on a rear-mounted rack adds a considerable extra load to the back axle and suspension.

Right: The chassis for this Lunar motorcaravan is being extended at Drinkwater Engineering works.

Right: Extending a chassis 'amidships' shifts the back axle rearwards, thus avoiding a large rear overhang.

chassis extended between the axles instead. One manufacturer who adopted this strategy was Lunar Motorcaravans, with work carried out by Drinkwater Engineering in Leyland.

This chassis conversion specialist is no longer in business but several vehicles are still in use with these modified chassis. If you purchase a Lunar built around 2000, for example, it may have one of these altered chassis. It is important to point out

that Drinkwater modifications met the approval of several vehicle manufacturers. Moreover, by extending the chassis amidships, there is an accompanying relocation of the back axle towards the rear of a motorhome. This was undoubtedly a successful way of extending a chassis without merely creating a long overhang at the back.

Chassis maintenance

One of the benefits of an AL-KO chassis is the fact that its components are hot-dip zinc galvanised rather than painted. Some AL-KO caravan chassis manufactured in the early 1980s were painted black, but this finish was soon superseded by galvanised treatments.

In contrast, standard base vehicle chassis are usually treated with paint and after several years rust starts to appear on the surface. Components like spare wheel cages and painted tow-bars are even more disappointing, and will become dreadfully rusty if left without periodic attention.

Traditional DIY work usually means crawling underneath a vehicle to apply a product like Hammerite. But remember: it is seriously dangerous to crawl under a vehicle elevated on a doubtful surface using unsuitable lifting gear. Serious injuries are not uncommon and you must never rely on jacks, poor-quality axle stands, insubstantial portable ramps or piles of household bricks.

Having spent several years carrying out periodic chassis repainting, the author recently had work carried out professionally. A commercial vehicle ramp afforded hitherto un-enjoyed access to the underside of a Fiat-based motorcaravan and the accompanying sequence shows how a truck and van specialist carries out routine chassis renovation work.

Suspension systems

Ride comfort in a motorcaravan is governed largely by the suspension and this can be a problem when the base vehicle was previously a commercial vehicle.

LEAF-SPRING SUSPENSION

Often described as 'cart springs', the typical leaf-spring arrangement used on commercial vehicles is fine for transporting bags of cement or crates of lemonade. But for a discerning motorcaravanner, this form of suspension is seldom satisfactory without some degree of modification.

It's main drawback is a 'harsh ride', which becomes increasingly apparent when a vehicle is driven on poor road surfaces.

Then there is the disconcerting feeling of body roll on sharp bends, twisting roads and small roundabouts. Tall vehicles with a high centre of gravity are particularly susceptible to body-lean on corners. Poor load distribution doesn't help, and the carriage of heavy items in ceiling lockers and an external roof box inevitably makes things worse. Disconcerting deflections are also experienced in

---

Load data

ALKO chassis weight limits

Motorcaravans built on an AL-KO Kober chassis and rear axle conversion will have a plate mounted in the engine compartment giving details about weight limits. The one shown here was mounted in a late 1990s coachbuilt. On more recent models, different loading terminology would be used as described in Chapter 2. For instance, Gross Vehicle Weight is now expressed as Maximum Technically Permitted Laden Mass (MTPLM). Irrespective of changes in words, the need to work within these limits is very important.

■ Gross Vehicle Weight (maximum total vehicle weight).
■ Gross Train Weight (maximum total weight of vehicle with towed trailer).
■ Maximum weight Axle 1 (permitted axle loading, front).
■ Maximum weight Axle 2 (permitted axle loading, axle number two).
■ Maximum weight Axle 3 (permitted axle loading, axle number three in the case of twin rear axle models).

Further details of the AL-KO Kober conversion are given in the AL-KO AMC Handbook which is included with the documentation accompanying a new motorcaravan. If mislaid, copies are available from AL-KO Kober using the address given in the Appendix.

AL-KO KOBER CHASSIS CONVERSION WEIGHTS (KGS.)	
G.V.W.	3400
G.T.W.	4800
AXLE 1	1650
AXLE 2	1900
AXLE 3	

Routine checks and chassis maintenance work

1. Although this 1999 Fiat Maxi chassis is protected with Waxoyl inside each member, external rust has developed on several fixtures and fitting.

2. The rear axle tube is deteriorating badly in several places and several lengths of brake pipe have had to be replaced on this 1999 base vehicle.

3. Preparation was carried out using 3M Scotch-Brite™ Roloc™ 50.8mm, 36 grade abrasive discs. These are a good size for reaching restricted spaces.

4. Safety guidance accompanying these 3M abrasive discs is particularly detailed. Eye, skin and respiratory protection should be worn at all times by users.

5. The under-floor spare wheel carrier is an item that has to be repainted quite often, and the removal of loose rust is an exacting task – even with power tools.

6. Particularly difficult to prepare are the outriggers that had been specially made to fit the standard chassis. They often need attention and access isn't easy.

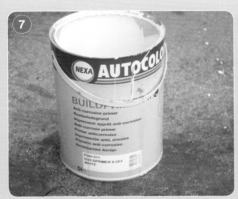

7. Many paint products are available, but this chassis specialist uses NEXA Autocolor Build Primer II for anti-corrosion treatment as it is easy to apply.

8. The bespoke tow-bar from Watling Engineers often needs repainting but its sections are fairly easy to reach – even without lifting the vehicle.

9. The benefit of a commercial ramp becomes particularly apparent once the repainting work commences. Even the outriggers are easy to reach.

Acknowledgement: *Photographs taken with the co-operation of the North East Truck and Van Company, Billingham.*

side-winds and when a high-sided vehicle overtakes a motorcaravan on a fast road.

To reduce these unpleasant characteristics, some manufacturers fit anti-roll bars; other strategies include the installation of stiffer shock absorbers on the front.

Making improvements by the addition of air-assistance products can also help. However, don't overlook the later comments regarding braking issues; problems can arise when spring assistance products are fitted retrospectively on older vehicles that are not equipped with ABS braking systems. On a further note, make sure you recognise the clear distinction between air suspension and air assistance. The differences are succinctly explained in the Technical Tip on page 69.

COIL SPRINGS

Although these are fitted to the rear suspensions of many cars, coil springs have not been widely used on commercial vehicles. However, the T4 Volkswagen Transporter is an exception because it has an independent suspension system at the rear which uses mini coil springs and a semi-trailing arm configuration. The refined ride has been acknowledged with satisfaction in many independent motorcaravan test reports and the newer T5 continues to receive favourable praise. Its springs are short coils mounted at a slight angle in order not to intrude far into the vehicle's interior. Rear coil springs on a car, for example, typically take up space in the boot, hence Volkswagen's decision to use shorter springs. Moreover, the semi-trailing arm is not unlike a wishbone configuration and independent springing undoubtedly provides a pleasing ride.

Examples of conversions based on Volkswagen Transporters include the Auto-Sleepers high-top Trident, Bilbo's high-top Nektar, the Middlesex MC Matrix, and many more.

If a conversion is based on a 'people carrier', this is also likely to have coil spring rear suspension. Wheelhome is one of the manufacturers that converts 'people carrier' vehicles.

TORSION BAR

Different again is a system that uses torsion bars. In this arrangement, a swinging arm suspension unit provides the mounting point for a wheel hub

at one end, and there is a long fixed bar at the other. When a vehicle rides the bumps, its bars are subjected to a twisting action that they naturally resist. Torsion bar suspension has been employed in many popular vehicles and the Renault 5 hatchback of the early 1980s is a good example.

An engineer might point out that the twisting action resisted by a long bar is little different from a similar twisting action that a coil spring has to resist. In effect, a torsion bar could be regarded as a coil spring that has been unwound to form a long rod.

When setting up a vehicle, inducing an initial twist can tighten up a torsion bar, which alters its ride height and driving characteristics. On the road, torsion bar systems work well – although the bars take up space. On a Renault 5, for example, the front torsion bars are 1.22m (4ft) long, although they are conveniently hidden behind the sills of the car.

If this seems a clumsy arrangement, it is no problem in respect of the rear suspension used in an AL-KO Kober AMC conversion. In this application, the torsion bars are mounted within the axle tube. These unseen bars have splines on one end that fit into the pivot point of the swinging

---

Servicing

AL-KO Kober torsion bar system

The rear axle of a motorcaravan built on the AL-KO Kober torsion bar system must be lubricated every 20,000km (12,500 miles). The procedure that a workshop engineer has to carry out is as follows:

1) Jack up the vehicle and provide support so that the wheels are clear of the ground.
2) Identify the grease points on the outer ends of the axle tube on either the forward-facing side or the underside. They lie just inside the main longitudinal chassis members.
3) Pump in grease using a pressure gun – about six pumps, ensuring that there is no likelihood of overfilling (a hand gun is not adequate).
4) Use a product such as Shell Retinax LX grease.
5) Record the mileage at the time of greasing in the service record.

Right: Participants on an AL-KO Kober training course are shown different grades of torsion bar used in the AMC axle tubes.

Far right: The all-important greasing points on an AL-KO torsion bar suspension are situated at the outer ends of the axle tube.

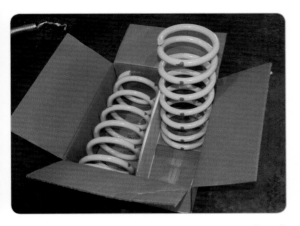

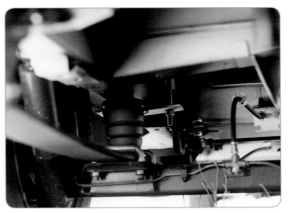

arms and telescopic shock absorbers are employed to dampen the movements.

The AL-KO Kober torsion suspension undoubtedly provides good road handling, and weight options of 3,200, 3,400, 3,500 and 3,850kg can be specified. In other words, the payload can be increased to suit a motorcaravan designer's specifications – ultimately providing the user with more, or less, scope when loading up.

In motorcaravan tests, the ride achieved in vehicles fitted with an AL-KO Kober torsion bar system is often favourably reported. However, to ensure the ongoing performance of the product, grease has to be injected periodically into the axle tube via nipples at its outermost ends. Guidance is given in the accompanying servicing panel.

As a footnote, it is most regrettable that some motorcaravan converters have occasionally mounted under-floor water tanks that completely obscure a suspension's greasing points. It is essential that grease is applied periodically to the axle tube and an AL-KO Kober Warranty is null and void if this is ignored.

SPRING ASSISTANCE AND BRAKING

As they get older, springs lose their resilience and it's not unusual to find that the rear end of an elderly motorcaravan has started to sag. When this occurs, the best answer might be to have new springs fitted and some owners take this opportunity to have heavier duty springs installed.

Not that springs have to carry the entire load. Some coachbuilt models have compressible rubber assisters fitted by their manufacturer to augment the work of their leaf springs. However, many motorcaravanners decide to have auxiliary inflatable boosters fitted in the place of these rubber buffers.

This strategy might be effective, but some suppliers wrongly infer that these additions provide the owner with an 'air suspension' system. This is incorrect; it would be more accurate to describe the modified configuration as a hybrid suspension system because it combines two different products. So be aware of misleading claims. In truth, there is a significant difference between 'air assistance' and 'air suspension' systems – as the Technical Tip box explains.

Air assistance units are usually installed centrally on a leaf spring. The step-by-step sequence overleaf shows a pair of ALKO 'Air Top' products being retrospectively fitted at the Company's Warwickshire factory. Their function, of course, is to bear some of the weight hitherto taken entirely by the springs, and this can help to elevate a motorcaravan whose rear end is inclined to sag. However, it's important to recognise that a retro-fit installation usually has to take into account the calibration of a vehicle's braking system.

Technical Tip

Air assistance or air suspension?

Air assistance describes inflatable devices designed to work in conjunction with the original springing system. For instance, if leaf springs have lost their resilience, a motorcaravan might develop a sag at the back. The addition of inflatable units may help to overcome this and give additional support to a deteriorating suspension. However, check the comments in the main text about the detrimental effects that incorrectly installed air assistance products can have on braking operation.

Assistance devices are frequently installed at the central point of a leaf spring.

Air suspension is installed on vehicles which need to provide supreme comfort (such as accident and emergency ambulances) or provide an extremely smooth ride (in lorries transporting sensitive loads such as aero engines). The original spring suspension system on these vehicles will have been completely removed and scrapped. The replacement suspension comprises air chambers, a compressor pump, an air reservoir, a computer-controlled monitoring system and a revised brake compensation system. These systems are fitted on high quality motorcaravans.

Large air chambers have been fitted in the place of leaf springs on this Drinkwater suspension.

Installing air-assistance products

1. The Air Top from AL-KO includes two air chambers, two pressure gauges and coupling tubes.

2. This pair of air assistance chambers fits Fiat Ducato and Peugeot Boxer motorcaravans.

3. The air pressure gauge panel can be mounted where it's most convenient inside a vehicle.

4. Once the concertina bump stop had been unscrewed, an air chamber is eased into place.

5. A chamber straddles the spring below and couples to a plate fixed to the chassis above.

6. When the two chambers have been fitted, the air tubing is coupled and routed where appropriate.

7. The brake proportioning bracket on the axle will not be used, nor its connected control valve.

8. With the old system disabled, non ABS systems are fitted with a brake-limiting valve in the system.

Acknowledgement: Photographs taken with the co-operation of AL-KO Kober Ltd, Southam, Warwickshire.

The point to recognise is that brakes do not normally provide balanced 50–50 front/rear braking. Usually a greater proportion of the braking is applied to the front wheels. However, vehicles may also be fitted with a device that automatically adjusts the front–rear balance in order to suit the load being carried. Put simply, the device registers the depression of the rear suspension and reacts by altering the braking to achieve optimum performance under that load condition. This facility isn't just fitted to commercial vehicles; estate cars and even some small hatchbacks and saloons have these brake control units.

In the case of a motorcaravan with a depressed rear, the brake-balancing device interprets this as a sign of heavy loading and responds by setting the balance of front/rear braking to suit that situation. However, it stands to reason that if the sagging rear of a heavily-laden motorhome is subsequently elevated by fitting a height-raising product, a brake-sensing mechanism that hasn't been appropriately readjusted is fooled into interpreting the revised ride height as an indication that a light load is being carried. The balance of braking applied to the front/rear wheels is then automatically set to suit a lightly-laden situation, when in reality, the vehicle might be heavily-laden.

This problem doesn't arise on recent vehicles equipped with ABS braking systems. It is normally only an issue on older base vehicles, and when air assistance units are added, the brake load sensing system must be adjusted in accordance with the base vehicle manufacturer's guidelines. If this all-important feature is ignored, braking performance could be compromised.

For this reason, if you consider having a spring assistance device fitted on a non-ABS braked vehicle, it is important to ascertain what the installer will do to re-calibrate the load-sensing system so that the correct proportion of front/rear braking is applied. Equally, you need confirmation that both the new product and its installation method receive the base vehicle manufacturer's approval. Unfortunately, some advertisements make convincing claims about ride improvement, better road holding and reduction in body roll, whereas the subject of the braking set-up is seldom mentioned at all.

These concerns will not occur when weight-reactive, computer-controlled air suspension systems are installed. In this type of suspension, a sophisticated brake sensor and control unit forms part of the set-up, as the following section now explains.

AIR SUSPENSION

In spite of the extensive use of air suspension in ambulances, public service vehicles such as buses, and in lorries that have to transport sensitive loads, the product is seldom used in British-built motorcaravans. It's true that air suspension has been offered as an option in Lunar motorcaravans and the author has a VB reactive system installed on his self-built motorcaravan, but few UK leisure vehicle are thus equipped.

In Germany, the situation is different. The benefits of air suspension are more widely recognised and motorcaravans are often equipped with load reactive systems, some of which include on-site levelling facilities. It is also true that an AL-KO chassis can be fitted with the Company's air suspension system and examples have been displayed at several exhibitions held in this country.

Not surprisingly, there are different versions of air suspension packages. In Europe, for example, some air suspension units are just fitted to the rear axle while coil springs are retained at the front. However, full air suspension systems are available, too, although these are usually only installed on high specification motorhomes.

When air units are mounted to support the back axle, this permits fore and aft levelling. On a sloping pitch, for example, as much air can be released as is necessary to level a vehicle. Alternatively, the motorcaravans fitted with front and rear chambers can also achieve lateral levelling. However, on-site levelling is only one of the advantages of having an air suspension installation.

Without doubt, the comfort achieved when 'riding on air' is hard to beat. In fact, this type of suspension is considered essential for users with certain disabilities. Equally, the use of air suspension in front-line ambulances is a well-established practice. Ride comfort is crucial in these contexts and it is no surprise that many owners of leisure vehicles prefer a smooth driving experience.

Where comfort is concerned, the desirability of air suspension systems is undoubtedly compelling. In addition to its benefits when setting-up on-site, the operating functions enable a motorcaravan to attain a level stance when being driven. Even when a heavy scooter has been loaded onto the back, the automatic monitoring sensors respond by activating the air inflation/release facility to compensate for this new addition. Conversely, when items are removed, the reduced load is again recognised and air is duly released automatiaclly, which means that the vehicle assumes a level stance on the road. But the benefits don't end there. The weight-sensing facility takes account of the load and can make appropriate adjustments to the brake operation.

Inevitably, a retrospective installation of a rear air suspension system typically entails removal of the original springs, and this is not a task to be taken lightly. However, VB-Airsuspension supplies conversion kits and there are products to suit a wide range of vehicles. The Company has a base in Blackburn, and the quality of both VB air assistance units and air suspension systems has been recognised for several years in mainland Europe. Currently the products are installed at several UK commercial vehicle workshops and the accompanying illustrations show a VB-Air suspension kit being fitted to a 1999 Fiat Ducato Maxi. The installation was undertaken in 2009 at the North East Truck and Van Engineering Division in Billingham.

Installing a VB-Air suspension system on a Fiat Ducato 2.8TD Maxi

This weight-reactive, ECU controlled system with an internal compressor is installed on the rear of a 1999 motorcaravan.

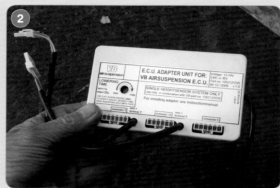

1. Key items in the kit are laid out and include: two air bellows, the main cross-member, a compressor, the panhard rod, shock absorbers, height sensor, cabling, controls, and air pipes.

2. Electronic control units are the brain behind the system and these are 'plug and play' items. Fine-tuning the operations of this unit includes an adjustment of lowering times.

3. This product operates without a separate air tank and the bellows are directly inflated by an air compressor. This was mounted under the driver's seat.

4. As a preliminary task, the air bellows are secured to the main crossbeam. Air tubes are also connected here and the instruction manual gives clear illustrations.

5. The upper-mounting of the shock absorbers is completed, after which the crossbeam is offered-up. The operation is really only feasible when a vehicle is raised on a ramp.

6. The ride height sensor can be fine-tuned to suit requirements and this is mounted on a bracket attached to the top of the main crossbeam.

7. In the absence of ABS brakes, this load-sensing valve replaces the original brake-balancing device. Pressure in the air bellows now dictates and sets the braking required.

8. When the setting-up checks were complete, the bellows were fully inflated and the vehicle was ready for use. Note the air bellows, the shock absorber, bump stops and new spring.

Acknowledgement: *Photographs taken with the co-operation of the North East Truck and Van Co, Billingham.*

Shock absorbers

When considering a suspension system, many people presume – quite wrongly – that fitting higher specification shock absorbers will stiffen the springs and increase ride height. This reveals a misconception about the function and design of products commonly referred to as 'shockers'.

Driven without shock absorbers, a vehicle bounces along in wild leaps – as any Banger Racing enthusiast will have noticed when a shocker fails on the racetrack. Irrespective of whether a telescopic shock absorber is filled with gas or oil, the component's job is to dampen down movements when a vehicle rides the bumps. In other words, shock absorbers simply do what their name implies and a standard product is not a spring-stiffening device.

Since the majority of motorcaravans are generally heavily laden, several specialists have developed replacement shockers especially suitable for leisure vehicles. The accompanying photo sequences give a brief insight into the installation of OMA high-performance units. These are constructed so that both internal chambers are filled with oil, thereby increasing strength as well as enhancing their damping performance. The units can also be dismantled for later renovation, whereas many sealed shock absorbers are throwaway components. These OMA products are manufactured in Italy and Nova Leisure, Northamptonshire supplies them to UK motorcaravan dealers.

The installation here was carried out in the Heart of England Motorhome Service workshops in Northamptonshire, NN6 7PP and the vehicle was a Peugeot Boxer 1997 coachbuilt model. Note that OMA ISO-certified products are made to suit many makes of base vehicles including Fiats, Ford Transits, Mercedes Sprinters, VW T4 and T5s, Renault Masters and their re-badged equivalents.

Footnote: Sturdy spring compression clamps are needed when dealing with commercial coil springs and if one suddenly becomes detached unexpectedly, injuries can be quite serious. This is a job best entrusted to an experienced mechanic.

In this installation, it was also necessary to remove part of the fascia inside the cab in order to obtain access to the upper fixings of the front shock absorbers.

Towing

Many motorcaravans are powerful enough to tow a sizeable trailer carrying a reasonable load. A base vehicle's commercial origin usually means its engine has good pulling power at low revs and this characteristic is especially evident with diesel engines. However, the weight of a loaded trailer must be checked on a weighbridge; the Actual Laden Weight (ALW) of the towing vehicle must similarly be confirmed. This data is needed when carrying out the following calculations.

Touring caravanners work on the basis that to

Replacing shock absorbers on a Peugeot Boxer motorcaravan

1. To achieve good access and to ensure that a vehicle is secure, this work is much easier when a workshop ramp is available.

2. It can be a tough task to loosen the fixing bolts on a vehicle that has never had its shockers removed before.

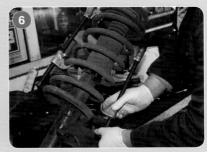

3. Removal of the rear wheels yields access to the upper fixings and this bolt is usually fitted first.

4. Aligning the lower coupling point often needs gentle persuasion but rear shockers are usually quite easy to fit.

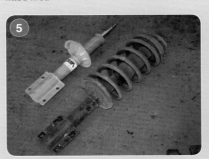

5. Most modern vehicles have a combined coil spring and shock absorber at the front, which are harder to replace.

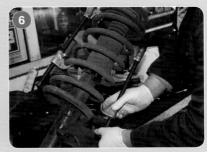

6. A spring has to be compressed before it can be detached and this is a potentially dangerous operation.

7. The upper end of the assembly is often a headache to reach. Forming the lower connections usually needs an alignment tool.

8. Job finished. It took this motorcaravan technician three hours to complete his first shock absorber replacement job.

Acknowledgement: *Photographs taken with the co-operation of staff at the workshops of Heart of England Motorhomes Service Centre, Long Buckby, Northants, NN6 7PP.*

Above: Many motorcaravan owners want to tow, but the weight of a trailer and its load must not exceed the gross train weight listed for the towing vehicle.

achieve an ideal match from the point of view of towing stability, the total weight of a trailer should not exceed 85% of the ALW of the towing vehicle. This ensures that the 'tail doesn't wag the dog', and most motorcaravans are likely to meet this recommended weight ratio. However, this might not be the case if there is a heavy trailer load, for example, a cabin cruiser or a heavy motor vehicle. Similarly, a lightweight micro motorcaravan might also be unable to achieve the 85% vehicle/trailer guideline.

Although the 85% guideline is worthy of note, an experienced driver might be safe to tow a trailer whose loaded weight is the same as the ALW of the towing vehicle (*ie* a 100% match). However, you must ensure that a loaded trailer never exceeds the actual laden weight of the towing vehicle.

Another important issue relates to the towing vehicle's 'gross train weight' (GTW). Compliance with this limit is mandatory and the GTW is normally given in a base vehicle's handbook and on a data plate in its engine compartment. The GTW limit concerns the combined weight of both the laden towing vehicle

and its loaded trailer. Problems might occur if you want to tow something heavy, like a support car, so this usually calls for trips to a weighbridge. You need to establish the weight of your loaded motorcaravan and the weight of the trailer with its tow-car in place. These two weights should be added together to establish the train weight, thereby verifying that you are not exceeding your motorcaravan's GTW limit. Incidentally, some vehicles also have a further towing limit that relates to the power of their engine and its ability to tow heavy loads.

There are also issues concerning the tow-bar (or 'tow bracket') to take into account. For example, it is now a legal requirement under Directive 94/20/EC that all light passenger vehicles registered on or after 1 August 1998 can only be fitted with an EC Type Approved tow-bar. Bear in mind that when this directive was introduced, it did not apply to commercial vehicles. However, further legislation now makes it mandatory for tow-bars fitted to motorcaravans registered in 2012 and thereafter to have gained TUV accreditation. This clearly affects bespoke bracket designers, such as Watling Engineers, PWS and TOWtal whose products are not submitted for TUV testing. With so many different base vehicles on sale, the costs of gaining TUV approval would be prohibitive for small tow-bar companies such as these. So, at the time of writing, the future of one-off products looks uncertain.

The matter of mounting tow-bars and the potential difficulties is also something to consider, as described at the beginning of this chapter. Brackets that have been designed to suit a base vehicle might not fit after it has been converted into a motorcaravan. Similarly, TUV approved tow-bars designed to fit an AL-KO chassis cannot always be coupled-up to the chassis after some types of body structure have been installed.

Right: This TUV approved tow-bar fits without posing problems because it extends sufficiently far rearwards of the bodywork.

Far right: Under future legislation, products like this bespoke tow-bar will not be fitted to post 2012 models unless it passes TUV tests.

Right: It has been a recent requirement for tow-bars to be fitted with a data plate providing information like its nose weight limit.

Far right: The smart tow-bars from PWC are usually sold with a powder-coated finish but they have not passed TUV tests.

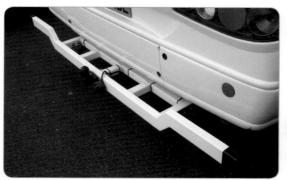

Left: Many motorcaravan owners use a trailer for pursuing hobbies and interests.

Trailers and A-frames

Many types of trailer are towed by motorcaravan owners and these are either for utility purposes or for hobby-related activities.

Information in *The Trailer Manual* (Haynes Publishing) explains that a laden trailer weighing in excess of 750kg must be fitted with a braking system. In most instances, the system is the type fitted to touring caravans and the auto-release brakes permit reversing to take place without the brakes halting the progress. Many additional requirements are also explained in *The Trailer Manual*.

Other information on towing is provided in *The Caravan Manual* (Haynes Publishing) and this includes detailed information on caravan 'over-run' brakes, wiring requirements, electrical couplings, stabilisers and the contrasting functions of secondary couplings and breakaway cables.

TOWING A SUPPORT CAR

When towing a trailer to transport a 'support car', the position is clear; to comply with the law, virtually all vehicle trailers are fitted with an over-run braking system as standard. Even smaller vehicles like the Smart for Two achieve an Actual Laden Weight (ALW) in excess of 750kg, and that's not including the weight of a trailer. Admittedly you don't have to purchase a large vehicle transporter because specialists like Bantam Trailers design

Far left: The compact Bantam Trailer designed by Alan Pierce is ideal for motorcaravanners; versions are made for several small cars.

Left: It is a requirement that modern trailers carry a data plate giving carrying capacities. Information like tyre pressures is useful, too.

Left: Made to measure. Several clever design features in this product make loading and safe securing fairly simple tasks.

Far left: Although one of the lightest cars currently on sale, this SECMA Fun Tech weighs 225kg with a full tank of fuel.

Right: Using an A-frame is a popular way to tow a car, but several points should be borne in mind.

Technical Tip

Towing with an A-frame

All but a few cars (such as the Fun Tech, QPod, and Aixam) weigh more than 750kg – and a trailer adds even more to the total trailed weight. When a car is towed with an A-frame, it is deemed to be a trailer and has to meet all legal requirements applicable to trailers. For instance, the fact that it exceeds 750kg means it must have independent brakes, just as a trailer does. Several devices, both mechanical and electrical, can be fitted to bring a towed car's brakes into play when needed. However, the question arises whether towing with an A-frame is legal throughout Europe.

■ **When The Caravan Club contacted all EU motoring organisations, it was established that a braked car towed behind a motorcaravan on a purpose-designed frame appears to be permitted in the United Kingdom and 'tolerated' in both Germany and the Netherlands. In other European countries, A-frame towing is normally reserved for the police and vehicle recovery operators.**

■ **Notwithstanding different rulings in EU countries, if a visitor travelling abroad is using a vehicle deemed acceptable in his or her country of residence, police of the nation being visited usually treat this as a special case and take no action. Unfortunately, where towing with an A-frame is concerned, police services in some EC countries appear to ignore this concession and a number of motorcaravanners report that they have been stopped. To avoid difficulties in these countries, transporting a support car with an approved trailer might be advisable.**

■ **An A-frame coupled with a motorcaravan doesn't articulate like a trailer. Moreover, the front wheels of a car faithfully follow its towing vehicle thanks to the 'castor effect', as long as it is moving in a forward direction. Unfortunately, this castor effect is immediately negated as soon as a coupled car is moved backwards. In consequence, reversing when using an A-frame is virtually impossible.**

■ **To prepare a vehicle for use with an A-frame, elaborate modifications have to be made in its engine compartment. Specialists like TOWtal have designed robust bracket assemblies for many years and the construction of supporting towing reinforcement is carried out with painstaking care. Modifications to any vehicle have to be reported to its insurers, and compliance with increasingly stringent automotive rules may soon prevent these types of adaptations.**

compact versions to suit the Smart Car, Toyota Aygo, Vauxhall Corsa and other small vehicles.

Only a few cars such as the French-manufactured Secma Fun Tech, Aixam and QPod weigh considerably less than models like the Smart for Two. A laden Secma Fun Tech, for example, weighs less than 250kg – though it might be claimed that this isn't a conventional 'car'. The Fun Tech or its QPod partner can even be towed legally on an unbraked trailer, provided the combined car/trailer weight doesn't exceed 750kg.

TOWING WITH AN A-FRAME

Trailing a car independently, by using what is known as an A-frame, raises a number of legal issues. Some of these are included in the accompanying Technical Tip panel, although this section is not claimed to be a definitive statement on the subject. In truth, the A-frame issue elicits countless differences of opinion.

To achieve braking compliance when using an A-frame, there are now several systems that bring a towed vehicle's brakes into play. This meets the braking requirement of a trailed car exceeding 750kg, but it must also be ensured that the combined weight of both vehicles does not exceed the gross train weight (GTW) displayed on a motorcaravan's data plate.

As stated earlier, virtually all small support cars, including the Smart for Two, weigh in excess of 750kg. In consequence, it is illegal to tow a Smart car on an unbraked A-frame unless a supplementary air brake system has been installed, or an electrical 'Brake Buggy' is used. Surprisingly, un-braked A-frames are often used by Smart owners and there are no signs of alternative air or electric braking mechanisms in use. This could lead to a conviction and is probably dangerous, too.

Note: *Auxiliary air brake systems are currently being marketed by some trailer specialists. The*

'Brake Buddy', imported from the USA, is an electrically-driven accessory which can operate a support vehicle's brake pedal.

Towing with an A-frame is often described as a 'grey area' and future legislation is expected to clarify uncertainties about these 'trailer-less' systems. The fact that the writer has towed with motorcaravans in the UK for many years using both trailers and braked A-frames is a matter of the past and not of the future. There is no doubt that a folding A-frame assembly is convenient to store. On the other hand, these products take a surprising amount of time to couple-up correctly. Even worse is the fact that you cannot reverse a car very far on an A-frame, which is a shortcoming that could lead to problems. This difficulty doesn't arise, of course, if you opt for a trailer instead – as long as you master reversing manoeuvres.

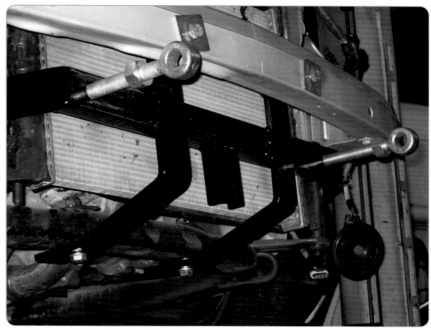

Right: Before this Vauxhall Corsa could be used with an A-frame, a robust and elaborate structure was constructed at the front..

Above left: Electric couplings have to be wired-up in the support car so that its road lights work in concert with the motorcaravan's lights.

Above: A folded A-frame assembly is easy to store at home; the unit from TOWtal also fits in the back of this 2002 Corsa.

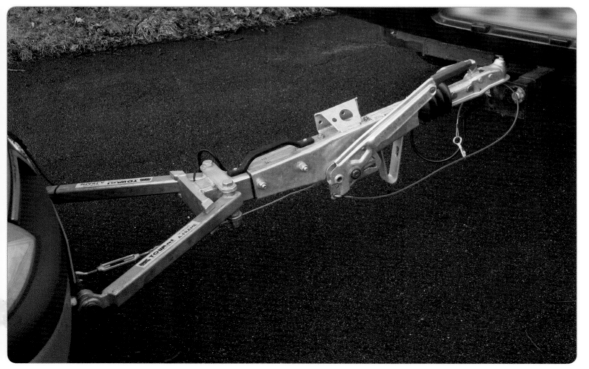

Left: This A-frame includes an over-run braking mechanism used on caravans, a safety breakaway cable, and electrical connections.

Tyres

Driving characteristics are dictated by chassis design and the suspension system, but the tyres of a motorcaravan are also important.

The pressures of tyres should be checked regularly when they are cold and the recommended settings should be given in the base vehicle's handbook. However, these recommendations might apply to commercial situations so also look at the pressure settings recommended in the motorcaravan manufacturer's owner's manual. If you purchase a pre-owned vehicle and the manuals are missing, owners' clubs can often provide the advice you need.

Recommended pressures vary because motorcaravans seldom run in a light state. In contrast, a commercial truck or a delivery van often returns to its base completely empty whereas motorcaravans are heavily laden most of the time.

It is also true that surprisingly few owners check their laden motorcaravan on a weighbridge and police roadside checks have established that some motorcaravans are grossly overweight. With this in mind, manufacturers of purpose-made motorcaravan tyres, such as the Michelin Camping XC, quote high-pressures for the tyres in their handbooks. As Michelin has pointed out in its Technical Guidebooks, 'Under-inflation has the same effect on a tyre as overloading *ie* under-inflating a tyre by 20% reduces its life by 26%.' (Source: Van Tyre Fitments Pressures and Technical Data, MichelinTyre PLC, P.7) However, if an owner is prepared to take weight checks,

and uses the data in conjunction with Load Index Tables, it sometimes transpires that a different pressure would be acceptable. These calculations are worth carrying out because a more precise, load-related pressure setting usually produces better ride comfort.

A further issue relates to a motorcaravan's pattern of use. Some leisure vehicles remain parked for extended periods, and if left in-store for several weeks, tyre sidewalls soon receive stress damage. The advice is to periodically move a vehicle a short distance one way or the other to ensure that a different section of the sidewall is distended during lay-up periods. Some manufacturers also recommend that tyre pressures are temporarily increased by 0.3bar (5lb per sq in) when a motorcaravan is taken out of service for a month or more.

Bear in mind that vehicles driven at irregular intervals usually need new tyres as soon as there are signs of deterioration. The accompanying photographs show the types of crack that can appear, and it is this element, rather than tread-wear, which signals the need for replacements. This is also the reason why products like Michelin's Camping Tyres are made with extra reinforcement in the sidewalls.

Before the need for replacement tyres is imminent, make a point of checking product availability. The seasonal nature of the motorcaravan industry means that tyres are often in short supply. Owners are often surprised to find that they have to wait 6–8 weeks for a product to be supplied. This can be devastating

Right: VancoCamper tyres from Continental are one of the purpose-made brands designed for the rigours of motorcaravan use.

Far right: This recent method of showing when a tyre left the factory reveals that the product was manufactured in the 26th week of 2007.

Right: The penalty of leaving a motorcaravan in store for long periods is the stress placed on its sidewalls – illustrated here by the cracks.

Far right: Cracking can be an indicator of a deteriorating tyre and is sometimes evident between the treads – even when a tyre's tread depth is good.

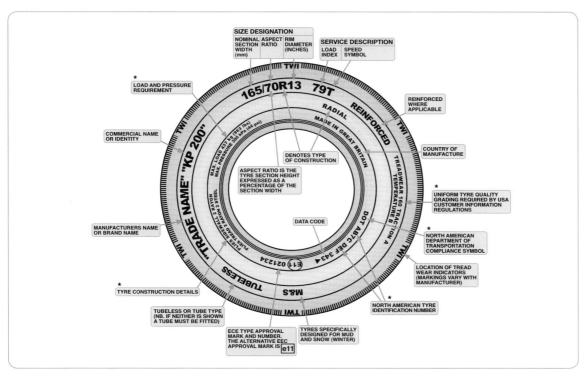

Car tyre markings (Reproduced with permission of the British Rubber Manufacturers' Association).

Some tyres have sidewall markings, eg 'loads and pressures', which are given in order to comply with North American requirements. They DO NOT apply in the UK and Europe; the examples shown here have an asterisk.

news if replacements are needed urgently for an approaching MoT test or a pre-booked holiday.

Similar concerns arise if one of your tyres has an irreparable puncture. If the spare is in good condition, a solution is immediately at hand. Unfortunately, some motorcaravans have recently been supplied without a spare wheel. In its place, a 'Fix'nGo' sealant injection kit has been included. This is a poor substitute because some types of tyre damage cannot be repaired by the injection of sealant.

Another reason for needing replacement tyres is age. However, the life expectancy of a tyre cannot be accurately predicted because its condition is determined by climatic factors (exposure to the sun, levels of humidity, temperature and so on). Conditions of use are equally influential, and these include the effects of unfavourable road conditions, vehicle loading, tyre inflation accuracy, and driving speeds. One manufacturer recommends that a tyre should be inspected five years after it was initially fitted or eight years after its manufacturing date, and this should be repeated at least annually.

A tyre's date of manufacture is usually given on its sidewall markings. The accompanying diagram explains some of these markings. One of the methods of recording the date is shown in the accompanying photograph.

Also, be aware that for safety and peace of mind, several owners are now having Tyron Safety Bands fitted. If one of your tyres suffers a 'blow-out' when you're driving, in a conventional wheel, the tyre will usually fall into the well. When that happens, the metal wheel rim comes into contact with the road and traction is immediately lost. The function of a Tyron band is to fill the well of a wheel, which causes a deflated tyre to remain roughly in place. This, in turn, means that part of the rubber casing maintains contact with the

road and the motorcaravan achieves reasonable adhesion while you bring the vehicle to a halt.

Lastly, owners should diligently observe all the legal requirements relating to tyres. Free literature is available from the British Rubber Manufacturers' Association (BRMA), and the customer service departments of leading manufacturers are also extremely helpful.

Left: The latest Tyron Safety Bands not only fill the well in a wheel, they also have a wireless device to relay pressure details to the cab.

Left: The installation of a Safety Band uses a compressing cage to provide access to the well; when inserted, the bands are bolted together.

CONTENTS

The electrical provision in a motorcaravan is more complicated than the electrical system in our homes. Not only is there a mains system, there's also an independent low-voltage supply.

This chapter looks at electricity in the living quarters. It comprises a 230V AC system, known as the mains supply; and a 12V DC provision, described here as the low-voltage system.

The system which serves the base vehicle is different yet again, and this is covered in textbooks that deal specifically with automotive wiring. For example, the Haynes Manual *Automobile Electrical & Electronic Systems*, by Tony Tranter, includes topics such as wiring procedure, ignition, electrical accessories and engine management systems.

Returning to the provision in the living quarters, the exact rating of the electricity supply needs clarifying. For example the 230V supply on a busy site sometimes drops below 200V, and this can affect the operation of appliances such as a refrigerator if the user has set the item to operate on mains. Similarly, a 12V provision is another misnomer. If a vehicle or leisure battery gives a meter reading of 12V across the terminals, this indicates that it is in a discharged condition. A battery in a full state of charge will give a reading of 12.7V. This is explained more thoroughly under the heading *Checking charge level* on page 91.

Not surprisingly, the subject of electricity in motorcaravans is wide-ranging and it is presented in this chapter using the following sections:
1) Low-voltage systems (12V DC)
2) Leisure batteries
3) Charging
4) Solar and wind generators
5) Portable petrol generators
6) Mains systems (230V AC)
7) Inverters

Technical Tip

Below: Control panels often include a battery selection switch and a meter shows the state of charge as well.

Below right: Like most control units, connections on a Zig battery selection panel are clearly marked

In most situations a battery provides 12V power for running appliances in the habitation areas. However, a built-in charger can also provide a 12V supply, as will be discussed in more detail later. Similarly, transformers/rectifiers are also available for motorcaravan use and the Mobitronic 230V-12V power-adaptor is an example. When connected to a mains supply, this adaptor provides a 12V DC source that can be used to run equipment, as long as the consumption doesn't exceed 5 Amps.

Although there are these other suppliers of 12V power, the provision in a living area is normally met by a 'leisure battery', (often referred to as an auxiliary battery), which is designed to run lights and other 12V appliances. If this fails, the vehicle battery can be used as an alternative. However, this should be regarded as only a temporary arrangement as vehicle starting could be affected if the charge level drops too low.

To change the 12V supply source, older motorcaravans are often equipped with a battery selection panel, which incorporates a charge level gauge or light display system, as shown here. Note: *Some micro-motorcaravans are very short of space and are equipped with so few 12V appliances that they draw all their power from the vehicle's starter battery. However, as explained in a later section, a vehicle battery is not designed for constant discharging and recharging, and its life is significantly shortened if it is required to run auxiliary items. For this reason, most motorcaravans are also fitted with a leisure battery.*

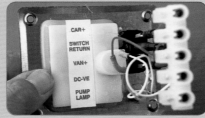

Low-voltage systems

A safe and efficient 12V system is dependent on a number of elements. A well-designed circuit is one feature; a dependable supply is another.

AN OVERVIEW OF CIRCUIT DETAILS

Source of the power

Nearly all motorcaravans use a large battery to supply the 12V appliances system in the living space. To be more accurate, *two* batteries are usually installed in the majority of motorcaravans, but one of these is principally for the base vehicle.

Fuse protection

Recognising the diversity of appliances that run on a low-voltage supply, a circuit designer now follows a practice that is adopted in the mains supply in our homes. The original feed from a battery is sub-divided into separate routes, which branch-out to supply different groups of appliances.

Each branch is independently protected by a fuse, the rating of which is appropriate for the appliances being served. For instance, a radio-cassette player has a low consumption, so is normally protected by a 5-amp fuse. On the other hand, a water pump has a higher consumption, and either a 7.5-amp or 10-amp fuse is usually fitted.

In some motorcaravans, the protection of appliances is sometimes achieved by fitting a separate fuse box. Two examples are shown alongside, one of which is installed in the Italian 2006 Mobilvetta models; the other is installed in a 2005 French-built Pilote Reference.

With regards to the construction of fuses, three types have been used in recent and older circuits; glass tube fuses, ceramic fuses and blade fuses. In older motorcaravans glass tube fuses used to be popular and these were inexpensive to replace. However, they are not particularly accurate, and sometimes their fuse holders make a poor connection when the spring contacts get slack.

Nowadays, the standard type used in automotive applications is a 'blade fuse'. These are notably accurate and are manufactured in a variety of ratings identified using the following colour-coding scheme:

1A – Black; 2A – Grey; 5A – Orange; 7.5A – Brown; 10A – Red; 15A – Blue; 20A – Yellow; 25A – White; 30A – Green.

Fused distribution units

Quite often the separate branches supplying accessories are fitted with a switch as well as a fuse. Control devices that are more elaborate than a simple fuse box are often referred to as 'fused distribution units'. The addition of a switching facility means that if you need to look at a troublesome water pump on a dark evening, you can switch off its power supply without having to interrupt the operation of the interior lights. This is undoubtedly convenient, although some of the older control units do not have switches. In this instance, you have to take out a fuse to isolate a particular supply.

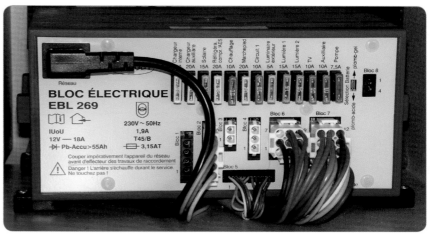

Left: Though not always completely clear, pictograms are a helpful way to indicate the circuits that each fuse protects.

Below: A rudimentary knowledge of French helps to identify these fuses, *eg* 'pompe' means pump and luminaires are lights.

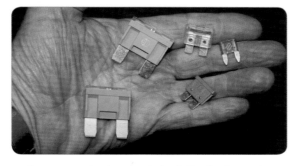

Left: Blade fuses are notably accurate and are identified by their colour; they are now used as standard in the motor industry.

As a general rule, a switched distribution unit will not merely provide control switches for the lighting, water pump and other appliances. It will also include:

- A battery selection switch
- Either a battery 'charge condition' gauge, digital liquid crystal display (LCD) or light indication system
- A gauge or light indicator showing water levels in the fresh- and waste-water tanks

The selection switch enables you to choose whether the supply is drawn from your leisure battery or the vehicle battery. Some selector switches have three positions, the centre of which isolates the circuit and draws power from *neither* supply.

The battery condition indicator warns when recharging is needed. A few units have a meter fitted to indicate a battery's state of charge and the markings on the scale can provide very precise information. However, most distribution units are fitted with light-emitting diodes. Typically a green light on the panel confirms that a battery is

Display panels recently fitted

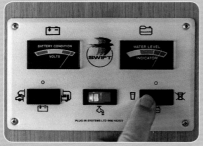

This panel fitted by Swift in the late 1990s has rudimentary gauges to show battery charge conditions and the fill-state of water tanks.

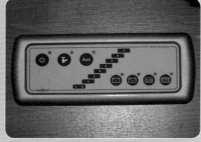

This Sargent display fitted in a 2009 Excel from Auto-Trail has a pump switch and a sloping display of LEDs to provide details about water levels and battery charge state.

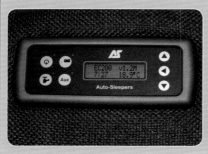

It is 18.9°C at 7:27am in this 2006 Auto-Sleepers Sandhurst. This panel from Sargent provides a lot of information, but don't lose its instruction manual.

Many of the motorcaravans imported from Italy have been fitted with this type of display. The pictograms are helpful and its operation is self-explanatory.

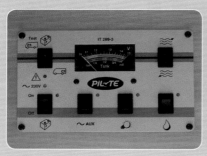

The display panel on this 2005 Pilote Reference uses a graduated gauge to provide information. The upper scale gives battery information; tank data is below.

This 2006 Dethleffs Esprit RT is equipped with graduated display gauges and after selecting the starter battery you can see that its charge is fractionally under 12.7V.

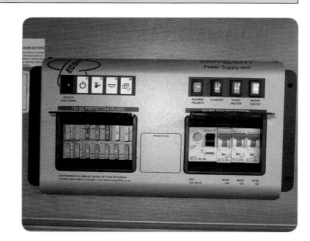

Right: Some motorcaravans are fitted with combined supply units which embrace both the 12V and 230V supplies in a single unit.

in a good state of charge; a red light warns that recharging is needed. Warning light systems are helpful but a discerning owner with a keen interest in battery performance undoubtedly prefers the detail given by a gauge with graduated markings.

Having a charge level warning display is also useful for other reasons. If the automatic shutdown on a water heater comes into operation, it is all too easy to assume that the gas cylinder is empty. On the other hand, if a battery warning light is on, this could mean there is insufficient power to operate the water heater's electronic circuits – hence the triggering of its automatic shutdown mechanism.

As the range of 12V appliances in motorcaravans became increasingly elaborate, some control units incorporated the fuses, switches and monitoring displays in the same casing. Others remained separate. Either way, information display panels vary. Some are extremely elaborate and can be set to show the internal temperature, the outside temperature, and the current draw (in Amps) from appliances in use. They usually include a digital clock, as well. The accompanying photographs show examples of different products fitted in the last few years.

Display panels
The display panels and control units fitted in British-built motorcaravans include products supplied by BCA Leisure, Kigass Electronics, Plug-in-Systems, Sargent Electrical Services and Zig Electronics. **Note:** *At the time of writing, neither Kigass nor Plug-in-Systems are presently supplying motorcaravan manufacturers, although their products are often found in older models. Van conversions from Murvi were sometimes fitted with Kigass products: Plug-in-Systems were widely fitted in motorcaravans from the Swift Group.*

Like many electronic products these may or may not be easy to operate. Sophisticated – and more expensive – panels provide a wealth of detail that some owners find very useful: others prefer a simpler display.

Combined supply units
In complete contrast with the products already described, some control units embrace both the 12V DC supply fuses/controls/switches and the 230V AC mains consumer unit. In some instances, a motorcaravan's fixed battery charger is also housed in the same unit. The idea of installing the entire complement of electrical elements into a single housing is not unusual and the illustration here shows a Sargent EC500 Power Supply Unit that is fitted in the 2011 Auto-Trail Tracker EK. But this is not a new strategy. The PMS combined supply unit from Plug-in-Systems was also being fitted in motorcaravans built in the 1990s.

Circuit wiring
Those with limited electrical knowledge may find 12V circuits hard to understand, and not all owners' manuals include wiring diagrams. The one here gives a broad picture of key elements.

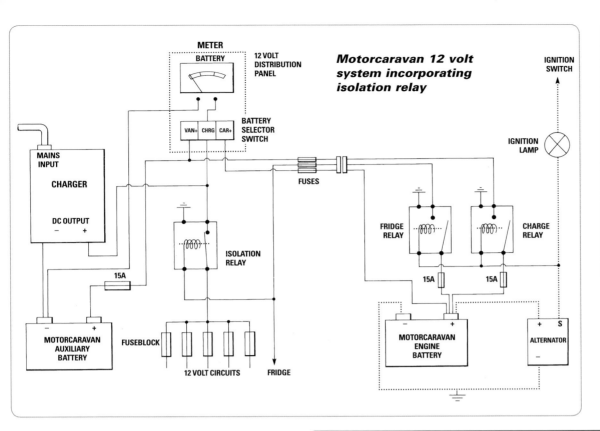

METER

BATTERY

12 VOLT DISTRIBUTION PANEL

Motorcaravan 12 volt system incorporating isolation relay

IGNITION SWITCH

VAN+ CHRG CAR+

BATTERY SELECTOR SWITCH

IGNITION LAMP

MAINS INPUT

CHARGER

DC OUTPUT
−   +

FUSES

FRIDGE RELAY

CHARGE RELAY

ISOLATION RELAY

15A

15A   15A

MOTORCARAVAN AUXILIARY BATTERY

FUSEBLOCK

12 VOLT CIRCUITS   **FRIDGE**

MOTORCARAVAN ENGINE BATTERY

ALTERNATOR
+   S
−

Technical tip

Some fused distribution control panels are only supplied to original equipment manufacturers (OEMs) rather than directly to the public. In addition, several electrical manufacturers (*eg* Plug-in-Systems) have ceased supplying products to the caravan and motorcaravan industry. This means that spares may have to be purchased from a breaking specialist like The Caravan Centre in Blaenavon, South Wales.

Left: Wiring for fridge, battery charging and isolating relays in a motorcaravan.

CABLE RATING

Whilst the layman often talks about 'wire', an electrician usually prefers the term 'cable'. Using the correct terminology is important; the panel on the previous page explains several other key words.

When coupling-up appliances, both the thickness of the connecting cable and its length are significant; thick cable is necessary for a good flow of current. A cable that is too thin causes a resistance to current flow, and this might cause its plastic insulation to overheat and melt.

The length of a cable-run also needs consideration; the longer the run, the greater the drop in volts. If your leisure battery is situated a long way from the vehicle's alternator, a significant voltage loss is inevitable when charging the battery

Below: Cable gauge is shown on the label here, but you can also work it out by counting up the strands.

Safety

■ The principal supply cable coming from a battery's live (positive) terminal to serve the low-voltage circuits *must* be protected by an in-line fuse fitted as close to the source as possible. However, when a leisure battery is installed in a ventilated locker, this fuse is usually positioned *outside* the locker as a safety precaution. The measure is taken because a battery sometimes emits a flammable gas while charging, and a fuse can produce a powerful spark when it fails; the resulting explosion can shatter a battery and cause acid to escape. Another alternative is to mount the main supply fuse inside a 'gas-tight' holder, as shown here.

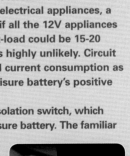

■ The rating of a battery supply fuse varies and some motorcaravans are fitted with a 15-Amp fuse. However, in a large model full of electrical appliances, a 20-Amp fuse is occasionally fitted instead. Obviously, if all the 12V appliances were being operated simultaneously, the total current-load could be 15-20 Amps and this could blow the fuse. This level of use is highly unlikely. Circuit designers usually consider 60% of the theoretical total current consumption as their guideline when prescribing the fuse to fit on a leisure battery's positive supply cable.

■ Some motorcaravan circuit designers also fit a master isolation switch, which allows an owner to cut off all power supplied by the leisure battery. The familiar red cut-off switches with a removable lever are often used in self-built cars for emergency situations. Some motorcaravan manufacturers also fit them, and Italian products in the Mobilvetta range sometimes have them mounted adjacent to the battery storage compartment. If a wiring fault suddenly becomes apparent, it is far quicker to isolate a supply with a master switch fitted at source than attempt to disconnect a clamp on a battery pillar.

Terminology

Volts, Amps and Watts

A practical illustration often helps a beginner to understand the theory behind electricity. For example:

To be hit by a fast-moving lead shot could be very unpleasant. It might only be small but the pressure it imposes at the time of impact would hurt. However, speed isn't everything. Being hit by a much slower object – like a double-decker bus – could be far worse since the size of the object comes into play. Now combine the two elements and the result is infinitely more potent. These mental pictures help to illustrate the difference between Volts (pressure), Amps (amount) and Watts (the amount and pressure combined).

Volts – This unit of measurement is concerned with pressure. However, in a practical situation, a cable offers a resistance that can lead to a loss of pressure – especially if the cable is too thin. Furthermore, the greater the length of a cable, the more you get a drop in the voltage.

Amps – Amperes or 'Amps' refers to the amount of electricity. This is also referred to as the 'current'. In practical terms, a motorcaravan fridge needs a large *amount* of electricity to work properly (8 Amps when working on its 12V setting) and requires a relatively thick connecting wire. In contrast, an interior strip light only needs a small amount of electricity (0.7 Amps), and works quite successfully with a much thinner connecting cable.

Watts – This is the rate at which electrical energy is used and some appliances are more greedy than others. Watts are a combination of both the pressure of flow (Volts) and the amount of current (Amps). The formulae to remember are:

$$\text{Watts} = \text{Volts} \times \text{Amps}$$
$$\text{Volts} = \text{Watts} \div \text{Amps}$$
$$\text{Amps} = \text{Watts} \div \text{Volts}$$

No of strands	Cross sectional area in mm^2	Max current rating in Amps	Application in motorcaravans
14	1.0	8.75	Interior lights
21	1.5	12.75	Wire to extractor fans, but check the model
28	2.0	17.50	Feed to fridge (minimum) See Technical Tip on page 85
36	2.5	21.75	Feed to battery from the charger Feed to a diaphragm water pump

• A cable that is too thin for a high-consumption appliance may start to get warm as a result of the cable's resistance. If the rise in temperature starts to cause the insulation to melt, there's a serious problem ahead. If several supply cables are wrapped together, for example, melting insulation could lead to a short circuit.

• A low-voltage supply doesn't pose a threat of electrocution like a mains supply, but if you've seen the powerful spark that is caused when there's a short circuit, you'll appreciate the acute fire risk that accompanies a 12V system. Melting insulation is sometimes the cause of short circuits. Fuses in a circuit are intended to prevent this risk but they have to be of the correct rating and appropriately located in the supply system.

while driving. The shorter the connecting cable, the better the charge rate. Accordingly, when a major motorcaravan manufacturer started to mount leisure batteries at the back of its long, coachbuilt models, the sheer distance from the vehicle's alternator justifiably led to fierce criticisms. Voltage loss is less pronounced if a much thicker cable is fitted, but some manufacturers fail to put this principle into practice.

Taking this subject further, the accompanying

Maximum current (Amps) permitted for cable of different cross-sectional areas on the basis of length

Cable size	Maximum cable lengths (supply and return)		
	4 metres	8 metres	12 metres
1.00 mm^2	9.4A	4.7A	3.1A
1.5 mm^2	14.1A	7.0A	4.7A
2.0 mm^2	18.8A	9.3A	6.3A
2.5 mm^2	23.5A	11.7A	7.8A

table quotes the maximum current in Amps that a cable can handle efficiently, taking into account the *total length* of both the live and neutral cables that connect an appliance to its power source.

As regards the type of cable needed, a motorcaravan low-voltage system is usually wired using automotive cable. This has good flexibility because it is made from separate strands, or 'filaments', and these normally have a standard thickness of 0.33mm. A flexible core made up of separate strands also achieves a more permanent connection when used in screw-fitted terminals. **Note:** *Single core copper cable, like the products used in household wiring, is more likely to shake loose from appliance connections in a motorcaravan.* The required flexible cable is not only sold by automotive electrical specialists, your local motorcaravan accessory shop is also likely to sell the small drums of automotive cable that are distributed by W4 Accessories.

As the table on the previous page shows, a low-consumption appliance like a fluorescent light only needs a thin cable, whereas a high-consumption appliance, such as a refrigerator working on 12V, needs a cable with a core of a much thicker gauge. But this is a simplification and a more precise specification is needed.

Cable rating is indicated on supply drums and this information usually includes its cross-sectional area in mm^2. A label also might quote an *approximate continuous current rating* in amps. However, if a label is missing, you can confirm a cable's rating by carefully counting its filaments, presuming the strands are of the standard 0.33mm thickness. The Terminology table on the previous page gives guidance on cable choice when coupling-up different types of appliance. Also note the accompanying Technical Tip box regarding 'three-way' refrigerators.

Additional electrical accessories are sometimes needed in a motorcaravan. It is not unusual to find that an extra spotlight or a 12V socket would prove useful. If you are competent in electrical work, the job is simple as long as the appropriate cable is chosen and the appliance is coupled correctly into the existing circuit.

For instance, if you wanted to fit a 12V socket to run a colour television, the older sets sometimes had ratings as high as 100 watts, so it would be quite wrong to run a feed to the new socket from an existing supply cable serving the lights. For example, a 0.7-amp fluorescent light draws around 8 watts, so the manufacturer would probably have originally connected this up using 1.0mm^2 cable (as shown in the Terminology panel on page 83). A colour television would be more appropriately served by a cable of 2.0mm^2. **Note:** *The Watt rating of appliances can vary greatly: for example, some of the compact portable flat-screen TV sets are rated at 20 Watts: other models can be higher.*

It is best, where possible, to route the cable for a proposed socket back to the distribution unit, as this usually has fuses serving different supply branches. However, visible cable pinned to the surface looks unattractive and could be obstructive, so time should be spent finding ways to keep it out of sight and safely located.

Coupling-up a spotlight is less of a problem because it is likely there will be a feed to another light fitting fairly close by. Forming the join is the next consideration and there are several ways to achieve this.

MAKING CONNECTIONS

There are many different ways to connect cables together, and in some situations electricians still prefer traditional soft-solder joints. However, auto-electricians are less inclined to connect cables this way and often use manufactured connectors instead. Three types of connector are currently popular:

- Snap locks (Scotchlocks)
- Crimp connectors
- Block connectors

Snap lock connectors create an electrical connection with an existing cable by means of a small metal tag that slices its way through the insulation sleeve on both feeds. By using a snap lock you avoid having to cut the original cable, although small incisions are made through the insulation sleeves of both cables. Some electricians dislike these products but the National Trailer and Towing Association (NTTA) asserts that these couplings *are* suitable for use inside vehicles in dry locations. However, the size of a connector must be correctly matched to the size of cable being used. As a guide, follow these recommendations:

	Main cable (mm²)	Joining 'tap' cable (mm²)
Red Scotchlocks	0.5–1.5	0.5–1.5
Blue Scotchlocks	1.5–2.8	1.5–2.8
Yellow	3.00–6.00	3.00–6.00

Left: Snap locks are colour-coded to indicate the size of the cables for which they are designed.

Some electricians working with 12V wiring systems prefer to use crimp connectors, and once again, these are sold in several sizes to suit cable of different diameters. These are generally easier to conceal than the bulkier snap lock fittings.

If you decide to use these products, it is worth purchasing a good quality wire stripper to remove the insulation accurately without cutting through the filaments inside.

Also be aware that there are inexpensive crimping tools available that do not always achieve good compression of the coupling collar. The type shown below has a special clamping mechanism that ensures the collar is fully compressed.

Alternatively, if you want to disengage the jaws midway through an operation, the illustrated tool includes a release lever.

Left: Although not the cheapest insulation stripper available, the tool here produces consistently good results.

Left: If you use these couplings quite often, it's worth buying a good-quality crimping tool.

Left: If the jaws need to be released in the middle of a crimping operation, this tool has a quick-release lever.

Right: Fitting a connecting
block is a commonly-used
way to add extra lights to a
motorcaravan.

Block connectors can be useful and have
the advantage that couplings can easily be
disconnected and joints reformed when needed.
Again, the size of the connector needs to be
appropriate for the gauge of cable. For instance, it
is not good practice to cut off some of the copper
filaments of a cable in order to insert it into the
coupling tube of a connecting block that is too
small for the job.

The choice of connector is usually determined by
its location. You will also need to secure the cables
and discreetly hide them if possible. Where access
is achievable, clips should be fitted as follows:

- On horizontal runs – at intervals no greater than
  250mm (10in)
- On vertical runs – at intervals no greater than
  400mm (16in)

Technical tip

**When bundling cables together to form a harness, never place mains cables and
12V cables together. In some industries, such as boat building, there are strict
rules regarding cable runs, although these tend not to apply to the automotive
practices employed in motorcaravans.**

**It takes considerable time to hide new cables when a product is fitted
retrospectively, so some installers use the seven or 13 multicore cables that
are used for coupling the electrical circuits in a caravan to its tow car. A new
appliance being fitted in a motorcaravan may only need a pair of cables, but the
unused cables held in the sheath are available for use at a later date.**

**The thickness of cables can vary, too, as explained in Chapter 3 of *The Caravan
Manual (4th Edition)* Haynes Publishing. For example in a 13 cable multicore
product there is a mix of 1.5 mm² and 2.5 mm² cables that would suit the needs
of different appliances that you may want to fit in a motorcaravan. Moreover,
there is also an opportunity to upgrade a feed cable serving an appliance by
joining two of the multicore cables together. If you join two 1.5 mm² cables
together, the resulting feed will achieve a 3.00mm² rating. Suffice to say, some**

**self-builders use multicore cable
when wiring-up their motorcaravans.
Not only are the cables in a multicore
sheath of the appropriate quality,
they have distinct colours, known
ratings, and provide a starting point
for a bespoke wiring harness.**

Left: This multicore cable contains 13
separate cables within its protective
sheath and is the type used when
coupling-up modern touring caravans.

INTERIOR LIGHTING

Motorcaravans were originally fitted with gas
lamps but these subsequently gave way to electric
lighting. Initially, 'car-type' bulbs with a tungsten
filament were used, and these are still found in
some motorcaravans today. Unfortunately their
electrical consumption, especially when related to
their output, is not favourable.

Greater efficiency was achieved in the 1960s
when an Essex firm called Labcraft found a way
to produce a fluorescent lamp fitting that would
run on a 12V supply. The casing of the units
incorporated a small inverter that converted 12V DC
to around 125V AC – the voltage needed to ignite a
fluorescent tube (see top left picture on page 103).

Note: *Since the voltage is considerably higher
in a motorcaravan fluorescent light fitting, always
switch off the supply before opening its casing to
fit a new tube.*

Many fluorescent fittings are still used in
motorcaravans but the light itself is sometimes
considered to look rather 'cold'. This is not the
case with halogen bulbs, which started to be
installed in motorcaravans during the 1990s.
Halogen fittings offer bright illumination with a
'warm' feel and are widely used today, but they do
have some drawbacks.

Not only does halogen lighting require a
surprising amount of current from a battery; the
fittings also become remarkably hot. There have
even been instances where a lack of ventilation
around recessed fittings in ceilings has caused
the cladding plywood to burn. In truth, this is not
very common, and halogen fittings are fine when
properly installed.

However, in the late 1990s luxury boat
manufacturers (whose budgets are often more
generous) started to fit lamps with light emitting
diodes (LEDs). These also appeared in a few
motorcaravans around the year 2000 but the fittings
were costly. This subsequently changed; LEDs
began to be manufactured in the Far East so the
prices quickly fell.

One of the benefits of an LED light unit is that
it doesn't get hot. No less important is the fact
that it draws a very small amount of current. As
one distributor points out, 8 LED light fittings use
roughly the same amount of power that is required
to operate *one* halogen light. And whereas the type
of light from LED units originally had a 'cold' look
reminiscent of fluorescent tube lighting, there are
now many colours, including 'warm white', reds,
greens, blues and so on.

A good quality LED is also robust. For example,
the red LEDs fitted on stereo systems that have
given service for several decades seldom need
replacing. Equally, the spread of light produced
from LED fittings is also becoming more effective,
sufficient for some new cars to be equipped
with LED headlamps. Vehicles have already been
equipped with red LED taillights for quite a while.

The significance of these developments
is evident by the eagerness of many
motorcaravanners to remove their existing interior

light units and replace them with LED fittings. In some instances, LED conversion products can be used to fit in place of halogen bulbs, so the owner doesn't have to remove the original lamp fitting.

A summary of these points is given in the accompanying illustrated panel.

ELECTROMAGNETIC COMPATIBILITY

Purchasers of recent motorcaravans have found that electrical appliances in the living quarters, with the exception of the refrigerator, will not operate while the engine is running; the interior lights are one such example. This can be a hindrance, but there is a good reason for this.

It has been prompted by a phenomenon referred to as 'electromagnetic compatibility', or EMC for short. Installers acknowledge that many forms of transport are reliant on electronic control systems; for instance, passengers travelling by air are not permitted to use certain types of electronic equipment during take-off and landing. There is a potentially similar risk in modern vehicles where electronic circuits control the operation of items like ABS brakes and engine management systems.

It is believed that the operation of these control devices could be detrimentally affected when other electrical equipment is used. So, the fewer items of auxiliary electrical equipment in use when a motorcaravan is being driven, the better – hence the introduction of an automatic 'isolation switch' in recent 12V circuits. This isolation switch is a component more commonly called a 'relay', and it automatically cuts off the supply of electricity to the living area if it detects that the engine is running.

The owners of older motorcaravans may not need such a system; sophisticated electronics in motor vehicles are comparatively recent. However, an attempt to bypass this control on a newer model could lead to a serious accident – caused, for instance, by interference with brake operation. This is not to say that the concerns regarding EMC are not acknowledged; there is a concession to keep a fridge running on a 12V supply while a motorcaravan is being driven. The manufacturers

Below: A relay is an electrically operated switch; a magnetic coil and contacts can be seen in this example.

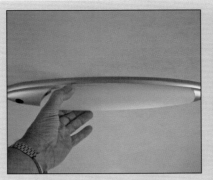

Recent fluorescent lamp fittings have a more attractive design than the bulkier fittings originally used.

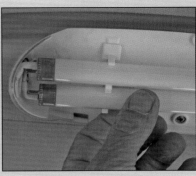

Unclipping the cover is easy and there's no difficulty changing a tube. But make sure the power to a unit is OFF.

This reading light can swivel in its holder and it is easy to change the 'car-type' tungsten bulb. Its consumption, however, is high.

Recessed halogen lamp fittings have become popular but consumption is high, the bulbs get hot and they break easily.

Good quality LEDs rarely need replacement and they consume very little current. This ceiling lamp has 78 warm-glow LEDs.

You reduce the life of a halogen bulb by touching its glass, but there's an LED conversion kit which fits some holders.

This is a 21 LED unit but there are smaller ones and products offering warm-glow illumination. These pins are spaced like the ones in the halogen bulb.

Although pins snap off as easily as the ones on halogen bulbs, an LED unit can be touched and eased home with a screwdriver.

of some fan-operated heaters have also challenged EMC, as the motors of their products are automatically disabled even though they have apparently been approved for continued operation. The debate on these matters continues.

Leisure batteries

Neither the base vehicle 'starter' battery, nor the auxiliary 'leisure' battery, should be seen as 'fit and forget' accessories. On the contrary, they need regular attention and special measures have to be taken if a vehicle is likely to remain unused for an extended period.

As regards a motorcaravan's leisure battery, it performs two different jobs. Firstly, it supplies 12V DC electricity to run a motorcaravan's accessories. Secondly, if you are coupled to a mains supply and the built-in charger is in operation, a leisure battery smoothes out irregularities in the 12V supply that comes from the charger. A smooth supply of power is important: irregularities or surges often damage electronically controlled components. For this reason, you should never operate a 12V supply without having a leisure battery connected into the system.

PATTERNS OF USE

Battery expectations, and the type of product you need to fulfil these expectations, are wholly dependent on the way you use your motorcaravan. For example, if you spend most of your motorcaravanning experiences using sites equipped with 230V mains hook-ups, your leisure battery is likely to receive continuing replenishment from its built-in charger. In this situation, even a cheap battery with a low Ah capacity would probably meet your needs. After all, the battery is merely smoothing out the charger's supply; it isn't being used as a *source* of power.

In contrast, other motorcaravanners seldom use sites offering mains supply points. Some use the simple Certificated Sites and Locations made available to members of the caravanning and motorcaravanning clubs. Others use minimal facility venues like the *Aires de camping-cars* (France), *Areas Attrezzata* (Italy), *Standplatz* (Germany), and *Areas de Servicios para Autocaravanas* (Spain)

and so on. Several motorcaravanners merely 'wild camp', and in these circumstances, a lack of mains hook-ups means that you need a good-quality 'deep cycling' battery. Some owners meet their requirements by fitting additional batteries or by installing large units offering 180Ah or more. Others purchase photo-voltaic solar panels in order to help with recharging.

Given these diverse requirements, let's look closely at the products themselves.

BATTERY CONSTRUCTION

In both construction and operational requirements, vehicle and leisure batteries are different. With the exception of AGM batteries, which are described later, the conventional 'lead and acid' starter and leisure batteries only perform one job well. Contrary to some of the claims made by distributors, a starter battery performs poorly as a leisure battery: conversely, a leisure battery is poor when required to start an engine. Research specialists working in this field are quite candid when affirming that at the present time, there is no such thing as a dual-purpose standard battery. If you want a battery to perform both jobs effectively, prepare to pay a high price for an AGM product. So what prevents this lack of versatility?

Firstly, be aware that a vehicle 'starter battery' is designed to produce a surge of power to operate a starter motor. This is a demanding task, but once an engine is running, the battery gains an immediate recharge from the vehicle's alternator. In consequence, its original level of charge is quickly reinstated and its internal construction is built to suit this particular performance pattern. For example, the lead plates inside are significantly thinner than the plates fitted in a purpose-made leisure battery.

In contrast, a leisure battery has to provide a steady flow of current over an extended period – and time sometimes elapses before recharging is possible. However, a recharge mustn't be delayed too long; battery manufacturers advise strongly against completely discharging a battery because this can cause permanent damage. It is also strongly recommended to recharge as soon as a battery becomes 50% discharged. Complying with this effectively means that a 90Amp-hour battery will be acting as if it is merely a 45Ah product.

Right: To achieve electrical independence for long periods, this owner fitted a bank of three 110Ah batteries.

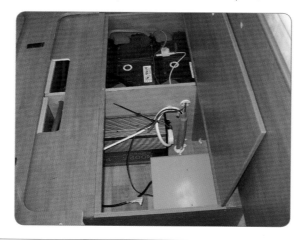

Far right: The lead plates in this budget battery are so thin that a spring is needed to compress them in each cell.

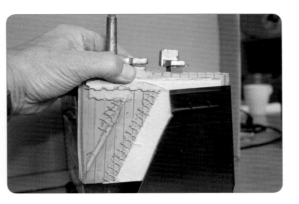

Far left: Starting with a plate with a grid construction, lead oxide paste is used; here are the finished positive and negative plates.

Left: Repeated deep cycling soon damages the plates in a starter battery and the all-important paste falls from the grid.

Far left: Each lead plate is normally held in a microporous plasticised envelope (sometimes called a 'separator'); a starter battery has nothing else contained in this envelope.

Left: In a leisure battery, glass fibre sheets are included in each microporous envelope to press against the lead oxide paste.

A leisure battery's relentless pattern of heavy discharge followed by recharge (referred to as deep cycling) is something that a vehicle battery cannot endure for long. The relatively thin lead plates used in starter batteries react and the all-important lead oxide paste held within their grid becomes detached and falls to the bottom of the casing.

In a purpose-made leisure battery, the plates are not only thicker; they also have a layer of glass fibre mat firmly pressed against their sides in order to hold the lead oxide paste in the grid more effectively.

This is reflected in the higher cost of the product but is one of the reasons why a leisure battery lasts considerably longer than a vehicle battery that is subjected to repeated deep cycling operations.

Starter and leisure batteries use a similar amount of fluid in each cell. This is diluted sulphuric acid, which in the battery context is referred to as the 'electrolyte'. In other types of battery the electrolyte is an acidic 'gel' that cannot be spilt. Then there are 'absorbent glass mat' (AGM) products where the cells are crammed tightly with a glass wool that completely absorbs all the sulphuric acid.

Summary of types used in motorcaravans:
- **Standard starter batteries** (sometimes called vehicle batteries, calcium batteries, cranking batteries, wet batteries, lead-acid batteries.) Also available in heavy-duty form for large goods vehicles.
- **Leisure batteries** (also described as semi-traction batteries, auxiliary batteries, wet batteries.) Also used for golf buggies, electric wheelchairs, and forklift trucks.
- **Absorbent Glass Mat (AGM) batteries**
- **Gel batteries**

Technical comments on these batteries:
- Provided a starter or leisure battery is not charged at a rate in excess of 14.6V, it will seldom need topping-up with de-ionised water. For this reason, some manufacturers describe them as 'maintenance-free', which can be misleading. Other manufacturers reserve this description specifically for sealed batteries that cannot be opened.
- Whereas each lead plate is placed in a perforated, plasticised separator, in both starter and leisure batteries, the latter type also has a glass fibre mat within these envelopes.
- Independently monitored tests have found that some batteries sold for leisure use have the internal construction of starter batteries. Discharge tests have further established that the products subjected to scrutiny in laboratory conditions seldom achieve the Ah rating claimed by the suppliers.

Left: Working with brand-new, fully-charged batteries, testers subjecting products to a discharge test often find disappointing Ah performances.

Right: The AGM batteries in the Optima range have a distinctive shape; the cells include tightly packed glass mat wadding.

From an electrical viewpoint, battery specialists are quite adamant that conventional lead-acid starter or leisure batteries (ie 'wet' batteries) are notably good performers, albeit when used solely for the purposes for which they are designed.

From the electrical perspective, a gel battery is unlikely to be any better than a 'wet acid' counterpart. This type of battery scores in user situations where a vehicle, or boat, could overturn. Quad bikes, jet skis, and a few motorcaravans are sometimes fitted with a gel battery.

Since the casing of a gel battery is sealed, there is no venting facility to release hydrogen gas when charging takes place. Correspondingly, a gel battery should *never* be charged using a voltage greater than 14.2V. That is when gas is sometimes created in a battery's cells.

The AGM battery is not only filled with highly compressed glass wool to absorb its acid: air is drawn out of the casing during manufacture and a pressure-release valve is fitted. Though comparatively costly, an AGM battery like products in the Banner Running Bull range can be recycled many more times than a standard product and thus have a much longer working life.

Some AGM batteries are built using a conventional rectangular polypropylene case. The models from Optima are an exception; these products are constructed using an assembly of cells with an appearance reminiscent of a six-pack of drink cans. Inside, the compressed glass wool is fitted in a roll configuration.

GUIDANCE ON USE

To get the best from a leisure battery, manufacturers suggest the following recommendations:

Terminals should be smeared with grease or petroleum jelly, such as Vaseline. Failure to do this can lead to a powdery deposit building up on a pillar terminal and in extreme cases this can lead to the pillar breaking apart.

On a non-sealed battery, check the electrolyte periodically. Before carrying out the check, ensure there are no naked flames or cigarettes nearby. It is also advisable to wear eye protection. If the acid level has fallen below the top of the plates, top it up with de-ionised water. This is sold in car accessory shops.

A battery must not be left in a discharged state – failure to promptly recharge will permanently ruin a battery. When left discharged, a condition known as sulphation occurs and a white deposit forms on the battery plates. In a mild case, some types of charger may be able to revive a battery, although it is seldom reinstated to 'full health'. In most instances, it is rendered useless.

If your motorcaravan is parked for an extended period, make provision for keeping the leisure battery in a charged condition. This might involve transferring it to a bench for charging; alternatively some use a trickle charger, which is left permanently connected. Products from

Right: A lack of grease on a terminal of a battery in this Frankia motorhome caused an excessive deposit to form.

Far right: If the electrolyte drops low in a cell, add de-ionised water.

Right: This battery failed prematurely after being left discharged; sulphation had affected all the plates.

Far right: The Carcoon trickle charger includes a short lead with eyelets which can be left permanently on a battery.

Carcoon are intended for use on classic cars, but are equally useful for maintaining the charge state of a motorcaravan's batteries.

■ Completely sealed non-spill gel electrolyte batteries, such as the Varta Drymobil, are fitted less often and it is important to seek the manufacturer's advice about care and maintenance. Many chargers that are designed for 'wet' lead acid batteries are *not* suitable for use with gel batteries.

■ When removing a battery on a 'negative earth' vehicle, disconnect the negative terminal first; when installing a battery, connect the negative terminal last.

■ Notwithstanding the cautionary advice about avoiding a total discharge, it is appropriate to add that a leisure battery installed in a motorcaravan is more likely to receive a periodic charge than a battery in a touring caravan. This is because a touring caravan is often left on a pitch for an extended period and if there is no mains hook-up, recharging a leisure battery can pose problems. In contrast, most motorcaravans are regularly driven off-site, so there is a periodic recharge from the alternator.

CHECKING CHARGE LEVEL

A reference to the 'condition' of a leisure battery normally refers to its state of charge. This is certainly the case if you see a meter installed in a motorcaravan bearing the words 'battery condition'. Frankly, the term is confusing because an ageing battery with cracked casing and whose reliability in electrical terms has clearly diminished could equally be described as being 'in a poor condition'.

It is usual to check a battery's state of charge with a meter, although testing with a hydrometer is an alternative. When using a meter it is best to take a voltage reading directly across its terminals, but there are several points to bear in mind.

■ The use of a digital voltmeter is recommended since these are easy to read and their accuracy is usually good. At one time these were expensive, but prices have dropped considerably.

■ Make sure all the motorcaravan's appliances are disconnected – even a permanently connected clock can falsify the reading.

■ If a battery has just been disconnected from a charger, or you've recently been driving your motorcaravan, the reading will be high, but this isn't a true indication of its state of charge once it has stabilised. You need to let it settle before carrying out a voltmeter test, which means waiting for at least four hours – longer if possible. The reason for this is that an elderly battery in poor condition has a problem holding its charge. Once a charger has been disconnected it's no surprise to see a good reading; but this can be misleading as it might drop to a much lower reading a day or two later, and that's what counts. In contrast, a battery in good condition that isn't supplying power should be able to hold its charge level for two months or more.

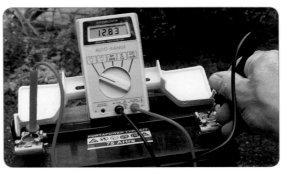

Left: A digital multimeter is used to take voltage readings directly across this battery's terminals.

■ Even though a leisure battery is described as providing a 12V power supply, this description is merely nominal, and many motorcaravanners are surprised to learn that a reading of 12V indicates a poor charge level. The following table clarifies the situation:

Voltmeter reading	Approx. state of charge
12.7V or over	100%
12.5V	75%
12.4V	50%
12.2V	25%
12V or under	Discharged

■ Another way to diagnose battery condition is to use a hydrometer. These are inexpensive test items but you should *always wear safety glasses when carrying out a test of the electrolyte. It makes sense to wear protective gloves as well.* Insert the nozzle of the hydrometer into the acid and then draw and release the electrolyte vigorously several times. If the acid goes black, this is an indication that it is 'cycled out'. This means that the oxide in the lead plate grids has started to fall away and the battery is virtually ready for scrapping.

■ If the acid is not badly discoloured, check the reading on the hydrometer's scale. Then refer to this table:

Acid density (specific gravity)	Voltage (no load)	Level of charge
1.280 SG or greater	12.7V or more	100%
1.250 SG	12.54V	75%
1.240 SG	12.40V	50%
1.180 SG	12.18V	25%
Below 1.120 SG	Below 11.88V	0%

Note: *The sulphuric acid in a battery is highly corrosive and if it gets on your hands, wash it off at once with water. Better still – wear protective gloves. If it gets on to your clothes, burnt holes soon appear, as the author discovered a long time ago.*

Left: Clean electrolyte and a specific gravity reading of 1.28 on this hydrometer show that this battery is 100% charged.

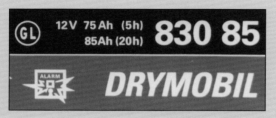
BATTERY LIFE BETWEEN CHARGES

The capacity of a battery is expressed in Amp-hours (Ah), and this indicates how long it can provide an output before needing a recharge. As a rule, the external dimensions of a leisure battery are related to its Ah capacity, and whilst a 90Ah battery needs a recharge less frequently than a 60Ah version, there isn't always sufficient stowage space for one.

The assigned location for a motorcaravan leisure battery is often unable to accommodate larger products.

In practice, this may not present a problem. Motorcaravanners who are constantly on the move are unlikely to be affected too badly. It is only when you park a vehicle on a campsite for an extended period – perhaps because you're travelling out of the site by other means of transport – that you realise a 90Ah battery would have been better. Moreover, the demand on a battery during cold dark winter nights is very different from the situation in the summer. But what does the Ah capacity rating mean in practical terms?

Right: Inspecting cells in a leisure battery can be difficult when it's fitted under the driver's seat.

To get a rough estimate of how long a battery will provide power between charges, make the following simple calculation:

1 Establish the wattage of appliances. Typical examples are: a single tube strip light – 8 watts; a spotlight – 10 watts; a water pump – 50 watts; a colour TV – 50 watts (can vary – some TVs like the Roadstar CTV 1020 are as low as 30w).
2 Work out how many hours (or fractions of an hour) they will be used in a 24-hour period.
3 Calculate watt hours for each appliance by multiplying wattage by hours in use.
4 Add together the total of watt hours.

This is shown in the following table:

Equipment	Rating in watts	Hours in use	Watt hours
Two 8 watt lights	16	5	80
Two 10 watt spot lights	20	1	20
Water pump	50	0.2	10
Colour TV	50	5	250
Total watt hours	**360**		

Divide watt hours by volts to get ampere hours:

360 ÷ 12 = 30Ah

So if your motorcaravan is fitted with a 60Ah battery, at this rate of use (30Ah consumed in 24 hours) and an ambient temperature of 25ºC (77ºF), it will be 50% discharged within a day. At that point, battery manufacturers recommend that it will then benefit from a recharge. Obviously it might provide power for a second day, but as stated earlier, running a battery to the point of total discharge is bad practice.

Newcomers to motorcaravanning are often surprised at how quickly a leisure battery loses its charge. The above guidance clarifies the position and also confirms the merit of fitting a larger capacity 90Ah battery where there is enough space for its bulkier casing. Some owners even fit a 180Ah battery to suit their requirements.

LEISURE BATTERY LOCATION

The closer a leisure battery is to the alternator, the better the charge rate when you're driving, and provided there's ventilation and adequate space, the engine compartment undoubtedly meets this requirement. In practice, there isn't enough space under most bonnets, so an alternative option is under a cab seat – presuming that the base vehicle has its engine at the front. (Older VW base vehicles had rear engines.)

The reason for this, as discussed earlier, is that a long run of connecting cable leads to a fall-off in voltage and a poorer charge rate as a result. Admittedly a thicker gauge of cable helps to reduce voltage loss on long cable runs, but putting a leisure battery in a locker right at the back of a vehicle or in a distant wardrobe is not advantageous from an electrical standpoint. Regrettably, some manufacturers disregard this point.

Other points regarding location are as follows:

- A battery must not share a locker with gas cylinders – a spark from a battery terminal next to a leaking gas cylinder could cause an explosion. The ideal location is in a separate locker, sealed from the interior, but vented to the outside of the vehicle. It is curious that purpose-made battery compartments are fitted in touring caravans but you seldom find them in motorcaravans. One of the few exceptions occurred in the 2012 Bailey Approach range and boxes from BCA Leisure have been purposely designed for these coachbuilt models.
- Avoid using crocodile clips on battery terminals. A clip might become dislodged and a spark across a poor connection can be powerful. Traditional bolt-on clamps sold in auto shops are recommended, although clamping clips sold at motorcaravan accessory shops are satisfactory as long as they don't rust.
- Recognising the point made earlier about the loss of Ah capacity in temperatures lower than 25°C (77°F), there is undoubtedly a benefit if a leisure battery is fitted in a location that receives warmth from the living area. In reality, that is often hard to achieve.
- Many owners are desperately eager to create a bank of leisure batteries but do not wish to lose existing storage space. One answer employed by owners of coachbuilt motorcaravans is to have an under-floor Beeny Box fitted. These are made individually, installed at the Cornwall factory, and are strong enough to carry surprisingly heavy items such as batteries. Further information on Beeny Boxes is given in Chapter 10.
- A battery location must have ventilation if the battery is a standard 'wet' leisure product. The reason for this is given in the safety panel (above right).

PURCHASING CONSIDERATIONS

When purchasing a battery, it is very important to recognise how you normally use your motorcaravan. This was explained at the commencement of this section. Consideration of the different types of battery is also important, not forgetting that only AGM types can be truly described as dual-purpose products.

Above: Beeny Boxes are manufactured individually for clients and can be installed on most coachbuilt motorcaravans.

Motorcaravanners also have to be mindful of weight issues and here lies a difficulty. Whereas a light battery makes less impact on your vehicle's payload, this is usually an indication that the lead plates inside are merely the kind used for starter batteries. A good leisure battery will be heavy.

It is also evident that some batteries currently on sale claiming to be for leisure use are non-regulated products. For instance, some of the products imported from the Far East are retailed at attractively low prices, but it often transpires that their performance is disappointingly poor.

The labels fixed to a number of batteries are also rather misleading. One product recently sold in the UK has been described as the 110 model but smaller print on the label states that it has a 90Ah capacity. Independently monitored laboratory testing has also established that a brand-new example of this product achieved a 54Ah rating.

Fortunately, there are other products that *do* achieve the claimed performance. For instance, manufacturers whose batteries are built to the standards set down in EN50342, sometimes achieve an Ah rating that is *greater* than the figure on the label. At present, however, there are disappointingly few leisure batteries that comply with EN50342; examples include models from Banner, Exide and Varta.

Not surprisingly, these are not the cheapest batteries sold by dealers and not many motorcaravan manufacturers fit them as standard. One exception is the Approach range launched in 2011 by Bailey Motorhomes, which have been equipped with Varta batteries. Hopefully, others will follow.

Leisure batteries built to EU 50342 specifications

Charging

A leisure battery can be charged using these supply sources:

- ■ a portable or fixed mains charger
- ■ an engine alternator
- ■ a petrol or diesel generator
- ■ a wind or solar system

MAINS CHARGERS

Portable chargers, permanently installed chargers, different charging patterns and the needs of different types of battery should all be considered. For example, a 'deep-cycling' leisure battery is best served by a charging pattern that is different from the one required by a vehicle battery. In reality, inexpensive battery chargers are not usually designed to meet both of these requirements, although a few types do have a two-way charge selection switch. Some of the latest sophisticated chargers go even further and offer a variety of charging patterns to meet the contrasting requirements of many types of battery. The relationship between chargers and batteries is important to get right.

Not surprisingly, the amp output of a charger influences how long it takes to restore a battery to its full state of charge. In addition, a charger's performance needs to be appropriate for the Ah capacity of a battery undergoing a recharge. An often quoted rule of thumb recommends that the current output (Amps) of a charger is approximately 10% of a battery's Ah capacity. However, some of the latest electronically controlled 'stage chargers' (sometimes called 'smart chargers') have more advanced capabilities and models with a low current output can sometimes be matched with a larger Ah battery than was previously recommended.

As regards the battery receiving attention, it is sometimes possible to 'over-charge' it. When this occurs, the water content in its electrolyte (the diluted sulphuric acid in its cells) may start to evaporate. If this happens, it is necessary to top up the battery as soon as possible using deionised water.

There are six separate cells in a conventional 'wet' leisure battery, each of which has a removable cap for inspecting and topping-up its electrolyte.

Sometimes a cell can fail and this upsets some charger sensing systems. Instead of switching off a charging operation automatically when the other cells are recharged, some chargers continue to provide a charging current on account of the failed cell.

As pointed out earlier, charging patterns, often described as charging 'regimes', can vary. So do the voltages of different charging devices. (It was described earlier in the chapter that whereas an *amount* of electrical power is measured in Amps, the *pressure* of a supply is measured in Volts.) Whereas a lead-acid or 'wet' battery is well-served by a voltage as high as 14.8V or more, both gel and AGM sealed batteries must have a lower voltage.

For example, manufacturers of gel batteries usually state that a charge level should *not* exceed 14.2V (although some product data sheets suggest 14.4V). Manufacturers of sealed AGM batteries usually quote a limit of 14.4V, but again, check the recommendation from your battery manufacturer/supplier.

Another issue to consider is how long a standard charging device should be left connected to a battery. It was usually the case with older chargers that they should be switched off as soon as a battery achieved its full state of charge. On the other hand, modern products (often called 'smart chargers') incorporate a battery condition sensing facility and these contain their own built-in switching function. Moreover, when a battery regains a good state of charge, it is also good practice to maintain it in this condition. The later section on trickle charging provides advice.

BUILT-IN MAINS CHARGERS

When a motorcaravan is connected to a mains hook-up, many owners keep its built-in charger running constantly. This is fine when a charger incorporates battery condition sensing circuitry but some manufacturers advise that a charger should be switched off as soon as a battery regains its fully recharged state. This particularly applies to older products, so check the recommendations given in your motorcaravan owner's manual.

Bear in mind that when a built-in charger is running, it is not only charging a leisure battery; its output is often being used simultaneously to run 12V accessories. In order to enhance its charging performance, a motorcaravan's charger is usually designed to provide a 13.8V (maximum) output. In practice, most 12V accessories can operate on a 13.8V supply without risk of damage – but not on anything greater. Unfortunately, that voltage is not high enough for the needs of most batteries. The manufacturers of lead acid vehicle and leisure batteries often point out that a voltage around 14.8V voltage is needed in the early stages of a recharge operation and failing to provide this higher voltage prevents a battery from ever becoming fully recharged. However, it is possible to achieve this if you disconnect it from your motorcaravan's 12V supply circuit and then couple it up to a high output stage charger.

In response to the charging and system supply disparities; BCA Leisure developed a built-in power supply product called the 'Duo Charger', which gives two separate outputs. One is limited to

Right: Both vehicle and leisure batteries have six cell compartments.

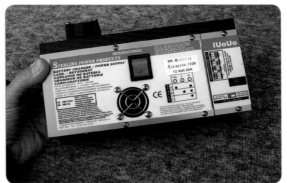

Far left: A display which shows the two output voltages from the BCA Leisure Duo Charger.

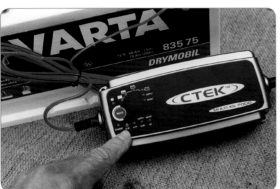

Left: The battery charger and power supply units from Sterling are often used in cabin cruisers.

Far left: The CTEK Multi XS 7,000 pulse charger offers up to six charge level steps and a maximum boost of 16V.

13.8V maximum and supplies a motorcaravan's 12V accessories; the other achieves a higher voltage and is intended solely for battery charging. Although BCA Leisure is principally concerned with supplying these products directly to manufacturers, many touring and motorcaravans are fitted with this Company's 12V supply systems.

Although there are occasions when a battery might be disconnected to receive a boost charge operation, do not use your motorcaravan's 12V systems without having a leisure battery in circuit (in other words, drawing power exclusively from the charger as if it were a transformer/rectifier). This is not recommended because the output from many chargers tends to fluctuate and some 12V appliances *must* be given a stable supply. Having a battery connected within the circuit smoothes out irregularities and prevents damage to appliances.

In addition to the points above, it is also helpful to have an understanding about the conditions that cause a battery to emit an explosive gas when being charged.

Left: Banner trickle chargers include products that will keep a leisure battery in a fully topped-up state.

Left: To maximise output from an alternator, some manufacturers are fitting the Sterling 4 Step Alternator Regulator.

GASSING

When the output from a charger exceeds 14.4V, a lead acid battery starts to 'gas'. This refers to a situation in which the dilute sulphuric acid electrolyte emits hydrogen, which is a flammable, explosive gas. This is why you should never be smoking or have a naked flame in the vicinity of a charging battery. Even when a charging operation is complete, residual gas often remains in the cells for a short while afterwards. Do not treat this lightly. When an explosion occurred in a local garage, the author was invited to inspect a battery casing that had completely blown apart. Fortunately, the highly

Technical tip

Vehicle battery charging

Although a motorcaravan's built-in charger looks after the leisure battery, it may not be switchable to charge the vehicle battery. To achieve this, some motorcaravanners carry a conventional portable charger.

Another solution is to fit the Van Bitz Battery Master, which provides a trickle charge to the vehicle battery that comes from the leisure battery. It is completely automatic in operation. Installation involves coupling the positive terminals of both the vehicle and leisure batteries via the Battery Master control relay product. The device monitors the charge

in the leisure battery and whenever it achieves a higher voltage than the vehicle battery, it diverts some of its power. This happens, for example, when the leisure battery is being charged. A red LED indicates when the sharing is taking effect.

corrosive acid had only hit the service technician's clothes. When he was disconnecting charger clips from a battery's terminals, he was smoking and wasn't wearing eye protection.

Bearing in mind that some motorcaravan manufacturers fit batteries in rather thoughtless places in the living space, this raises concerns. For instance, if a leisure battery is mounted under a cab seat and its gas relief tube becomes detached, which it often does, hydrogen could escape whenever it's being charged. Since hydrogen rises, anyone smoking nearby could conceivably cause an explosion. It would be much better if sealed, purpose-made battery compartments with external venting were used more often. Paradoxically, they are fitted as standard on touring caravans.

Another reason why fixed battery charges are limited to a 13.8V output is that this charge level normally only initiates gassing if one of the cells in a battery fails. Of course, these comments might make it sound that gassing should be avoided. That's not entirely true. Over a period of time, the performance of a leisure battery deteriorates, and this often occurs when sulphate builds up on the plates. However, the use of a starting voltage around 14.8V causes gassing to commence and this helps overcome this condition. It is even claimed that many leisure batteries are scrapped prematurely because of mild sulphate deposits – a condition that can *sometimes* be alleviated by using a high output charger. Of course, a gassing battery needs good ventilation and an environment free of sparks, naked flames and lighted cigarettes. Equally, a battery that gasses frequently needs a regular top-up with de-ionised water.

SMART CHARGING PRODUCTS

It stands to reason that if an owner periodically transfers a leisure battery to a bench situated in a suitably safe environment, a high output charger with a stepped regime can then be used without risk. For instance, RoadPro retails Sterling chargers that are often used in the marine industry. These products create different regimes to suit those recommended by battery manufacturers; for instance, they offer settings for gel batteries, which normally mustn't be given a charge voltage exceeding 14.2V. However, this type of high specification product is considerably more expensive than a basic, single-function charger.

Other stepped chargers include CTEK products that are designed to charge several types of lead acid and gel batteries, including the kind fitted on motorcycles. CTEK chargers are unusual in that they create a pulsed output in certain operating modes and the Multi XS 7000 model operates with up to six charge level steps. A maximum boost setting of 16V, which operates for a timed period of four hours, can also be chosen for batteries that have been neglected and need extensive reconditioning. CTEK products employ automatic timing and current-controlled charging, so that the needs of a battery are identified and met by an appropriate stepped charge regime.

At the time of writing, RoadPro catalogues contain a table listing 16 different CTEK models and a detailed table of each charger's capacities, stage operations, maximum charging current and battery application.

TRICKLE CHARGING

The chapter so far has focussed on procedures for dealing with a discharged leisure battery. However, there is also the matter of *maintaining* the level of a fully charged battery – during a period of storage, for example. It mustn't be overlooked that even when a vehicle is not in use, instruments like a clock and electronic alarms make a constant (though very small) demand on a battery. However, these add up over a period of time and a battery inevitably loses its charge.

In order to keep a battery fully charged, it is wise to couple-up a trickle-charging device. As its name implies, this only provides a small charge and modern versions with electronic sensing systems are automatically activated or deactivated using information received from the battery itself. Purpose-made trickle chargers are sold by car component specialists. On the other hand, if you own a modern 'smart charger' with a stepped regime facility, the product is likely to include a trickle charging function among its various operating modes. This setting is usually activated automatically as soon as a full recharge cycle has been completed.

THE ENGINE ALTERNATOR

When a motorcaravan is being driven, its alternator is able to charge a leisure battery as well as the vehicle battery.

To enable a leisure battery to receive a charge while an engine is running, it isn't merely a matter of linking the vehicle batteries together in parallel (parallel is where the terminals are connected positive to positive and negative to negative). If those connections were made, current would be pulled from *both* batteries when starting the vehicle. This can damage a leisure battery and sometimes a fuse can blow in the process.

The batteries have to remain isolated whenever the engine isn't running, but if a special relay is fitted, a connection can be achieved automatically as soon as the vehicle has been started. A 'relay', as illustrated on page 87, is an electrically operated switch, and when wired into the system, the two batteries retain their independence until the engine is running. In this situation, power from the alternator triggers the relay and the link between the two batteries is achieved. Incidentally, a similar relay is also fitted if you need to run a refrigerator on a 12V supply when you're on the road.

Several electrical suppliers sell suitable relays, including Hella, Lucas, Ring, Ryder and Towing Electrics. Equally, installation kits are made for both motor and touring caravans. Full instructions are provided and the wiring diagram on page 83 shows how a fridge relay, a battery charging relay and an isolation relay for the low-voltage supply in the

living quarters are all connected up.

On older vehicles, the fridge and charging relays are activated by connecting into the ignition light supply from the alternator. In practice, forming this connection isn't always easy and an auto electrician at a franchise dealer *must* be consulted. The wiring in modern vehicles is far more complex than it used to be and dealer advice is essential. Taking a supply from an ignition-controlled accessory on the base vehicle may not be a suitable alternative either. Some accessories are activated as soon as the starter is cranked and that means that the vehicle battery is inappropriately augmented by power from the leisure battery. That can cause damage.

Some auto electricians prefer to fit electro-magnetic relays for circuit isolation switching, battery charging and fridge operations. Alternatively, combination relays can be fitted. A popular product is the TEC3M unit from Towing Electrics.

Finally, fitting a battery-to-battery charger can enhance the charging rate given to a leisure battery by an alternator. Models are included in the CTEK and Sterling product ranges and an increasing number of motorcaravan owners are reporting their approval of these products. Full explanations of battery-to-battery functions and installation details are available from their manufacturers. Advice is also contained in many product catalogues.

PETROL AND DIESEL GENERATORS FOR CHARGING

A generator is useful for running mains appliances but many types deliver a fluctuating supply and power surges are not unusual. For example, when a low-wattage 230V electric kettle automatically switches off when the water boils, there's a momentary surge of power. That might cause problems. Not only are there electronic products that need a smooth supply of mains electricity (such as laptop computers), there is also widespread use of 'switched-mode' battery chargers in motorcaravans. Switched-mode chargers are conveniently light in weight but a surge in the supply can damage their sensitive electronic circuits. The chargers fitted to motorcaravans in the 1980s used a transformer, which is less susceptible to damage. However, these older products are heavier than the switched-mode chargers that have superseded them.

To avoid causing damage:

■ If you just want a generator to charge your battery, some of the better models provide a separate 12V output. This gives a coupling point for a lead that would run directly to the battery terminals, thereby eliminating the motorcaravan's built-in charger from the system.

■ The risk of damage occurs if you plug the 230V output from a generator into your motorcaravan mains input socket (as you would a mains hook-up lead), completely forget to switch off the consumer unit and appliances, and then start the generator. To avoid a generator's start-up surge, it is essential that you have all the electrical items switched off in the motorcaravan, including the main switch on the consumer unit. However, the hook-up lead between the generator and the motorcaravan inlet socket can be coupled. Then start the generator in accordance with its instructions. Wait until it reaches normal running speed. Then – and only then – switch on the master control at the 230V consumer unit, and also the power supply switch to the charger, if there is one.

■ Perhaps the smoothest supply from a generator is obtainable from recent products like Honda's EU10i and EU20i models. These employ a completely different method of creating mains power and their supply is claimed to be surge-free and more stable than a normal mains supply. To achieve this, Honda's products

Right: This Honda generator is secured with a robust chain to a towing bracket to discourage theft.

generate 12V DC power, which is then passed through an inverter to raise and rectify the supply to 230V AC.

■ To be certain that the correct use of a generator is not going to damage a charger, it would be prudent to confirm the situation with your motorcaravan's manufacturer. You must also follow the instructions to your generator.

Note: *Good quality generators are expensive and when they are in operation on a site, it is prudent to ensure that they are suitable protected against theft. Some models are noisy, too, so use them with consideration for others.*

SOLAR AND WIND GENERATORS FOR A 12V SUPPLY

The idea of getting 'something for nothing' is very attractive. On the other hand, solar and wind generators only provide a trickle charge for a battery. They do not create mains electricity. Only

in domestic installations, where you have a large array of panels on a household roof and an inverter in the system, is a 230V supply produced.

Strictly speaking, the term 'solar' is inaccurate because photovoltaic (PV) cells produce power from light, and also produce electricity in cloudy weather; they don't depend on sunshine. Solar panels are popular products and a number of specialists fit them to the roofs of motorcaravans. Portable units are also gaining popularity as they can be easily transferred to another motorcaravan. However, there have been instances where portable panels have been stolen. With both wind and solar products, a regulator is needed to ensure that a battery isn't overcharged. For example, an abnormally high output produced by a wind generator during a gale could lead to damage. Similarly, the output from a large solar panel on a bright day can exceed the safe limit. In good weather, it's not unusual for a panel to produce a supply around 20V, so this has to be checked by a voltage regulator. The more expensive regulators also supply information on an LCD screen.

Several types of solar panel are available, complete with installation kits, although large panels are costly. They are heavy, too, although the semi-flexible units that are not built using a solid frame are considerably lighter. They're also easy to mount on a roof because no holes need drilling to secure the product; semi-flexible units are bonded using an adhesive sealant, as shown in Chapter 10.

There is no doubt that a reasonably large solar panel like a 70-Watt unit can provide a helpful trickle charge to a leisure battery. However, a battery usually works hardest during long dark winter evenings, which is precisely when solar panels are least productive.

Mains systems

This section describes the components used in a mains supply system and provides general safety guidance, including procedures for coupling-up on-site. It is only older motorcaravans that were not built with a mains supply system as standard. However, comprehensive wiring kits are available for retrospective installation. Many owners would entrust this work to a qualified electrician, but some DIY enthusiasts undoubtedly have the knowledge and ability to fit a 230V mains kit themselves.

Right: Portable solar panels can be transferred to another motorcaravan but they are also subject to theft.

Right: This Steca solar charge controller also displays attained Ah levels and even gives a summary of gains over long periods.

Far right: The semi-flexible, frame-free panels from GB-Sol don't need fixing holes because they are bonded to a roof using an adhesive sealant.

Above: A Powerpart 230V mains wiring kit is supplied with full fitting instructions.

Safety note: *DIY installations must be tested by a qualified electrician and should have a signed test certificate to verify compliance with the current IEE regulations. Contact the NICEIC or ECA for details of approved inspectors in your area.*

The kit itself should include:
- Suitable cable for a supply circuit that meets IEE standards. This means 2.5mm² flexible cable to connect the input socket to a residual current device (RCD); 1.5mm² flexible cable for supplying all the circuits that are served by miniature circuit breakers (MCBs).
- A mains consumer unit manufactured with a residual current device (RCD); this immediately cuts off supply if anyone touches a live wire in the motorcaravan. It also includes miniature circuit breakers (MCBs) to protect individual circuits – there is usually one MCB for the fridge and another for the sockets. Three MCBs are fitted, however, to suit the more extensive circuit provision found in larger motorcaravans.
- An earth wire, covered with green and yellow sheathing. This has to be connected from the earth bar in the consumer unit and bolted to the chassis. A warning plate should also be provided and this has to be attached to the earth wire's point of fixing.
- 'Three-pin' 13-Amp sockets. In a more expensive mains kit, these will be switched sockets, and ideally would also feature double-pole switching, although few manufacturers install this type of socket.
- A coupling input socket (for the 'hook-up' cable) which complies with BS EN 60309-2.
- Some kits also include the connecting hook-up cable, which should comply with BS EN 60309-2. Otherwise a coupling cable can be purchased separately. This should not exceed 25 metres and it should include three flexible core cables for live (positive), neutral (negative) and earth connections, each of which must have a cross-sectional area of 2.5mm². Incidentally, you are NOT recommended to link up more than one extension lead when coupling-up to a site supply.

Above: An earth cable bolted to the chassis must be clearly labelled.

Note:
1 An MCB is a trip switch providing over-current protection. This is a modern equivalent of the old-fashioned rewirable fuse.
2 An RCD used to be called an 'Earth Leakage Circuit Breaker' or a 'Residual Current Circuit Breaker'. In recent years, these incorporate double-pole switching, which means they control current flow on both live and neutral connections. Bear in mind that the RCD affords no protection from a shock received from the site pillar, the hook-up lead and that short length of cable linking a motorcaravan's inlet socket with its consumer unit.
3 Most consumer units fitted in motorcaravans deal solely with 230V electricity. However, there are some control units, such as the Plug-In-Systems PMS3 (fitted in Bilbo's conversions) and the Sargent EC500 pictured earlier in the chapter that embrace mains, charging and 12V systems in a single control box.

The system fitted in a motorcaravan is designed to connect with site hook-up pillars in the UK that are fitted with an industrial socket. If you want to connect the supply lead to a 13-Amp socket at home, check the later section. Similarly, adaptors are needed to connect into the many different types of hook-up pillars found on the Continent.

Below: Bilbo's models often have a Plug-in-Systems power unit which combines mains and 12V controls in a single unit.

Mains hook-ups

A site hook-up is limited in its supply. Some supplies are as low as 5 Amps; others are as high as 16 Amps. Some sites offer two levels of supply and charge accordingly. On arrival at a site you need to ask the site warden about the amperage rating.

Using the figure given (Amps), multiply this by 230 (Volts) to establish the total wattage it can supply. For instance if a site offers a 10 Amp supply, 10 x 230 = 2300 Watts. Now look closely at your appliances to see their wattage rating. Typically these are:

Light bulb	60W	Battery charger	100W
Small colour TV	50W	Microwave cooker	1,200W
Fridge	125W	Domestic kettle	2,000W

Now add up the wattages of the appliances you expect to have in use at any one time to assess whether you'll overload the site supply.

Note 1. If you overload the system, you'll activate the hook-up pillar's trip switch and on many sites the warden will be summoned to reinstate the supply.
Note 2. A site is not able to supply all hook-up pillars simultaneously with a maximum or near-maximum output. Advice posters often encourage users not to operate 230V items unnecessarily. This is especially true in winter when central heating systems are often run on electricity rather than gas and many owners spend long evening hours watching television and using interior lighting.

CONNECTING UP TO A SITE SUPPLY

When you've gained a site official's approval to use a mains supply, always follow this hook-up routine:

1　Switch off the residual current device (RCD) master switch on the consumer unit and all 230V appliances.
2　Uncoil the hook-up lead. Never leave it coiled on a drum because this can lead to overheating.
3　Insert the hook-up plug with recessed tubes (female) into your motorcaravan input socket.
4　Insert the opposite end with pins (male) into the site supply point. On some sites you have to rotate the connector clockwise until it locks and this action activates the flow of current.
5　Inside your motorcaravan, go to the mains consumer unit. Turn on its master switch, which is protected by the RCD to activate the 230V supply.
6　Then, as a safety check, press the trip button to confirm that the RCD cuts out, as it should.
7　Provided the trip facility works as intended, reset the RCD switch again to reinstate the supply.
8　Check the polarity of the supply. Sometimes there is a reverse polarity warning light on the consumer unit. If there isn't, make sure you purchase a socket tester from a dealer or electrical factor.

When disconnecting a supply, switch off all the mains appliances and the RCD control switch. Then withdraw the supply plug from the site's hook-up pillar. In the case of the twist-socket fitted on several sites, you need to depress a red button to release the connector.

Right: Before coupling-up to a mains supply, switch off the RCD master switch on the consumer unit.

Far right: Leaving a hook-up lead tightly coiled can create sufficient heat in the cable to melt the insulation sheath.

Right: When the power is on, a test device confirms if the system has polarity reversal or any other fundamental faults.

Far right: On some UK sites, a red button on a hook-up socket has to be depressed in order to retrieve the plug.

Similarly, the inlet sockets on some motorcaravans are also fitted with a plug release catch.

CONNECTING UP TO A MAINS SUPPLY AT HOME

There may be occasions when you want to connect your motorcaravan to a 13-Amp socket at home. This might be to pre-cool a refrigerator before leaving for a holiday. Or it might be to operate a battery charger in the vehicle when it is parked for an extended spell.

An appropriate way to do this is to use your mains hook-up lead and to operate the required appliances with the safety afforded by your motorcaravan's mains consumer unit. However, the coupling lead itself does not benefit from the consumer unit's protection, since it is drawing current from your house. Some properties have RCD protection as part of the household supply system but others don't. In order to ensure that the mains coupling lead running out to your motorcaravan is safe, fit a portable, plug-in RCD to the supplying 13A socket. These are sold at DIY stores and the accompanying photograph shows one of these products.

POLARITY

In the UK, it is normal practice for a switch to create a break in the live feed serving an appliance or lamp fitting. In other words, if a light is switched off, no current will reach the bulb, its holder or the fitting itself.

However, in many other European countries, a switch operates on both live *and* neutral connections: a system known as double-pole switching. This is undoubtedly very safe, but it seems that less urgency is exercised abroad when contractors install campsite hook-ups. Live and neutral feeds are often reversed, although the situation, called 'reverse polarity', is not such a safety threat in countries where all electric controls adopt double-pole switching.

On the other hand, reverse polarity is potentially very dangerous for the UK tourist whose motorcaravan is normally fitted with only single-pole switches. When you switch off an appliance with a reversed polarity supply it's true that it ceases to function. But – if we take a light as an example – *the light fitting remains live* because switching is now on the cable leading *out* of the unit.

If you encounter a reversed polarity supply, you are strongly advised not to use a mains hook-up just in case you were to accidentally touch a live connection. However, some owners create a practical solution for dealing with reversed polarity by intentionally wiring up a continental adaptor with its live and neutral connections reversed. This is

Above left: On some motorcaravan mains inlets, you cannot remove the plug until you've depressed a release button.

Above: To draw a mains supply from your home, purchase a plug adaptor and a portable RCD protection device.

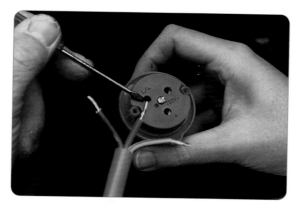

Right: To deal with reversed polarity some owners wire-up a plug with the live and neutral connections reversed.

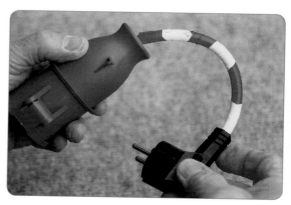

Far right: Red and white stripes remind the user that this foreign adapter has been specially wired to deal with reversed polarity.

then marked with bright tape to indicate that it is a reverse-wired adaptor.

Obviously you cannot buy a 'wrongly wired' adaptor but getting one of these made-up enables you to remedy the problem at source, namely your pitch supply socket. By carrying both adaptors when touring abroad, together with a polarity tester plug, the situation can be immediately resolved.

Motorcaravans manufactured since 1993 have double-pole switched RCDs so the problem is less acute. But regrettably, single-pole switched 13-Amp sockets are still fitted in motorcaravans – even though double-pole 13-Amp switched sockets have been available for some time.

PETROL AND DIESEL GENERATORS FOR A 230V SUPPLY

Earlier it was explained how to use a petrol generator to charge a leisure battery. In this section, the focus is on 230V supply systems.

Right: The generator covers manufactured by Sew 'n Sews are not only rain protectors; they also double-up as carrying cases.

right: This permanently-fixed 2.5kW Electrolux generator was mounted in a Murvi van conversion as a special project.

Far right: Starting and operating a permanently installed generator is sometimes controlled by a remote panel.

From the outset, it must be recognised that a generator's Amp output is far lower than the output obtainable from a mains supply hook-up. For example, a site providing 16 amps is able to operate appliances whose combined rate of consumption adds up to roughly 3,680 Watts. This is considerably more than the output from a Honda EU10i generator, which has a rated output of 900 Watts. This isn't a problem if you want a generator to run mains lighting, a TV, a mobile phone charger, a shaver, or even a low-wattage electric kettle. However, many owners expect a mains supply to be able to run portable heating appliances and a microwave oven. It's the product mentioned last, which is usually rather misleading.

To explain this issue, imagine that you own a compact microwave oven that is rated at 600 watts (sometimes referred to as 600 watts cooking power). The trouble is that this figure relates to the oven's *output* as opposed to the *input* it requires. In order to establish which types of generator will be powerful enough to run your microwave oven, the usual advice is to double the oven's quoted output wattage and then deduct 10%. Hence a microwave oven rated at 600 watts would need a generator producing at least 1,080 watts. This is beyond the capability of the Honda EU10i, although it falls within the scope of a Honda EU20i. Both of these models are pleasingly silent, whereas industrial machines that offer a higher output are considerably noisier and less compact than leisure machines.

Provided this is understood, generators have a useful place and some motorcaravans have a

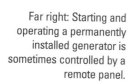

102 **The Motorcaravan Manual**

Far left: Labcraft discovered that a fluorescent tube light could operate using a 12V supply if a tiny inverter was fitted in the casing.

Left: Compact inverters like this 350W ProPowerQ quasi sine-wave model are included in the range from Sterling Power Products.

metal-lined locker to transport one. But don't be misled: these lockers are not vented, so you cannot operate a portable leisure machine when it's left in its locker. Also be aware that leisure generators mustn't get wet, so a ventilated cover is needed when a generator is running in the rain.

On larger motorcaravans, a special compartment is made to house a permanently mounted generator. Dometic and Onan generators are often fitted in large motorhomes, and they usually have a remote control panel situated somewhere inside the living area. Of course, on large American RVs, a built-in generator is quite common. However, before purchasing this type of generator, check what it weighs and relate this information to your motorcaravan's spare payload. They really *are* heavy accessories.

INVERTERS

Another way to gain mains power is to take a 12V DC supply from a leisure battery and to convert it into 230V AC using an inverter. It shouldn't be forgotten that fluorescent lighting wasn't possible until Labcraft created and fitted a miniature inverter in the casing of its lamp fittings over 40 years ago. As mentioned earlier in this chapter its function was to raise the voltage to a level that would ignite the gas in the tube.

Inverters have played a part in caravanning contexts for some time. They have also been installed in boats, and inverters in the Sterling Power Product range are now being sold to motorcaravanners as well.

There are two types of product: the more expensive replicate the characteristics of mains power and are referred to as 'pure sine-wave inverters'. Their main benefit is the fact that they will operate virtually any type of 230V equipment that falls within their output range. Considerably less expensive are 'quasi sine-wave' inverters, which are still able to operate a number of mains appliances including hair dryers, microwave ovens, electric heaters, and power tools, to name a few examples. However, you again need a model with sufficient output to meet the needs of different types of equipment.

The quasi sine-wave product shown here is rated at 350 Watts but around 10% of this (35W) is used by the inverter itself. And even though an inverter should be situated as close to the supplying battery as possible, voltage loss

will still occur. Add to this the fact that some mains appliances demand more power for that brief period when they are starting-up, it is soon apparent that this inverter's 350W rating is going to be far less useful than might have initially been assumed. As a rough guide, if you want an inverter to operate a 1,000W appliance, you might need one rated around 1,500W. However, the concerns do not end there.

There is also a very significant draw of current (Amps) from a supplying battery. Whereas a 1,000W hair dryer might take 4.3A when running on 230V AC supply, the demand when the same dryer is running on 12V is around 84A. That represents a very substantial drain on a typical leisure battery with a 84Ah capacity.

Where lighting is concerned, an inverter can be more useful, especially if you want to use a couple of long-life bulbs. These might take around 30–40W, and it is interesting conducting simple experiments like the one below to find out precisely how long a battery will last before it needs a recharge.

Of course the trouble with lighting is that it will be in use for an extended period, whereas an appliance like an electric shaver is only in use for several minutes. As for the low wattage kettle shown in this test, it didn't work at all when matched with the 300W inverter.

In summary, an inverter can carry out useful tasks, but be prepared to accept that it is a very poor alternative when compared with the power that is available from a 230V hook-up pillar.

Below: Experiments with inverters soon prove their limitations and the speed at which they discharge a 12V leisure battery.

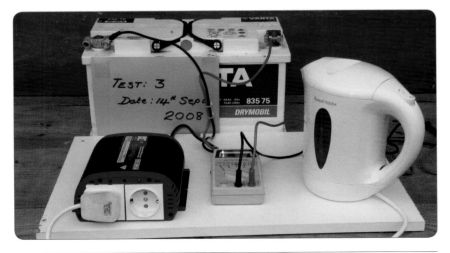

6 Gas supply systems and heating appliances

The most common fuel for heating and cooking in motorcaravans is liquefied petroleum gas (LPG). This is produced in two different forms and an understanding of its characteristics, storage and supply ensures that the fuel is used efficiently and safely.

CONTENTS

Characteristics of gas

Supply

Storage

Pressure regulation

Pipework and installation

Cooking appliances

Space heating appliances

Water heating appliances

Gas is not the only fuel used in a motorcaravan; for example, electricity is sometimes used to run heating appliances. In recent motorcaravans, for example, you might find a 230V hotplate fitted alongside the gas burners on the hob.

In practice, electricity is only one of several alternative fuels. Another option is diesel, which has been used for many years to heat the cabs in heavy commercial vehicles. Today, petrol and diesel heating appliances are used in motorcaravans, too. All types of heating system have points in their favour but at present, gas is by far the most common fuel used in leisure vehicles.

Right: The cooking hob on this 2011 Auto-Trail TrackerEK is equipped with a 230V hotplate and three gas burners.

Safety

■ It is critically important that gas supply systems in motorcaravans achieve high standards of safety with regard to installation and use. For several years, manufacturers of motorcaravans have worked within British Standard (BS)/European Norm (EN) 1949:2002. However, in 2011 the British Standards Institute published a revised LPG installation standard; BS EN 1949:2011. The National Caravan Council (NCC) in conjunction with The Gas Safe Register will implement the new standard on 1 September 2012. In effect, this will concern motorcaravans designated as 2013 models. **Note:** *The Gas Safe Register is the agency that verifies the integrity of installations; previously this work was carried out by the Council of Registered Gas Installers (CORGI).*

■ At the time of writing, a Code of Practice (CoP) is in the final stages of preparation regarding fixed or underslung LPG tanks fitted on motorcaravans. The content of this CoP embraces issues such as design, installation, maintenance, user instructions and decommissioning. Following consultations with industry experts, it is anticipated that the final CoP publication will be available early in 2012.

■ From 1 September 2011, all motorcaravans that are submitted for NCC certification will have to be equipped with a Carbon Monoxide (CO) alarm. In effect, this will be applicable to motorcaravans designated as 2012 models. Many manufacturers and owners have already installed CO alarms voluntarily. Others have also voluntarily installed gas leak detection devices. **Note:** *See illustrations and advice in the later section 'Leak Detection'.*

Characteristics of gas

The full name for this fuel is Liquefied Petroleum Gas, or LPG for short. To meet the needs of leisure users it is supplied in portable cylinders, although some motorcaravanners choose to have a refillable bulk tank fitted underneath their vehicle.

Below: Refillable gas tanks are sometimes installed; these should comply with the recently established Code of Practice.

For owners embarking on long continental trips, either a tank or permanently fixed refillable cylinders have their merits.

Although both fixed tanks and portable cylinders are available, most motorcaravanners use the latter. However, their benefits are hindered by the fact that portable cylinders sold in the UK and abroad have a prodigious array of couplings. This lack of standardisation can pose problems when you need to exchange an empty cylinder for a full one.

Couplings pose challenges, but firstly let's consider the gas itself. LPG in its natural state is neither poisonous, nor does it have a smell, which means a leak could occur unnoticed. This would be dangerous because LPG is highly flammable, so a 'stenching agent' is added to the gas during processing. The resulting odour is distinctive, very unpleasant, and it ensures that leaks are detected at once.

In addition, LPG is denser than air and sinks to the floor. As a result of this, 'drop-out' holes (sometimes called gas dispersal holes) are built into a motorcaravan's structure to provide easy escape routes for leaking gas. The same provision has to be made at the lowest point in gas cylinder lockers. It is obviously most important that vents built into the floor and under gas appliances are never covered.

Anyone buying a pre-owned vehicle should carefully check that the previous owner kept all the ventilators unobstructed. These vents can be draughty, especially in windy conditions. If this leads to discomfort indoors, it is not difficult to fit an external shield to divert wind without interfering with the gas escape function of the outlets.

Of course, a well-finished motorcaravan should have draught excluders already in place.

As stated in this chapter's opening sentence, there are two types of LPG: butane and propane. Their characteristics are different but the appliances fitted to motorcaravans built in Europe are designed to run on either gas without need for adjustments. The differences between butane and propane are as follows:

BUTANE:

- **Butane** has a higher calorific value than propane, which means it is a more efficient heat producer. Accordingly, butane is a popular choice – except when the weather is cold.

Above: Permanently installed Gaslow cylinders sold in the UK are refilled at service stations equipped with LPG pumps.

- **Butane** does not change from its liquefied state to a gas vapour when temperatures are lower than 0°C (32°F) at atmospheric pressure. Even a cylinder brim-full with liquefied butane cannot equip a motorcaravan's supply system when temperatures fall below freezing, so it is seldom used in the winter.
- **Butane** is denser than propane, so although the smallest Calor Gas cylinders for the two products are the same size, the propane version holds 3.9kg (8.6lb), and an equivalent cylinder filled with butane holds 4.5kg (10lb) of liquefied gas.

PROPANE:

- **Propane** changes from a liquefied state into a gas in temperatures as low as -40°C (-44°F) – so it is better for use in winter. It is unfortunate that suppliers on the Continent sell mainly butane, although processing companies sometimes add a small quantity of propane to butane cylinders in order to give improved cold weather performance.
- **Propane** in its liquefied state is less dense and therefore lighter than butane. That's why, in two cylinders of identical size, there is less propane by weight than butane.
- **Propane** is better for running a system in which several gas appliances are operating

Far left: Never cover a gas 'drop-out' hole; if a gas leak were to occur, this is one of the escape points.

Left: A manufacturer's deflector shield prevents this gas 'drop-out' hole becoming a source of draughts.

simultaneously and where the demand for gas is high. When describing this feature, technical specialists often say that a propane cylinder has a better 'off-take rate' than a similar butane cylinder.

- **Propane** has a vapour pressure between three and four times that of butane at 15°C, and for this reason, different regulators are normally required for these two gases. But note the following paragraph.

When changing from a liquefied form into vapour, butane and propane attain different pressures. To ensure that a motorcaravan's appliances are supplied with gas at the required pressure, a device called a 'regulator' is required.

Until recent alterations in regulator construction, gas supplied from a butane cylinder required a butane-specific regulator: conversely, gas supplied from a propane cylinder needed a propane-specific version. Furthermore, to ensure that you use the correct regulator, butane and propane cylinders have different couplings. However, in 2003, a new type of regulator was introduced that can deal with either butane or propane, and this will be discussed in more detail later. The only point to emphasise here is that dual-use regulators should only be used in conjunction with purpose-built appliances fitted in motorcaravans built from 2004 onwards. Motorcaravans built prior to that date need a cylinder-mounted regulator that matches the owner's choice of gas and the appliances originally installed.

Safety

- **Before taking to the road, it is important to turn off the gas supply at source. Even though there are isolation valves in modern motorcaravans for controlling different appliances, the best precaution is to turn off the supply *at the cylinder*. Prior to starting the engine, turning off the supply should always be part of a motorcaravanner's routine. This precautionary measure ensures that no appliances (especially a fridge) can be accidentally left running on gas. When you drive into a filling station for fuel, it is strictly illegal for a motorcaravan to have a naked flame and this would pose a very serious threat to people's safety.**

Always turn off your gas supply at the cylinder before embarking on a journey.

- **Always transport a cylinder in its *upright* position. If a cylinder is laid on its side, the liquefied gas *might* prevent the pressure relief safety valve from functioning correctly. Gas can also escape from a faulty valve. When it's acknowledged that in the transfer from liquid to vapour there's approximately a *two hundred times increase in volume*, the potential hazard arising from a leak is clearly apparent.**

Note: *A recent development has led to the introduction of safety devices that permit a gas supply to remain in use while a vehicle is being driven. This, in turn, enables a motorcaravanner to operate certain types of specially-designed heating appliances. Notwithstanding the benefits, it is essential that no naked flames are in operation when a vehicle enters a filling station. For safety's sake, turning off a gas cylinder remains the best course of action.*

Supply

Portable LPG cylinders are sold in several sizes, some of which are more suited to a motorcaravanner's needs than others. To obtain a Calor cylinder, you have to sign a hire agreement document and pay a fee. Under this arrangement, every cylinder remains in the ownership of Calor Gas Ltd. Subsequently, if you cease being a Calor customer, the initial hire fee can be reclaimed, provided you are able to present your copy of the original agreement form.

The Campingaz system is different. In this case you *do* have to purchase your first cylinder and when it's empty, you pay to exchange it for a full one again.

In recent years, an increasing number of suppliers have also started marketing lightweight cylinders for use in touring caravans and motorcaravans, some of which consist of glass fibre reinforced plastic containers. These new products have provoked widespread interest, although Calor Gas Ltd is still a large UK provider of LPG to domestic, industrial and leisure markets. In the domestic context, large cylinders are often used by home owners whose properties are not served by a gas main. However, Calor's 19kg domestic propane cylinder is too heavy and bulky to transport in a motorcaravan.

Irrespective of your choice of cylinder, there are safety considerations to take into account, two of which are set out in the accompanying safety panel. The careful handling of cylinders is important, too, and it is an owner's responsibility to ensure they are mounted securely in a motorcaravan gas locker. Be aware that some of the strap systems provided by motorcaravan manufacturers have a tendency to shake loose when roads are bumpy.

The Calor Gas range of leisure cylinders is listed in the table on page 109. It's an impressive array, and a pity that Calor products cannot be obtained abroad.

In contrast, Campingaz is available in over 100 countries including most of Europe. But there are exceptions. Campingaz is not available in Finland or Sweden and is seldom stocked in Norway.

Also bear in mind that Campingaz cylinders are purported to contain butane – which can present a problem for winter caravanners. It is believed, however, that a small amount of propane is added to improve performance in cold environments but this strategy is not revealed on the cylinders' markings. Furthermore, the 907 cylinder is the only one suitable for meeting typical consumption requirements in modern motorcaravans. This is the *largest* cylinder in the Campingaz range, but it only holds 2.72kg (6lb) of butane: even the *smallest* butane cylinder in the Calor Gas range holds 4.5kg of butane.

Both Calor Gas and Campingaz are popular in the UK but product choice increased further when BP introduced two 'Gas Light' cylinders in 2006. These have been marketed in conjunction with Truma UK and the corrosion-proof, glass-fibre-reinforced cylinders are claimed to be half the weight of an equivalent steel cylinder. Part of the structure is

Far left: Always make sure that a cylinder security strap is tightly attached.

Left: In some motorcaravan lockers, the smaller 5kg BP Gas Light cylinder is accommodated more readily than its taller partner.

Far left: This adaptor may be needed to couple-up to the Gas Light 27mm clip-on valve; alternatively clip-on regulators are also available.

semi-transparent, too, so you can see the level of the liquefied gas inside.

The Gas Light cylinders hold 5kg and 10kg of propane respectively. Both measure 305mm in diameter and some motorcaravan lockers might not be able to accommodate the larger product which is 587mm in height.

To couple-up, Gas Light cylinders have a 27mm clip-on valve, and many owners purchase the type of adaptor shown alongside. Alternatively, you can purchase a clip-on regulator for direct cylinder mounting.

In response to BP's weight-saving initiative, Calor subsequently launched a new lightweight cylinder in autumn 2007. Known as the Calor Lite, this is filled with propane; it is made using recyclable lightweight steel and a plastic collar provides comfortable lifting points. The Calor Lite cylinder is also fitted with a level indicator that uses the float mechanism first introduced in 2005 on Calor's Patio Gas propane cylinders.

Though slightly taller, Calor Lite 6kg cylinders are otherwise the same dimensions as existing 6kg Calor Gas 'heavy' cylinders; they also employ the screw-thread 'pole' couplings fitted on the Company's 3.9kg, 6kg and 13kg 'heavy' propane cylinders. When filled with 6kg of propane, a Calor Lite cylinder weighs a total of 10.52kg.

So how does this compare with the heavier steel cylinders of this size? The alloy collar on Calor's equivalent 'heavy' cylinder records a tare (ie cylinder-only) weight of 17lb 6oz – ie 278oz.

Multiplying 278oz by 0.0283495 converts it to 7.88kg, and when that figure is added to the gas content (6kg), it totals 13.88kg. In other words, a new Calor lite cylinder when full is 3.36kg (c.7.4lb) lighter than its heavier brother. This is a significant saving in weight.

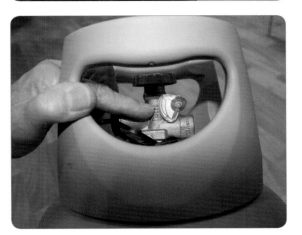

Left: Though fractionally taller, Calor Lite propane cylinders usually fit a locker that can accommodate Calor's standard 6kg cylinders.

Left: Although a float system works more accurately during the later stages of consumption, this is a useful facility on Calor Lite cylinders.

Left: It is a tradition that a Calor Gas cylinder collar shows the empty cylinder weight in pounds and ounces.

Owner-refillable portable LPG cylinders

Notwithstanding the cost-saving benefits of owner-refillable gas cylinders, both The Camping and Caravanning Club and The Caravan Club adopted a policy NOT to encourage members to invest in such equipment. There are concerns over the acceptability and safety of refilling portable cylinders on an autogas forecourt; moreover, forecourt staff are seldom classed as 'competent' to carry out the task or give advice. This is likely to invalidate a Company's insurance.

Then in June 2007, a trade association known as the LPGas Association (since renamed UKLPG) also made the formal statement: *It is our advice that user owned (sic.), portable LPG cylinders should not be refilled at Autogas refuelling sites'*. This refers to cylinders which have to be removed from a motorcaravan for refilling directly from the nozzle of an LPG pump. The Association then added:

Vessels which are attached to a vehicle for heating or cooking (on camper vans or similar) present similar risks on filling to those for propulsion purposes and may be permitted to be refilled at Autogas refuelling sites provided they:
- *remain in-situ for refilling; and*
- *are fitted with a device to physically prevent filling beyond 80%; and*
- *are connected to a fixed filling connection which is not part of the vessel.*

Fixed systems which meet these criteria are available from Gaslow International Ltd., and RPi Engineering.

OWNER-REFILLABLE CYLINDERS

Cylinders refillable by motorcaravanners are another recent development, and several safety issues hindered their acceptance when they first went on sale. Concerns that were expressed are reported in the accompanying Safety Panel.

The main attraction of a self-fill product is that gas drawn from an LPG pump at a filling station is considerably less expensive than gas supplied with an exchange cylinder. For owners who use their motorcaravan regularly, especially in winter, they should be able to recuperate the cost of a refillable cylinder and its installation fairly quickly.

Benefits also arise if you travel abroad. Autogas stations that supply owners of gas-powered cars dispense propane. A coupling adaptor might be needed but these are available from gas specialists.

However, there are safety issues to consider, and some fuel stations do not permit members of the public to refill portable cylinders on forecourts. This hasn't been helped by the fact that some self-fill portable cylinders are not equipped with an automatic shut-off valve. This is an important safety device because a gas cylinder must never be filled more than 85–87% of its total volume. Overfilling can have disastrous consequences, especially if you drive with an over-full cylinder in your motorcaravan; a change in air pressure can cause the contents to expand.

For this reason, a refillable cylinder must be fitted with an automatic cut-off valve that operates as soon as the contents reach 80% of its total volume. When filling a glass-reinforced plastic cylinder that isn't equipped with one of these valves, a user has to monitor the rising level through a sighting point at the side. That can be difficult to judge with accuracy, especially when using a pump that dispenses liquefied gas at a brisk pace.

In response to this safety concern, Gaslow, a long-established gas specialist, embarked upon the design of a safe caravan- or motorcaravan-specific installation. The project started with the manufacture of yellow portable cylinders, which have to be installed to act as fixed tanks. Their capacities (in gas weight) are 6kg and 11kg respectively, and they carry a 15-year warranty. They also qualify for the company's replacement service after that period elapses on payment of a small fee. The complete Gaslow installation kit now being offered to motorcaravanners includes:

- A 6kg or 11kg cylinder fitted with a European Pi approved filler valve that shuts off when the cylinder is 80% full
- An over-pressure release valve
- A 0.6m length of semi-flexible, rubber-free, stainless steel pipe
- A filler coupling for mounting externally on the wall of a motorcaravan, which is the type used on many LPG converted cars

When carrying out the fitting work, the cylinder (or cylinders) must be installed in a motocaravan's locker and fixed permanently in place. The cylinder then has to be coupled-up to the stainless steel pipe, which must be appropriately secured and permanently connected to a wall-mounted filler. Three optional filling adaptors are available from Gaslow to match the coupling systems used in Europe.

To refill a cylinder in a Gaslow installation, a motorcaravan is driven up to an LPG pump at a suitably equipped fuel station and coupled just as

Right: This refill inlet mounted on the wall of a motorcaravan is the same pattern as the types fitted on many LPG-powered cars.

Far right: A Gaslow stainless steel coupling has a braided cover protecting a semi-flexible stainless steel ribbed pipe.

Cylinder gas content

Note: *The weight in kg with its approximate equivalent in lb relates only to the gas itself. On Calor products this is clearly marked on the cylinder. It does not relate to the total weight of both the cylinder and its gas content.*

BP Gas Light cylinders
5kg (11.02lb) propane
10kg (22.04lb) propane
■ BP Gas Light cylinders are coloured green and white

Calor gas cylinders
3.9kg (8.6lb) propane
4.5kg (10lb) butane
6kg (13.2lb) propane
7kg (15.4lb) butane
13kg (28.7lb) propane
15kg (33lb) butane
19kg (41.9lb) propane
6kg (13.2lb) propane Calor Lite
■ Calor Gas butane cylinders are painted blue
■ Calor Gas propane cylinders are painted red
■ Calor patio gas (propane) cylinders are painted green

Note: 1. The 19kg (41.9lb) propane cylinders are too large to transport safely in a motorcaravan. The 13kg propane and 15kg butane cylinders present similar problems although the gas lockers on some coachbuilt models are large enough to transport and secure cylinders of this size in an upright position.

2. An advantage with Calor Gas is that you can usually change from butane to propane and vice versa. In other words, an empty 3.9kg propane cylinder can be exchanged for a full 4.5kg butane equivalent without paying any more than the cost of the gas. Similarly a 4.5kg butane cylinder can usually be changed for a larger 7kg cylinder. Occasionally there are restrictions – notably when a particular size of cylinder is in short supply.

Campingaz cylinder sizes
0.45kg (1lb) butane
1.81kg (4lb) butane
2.72kg (6lb) butane
■ Campingaz cylinders are painted blue

Note: *Only the 2.72kg (type 907) butane cylinder is a practical proposition for motorcaravanning. The two smaller cylinders might be kept for emergency back-up to operate a cooker burner, but they are really intended for backpacking camping trips.*

Gaslow owner-refillable cylinders
6kg (13.2lb) propane
11kg (24.3lb) propane
■ Gaslow cylinders are coloured yellow

Left: Sold with a date stamp on the collar, Gaslow's cylinders have a 15-year warranty and an exchange facility.

Below: Several configurations are possible and this Gaslow installation has a manual rather than an automatic changeover.

a gas-powered car would be for refilling. However, since LPG stations are not always easy to find, some owners have only *one* refillable Gaslow cylinder installed and this is accompanied by a portable dealer-exchange cylinder.

CYLINDER STATE

Assessing the amount of gas remaining in some cylinders can be difficult and several retro-fit devices are sold to give an indication of the 'fill level'.

Some owners monitor consumption by weighing a full cylinder on bathroom scales before it is put into commission.

The information is noted down or recorded on a label that an owner attaches to the cylinder. Since the quantity of gas in a full cylinder is expressed in weight, it is easy to calculate what proportion of the gross figure is gas and what proportion relates to the weight of the empty cylinder (called the 'tare' weight). When later embarking on trips with a part-empty cylinder, subsequent checks using accurate bathroom scales indicate how much

Left: In order to track the declining amount of gas, weigh a full cylinder before it is put into commission.

Right: The internal locker in a van conversion must be effectively sealed from the living quarters.

Far right: Gas drop-out holes in some motorcaravan lockers are far too easily obscured; this one is much better than most.

Far right: Even this short wheelbase 2006 Orian Gemini was equipped with a gas locker large enough to house two cylinders.

weight has been lost since a cylinder was new, thereby revealing what weight of gas remains.

In the case of a cylinder's tare weight, Calor indicates this on the aluminium collar mounted near the connection as shown in the earlier illustration. The only unhelpful feature is the fact that tare weight is expressed in pounds and ounces. **Note:** *The formula for converting this to kilograms and a sample calculation was given earlier when assessing the weight-saving benefit of a Calor Lite cylinder.*

To produce a quicker indication of how much gas is left in a cylinder, some products are fitted with a float and an inspection gauge. Others have translucent sides and the level of the liquefied gas is clearly evident. Alternatively, the gauges marketed by Gaslow provide a visual indication of a cylinder's supply capabilities. However, gas appliances need to be operating before one of Gaslow's gauges can provide this information.

Storage

The design of a motorcaravan gas locker should incorporate an effective means of securing a cylinder and there are distinct disadvantages if there is insufficient room to accommodate a back-up supply cylinder. A few small motorcaravans only have single cylinder lockers, which is most unsatisfactory. Moreover, many van conversions only have *internal* access to their gas cylinder locker.

In this case, an access door must be carefully constructed and fitted with a gas-proof seal to ensure that the locker is completely sealed-off from the living area. In addition, it is good practice to construct a compartment that is lined with thin galvanised steel sheeting. The location of a gas locker should be marked with an approved red label depicting its function, and the locker must have substantial drop-out ventilation at the lowest point.

In the case of coachbuilt motorcaravans, it is usually relatively straightforward to construct a gas cylinder locker with external access. These compartments vary in size and most are large enough to accommodate a pair of 6kg Calor cylinders.

This is a job-specific enclosure and electrical products such as a leisure battery or a light should never be installed in a gas locker. Leaks *can* occur at a cylinder valve, and if a spark is generated when coupling the terminals of a battery, there might be an explosion. **Note:** *Sealed LED illumination has sometimes been used and the connections for the fitting are formed outside of the compartment.*

On returning home, many owners remove gas cylinders from a vehicle as a precautionary measure. This is logical, but the storage of cylinders at home introduces further safety issues. Under no circumstances should cylinders be left in a cellar because leaking gas would have no means of escaping. Moreover, *Gas Safety Regulations (Installation & Use)* clearly state that propane cylinders must not be stored inside any dwellings; nor should they be stored anywhere that lacks low-level ventilation outlets. A shed or outhouse might prove suitable, but it is safer to adopt the practice of gas suppliers whose cylinders are kept in a roofed storage cage that is intentionally situated well away from any source of flame. And remember: cylinders must always be stored upright.

Pressure regulation

A key component in a motorcaravan's gas supply system is the regulator. This device ensures that gas is delivered from a cylinder at a stable and constant pressure to suit the fitted appliances. This means a new replacement cylinder will not deliver gas at a higher rate than one which is nearly empty.

Regulators are set at the time of manufacture and must not be dismantled. Inside the sealed casing, a diaphragm moves up or down to operate a lever mechanism that controls the flow of gas. There is *nothing* to adjust, which is why regulators are sealed at the time of manufacture. They give several years service, but if one gets damaged, replace it. Some specialists advise you to change a regulator as a matter of course every three years.

Gas supply arrangements in motorcaravans built towards the end of 2003 underwent a radical change. The alterations were prompted by an obvious need to standardise practices in all European Community member states. Changes were as follows:

a) European Norm (EN)12864:2001 led to the publication in March 2002 of BS EN 12864:2001, which is the official English language version. This particularly focusses on regulators.
b) European Norm (EN)1949:2002 led to the publication in September 2002 of BS EN 1949:2002, which is the official English language version. This specifies LPG installations, including pressure regulation.

Note: *Information on recent codes of practice is given on the opening page of this chapter.*

It took many months to get these standards agreed and published, and also took time to manufacture new gas products. However, a few German motorcaravans were quick off the mark and their motorcaravans released in the summer of 2003 were already fitted with new systems. In Britain, the National Caravan Council's (NCC) member-manufacturers were required to implement the new systems from 1 September 2003 – which effectively means the 2004 model ranges. Many non-member manufacturers also elected to adopt the new standards even though compliance was not obligatory.

Moreover, there is no requirement for pre-2004 models to be altered, so there are now two distinct systems in use. There are many pre-2004 motorcaravans that employ cylinder-mounted, gas-specific regulators: there are also more recent models with a permanently installed dual-gas regulator that forms an integral part of the supply system. Since this manual is compiled to assist owners of new and older vehicles, the strengths and weaknesses of both systems are described here in detail.

CYLINDER-MOUNTED REGULATORS

Until 1 September 2003, when Britain's 2004 models were introduced, anyone purchasing a new motorcaravan was obliged to buy a regulator to suit the fitting on the cylinder that he or she intended to use. These regulators are compact, inexpensive and specific to either butane or propane.

(**Note:** *The term 'cylinder-mounted regulator' is used in this manual to differentiate these products*

Technical Tips

Cylinder-mounted regulators

- Remember to buy a supply of sealing washers if you use a Calor screw-on butane cylinder-mounted regulator. Contrary to popular belief, the washer that comes in the black screw-on blanking cap that you get with a new cylinder must not be transferred for use in a regulator. It is not made of a suitable material.
- A cylinder-mounted butane regulator is rated at 11.2 inch water gauge (28m bar); a propane regulator is rated at 14.8 inch water gauge (37m bar). So if a service engineer connects a glass U-tube holding water to a butane supply, the pressure is sufficient to force the water 11.2 inches up the tube; propane would force the water 14.8 inches up the tube. The device which employs this water-gauge test principle is called a manometer.
- A regulator has a tiny hole in the casing. If this becomes blocked, the diaphragm is unable to move inside. The problem sometimes occurs in windy and dusty conditions. A similar situation arises in winter if moisture gets into the breather hole and then freezes. When this happens, the diaphragm can get stuck in its fully open position. Should you find that the flame on a cooker becomes far higher than normal, this 'over-gassing' situation is nearly always the result of a regulator malfunction.

Sealing washers for this type of regulator must be changed periodically and are sold in packs.

The sealing cap washer supplied with this type of cylinder is NOT suitable for use on a regulator.

The label on this cylinder-mounted propane regulator confirms its 37mbar output pressure.

A regulator will fail to work properly if the breather hole on its casing gets blocked.

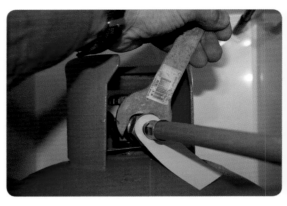

from the 'fixed regulators' whose introduction was prompted by the 2001 and 2002 standards mentioned above.)

Cylinder-mounted regulators are made to suit particular appliances. In Britain, for example, gas appliances in 2003 and earlier models were designed and built to run on gas supplied at a pressure of 28–37mbar. Accordingly, a cylinder-mounted butane regulator delivers gas at a pressure of 28mbar and a propane regulator delivers gas at a pressure of 37mbar. However, in Germany, the jets fitted in appliances required gas to be delivered at a higher pressure. For that reason, imported German motorcaravans sold in Britain prior to summer 2003 had to be fitted with replacement gas appliances that suited the lower pressures adopted in British motorcaravans.

That aside, it had been the practice for a regulator to be coupled directly to the top of a cylinder. The trouble is that there are so many different types of cylinder fittings.

Standardisation of some kind was clearly needed, which was why the new European Norms (ENs) were introduced. Without doubt, the revised supply system certainly helps anyone travelling abroad because non-British gas cylinders can be easily connected to a British motorcaravan merely by purchasing the appropriate coupling hose. However, owners of pre-2004 models cannot have their motorcaravan fitted with this revised gas system without major alterations.

As it happens, many motorcaravanners wouldn't want to do this anyway and are thoroughly content with the safe, simple, inexpensive cylinder-mounted regulators which have served them well for many years. Here are some of their key features:

1 When a regulator fits directly to a cylinder, its design includes a ribbed nozzle to accept a length of low pressure flexible hose for coupling to the nozzle on the metal pipes of the gas supply system. The hose should be secured using hose clips.
2 The Calor butane and propane cylinders with threaded couplings are made with a reverse thread. This means that to tighten a coupling, the flanged nut on the regulator has to be turned anti-clockwise. A spanner is also needed and you can buy an inexpensive one at an accessory shop. However, these don't always have the rigidity to undo a really tight connection – especially on a propane cylinder.
Note: Gaslow can now supply 'spanner-less' propane coupling hose that is fitted with a red hand-wheel.
3 To connect to a propane cylinder, the regulator is manufactured with a carefully machined threaded insert (male – sometimes called a 'pole' fitting), which has to engage tightly in the receiving socket (female) of the cylinder. No washer is used so there must be a close metal-to-metal register to achieve a leak-proof connection.
4 There are various types of butane coupling:
   ■ A Calor screw-on butane regulator to suit 4.5kg cylinders – for which an open-ended spanner is needed.

Disconnecting a 541 regulator from a 7kg Calor Gas butane cylinder

When the regulator switch is in the 6 o'clock position, the gas supply is turned ON.

To stop the gas flow, turn the switch to the 9 o'clock OFF position; wait for all gas flames to go out.

With the switch in the OFF position, the disconnecting lever can be lifted and the regulator removed.

The orange safety cap must always be replaced – even if the gas cylinder is empty.

If all new motorcaravans were equipped with 30mbar wall-mounted regulators in accordance with EN 1949:2002, gas installations in leisure vehicles from European Community member states would be standardised. This strategy has met with a favourable response from almost all manufacturers. Surprisingly, however, a few German motorcaravans have continued to be equipped with a 30mbar *cylinder-mounted* regulator rather than a wall-mounted product; inevitably this would fit only one of the many variations of cylinder coupling. The 2006 Dethleffs Esprit is one example and this range of motorcaravans has been imported and sold in the UK.

■ A Calor clip-on butane regulator with on/off control to suit 7kg and 15kg cylinders.
■ A Campingaz butane regulator with on/off control to suit threaded couplings.

5 Calor propane cylinders and Calor 4.5kg butane cylinders are the only types to have a hand wheel on the top for opening or closing the gas supply valve. The larger butane Calor cylinders just have a clip-on coupling and this means that a control tap has to form part of the regulator.

6 A Campingaz regulator is also made with a control tap. However, many people buy an adaptor (made with a control tap) from a dealer to pair-up with their Calor 4.5kg butane cylinder-mounted regulator.

7 Check the accompanying photographs and Technical Tips panel for further information.

PERMANENT 'UNIVERSAL' REGULATORS

The attempt to harmonise the gas systems fitted in motorcaravans throughout Europe was well-intentioned and two important changes were made. Firstly, the operating pressures of appliances running on butane and propane had to be brought in line throughout EC countries. Secondly, it was considered necessary for all new motorcaravans to be equipped with a permanently mounted regulator that would, a) serve the standardised appliances, and b) accept either butane or propane without need for adjustment.

Meeting the technical requirements was onerous, but 'universal' butane/propane regulators were designed and manufactured by CLESSE (for Comap UK), GOK (for Truma UK), and RECA (for the Cavagna Group). A motorcaravan manufacturer has to couple these directly to the copper or steel supply pipe-work and mount the regulator in a gas cylinder locker.

In addition to accepting butane and propane, the output from one of these regulators must

Coupling-up directly to non-Calor cylinders

One of the alternatives for a Campingaz 907 butane cylinder is to fit a purpose-made Campingaz regulator with on/off control.

Another alternative on a Campingaz 907 cylinder is an adaptor that offers a threaded coupling to accept this type of cap nut.

This propane 37mbar regulator fits the push-on connection of a BP Gas Light cylinder for coupling to systems prior to 1 September 2003.

Gaslow sells a wide range of regulators and this adaptor type fits Norwegian, Spanish, Portuguese, and Southern Irish cylinders.

Left: These three makes of universal regulator complied with the recommendations regarding dual-gas, wall-mounted products.

Left: Recognising that spanners can get lost, Gaslow now offer a high-pressure propane hose that employs a red hand-wheel tightening facility instead. The example here has been coupled to a Gaslow pressure gauge that also has a hand-wheel.

Technical Tips

Flexible hose

- This is made from a special composition to comply with BS EN specifications. It is not rubber.
- There should only be one flexible hose in the entire system – to couple up with the gas cylinder. Elsewhere, metal pipes have to be fitted and copper is the most common material.
- In a pre-2004 system, a low-pressure hose is pushed onto ribbed unions (nozzles), but the standards recommend that hose clips are used to secure the hose tightly.
- Flexible hoses deteriorate very little when kept in stock by an accessory supplier. In use, however, it is affected by LPG and will need changing periodically. It is also affected by ultraviolet light, for example when a cylinder is used in sunlight to serve a gas barbecue.
- The hose bears a date to indicate when it left the factory; this may be a year or so before you purchase it from a dealer, depending on stock turnover.
- It is important to note the precise date when a new length of hose is installed. The *Calor Gas Dealer Directory 1995* recommends that it is replaced at intervals of five years, or more frequently if there is evidence of deterioration.

Right: Flexible gas hose is stamped with a date on the side which indicates when it was manufactured.

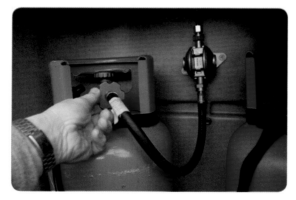

Right: After 2003, a butane/propane regulator is fixed to a wall and a factory-made high-pressure hose is needed to couple-up with the cylinder.

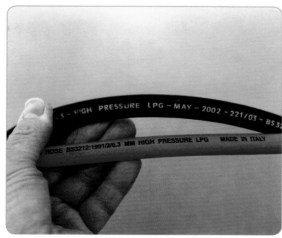

Right: Motorcaravans built to the 2002 gas standards must have high pressure coupling hose; this is made in several colours but it's always appropriately stamped on the side.

Far right: High-pressure hose cannot use standard hose clips; it has to use factory-fitted bonded or crimped couplings.

comply with the standardised European pressure of 30mbar. In addition, gas appliances fitted in motorcaravans equipped with one of these regulators have to be manufactured and fitted with a data plate to confirm that they are built to operate at 30mbar. Retro-fitting a permanently mounted universal regulator to a pre-2004 motorcaravan model is not approved by specialist gas engineers. The Calor Gas leaflet *New Requirements for LPG in Caravans,* distributed in 2003, states: 'The gas pressures of the new regulator and your existing installation are NOT compatible. You should continue to use the appropriate cylinder-mounted regulator...'

USING A MOUNTED UNIVERSAL REGULATOR

To use the post-2004 system, an owner has to purchase a special coupling hose – sometimes called a 'pig-tail' connector – to link up the chosen cylinder to the permanently mounted regulator.

This will subsequently convey gas coming from the cylinder at *high pressure* and is more expensive than a clipped length of low-pressure hose used in the pre-2004 system. A pigtail connector comprises high-pressure hose and bonded or crimped couplings, which are factory-fitted.

A hose-clip system would *not* be acceptable. In addition, the new standards specify a permitted maximum length of 450mm (about 18in), unless the cylinders are stowed on a pull-out tray. Where a sliding tray is used, a hose up to a maximum length of 750mm (about 30in) is permitted. In reality, sliding tray systems are uncommon, although they *are* fitted on some Dethleffs coachbuilt motorcaravans.

These connectors are well-made, reasonably priced, and versions are available to suit the cylinders sold in a number of European countries.

However, with so many different types of cylinder, there is still a need to buy adaptors to suit less popular couplings.

An important benefit of this system is that you can obtain cylinders in countries you would like to visit and only need to purchase the appropriate coupling hose. Under the former system, which used cylinder-mounted regulators, you had to purchase a new regulator as well. The only problem that could arise

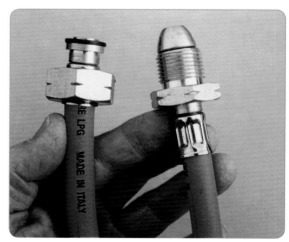

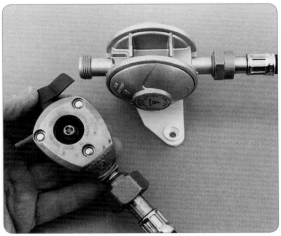

Far left: Under the most recent gas standards, connecting hoses are made to suit cylinders used in many European countries.

Left: Unfortunately, there are so many different cylinder couplings that adaptors are occasionally needed in post-2003 gas installations

when touring through several countries is the fact that you might start collecting a variety of different gas cylinders, together with coupling hoses.

CHANGEOVER SYSTEMS

Running out of gas is always inconvenient. Even if you have a back-up cylinder, the business of disconnecting an empty cylinder and coupling-up its replacement is unpleasant in the dark, especially if it's raining. It is also a nuisance if a meal is being cooked or you need to keep the heating on. This is why a changeover system is useful – especially a completely automatic one.

Changeover products are available from Gaslow, whose manual and automatic systems have been used in conjunction with transferable regulator systems for many years. Products have also been offered in Truma's range of gas accessories.

GAS BLOCKAGES AND STARVATION

The idea of installing a wall-mounted regulator and high-pressure coupling hose made sense when it was first introduced in 2004 motorcaravans, but unexpected issues subsequently arose. A number of touring caravan and motorcaravan owners found that their vans sometimes suffered from gas starvation. It is difficult to know the extent of this problem but the NCC estimated that it was occurring in 4% of models.

Preliminary investigations showed that wall-mounted regulators in vans troubled by blockages were not working properly, and an 'oily substance' was getting into their regulating mechanism. The liquid was also found in some of the adjacent hoses and pipes.

Since liquefied petroleum gas is an oil-related product, some investigators speculated that there might be contaminants in the gas itself. However, when samples of the so-called oily liquid were subjected to laboratory analysis, it was found that the 'mystery substance' contained phthalates. These are plasticising agents used in the manufacture of flexible hoses.

Close investigations also revealed that condensation sometimes forms in the short length of *high-pressure* hose that is used to link

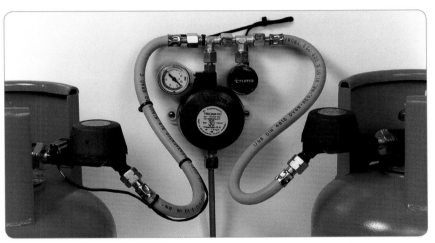

a cylinder to a wall-mounted regulator. It seemed likely that the moisture was absorbing some of the plasticising agent that was being leached out of the hose. Then, as gas was drawn from the cylinder, the liquid subsequently entered the regulator. It seemed likely that this oily liquid was upsetting the regulator's diaphragm and operating mechanism – thereby hindering the passage of gas.

Another interesting point was the fact that neither gas blockages nor contaminating liquids had been observed in pre-2004 touring caravans and motorcaravans. As reported earlier in this chapter, older vans are fitted with a cylinder-mounted

Above: Some motorcaravanners have had an automatic changeover device such as the Truma Trionic fitted.

Left: Models with reported gas starvation had an oily liquid in the supply hose, regulator and fixed pipes.

Tecnical Tip

The problem of gas blockages has been largely remedied, but Truma has continued to research the accumulation of 'oily' residues in gas regulators. This has led to the development of a small component intended to intercept oily substances *before* gas enters a regulator. This 'oil trap' contains a filter, and prototypes were used in monitoring tests during autumn 2011 with the intention of introducing finished products in 2012.

Above: Oily substances entering a regulator can upset its operation.

regulator, which reduces the pressure of gas *at source*. In consequence, gas is delivered at a reduced pressure into the short length of *low-pressure* hose that couples to the main supply pipe. Investigators also speculated that condensation might be more prevalent when gas is delivered at high pressure.

Curiously, researchers were not able to recreate the formation of the 'oily liquid' in laboratory conditions. It was also noted that problems were not being reported when Clesse regulators had been installed. When used by Avondale, Clesse regulators were always mounted high up in a gas locker box.

All these findings and observations prompted the National Caravan Council (NCC) to circulate a statement indicating probable causes of the reported gas blockages. In this publication (January 2007), the Council's technical specialists also suggested curative measures that a dealer should be able to carry out. The recommendations were:

■ To remount a fixed regulator as high as possible in its locker, to achieve a position *above* a cylinder's outlet.
■ To consider fitting an elbow joint on top of a regulator if this improves the chance of increasing its height.
■ To position the high-pressure coupling hose so that it achieves a steep slope, thereby encouraging condensation to drain back into a gas cylinder rather than entering the inlet of a wall-mounted regulator.

As a routine practice, the NCC also recommends that users should always shut down a gas supply at the cylinder when leaving a motorcaravan unused for a while.

In addition to the NCC suggestions, some owners have replaced the flexible high-pressure hose with a semi-flexible stainless steel 'rubber-free' pipe, thereby eliminating the presence of plasticisers. Gaslow supplies this pipe and offers upgrading kits that include a Clesse regulator (guaranteed for up to five years), a 750mm stainless steel flexible butane pipe and an adaptor for propane cylinders.

In addition to these strategies, some regulators have also undergone minor modifications, and there is a sense of optimism that gas starvation shouldn't be a problem in future. This is pleasing, although it is not of much help to members who purchased models manufactured in the early days of wall-mounted regulators. So have a look at the way your regulator has been fitted, and if necessary, consider the advice above.

Of course, if your caravan or motorhome has an old-style cylinder-mounted regulator, gas blockage problems seem unlikely. Similarly, imported German models with 30mbar cylinder-mounted regulators should be trouble-free, too.

Pipework and installation

Moving 'downstream' from the cylinder, regulator and flexible coupling hose, a gas system is built using rigid pipes – copper being the most popular material. The following points about a supply system should be noted:

To avoid a serious accident, neither the rigid gas supply system nor the connections to gas appliances should be modified, repaired or coupled-up by an unqualified person. In the *Calor Caravan Check Scheme* booklet (May 1995 edition) it states: *'Gas installation is an expert's job and by law must only be undertaken by an experienced gas fitter.'*

This principle is endorsed here and the following technical descriptions are provided for information only. In practice, the task of connecting up copper gas pipe using a proprietary pressure fitting is not difficult – particularly for anyone familiar with similar pressure fittings used in domestic plumbing; but an inexperienced person will not know how much to tighten a coupling to achieve a leak-free joint. Over-tightening can deform the pipe and a leak is inevitable. This is also the case if the coupling is under-tightened. It's a job to leave to a qualified LPG fitter.

Copper pipe for gas systems is made in the following sizes:

- 5mm (^{3}/$_{16}$in) outside diameter (OD) = feed to a gas lamp as used in historic models
- 6mm (^{1}/$_4$in) OD = feed to many types of appliance (such as the fridge)
- 8mm/10mm (^{5}/$_{16}$in) OD = main trunk feed in a motorcaravan; feed for space heating appliances

Note: *Some fittings designed for metric pipes will not fit imperial pipes.*

Pressure couplings are made to suit specific pipe diameters, and there are reducing fittings because a branch supply normally uses a narrower diameter pipe than the main trunk-way. The accompanying diagram shows the key components such as the 'olive' and the 'cap nut'. *The Dealer Information Booklet*, published by Calor Gas, points out that jointing compound should not be used. Jointing compound is only intended to seal thread-to-thread couplings.

Bending copper gas pipe is often done by hand; but for more precise work, especially when forming a tight bend, a pipe-bending tool is used. This supports the walls of the pipe and prevents kinking. It follows the same principle of operation as a pipe bender does for domestic copper water pipes.

As regards the final coupling to appliances, this often employs a thread-to-thread union rather than a compression fitting. In this instance, a special LPG jointing paste is required to seal the threads; Calortite is one such product.

In modern installations, it is also necessary for individual appliances to be controlled by a separate isolation valve. If an oven were to develop a fault on holiday, for example, the supply to this appliance could be completely shut-off while other appliances remain in use.

Left: Compression fittings have three principal items: the component itself, a cap nut and an olive.

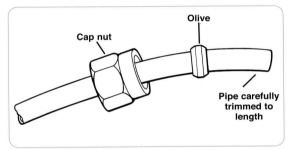

Left: When connections are formed, the cap nut is fitted on the supply pipe first, followed by the olive. The pipe is then inserted into the coupling as far as the stop point and the cap nut tightened.

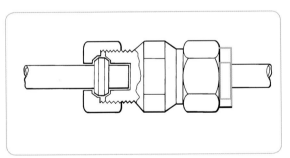

Left: As a cap nut is tightened, the olive bears harder against the shoulder of the fitting and is squeezed inwards, gripping the gas pipe tightly.

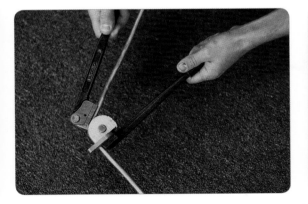

Far left: Bending copper gas pipe can be done by hand; but a pipe-bending tool is used for more precise work, especially when forming acute angles.

Left: In a modern installation, isolation valves are fitted so that individual gas appliances can be controlled separately.

Versions of Gaslow gauges

To suit motorcaravans with pre-2004 supply systems, there are cylinder-mounted regulators that incorporate a Gaslow gauge.

The connection on this butane Gaslow gauge fits the threaded outlet on a Calor 4kg cylinder.

This propane gauge is paired with a propane high-pressure hose to couple-up to a wall-mounted regulator.

If you have a twin-cylinder system with a manual changeover, this gauge links with both hoses.

Installing and using an Alde detector

The red button on an Alde detector is pressed down in order to carry out a leak test.

Depression of the red button causes gas to be diverted via the liquid chamber below.

Before the device is installed in a run of gas pipe, the plastic reservoir has to be unscrewed.

The reservoir is then filled with a glycol mixture to prevent it freezing in cold weather.

Safety Note: *The installation of an Alde leak detector must only be carried out by a quaified gas fitter.*

LEAK DETECTION

DIY enthusiasts should not undertake work on gas supply systems, but an owner should ensure that a system is safe and working correctly. Anxious to know that a gas supply is in good condition, some owners arrange for a leak-detection device to be fitted. Similarly, if reassurance is needed that couplings are sound, competent owners with practical interests sometimes check them using a leak-detection liquid.

Before carrying out an inspection, make sure that cigarettes and naked flames are extinguished. Check that all appliances are off and then switch on the supply at the cylinder. If there is any hint of a gas smell, continue with extreme caution. Systematically smear a coupling, or a group of adjacent couplings, with either a proprietary leak-detection product or diluted washing-up liquid. When this has been applied, check for bubbles, which reveal that a joint has a leak. It is usual to apply the mixture with a small brush and hold your fingers around the joint to prevent the fluid running away. If you have any doubts at all about the integrity of a coupling, switch off the system at the supply cylinder and get a gas fitter to tighten or replace the faulty fitting before operating the system again. It is also wise to have the complete system pressure-tested. Remember to request a signed and dated certificate to verify the results of the test procedure.

Note: *The use of diluted washing-up liquid for checking gas joints is common practice. However, this product contains salts that can corrode some of the components used in gas systems. If a proprietary leak-detection fluid is not available, use the alternative approach, but ensure that all traces of it are carefully removed from fittings, using clean water and a suitable cloth.*

Regarding routine monitoring of a system, a convenient way to do this is to have a Gaslow gauge fitted at or near the gas supply cylinder. These products were mentioned earlier because they are also used to indicate the pressure in a cylinder. The test procedure is as follows:

- Turn off *all* gas appliances.
- Turn *on* the gas supply cylinder; the gauge should show a green segment.
- Turn *off* the gas supply at the cylinder.
- Provided there is no leak, gas will be held in the supply pipes and the gauge will continue to show the green segment.
- Using a standard Gaslow product, if the gauge remains green for at least a minute, the system is considered sound; over a longer period, the gauge will eventually return to the red sector.

Another way to monitor this long-term is to have an Alde leak detector connected into the supply pipe by a qualified gas fitter. This should be installed as near to the supply source as possible because it confirms the integrity of connections 'downstream'

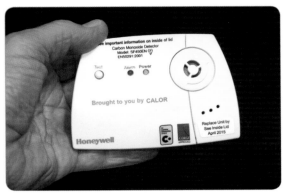

Far left: The Strikeback gas alarm from Van Bitz draws its 12V supply from the leisure battery.

Left: The carbon monoxide alarm manufactured by Honeywell is sold in the UK by Calor Gas Ltd.

from its location. In view of this, it cannot indicate 'upstream' faults in items like a flexible coupling pipe to the supply cylinder.

The device incorporates a glass-sighting chamber filled with a glycol liquid that doesn't freeze in low temperatures. To conduct the test, you switch the gas supply on and turn off all appliances. When a red test button on the top of the detector is depressed, a flow of bubbles in the sighting chamber shows that gas is escaping somewhere in the system.

Different again are leak detectors that give an audible warning when a sensor detects gas. These types of device are often fitted by DIY owners and a piercing siren is activated whenever gas is detected. Products like the Strikeback alarm from Van Bitz are installed in many motorcaravans, and these have good sensitivity.

When the author was applying a small amount of cellulose paint to a rusting component inside his motorcaravan, the Strikeback alarm suddenly burst into life. It hadn't been anticipated that gas contained in an aerosol spray-can would also trigger this alarm so promptly.

Units like this have to be connected to a 12V DC supply and should be fixed to a secure base in an appropriate location. Their main function is to issue a warning of an LPG leak, and since this gas is denser than air, the alarm should be fitted low down in a van.

Carbon monoxide detectors are different in their detection function. These detect CO that can be emitted by a faulty gas appliance – typically when the burners need adjustment. Any burner with an exposed gas flame – such as those on a hob or a grill – could pose a serious threat to the wellbeing of occupants. Nowadays, the burners in appliances such as space heaters are completely 'room-sealed'. This doesn't mean that they cannot move out of place; nor does it imply that they cannot emit CO gas. However, exposed flames need particular attention because their fumes discharge straight into the living area.

Installation instructions and recommendations regarding the location of warning devices must be checked with care. As stated in the Safety Panel at the commencement of this chapter, all NCC certificated motorcaravans built from 1 September 2011 are obliged to be equipped with a carbon monoxide alarm as a standard item of equipment.

Cooking appliances

Cooking facilities in a British-built motorcaravan include a hob as standard; larger models have domestic sized ovens as well. As a general rule, a grill is included as part of the hob.

Motorcaravans built abroad are usually different. For instance, the overall space devoted to food preparation is usually much smaller in motorcaravans designed in mainland Europe. When checking the appliances, you'll also find that a grill is seldom included; presumably these are made for people who don't care for toast. The contrasts are sufficiently acute for the importers of foreign products to fit different appliances in order to make motorcaravan kitchens more acceptable to British clients.

Some imported motorcaravans also lack electronic ignition devices to light their hobs, a

Above: Like many UK coachbuilt motorcaravans, this 2006 Swift Sundance is fitted with a full-size cooker.

Left: A grill is standard in UK motorcaravans, whereas many imported models are not equipped with this facility.

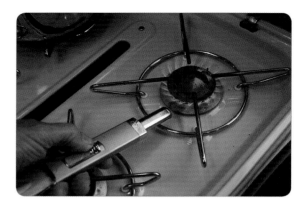

facility that has been commonplace on UK models since the early 1990s. Many Cramer hobs, for example, require an owner to keep a box of matches or a hand-held lighter in the kitchen.

Traditions are obviously different, and it is sometimes suggested that many continental motorcaravanners are disinclined to cook indoors, they instead prefer to eat in restaurants or prepare barbecue food.

COOKER AND KITCHEN SAFETY ISSUES

■ Flame failure devices

Since 1994 it has been mandatory to have a flame failure device (FFD – sometimes called a 'flame supervision device') fitted to each gas burner. If a burner blows out in a draught, the device immediately cuts off its gas supply. One of an FFD's components is a small bi-metallic probe that projects into the flame of a burner. When this is hot, an electric current is generated; this flows to an electromagnetic gas valve, which is held open all the time the probe is hot. However, if a flame is blown out, the probe quickly cools and a current is no longer produced. As a result of this, the electromagnet in the gas valve fails and a small spring closes off the supply.

With this safety system, when you want to light a burner, the spring has to be compressed to open its gas valve. This is done by depressing the control knob and holding it down until the newly lit flame has made the probe hot again. When a system fails to operate properly, it is often found that the probe has become dislodged and is no

longer achieving close contact with a burner flame. A probe can also get dirty, especially if a saucepan has boiled over. Alternatively, the general vibration in a motorcaravan occasionally causes one of the electrical connections to loosen. This results in a break in continuity between the probe assembly and the electromagnet that opens up the gas valve. Re-tightening the connections on both ends of the metal linking conductor often solves the problem.

■ Appliance approval

Since 1 January 1996, it has been mandatory for all gas appliances installed in new motorcaravans to meet standards laid down in the EC Gas Appliance Directive 90/396. Approval is confirmed by the CE label, which stands for *Commonauté Européene*. Other European standards concerned with gas systems and ventilation requirements include the following: EN 721 Ventilation requirements in leisure accommodation vehicles; EN 722-1 Liquefied fuel heating in caravans; and EN 1949 LPG Installation in leisure accommodation vehicles.

■ Carbon monoxide issues

If a gas flame flickers yellow and soot is left on saucepans, this is usually a sign of an incorrect gas/air mixture. The condition is symptomatic of incomplete combustion, and when it occurs, there may be a release of carbon monoxide. This can be serious so a competent gas engineer should check the appliance. The fault *must* be remedied before the burner is used again.

■ Fire risk

A hob must not be used to heat a motorcaravan. Unlike a room-sealed heating appliance, it doesn't have a specially designed flue and its flames are exposed. If a burner is alight, make sure there is a kettle or pan in position. Although there are minimum distances required between a hob and ceiling level cupboards, these compartments soon get extremely hot if a the flame on a burner is left uncovered.

Also recognise that the diameter of a pan or kettle must be related to the size of a burner. If you use a pan that extends more than a centimetre or two beyond a burner's pan support grid, the flame can be diverted horizontally outwards. In some cases the spread of the flame can burn the rubber caps covering the screws that secure a hob in place.

Safety

■ Make sure your kitchen is equipped with a fire blanket and a dry powder fire extinguisher (which is well within its user expiry date).

■ Check that the fire blanket and extinguisher are easy to reach *without* being too close to the stove.

■ Use a fire blanket on fat fires. If it isn't fitted with holding tapes, roll it over at the sides to cover your fingers – thus providing protection from the flames. It is well worth practising this holding technique.

Right: Part of a flame failure device is a small probe that heats-up in a burner and creates electricity that holds open a gas supply valve.

Far right: Although cupboards are placed well above a hob, don't leave a burner alight without it being covered by a saucepan.

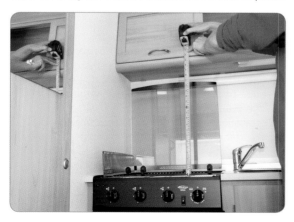

When this has been reported, it is usually found that an ill-advised owner has been taking large domestic saucepans from home and using them on the small burners in a motorcaravan.

Ventilation

Ventilation is essential in a kitchen and a professional manufacturer will have installed permanent vents. These are needed to provide oxygen for combustion and to create an escape route for the products of combustion. Additionally, the ventilators help with the removal of the steam that leads to condensation. A good improvement project is to fit a fan-assisted cooker hood over a hob. A model manufactured by Dometic helps to extract steam by venting it outside.

Safety checks

Like all gas systems and related equipment, cooking appliances *must* be checked periodically by a competent gas engineer in accordance with manufacturers' instructions. This is one of the tasks that should come within an annual service operation. Apart from cleaning, there are no servicing tasks that an owner can carry out.

Space heating appliances

It was on safety grounds that open-burner 'gas fires' ceased to be used in motorcaravans. Exposed burners are considered unsatisfactory for the following reasons:

- something could fall onto the exposed flame
- oxygen is taken from the living space while the heater is in operation
- waste products from combustion are discharged into the living area
- in extreme cases, a faulty burner could produce carbon monoxide
- when LPG burns, vapour is emitted and condensation forms on cold surfaces

In response to this, motorcaravan heating appliances are now referred to as 'space heaters' rather than 'fires', and they must be 'room sealed'. In consequence, the burners are housed in a compartment that is completely sealed off from the living area. Combustion air is drawn directly into this sealed enclosure from outside, and in a similar way, exhaust gases are subsequently returned to the exterior via a flue.

Heat generated in this combustion chamber then has to be directed into the living area. This is achieved by directing the hot air through a heat exchanger, which is designed to release its heat as efficiently as possible. Many heat exchangers are therefore manufactured with moulded fins – rather like the fins on an air-cooled motorcycle engine.

In other words, it is a metal heat exchanger that warms the air in a living space rather than the gas flames directly. To assist in the distribution of heat, many appliances also have a fan that drives the warmed air along a network of ducts. Outlets in the ducting then ensure that heat is released at key points. Rooms that are usually closed off from the main living spaces, such as a shower cubicle, can then receive a share of the warm air coming from a space heater. Of course, this presumes that a flap on the heating duct has been opened.

If an older motorcaravan is purchased, it is not unusual to find that it has been equipped with a wall-mounted Carver space heater matched with a 12V Fanmaster to distribute the air around the

Far left: When a large saucepan was used on this burner, the spread of flame set this screw's rubber cover alight.

Far left: This display using a Truma room-sealed space heater shows how both the combustion air intake and the exhaust flue are ducted directly to the outside.

Left: The heat exchanger in a room-sealed appliance usually has fins moulded on its casing to release its heat efficiently.

Trumatic S Series heater detail

Many UK motorcaravans are fitted with Trumatic S series space heaters as standard; they can also be retrofitted to replace products like Carver's.

In this cut-away model used for training purposes, the removal of the upper part of its heat exchanger shows the ignition burner alight but not the main burner.

On modern space heaters the burners are completely enclosed in a sealed heat exchanger. To confirm that a burner's alight the flame can be checked through a viewing port.

The control wheel on top of a heater is coupled to this assembly by a steel spindle. A copper thermal sensor tube controls the main burner and mustn't get covered by carpet.

This heater has been removed and inverted for servicing. Operation is often upset when spiders/moths get into the copper (or stainless steel) air intake.

The air intake is now removed for cleaning-out. The main burner is on the left; the ignition burner has a spark igniter, and the tip of a thermocouple element is visible at the rear.

To run the automatic ignition system a small battery is fitted which triggers a microswitch. One of the tasks during a full service is to replace the battery and clean its contacts.

The electric auxiliary Ultraheat unit fits to the rear of a heat exchanger and helps raise the temperature quickly; many motorcaravanners leave it on a low setting at night.

living space. This Fanmaster addition has a 1.5-Amp, 18-Watt motor protected with a 5-Amp fuse.

Later Fanmaster products went a step further to include a mains-operated electrical element that draws 8 Amps at 2kW; so the product does more than just *distribute* heat with a fan. It also *warms* the air using a built-in 230V heating element that produces a manually controllable output ranging from 0.1 to 2kW. However, there is one point that must not be ignored: Carver space heaters fitted with this later Fanmaster must NOT be operated using gas and 230V heating simultaneously. You either use the gas heating option or the mains heating facility.

Carver products were deservedly popular, but Truma subsequently purchased the gas appliance division in autumn 1999, and products like the Fanmaster were discontinued. However, Truma sold spare parts for most of Carver's products for several years beyond that date. Pre-used components can also be sourced at specialist breakers, such as The Caravan Centre at Blaenavon in South Wales.

The operation of a wall-mounted Truma Ultraheat is similar to the Carver products, although this appliance *can* operate on gas and its 230V element simultaneously. This is achieved by affixing a 230V element directly to the heat exchanger instead of it forming part of a fan assembly fitted to the rear of the casing. Its output is:

- 500, 1,000 or 2,000W from the electric element
- 3.4kW from the gas burner
- 5.0kW from the combined systems

For a quick warm-up, both gas and electric systems *can* be used together. However, when the heater reaches 2kW the electric heating element is switched off automatically. This is a safety feature of the Ultraheat system. However, Truma points out that to enjoy the full benefit of the 230V option, you need to stay on a site where the hook-up offers a minimum supply of 10 amps – which is quite substantial.

To give a closer insight into this type of Truma heater, a detailed illustrated panel alongside shows some key features of a Trumatic S Series heater.

Many owners of older motorcaravans also add new or extended ducting systems. The task can be fairly straightforward using Truma components. Hiding the ducting is the main challenge, although it *is* possible to obtain specially reinforced sections to take a duct under the floor without too much loss of heat.

There are other methods of heating, too. Some large motorcaravans have 'wet systems' that use radiators. The 3000 Compact central heating system from Alde, for example, has been installed in Buccaneer motorcaravans. This motorcaravan also incorporates the Alde 2968 engine heat exchanger, which operates in conjunction with a Fiat engine's heating system.

In small motorcaravans, compact heaters are more suitable. These are completely enclosed

Heating appliance care and attention

- There are no servicing tasks on gas heating appliances that unqualified or inexperienced owners should attempt.
- Space and water heating appliances must be checked by a qualified gas engineer in accordance with the manufacturer's instructions – a task which should be carried out as part of an annual habitation service check.
- In addition to checking an appliance, its flue should also receive a safety and efficiency inspection.
- Typical jobs include; confirming that the gas flame pattern is correct and that there are no dust, cobwebs, insects or spiders interfering with the burners, flue system, or combustion chambers. It is always surprising to learn that a spider is able to upset the operation of a gas appliance; filaments of a web across a pilot light can distort the shape of the flame and this can prevent a main burner from igniting. It's the same with a flue. A spider's web spun across a flue near its outlet can sufficiently upset the exhaust efficiency to prevent a space heater switching from the pilot flame to the main burner. For this reason, general cleaning is one of the servicing tasks.
- After an appliance has been checked and serviced, always insist that you are given a written, dated and detailed account of the servicing work that has been carried out.
- Space heaters usually have an automatic cut-out that comes into operation if they overheat. This can occur if all the outlet ducts are closed

If an overheat situation arises on a Carver Fanmaster, the system shuts down. Later the reset button needs activating.

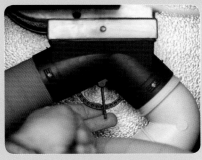

On some of the space heaters from Carver and Truma, the distribution of warm air released into the ducts can be easily adjusted by means of a control lever.

or accidentally obstructed. However, on a Carver Fanmaster there is a reset button, which owners can activate themselves. Firstly, you wait for the appliance to cool down, then open all the outlets and disconnect the mains supply at your consumer unit. After that you have to reset the trip button situated on the side of the fan casing, bearing in mind that in some motorcaravans, access to this part of the unit isn't easy. Then switch the mains supply back on. Truma products have similar overheat safety devices and the owner instructions explain the routines.
- Many space heaters used to have a piezo ignition system where you depress a button to create a spark at the burner. Today, electronic ignition systems have taken over and a wall switch triggers the spark. Regarding compact heaters, the Truma E-series employed electronic ignition as long ago as the 1980s.
- Most ducted systems have two main branches serving opposite ends of a motorhome. However, many owners do not realise that if there is an imbalance in the heat flowing down these branches, the heat distribution can be adjusted using the control lever on the back of a wall-mounted appliance.

(apart from the air intake, air distribution outlet and flue) and an integral fan distributes the warm air. One great benefit of these products is that they can be mounted in lockers and small wardrobes.

Models made by Truma are long established and operate with remarkable efficiency. Ignition is electronic, and in spite of its compact size, the heat output from a Trumatic E2400 model is a noteworthy 2.4kW. Heat from the unit is transmitted through ducting and, like most room-sealed heaters, it can be left on all night. Output is thermostatically controlled to ensure that warmth remains at a consistent level.

Similar products include Propex heaters and the Carver P4 compact blown air unit. The P4 is a self-contained unit featuring a low-profile side wall flue. With 1.2kW or 2.2kW output settings, the specification includes automatic ignition, thermostatic control, and operation on either butane or propane. However, it is no longer available and spare parts are increasingly difficult to obtain.

After forming a co-operative link with Propex, Whale introduced a new gas and 230V space heater in 2010. Then, a year later, the range comprised four compact heaters, two of which are designed for mounting underneath a vehicle so that space can be saved in the living area. Even on the

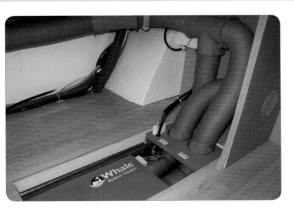

Left: This under-floor version of the Whale gas and electric space heater was fitted by Elddis in one of its 2010 models.

Left: Although DIY enthusiasts shouldn't repair a gas appliance, trained persons like the ease of access to the circuitry on Whale's space heaters.

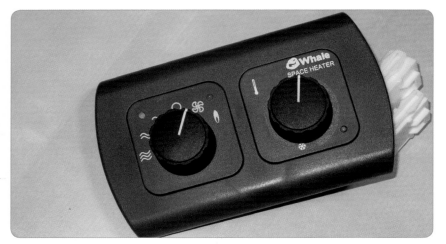

Above: The self-explanatory control panels designed for the Whale space heating appliances are especially easy to use.

Right: Air ducting in 65mm and 75mm is coupled-up to the cold air IN and hot air OUT connections on the heater casing.

models installed indoors, components like the fresh air inlet and the flue do not encroach into the living area – they are simply directed straight through the floor.

As regards the Whale under-floor heaters, these are supplied with a galvanised, sealed and weatherproof casing, and on account of their space-saving features, Elddis installed one of these in a compact 2010 model. Both internal and external types are sold in gas-only versions or in gas *and* 230V models. The electric model has settings of 500W (quiet night-time setting), 1,000W (standard setting) 2,000W (heat boost setting) and a frost-protection setting. However, you cannot run these heaters on gas and electricity simultaneously.

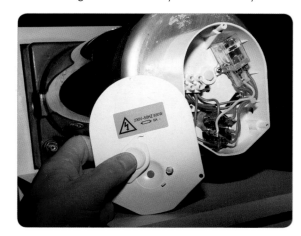

Right: If a Carver Cascade 2 overheats it has an emergency cut-out; a reset button is on the end of the casing.

Water heating appliances

In small 'campervans', where space is at a premium, there often isn't room for a water heater. There usually isn't room for a shower, either. In consequence, the needs of most owners are often met by boiling a kettle.

The situation is different in coachbuilt models and many motorcaravanners simply wouldn't tolerate living without a continuous hot water supply. To fulfil this requirement, two main types of appliance are installed:

1 Stand-alone storage water heaters (*eg* Carver Cascade, Rapide GE, Maxol Malaga, Truma Ultrastore and Whale water heater).
2 Water heaters combined with a space-heating appliance (*eg* Trumatic C ranges, Atwood Confort 3, Alde 3000 Compact).

Note:
■ *American manufacturer Atwood ceased marketing products in Europe in 1997. Spares are now difficult to obtain.*
■ *The National Caravan Council (NCC) has recommended that old instantaneous water heaters with exposed burners should be replaced by an approved storage heater.*

STORAGE WATER HEATERS

These hot water appliances are usually mounted inconspicuously in a cupboard and operated from a remote control panel. Their balanced flue is discreet, and recent models also incorporate a mains heating element. On some models you can use both the gas and electrical elements simultaneously so that hot water is quickly 'on tap'. One of the first storage water heaters to gain widespread interest was the Carver Cascade, launched in the mid-1980s.

The Mk1 Cascade was eagerly received, but it took a long time to drain down its water when frosty weather was expected. The problem was remedied in later models, such as the Cascade 2 Plus, in which an air relief point was added. Another improvement on these gas storage heaters was the introduction of a mains heating element. The first of these was the Cascade 2 Plus GE, which included a 680W mains electricity heating element. The later Cascade Rapide introduced an 830W heating element, and if you had to purchase a tank replacement kit after frost damage, this included a replacement 830W element as standard. Incidentally on the later models, an overheat reset button was situated behind a cover flap, as shown in the accompanying photo.

Notwithstanding the popularity of this appliance in the UK, motorcaravanners were disappointed and surprised when the product was withdrawn from sale. In response to this, a 'virtual replica' was later introduced, and known as the Henry GE water heater. This has all the main features of the former Carver Cascade product and is currently available from Johnnie Longden in Poole, Dorset.

Although Carver Cascades were popular, the Maxol Malaga and its partner the Malaga E with a 230V heating element, were also fitted in the mid-1990s. Today, the Malaga MkIIIG and GE 13.5-litre models, are available from suppliers like C.A.K.

However, it is the Truma Ultrastore that is most often installed in recent motorcaravans manufactured in the UK and mainland Europe. There are 10- and 14-litre versions, both of which can be equipped with an additional 850W (3.7A) electric heating element.

Although these are well-engineered products supported by good after-sales support, the poor level of thermal insulation around the water tank prompted Whale to design an alternative product.

The first Whale water heater was introduced in 2010 and its 13-litre tank was liberally protected with a generous layer of moulded insulation. The product offers either a gas or 230V heating operation and the manufacturer claims that it produces a larger quantity of hot water in 5½ minutes than any similar product.

Of further interest is an optional adaptor wall plate that allows a motorcaravan hitherto equipped with an old Caravan Cascade to be fitted with a new Whale heater without needing major modifications.

Equally unusual is the fact that the appliance is already mounted on a plywood base – so installation work is easier than ever. It is therefore no surprise to learn that several DIY installers have fitted these appliances, even though it is always

recommended that an experienced gas specialist undertakes final gas coupling work.

The angular shape of this water heater lends itself well to installation in a rectangular cupboard and means space wastage is kept to a minimum. Then, to take the space-saving point further, Whale later announced that a smaller 8-litre version would be introduced in 2011. The first impressions of these products are pleasing and the attention paid to insulation and heat retention certainly cannot be ignored.

COMBINED SPACE AND WATER HEATERS

Appliances which integrate space and water heating functions in a single casing are usually fitted in larger vehicles.

For instance the Alde 3000 with its radiator system was fitted in Buccaneer's 1998 models. The Atwood Confort C was fitted to the Murvi Morello in 1996 and 1997 models. The Trumatic C Combi heater has been fitted in several Swift coachbuilt models, such as the 2002 Gazelle F63 High. Upgraded versions of Truma's heaters were also introduced around 2006 and are fitted in many high-specification coachbuilt models, including the Bailey range of motorcaravans introduced in 2011.

Combined space and water heaters are also fitted with a release valve that empties the water heater reservoir automatically when air temperature drops to 2°C. This is a good safety feature,

Above left: This cut-away Ultrastore water heater shows the gas burner and the mains heating elements above.

Above: This Whale heater has a 13L tank, gas and 230V operation and it is pre-mounted on a wooden baseboard.

Above: An adaptor plate is made to fit in a Carver Cascade aperture when a Whale water heater is being fitted in its place.

Far left: The combined heaters from Truma are impressively engineered but are too large for small motorcaravans.

Left: The red drain down button on this Truma Combi heater also activates automatically when temperatures fall to 2°C.

although in certain circumstances an unexpected loss of hot water can be a nuisance. Suffice to say, this facility can be overridden if a motorcaravanner is in residence and monitoring the temperature with care.

Whereas the water heating facility in 'Combi' heaters runs on gas or mains electricity, some models have not been fitted with a 230V *space heating* feature. Some owners discover this too late, with considerable dismay. Normally it's an optional extra that can only be specified at the time of purchase. So if the gas supply runs out, you simply get cold.

OWNER CARE

It is important that a water heater is cleaned and checked as part of an annual habitation service. Together with other gas-operated appliances, servicing and repair work fall outside the scope of DIY endeavour. Draining-down work, however, is different.

Frost can severely damage a water heater, so steps have to be taken if you do not use your motorcaravan for extended periods when the weather is cold.

There are two ways to protect the system from frost. One is to drain down the entire system and leave it empty until the cold weather is over. The other is to fill the water system with a purpose-formulated non-poisonous anti-freeze – but check first that your appliance manufacturer approves this.

Prior to a lay-up period, filling a water system with special anti-freeze is seen as a seasonal task in the United States. In fact, an American winterising product called 'WinterBan' is available in the UK under the Camco accessory range and is available from Recreational Vehicle (RV) specialists such as ABP Leisure. You merely have

to pump a recommended quantity of this fluid into the system and leave it there until you are ready to use your motorcaravan again.

The other option involves draining down a system and leaving it dry during winter storage periods in accordance with its manufacturer's instructions. If you have a Truma Ultrastore, for example, you should:

1 Switch off the water pump.
2 Open all taps, or in the case of lever types, make sure the lever is raised and left in its central position.
3 Open the appliance's safety drain valve and leave in the vertical position.
4 Ensure that water draining outside doesn't cause inconvenience – and be careful if it is still hot.

DIESEL-FUELLED HEATING SYSTEMS

Eberspacher heating systems used in boats and long distance lorries have recently been re-engineered for motorcaravans. Murvi helped with this development work and an Eberspacher system was shown on a Murvi motorcaravan at an Earl's Court Exhibition in 1998. Since then it has become a popular choice of heating by many people ordering a Murvi. Other manufacturers fitting Eberspacher products include Autocruise CH, Auto-Sleepers and Romahome. Diesel heating appliances from Webasto are similar, and several van converters fit the Company's small space heater under a driver's seat.

Eberspacher's Hydronic system is a top-of-the-range installation providing both space and water heating. To explain how it works, it's helpful to liken the product to the heating system fitted in a car. Water heated by a car's engine is diverted to a small radiator behind the dashboard that is fitted with a fan. When the driver operates its blower switch, the fan pushes air through this radiator (often called a heater matrix) and ducts then convey the warmed air to screen outlets, face vents or footwell outlets, according to requirements.

It's the same idea in a hydronic system, except that additional pipes take engine-heated water to similar fan-operated radiators that heat the living area. However, another flow and return pipe is directed to a small copper cylinder, storing water for domestic use. Hot water from the engine is passed through a coiled pipe running down the centre of the cylinder, thus heating the domestic

Right: It is very important to drain off the contents of a water heater when a motorcaravan is not in use during frosty conditions.

Right: The compact warm air heater from Webasto is often installed under a cab seat in small van conversions.

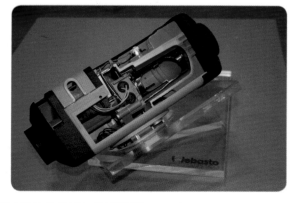

Far right: This Eberspacher Airtronic compact space heater is paired-up with a 230V mains heating unit in the warm air supply duct.

water around the coil. Many people have a similar water-heating cylinder in their homes, which is usually fitted in an airing cupboard. The two gallons of water in an Eberspacher cylinder become extremely hot and a blender valve is fitted to mix cold water into the supply automatically.

From the description so far, you will note that this system can operate only when the engine is running. In fact you don't have to drive far before the domestic water in a motorcaravan is hot; equally, the living area can be heated via the additional heater matrix units while you are driving.

However, it stands to reason that the heating operation described must cease as soon as the engine is switched off. So an Eberspacher Hydronic installation includes a small diesel- or petrol-fuelled heater mounted under the floor or low down in the engine compartment. This is smaller than a shoebox, and its fuel is drawn via a small pipe that has been connected into the vehicle's fuel tank. You switch this unit on when required and it performs the same heating functions as the engine.

A digital control panel provides a wide range of options. This can be programmed so that the heating comes on automatically for a selected period of time, and it can do this on up to three occasions during a 24-hour period on any chosen day(s) of the week. This rolling operating timetable is very helpful when a vehicle is laid-up in winter.

In the summer, you can disregard the space heating function altogether and just select the water heating option. Incidentally, although water heating is normally achieved through the engine or diesel heater, the hot water cylinder can also be fitted with a 230V immersion heater that has to be wired into the mains supply.

An Eberspacher installation can also be linked with a base vehicle's original cab and screen heater, thus augmenting the heat output from outlets in the living area. That is useful in motorcaravans with a cab forming part of the living space, but there is also a benefit from coupling-in the screen vents. It means the system can defrost the screen in advance of departure. Furthermore, you can also select an engine pre-heat programme for easy starting.

To derive the full benefit from these many facilities, a hand-held remote control unit is an optional accessory. This enables a motorcaravanner to switch on the heating during the night without getting out of bed. Equally, if your motorcaravan is parked outside your home, the remote control is powerful enough to activate the heating and the screen-defrost facility from inside the house – even while you are having breakfast.

Eberspacher operating modes are unusually versatile, and these heating systems are also noted for their frugal fuel consumption. Even with the largest 5kW hydronic heater working with maximum fan speed and heat demand, the consumption is listed as 0.62 litres of diesel an hour. On the other hand, a leisure battery with a generous Ah capacity is needed to operate the heating fans. It is also appropriate to point out that an externally fitted hydronic oil-fired heater is noisier in operation than

Oil-fired heating hydronic 12V system

a gas appliance. This is seldom noticed inside a motorcaravan, but could be distracting for someone using a tent on the next pitch.

In addition to Eberspacher's hydronic 4kW and 5kW water and space heaters, the company also supplies compact oil-fired warm-air heaters, fitted by several manufacturers including Romahome and Auto-Sleepers. These are referred to as Airtronic units and mustn't be confused with the water-based Hydronic systems; there are 2.2kW and 4.0kW output versions currently available and these can be discreetly installed in a blanket locker. They provide precise temperature control and, again, a digital timer offers seven-day programming possibilities. A mains heating unit can also be fitted in line with these diesel heating products.

Both Eberspacher and Webasto products have been installed in commercial vehicles and boats for a long time. Now these appliances are providing motorcaravanners with intriguing heating alternatives.

This compact diesel-fueled heater is mounted in the engine compartment to provide heating whenever the engine isn't running.

Hidden in a cupboard is a compact radiator or 'heating matrix' together with a fan that distributes warm air to the interior.

Some of the water is diverted to a coil in a copper cylinder which then heats 2 gallons of domestic water. (There is also a 230V immersion cylinder.)

A panel controls the operation of an Eberspacher system and its timers can be programmed in 24-hour periods over a repeating seven-day pattern.

7 Fresh and Waste Water systems

CONTENTS

Motorcaravans have two separate water systems. One is concerned with the supply of fresh water: the other removes waste water from a sink, wash basin or shower tray. Their operational success depends on efficient components.

Water systems in motorcaravans vary in a number of ways. The type of pump, the taps, the refilling facility, the filter system and the waste water disposal arrangements all differ from model to model.

The supply system

Even the procedure for supplying fresh water and collecting the waste can vary. Most motorcaravans have fixed water tanks, but a few models use portable receptacles instead.

PORTABLE CONTAINERS
It is not unusual to find camper vans that have been built without fixed water tanks simply because they take up too much space. Micro-van conversions and elderly VW campers are examples. In consequence, some motorcaravanners adopt the practices used by owners of UK touring caravans, in which fresh and waste water portable containers are placed on the ground outside the vehicle.

An alternative strategy is to fit one or both of the portable containers indoors – a procedure followed in some of the conversions built by la strada, Middlesex Motorcaravans, Reimo, and Wheelhome.

The use of portable containers rather than a fixed tank certainly makes sense on sites that are not equipped with a motorcaravan service point. It's often far easier to walk to a tap to refill a container than to drive the entire motorcaravan.

Indeed, it is the absence of good motorcaravan service points on sites at home and abroad that

Above: In conversions manufactured by Middlesex Motorcaravans, two fresh water containers and a submersible pump are mounted indoors at the back.

Below: If a site lacks a motorcaravan service point, it is often easier to deal with water matters using portable containers.

Below: This VW van conversion uses external waste and fresh water portable containers.

Far left: Well-equipped sites have a motorcaravan service point that provides easy parking when you need to fill up or empty waste water.

Left: This cut-away display of the 2012 Bailey Approach shows its under-floor fresh and waste water tanks.

Left: On some coachbuilt models, the fresh tank is fitted under one of the seats. **Note:** *To drain this tank down you unscrew its red cap then pull out its overflow tube.*

prompts many owners of motorcaravans built with fixed 'on-board' tanks to carry a length of hose, a plastic water container and a bucket for refilling and emptying tanks.

ON-BOARD WATER TANKS

Notwithstanding these comments, the majority of motorcaravans *are* built with fixed, on-board tanks – one for fresh water, and the other for waste. Incidentally the word 'waste' in this context refers to water discharged from a sink or wash basin. Some people refer to it as 'grey water'. Only large American motorhomes have a special holding tank for sewage as well, which is often described as 'black water'.

There are two options for the location of a fresh water tank; either the tank is mounted below the floor, or it is fitted indoors. Some manufacturers, such as Auto-Sleepers and Bailey motorcaravans, mount both the fresh and waste water tanks under the floor in order not to occupy storage space indoors.

However, there is a disadvantage with this arrangement. In winter, water in externally fitted pipes and tanks soon freezes, which has severe implications if you want to use your motorcaravan during colder times of the year. This is why the second option is often adopted and manufacturers of large coachbuilt motorcaravans usually mount a fresh water tank within the living area.

The subject of winter motorcaravanning, is considered more closely later in the chapter.

Moving to the matter of emptying, the water level in waste and fresh water tanks needs

constant monitoring and it is customary to have a panel mounted in the living area as shown on page 82. Sometimes electronic depth probes are fitted, although any device fitted *inside* a waste tank (which is likely to contain water-borne food particles) can become unreliable. Alternatively, it is possible to install a waste tank that has been fitted with sensor studs instead of long probes, as shown in the accompanying photograph.

If a motorcaravan waste tank isn't fitted with a level indicator, you need to adopt the discipline of emptying it every time you top up the fresh water tank. This should prevent it from becoming overfull.

On the subject of emptying waste tanks, water must be emptied into a purpose-made gully or inspection chamber.

Emptying it on to a grass verge is unacceptable. However, a few sites are starting to offer pitches

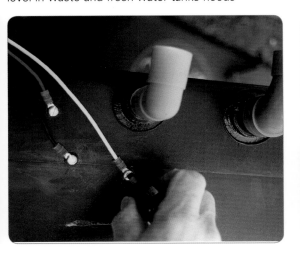

Far left: Some water tanks are fitted with sensor studs which send a reading to a water level display panel.

Left: Waste water disposal facilities are found on well-equipped sites like this one at Crystal Palace.

Right: This campsite in Northern Ireland has several pitches that provide occupants with their own fresh and waste water service points.

that enable occupants to couple-up directly to a fresh water supply and a permanently coupled drainage point.

TANKS AND FROST

When using a motorcaravan in winter, freezing tanks can make life difficult. Not many motorcaravans have the heated double-floor systems described in Chapter 4. However, if an under-floor fresh water tank freezes, at least it is possible to bring in water using a kettle, saucepans, bottles or a portable container. Matters are far worse if your waste water container and its linking pipes freeze. If this happens, waste water cannot be released from the sink, washbasin or shower tray, and there is no simple solution.

To avoid this situation, leave the drain outlet of the waste water tank permanently open so that discharged water runs straight through the tank and into a portable container. The receptacle obviously needs emptying regularly, but at least the tank remains clear.

Mindful of these difficulties, the manufacturers of la strada Nova models fit two waste tanks of roughly half the normal size. One is mounted in the warm interior; the other is mounted underneath. A controlling isolation tap keeps them either connected or separate. This is how the system works:

■ In summer the isolation tap is kept open and both tanks collect waste water.

■ In winter, the tap is closed. This means that waste water flows to the interior tank that benefits from heat in the living space and doesn't freeze. The outside tank – which *would* be likely to freeze – remains empty.

■ When the interior tank needs emptying, its isolation tap is opened together with the main release tap and water discharges straight through the outer tank into the emptying facility.

■ The isolation tap is then closed once again to ensure the under-floor tank remains empty.

Another strategy adopted by several manufacturers such as Auto-Trail, is to wrap externally mounted tanks in a silver 'insulating blanket'. This will delay freezing, but in really cold weather the contents will eventually succumb to low temperatures, and as external temperatures start to rise again, a tank-insulating jacket hinders the thawing-out of its water inside. This is the main disadvantage of an insulating blanket.

As for winter strategies for fresh water supplies, some owners rig up an alternative arrangement in which fresh water is drawn from a portable container that is temporarily placed in the shower tray. A submersible pump is lowered into this container and a new connection point is made to direct water into the normal supply pipes. In order to help owners make the necessary alterations, Carver used to sell the parts in a 'winterising kit'. Regrettably, Carver terminated its involvement with the motorcaravan industry in the late 1990s, but Caravan Accessories Kenilworth (CAK) can supply components to make modifications like this. Alternatively, if you prefer not to alter internal pipework, be aware that CAK also sells electric immersion heaters for fitting inside underfloor tanks.

WASTE TANKS AND DRAINAGE ODOURS

As many experienced motorcaravanners know to their displeasure, indoor life becomes intolerable when a living space is afflicted by drain odours. This occurs when smells from stale water in a waste tank enter the interior via sink, washbasin or shower tray outlets. This is usually attributable to a poorly designed waste system.

Right: When severe frosts were expected, this owner left the waste tank drain-down tap open and used a bucket.

Far right: Some motorcaravan owners who regularly travel to cold locations have tank immersion heaters fitted.

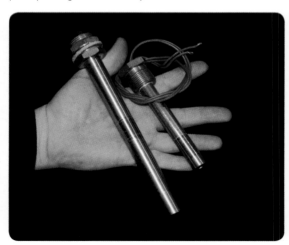

After all, the problem doesn't happen at home because there are deep water traps fitted under baths, sinks, shower trays and wash basins. An example of a large water trap can be seen at the bottom of all household toilet pans. Water retained in a trap creates a barrier that prevents smells from sewer pipes entering our houses. It's a simple but hugely important feature of modern plumbing.

The sinks, basins and shower trays in motorcaravans built by the author have similarly incorporated water traps. The waste pipes have also been constructed using 30mm (1.25in) domestic waste pipe – just like the products used at home. This is an inexpensive arrangement, and was used in Vanroyce touring caravans before their production ceased several years ago. What a pity that many motorcaravan manufacturers are less willing to adopt this practice.

If a trap is fitted, smells will not have an unhindered escape route into the living area. Furthermore, the use of a wide bore pipe ensures that water runs out of a sink considerably faster than it does when a narrow, ribbed hose is fitted. But how are these smells created in the first place?

One contributor to unpleasant odours is a badly-designed waste water tank. When an emptying tap is opened, the connections on a well-designed tank allow *every* drop of waste water *and* any food remnants to be released. Until recent changes were made to tank mouldings, this simple objective couldn't be achieved; residual water remains held in the bottom of many tanks – together with remnants of food, which soon start to rot. This causes odours to rise up the waste pipe and be released via sink or basin outlets into the living space.

It doesn't help when a motorcaravan is fitted with cheap waste hose with moulded ribs on its internal surfaces. These ridges often catch water-borne food particles and it isn't unusual to find short upturns in sections of a waste pipe run where water collects. Areas of residual water harbouring rotting food are another source of drain odours.

There are a number of ways to resolve this. As previously mentioned, the installation of a trap helps to prevent odours getting into the living area, but it is even better if something can be devised to stop the creation of smells in the first place. Let's consider the trap first.

TRAPS AND INTERCEPTORS

As long as a water trap is primed with water, it will halt the passage of smells. Obviously, in a leisure vehicle that has just been driven, water may have been shaken out of a trap. To reinstate its water when a motorcaravan is parked on a pitch, simply empty a cupful of water down each waste outlet to 'recharge'

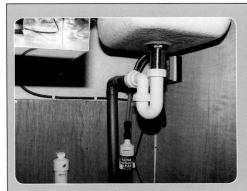

On this self-built motorcaravan, a deep-water domestic trap was coupled to a household waste outlet and PVCu 30mm waste pipe was used.

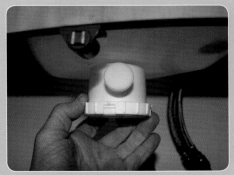

Many manufacturers now recognise the importance of fitting a water trap and food interceptor under sinks; this type was fitted on a Mizar Elite 2008.

The Auto-Sleepers Sandhurst (2006) was one of the earlier models to be fitted with a trap and interceptor manufactured by DLS Plastics.

A DLS trap with a removable bowl couples directly to a 28mm *rigid* pipe; CAK also supplies adaptors to couple with 20mm and 25mm Supaflex hose.

This CAK trap is available in two sizes to couple with a 20mm and 25mm waste hose respectively; it has to be removed to wash out the debris.

A grit interception trap is sometimes fitted in a pipe run just before it enters the tank; these are often fitted on Swift models like this Sundance.

the traps, which is hardly a chore. Alternatively, it can be refilled by briefly turning on a tap.

Another function of traps fitted under sinks is to intercept particles that get swept down a waste outlet. In some household installations, for example, a trap can sometimes be unscrewed in order to remove intercepted debris.

When constructing a self-build motorcaravan, it is usually possible to use (or modify) a sink so that it takes a domestic-size drain outlet. Then you can fit a standard household deep water trap as shown in the panel on the previous page. However, if you already own a motorcaravan, altering or replacing a sink is not a practicable proposition. On the other hand, miniature traps have recently been manufactured to suit the plumbing systems of leisure vehicles too – and most products can be fitted retrospectively.

It is always interesting to see which motorcaravan manufacturers are aware of these issues. Screw-capped traps are now being fitted in several motorcaravans imported from Italy. In the UK, the water specialist, CAK, has also had a compact water trap manufactured, which is sold through its mail order service. Similarly,

DLS Plastics is manufacturing a small water trap complete with a removable cap. Both products are shown here and their manufacturers' addresses appear in the Appendix.

In addition to those traps that perform a double function, namely blocking smells and catching debris, interceptors can usually be fitted in a waste pipe just before it enters the tank. Intercepting grit and food debris is their only function. They are constructed with a screw cap so collected 'muck' can be periodically removed. An example is shown in the panel on page 131.

Not surprisingly, fitting some of these components retrospectively is a little more involved than might be expected on account of the variety of waste pipes and hoses found in motorcaravans. Adaptors are often needed but, CAK is usually able to supply the appropriate couplings. To form a water-tight seal when coupling a plastic pipe or connector to a hose, smear some silicone sealant on the component; then tighten the hose using good quality clips.

WASTE TANK DETAILS

As a cost-saving strategy, motorcaravan manufacturers often purchase a batch of identical waste tanks and use them on several different vehicles in their 'line-up'. Since the required position for a drainage outlet will vary from model to model, they make the drain-down connection themselves. This involves cutting a hole in the chosen position and fitting a 'nutted' connector instead of getting the tank manufacturer to 'plastic weld' an outlet nozzle. The disadvantage of this approach is that outlets held by threaded plastic nuts cannot be installed as close to the bottom of a tank's sidewall as a factory-welded outlet. This means a tank that an owner believes to be empty is really retaining around 25mm (1in) of water – and that's how drain smells develop.

In recognition of this unsatisfactory situation, CAK designed a retrospective modification that permits the release of all residual water from a tank, providing it has a cleaning cap on the underside. A threaded cap, which is often red, usually represents the lowest part of a waste tank, and once a hole has been formed in the cap, fittings supplied by CAK are coupled-up to form a new outlet. Obviously this cannot be carried out on tanks without a cleaning port and cap – or on tanks that have been installed with the screw cap uppermost.

If intolerable smells continue to arise from a waste tank, the most realistic solution is to fit a better-designed product. A less costly strategy is to routinely empty the water by parking on an appropriate slope and to follow this up by using a proprietary tank cleaning product.

In more recent tanks, a moulded low-level take-off point forms part of a tank's design. This is a great improvement because it allows a drain-down hose or pipe to remove all but a few drops of water. However, as the illustration alongside reveals, it isn't always fitted as intended.

Below: Waste Master Superclean from F.L. Hitchman is formulated to clean tanks and waste pipes in motorcaravans.

Above right: To empty a waste tank completely, some owners fit a new discharge outlet by converting the red screw cap using a CAK kit.

Right: More recent tanks usually have a moulded low level discharge outlet that releases all water; this was used to good advantage on this Swift Sundance.

Right: On this Bessacarr model, the tank was positioned too close to a chassis member, so its low-level discharge outlet couldn't be used after all.

This robust drain tap fitted on a 2006 Swift Sundance is kept clean because the vehicle is fitted with mud-flaps; it can also couple-up to an extension hose.

The 2006 TEC Freetec employs a combined hose and pipe arrangement that enables users to discharge water into a hard-to-reach drain.

This plastic drain-down valve on a 2006 Orian Gemini looks fragile and it is positioned surprisingly close to the exhaust pipe.

Weak hose clips, which tend to rust easily, and a dangling pipe, are not endearing features on this 2006 Autocruise Starmist.

The 2005 Knaus Sun Ti has many good features, but its drain-down lever failed to release any water when tested.

This 2006 Swift Kon Tiki Vogue wasn't fitted with mud-flaps so it was no surprise when the drain-down tap seized-up during a user-test.

DRAIN-DOWN TAPS

The drain-down systems installed on motorcaravans can vary remarkably, as illustrated in the accompanying panel. Some drain-off a tank's contents with impressive speed; others get blocked; and others seize-up because the release tap gets covered in dirt thrown from a rear wheel. Also, on a number of models, emptying hoses can be poorly secured. This /is an important issue for motorcaravan users, but unfortunately the corresponding products are inexcusably poor. The panel above shows some contrasting systems.

INSTALLING TANKS

An experienced DIY enthusiast is unlikely to find the installation of a replacement water tank particularly difficult. However, it's an awkward exercise if you cannot elevate your vehicle safely. Under no circumstances should you crawl under a motorcaravan that is only supported by a jack or unreliable axle stands. If a safe means of access is unavailable, this is a job that should be carried out at a well-equipped workshop.

Of course, each installation is different and some operations are harder than others. It is important to purchase a tank of the right shape, capacity and depth. If this element isn't carefully checked, important ground clearance might be lost. Tanks are sold by Amber Plastics, CAK and Fiamma. In fact, in CAK's remarkably comprehensive catalogue,

there are illustrations of more than 150 tanks in different shapes and sizes. All these products are manufactured at the Warwickshire factory.

When placing an order it is advisable to specify the inclusion of a large port with screw cap for cleaning the inside. Several other associated components will also be needed, such as outlet unions, couplings, pipe, drain taps and level check facilities – all of which are listed in the CAK mail order catalogue. This manufacturer will also fit inlets and outlets in the exact places needed using a plastic 'weld' operation.

Water level gauges are also distributed by several UK manufacturers, as described in Chapter 5 on page 82. Moreover, a light-emitting diode indicator fitted in Murvi motorcaravans comes from Calira, a German specialist. As mentioned earlier, these have to be coupled-up with a sensor system fitted to a tank and many DIY builders use a CAK product that has already been fitted with stainless steel sensor studs for registering water level.

As a final warning, before tackling a tank installation project, always spend time reflecting on the merits of different locations. Water is heavy stuff: a litre weighs 1kg (2.2lb), or if you prefer imperial measures, a gallon weighs 10lb; so a large container inappropriately located may upset a vehicle's weight distribution and axle limits.

Also be aware that many motorcaravanners fill their fresh water tanks to the brim prior to leaving a

site – which obviously affects the payload. On the other hand, a part-filled tank might affect braking. It's true that some tanks have rudimentary baffles in their moulding, but a sudden surge of water could still hinder braking efficiency, especially if you need to carry out an emergency stop.

Above: At many large sites, you will often find full service pitches which provide an individual tap and emptying point.

Fresh water filling

When visiting a campsite, a motorcaravanner needs to establish how easy it will be to top up the fresh water tank. Not all sites have motorcaravan service points and it is often inconvenient to drive to a standard water tap. Most owners carry a short length of portable hose and this should be of food-grade quality so that it doesn't contaminate drinking water. Sometimes a funnel is needed too, especially when topping-up using a portable container. However, to avoid heavy lifting and water spillage, some models (eg some Swift Kon Tiki coachbuilts) have a 12V socket mounted alongside the motorcaravan's filler. This accepts a 12V Whale submersible pump which can be lowered into the water container as shown here. It's a very useful arrangement.

Left: This Swift motorcaravan has a 12V socket to run a submersible pump.

Below left: Here the pump is lowered into a portable water container.

Below: The feed hose is inserted into the fresh water inlet to top-up the tank.

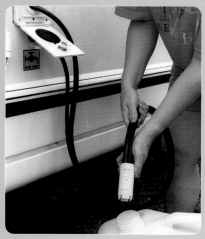

Direct supply and waste provision

In America, many 'camping grounds' provide visitors direct coupling opportunities to link their 'recreational vehicle' (RV) to the site's drainage and supply facilities. Pitches equipped with this provide fresh water, waste water and sewage connections.

This level of provision is seldom seen in Britain, although an increasing number of sites offer pitches equipped with a personal water tap and an emptying point for basin or sink (but not toilet) waste. Products like the Whale Aquasource, which couples into a Whale Water-master socket, includes a pressure reducer so that a permanently plumbed-in connection can provide water at the taps in your van. Similarly, there's the Truma Waterline, which couples into a Truma Ultraflow inlet. However, motorcaravans normally have built-in fresh water tanks and you cannot use direct connection accessories like these without modifying the original system and bypassing the tank.

For most UK motorcaravanners, a private supply on a pitch is fine for topping-up a tank rather than creating a fully plumbed-in arrangement. Filling a tank usually needs a coupling hose, and a pitch equipped in this way eliminates the need to drive a vehicle to a motorcaravan service point. Equally, it is often possible to rig up a coupling pipe to a waste tank's outlet so its contents go straight down a drain. A make-shift example is shown on page 130.

Pipework

The general plumbing arrangements in some motorcaravans are surprisingly disappointing. Although progress has been made in the last few years, many owners would still like further improvements. As the earlier photographs of drain-down taps and linking hose revealed, some products are surprisingly poor.

Above: No hope for a speedy flow rate on this 2006 Orian Gemini; the waste hose has ridges on its inside surface and there's a huge up-turn here in the pipe run.

WASTE WATER SYSTEMS

It is not unusual to find that the rate at which water empties from a motorcaravan sink or washbasin is very slow. The narrow bore of the waste pipe is partly to blame and sometimes there are up-turns that hamper the flow.

If that isn't bad enough, some manufacturers fit convoluted plastic hose with ridges on both the inside and outside surfaces. On better types of waste water hose, such as Supaflex products, the inside lining has a smooth surface that enhances the flow rate.

However, many manufacturers persistently fit the cheaper convoluted pipe, which, on gentle gradients, often catches food particles that could later cause smells. Add to this the omission of a water trap under a motorcaravan sink, and you can see why unpleasant drain odours sometimes creep into living spaces. This ought not to happen. The accompanying panel shows one way to improve a waste water system.

Below: The inside surface of this convoluted waste pipe has a smooth lining to improve the flow of water.

Laying-up tip

When leaving a motorcaravan for a prolonged period, remember to put plugs in the sink and basin outlets. This prevents smells from the waste water system creeping into the living space. Buy a spare plug for the shower tray as well.

Improving a waste water system using domestic pipe

In a motorcaravan, a waste water system can be improved by installing domestic 30mm (1.25in) PVCu waste pipe, which is sold at builders' and plumbing merchants. This is the type of 'plastic' waste pipe that many of us have under our sinks and washbasins at home. *Note: In smaller motorcaravans, some installers prefer to use 25mm (1in) PVCu pipe, which is the product often used for a domestic toilet cistern's overflow.*

When connecting up 'plastic' pipe, all joints are formed using a proprietary 'adhesive weld' sold for the purpose. With a brush mounted on the screw cap, it's easy to apply, but preparation is important. The collar of each coupling and the end of a pipe should be perfectly clean. If you rub the surface with a light grade of abrasive paper it will help the components 'key-in' successfully.

During construction, the inclination of flatter pipe runs should be checked with a spirit level to ensure that whenever the vehicle is parked level, there is a distinct fall throughout the system. The installation work demands patience rather than a high level of skill, and when the system is complete, water will flow along the pipes at a notable speed.

In some motorcaravans, making modifications to the entire system isn't possible without embarking on serious alterations to furniture and fittings. Pipes are often hidden, and there is also the problem that the waste outlets on sinks and basins are too small for coupling up to domestic waste pipe. However, in one of the author's improvement projects, most of the system was converted to 30mm PVCu pipe, while the original narrow convoluted pipe fitted to a sink was retained but cut about 300mm (12in) below its waste outlet. Roughly 200mm (8in) of this 'tail' of original pipe was then inserted into the larger domestic pipe (mounted vertically), thereby providing sufficient overlap to prevent a leak. Foam (sold in aerosol cans at builders' merchants) was carefully added to seal the small gap around the thinner ribbed pipe.

When pipe has been cut to the required lengths, contact surfaces must be cleaned or roughened-up using emery cloth.

This 'weld' adhesive has a brush in the lid. Coat both surfaces, insert the items, give a twist back and forth, and then wipe off surplus glue.

In previous caravan and motorhome upgrades, it has often helped to pre-form separate parts of the complete system on a workbench.

On some projects, sinks have been modified to accept a domestic waste outlet. Failing that, leave 300mm of the orginal hose to drape inside the new pipe.

FRESH WATER SYSTEMS

Like waste systems, many fresh water supply systems are equally disappointing. For instance, flexible 'hose and clip' systems are still fitted in a surprising number of motorcaravans.

The trouble with non-reinforced flexible hose is that over a prolonged period, kinks often develop, so that on older models it is not unusual to find that the fresh water flow rate is disappointingly slow. Typically, the pump gets the blame, but a closer investigation often reveals a constriction in one of the feed pipes where it turns a sharp bend or bears against a sharp edge. Once a section of flexible hose develops a kink, it is very hard to get it to regain its former shape.

Leaking joints can also be a problem. In a motorcaravan, a remarkable number of hose clips are needed to couple up branch pipes and appliances. Worm-driven clips are not always fault-free, and any hint of weakness will be aggravated by the movements when driving on bumpy roads. It's no surprise that a joint occasionally fails, and if the faulty coupling is hidden behind a panel, carrying out a repair can be quite difficult.

With this in mind, the case for installing semi-rigid pipe with push-fit couplings instead of a hose and clip arrangement is a very strong one. This type of product has proven reliability; for instance, it has been used to pump beer in clubs and pubs for over 40 years. Curiously, motorcaravan manufacturers have only used it in recent years.

Admittedly, there are occasions where, in a tight squeeze, it's easier to run a length of plastic hose, but that doesn't mean that you need to fit flexible hose throughout the entire supply because there are adaptors to link both types of pipe.

Similarly, there are unions that enable a length of semi-rigid pipe to be terminated with a threaded coupling nut. A threaded coupling is usually needed when connecting semi-rigid pipe to a diaphragm pump.

A particularly innovative item in the John Guest range of semi-rigid pipe-work components is a short length of plastic channelling, which has a moulded 90° bend. This is used in situations when a length of semi-rigid pipe has to be led around a sharp corner. Without this component, the pipe would kink irreparably, but when a section is pressed into the angled channelling, its sidewalls are supported.

Whale also distributes semi-rigid pipe and the range includes a pipe-cutting tool that ensures a measured section of the 12mm or 15mm (outside diameter) pipe is cut cleanly and squarely. This is important when forming a joint.

Hose and clip plumbing

- When replacing a failed joint, don't be tempted to reuse the old worm-drive clip – buy a replacement. (Worm-drive clips are often known as 'Jubilee clips', which was the original brand-name.)
- Buy good quality clips, even if they cost a little more. Poor quality imitations often have a ridged rack, which is all-too-easily deformed by the worm-wheel when the clip is tightened.
- Prior to fitting a new clip, apply a small drop of oil on the worm wheel and also on the ridges of the tightening strip.
- Make sure the end of the hose is trimmed neatly and squarely.
- To ensure the hose is flexible, immerse the end in very hot water for several seconds. If you work quickly, you'll find the Jubilee clip will pull more tightly into a warmed hose.
- Some clips may have a sharp edge that can split a hose if over-tightened.
- Most clips don't over-compress, but if you're connecting up to a rigid plastic tube on a component (such as the coupling nozzle of an in-line water filter) be careful not to crack it.

Push-fit semi-rigid plumbing

- Forming a joint is extremely easy with a push-fit system. Make sure the pipe is cut cleanly

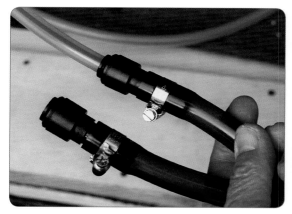

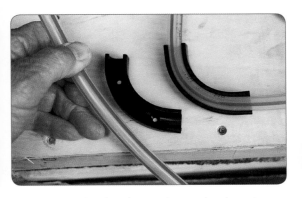

and squarely, then insert the section into the coupling and push it fully home. A watertight connection is immediately achieved. Take care, as sometimes it seems that the inserted pipe has been pushed fully into the coupling, but there is still a bit further to go.

- Inside each coupling there is a small collar known as a 'collet'. This can be removed if you want to see what it looks like – but it is usually left in place and shouldn't be taken out when forming a joint.
- The collet grips the outside of the pipe, so if you try to pull the joint apart, the collet is driven against the surface of the pipe with increasing force. Disconnection by muscle-power is virtually impossible.
- Notwithstanding the grip achieved by the interaction of these key components, the joint can be disconnected by holding the exposed part of the collet firmly against the coupling itself. While pushing the collet *towards* the coupling, the pipe will disconnect when pulled in the opposite direction.
- To ensure a coupling isn't accidentally disconnected by pressure on the exposed part of the collet, some systems have cover caps that are pushed over the finished joint to prevent unintended disconnection.
- Several years ago, Whale made minor improvements to its push-fit products, and the revised couplings didn't always exactly match-up with some of the earlier components. In consequence, mixtures of earlier and later couplings are sometimes hard to take apart if you want to disconnect a component.

System requirements for both types of fresh water system

Irrespective of the hose or pipe system installed in a motorcaravan, additional components might also be needed.

Non-return valve

Once a motorcaravan's pipes are full of fresh water, it would be a nuisance if gravity caused the supply to run back to a tank or water supply vessel every time a tap was turned off. Equally, if a Whale GP74 in-line pump were fitted, its 'primed state' would also be lost when this happens. The situation also arises when a submersible pump has been installed. Whenever a submersible pump

stops operating, water held in the pipes again drains back to the tank because it merely runs unimpeded through its operating mechanism. To prevent this from happening, a non-return valve is fitted in the main supply pipe as near to the tank as possible. One of these devices allows water to pass one way only, so it cannot then run back through the pipes.

However, where a diaphragm pump is installed in a motorcaravan (as described later in the section entitled *Water Pumps*), its mechanism does *not* allow water to drain through the chambers when its motor isn't operating – so in this instance, a non-return valve is not needed.

When a diaphragm pump or a non-return valve has been installed, residual water is retained in pipe runs *after* it has passed through these components. In normal every-day use, the retention of water in a supply system is helpful for the reasons given. On the other hand, residual water won't be very fresh if your motorcaravan has not been used for an extended period. Similarly, when frosty weather is expected and you want to drain-down the supply pipes, a non-return valve prevents you from carrying this out unless a drain-down tap has been fitted nearby. In the absence of a tap, the usual strategy for draining-off water held in pipes is to disconnect a coupling on the delivery side (ie 'output' side) of the diaphragm pump or non-return valve. That is hardly state-of-the-art plumbing.

Note: *Non-return valves used in hose plumbing are about the width of a pencil and 30mm (1.25in) long. They are inserted inside a section of hose near a joint and achieve a snug fit. Alternatively, there are valves of a similar size that couple-up with push-fit pipe. Since the majority of motorcaravans are equipped with diaphragm pumps, they are not often fitted.*

Right: This drain-down tap from the Whale range is designed so that it can be easily coupled up with semi-rigid pipe.

Drain tap

When a vehicle is not being used during extremely cold weather, a water system needs to be drained down to prevent frost damage. It is true that some owners never empty their supply systems, and the pumps, pipes and water filters manage to avoid damage. Flexibility in plastic components can sometimes cope with freezing water and the attendant pressure build-up when ice expands. Geography plays a part, too. Winter temperatures are much lower in Inverness than they are in Penzance. However, it is silly to take risks, and where water heaters are concerned, draining them down is absolutely essential, (as discussed in Chapter 6). Cartridge water filters often split their casings, too. It is therefore disappointing that some motorcaravan manufacturers don't fit drain taps to release water from the supply pipes. Fortunately, it isn't a difficult job for a practically minded owner to fit a drain-down tap, even though it ought to have been installed when the motorcaravan was originally built. A drain-down tap, (or taps), should be located:

a) Where it is easy to catch the drain-off water
b) At low points in the system
c) At a point (or points) 'downstream' (on the outlet side) of a non-return valve or a diaphragm pump.

Note: *When water freezes it expands in volume. In other words, water held in the downturn of a supply pipe expands and increases the pressure in that pipe. Sometimes the subsequent failure of a coupling or joint is caused by high pressure –*

and not always as a result of direct contact with expanding ice. Appendix C (page 201), which discusses pre-winter lay-up preparations, points out that taps and shower controls must be left open to release a pressure build-up.

Surge dampers

When a diaphragm pump is fitted, it is sometimes found that the motor operates with irregular pulses. Fitting a small chamber within the pipe feed known as a 'surge damper' can solve this. Several motorcaravan manufacturers now fit one of these as standard. But don't let the shape confuse you – this is not an in-line water filter, which sometimes has similar dimensions.

Note: *Some surge dampers have to be mounted vertically with their connection point at the bottom.*

Water pumps

Motorcaravan water pumps fall into two categories: models that need priming and models that don't.

Some products are unable to start the pumping action until water is introduced into the casing of the unit, thus expelling the air; this is what 'priming' means. Typically, a pump that needs priming is made with a small impeller, or paddle wheel, that spins around and pushes water through the casing and along the pipes. This is known as a centrifugal pump and submersible pumps are built with a small impeller. However, the priming process is easy for this type of centrifugal pump because the casing fills with water as soon as it is lowered into water.

In contrast, a self-priming pump usually incorporates pistons that move up and down within sealed chambers; this type of pump has the ability to draw water along an empty pipe even when its chambers are empty. The perception of most people is that the pump is able to 'suck' water up from a tank or portable container rather than merely pushing it along pipe with a paddle wheel. A physicist might politely point out that it's not a matter of suction but of vacuum creation and atmospheric pressure. This subtle difference is right, of course, but all that needs to be said here is that self-priming devices fitted in motorcaravans are called 'diaphragm pumps'.

Examples of the two different types of pump:

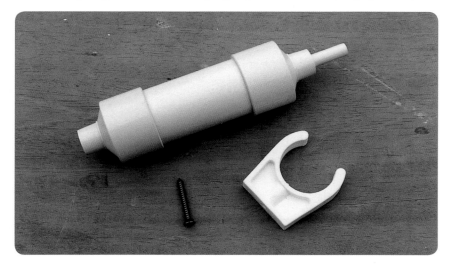

Below: A surge damper fitted in a fresh water supply system helps to prevent a pump from operating with a pulsing action.

- *Non-priming pumps* – Whale GP74 (seldom seen today), submersible pumps (made by Reich, Truma Ultraflow, Whale High Flow, and several other models).
- *Self-priming pumps* – Fiamma Aqua 8, Shurflo Trailking, Whale Evenflow, Whale Clearstream, Whale Smartflo, Whale Universal.

This chapter looks closely at submersible pumps and their more expensive counterparts, diaphragm pumps. However, there is another matter to consider before comparing these products. Irrespective of the type preferred, there has to be a switching arrangement.

PUMP SWITCHING

Before an electric pump can deliver water, the tap's outlet has to be opened and the 12V electric motor has to be switched into operation. One of three switching methods can be used:

1. Manual switch

A finger-operated 12V switch could be mounted in a kitchen to activate a pump whenever a tap top has been turned. Alternatively, a foot-operated push switch is also available. In practice, neither of these types is fitted nowadays, although they *could* be installed as a temporary cure if a fault were to develop elsewhere.

2. Micro-switch

A more popular type of switch used in caravans and motorhomes is a tiny unit fitted within the tap itself. These compact 'micro-switches' switch a motor into action whenever someone turns the tap top or lifts its lever. Damp is an enemy of a micro-switch and if water or condensation gets inside its casing, electricity can track across the tiny gap between its switch contacts. When this happens, the micro-switch will need replacing – a topic covered later under *Taps and shower systems*.

3. Pressure-sensitive switch

This type of switch can be mounted:

Micro-switch recognition

If you decide to buy a motorcaravan and need to confirm which type of pump switching has been fitted, look underneath the sink or bathroom washbasin. If you see cables coming down from the tap units, then these are undoubtedly linked to a micro-switch.

In Britain, micro-switched control of water pumps is usually only found in touring caravans. However, German motorcaravans are sometimes built with micro-switches in their taps as well. For example, some Arto A Class models have micro-switches, as do models in the Dethleffs Esprit range.

Cables coming down from a kitchen tap in this 2006 Dethleffs Esprit indicated that it used micro-switches to control the pump.

a) In-line, within the feed pipe itself
b) Integrally within the body of a diaphragm pump
c) As part of a water-inlet socket – more commonly fitted on touring caravans.

A pressure-sensitive switch responds whenever a tap top is turned or an operating lever is raised. The action causes an opening to appear in an otherwise sealed supply system, which leads to a pressure drop in the supply pipes. This drop in pressure then

Different locations of pressure-sensitive switches

1 Within the pump: Adjusting point on a Whale Clearstream pump.

2 Within the pump: Screw hidden by silicone on a Whale Evenflow.

3 Within the pump: Centre screw (of five) on a Shurflo Trail King.

4 In-line: Whale pressure switch with adjusting wheel on top.

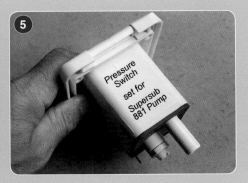

5 In wall socket: There's switching in this Whale Watermaster inlet.

6 In wall socket: Setting adjustment screw on a Watermaster inlet.

If your water pump isn't working, this might be the result of a faulty micro-switch. Firstly confirm that the isolation switch on the control panel is on. Then establish whether your taps have micro-switches by looking for cables under each tap's mounting point. If the cables can be detached from the tap, touch the terminals on the cables together. In effect, bringing the cables together is replicating the action of the micro-switch. If the switch is faulty, touching its feed cables together should activate the pump. If it doesn't, the fault is elsewhere in the system.

Alternatively if your motorcaravan has micro-switches and the pump motor won't *stop* running, ensure that all the taps are turned off (either tops closed tightly or levers lowered). As the motor continues to run, systematically disconnect the micro-switch cables attached to all the taps, including the shower control. The pump motor will continue to run until you get to the one whose micro-switch is not interrupting the flow of current. This fault occurs when sufficient damp gets into its casing to create a continuing passage of power between the make and break contacts inside the micro-switch – even when they're parted in their off position.

Everything is small inside a micro-switch enclosure and most casings are sealed. Consequently, you cannot clean the dirty or damp contacts, and the usual solution is to purchase a new switch. These are not costly items.

activates the switch mechanism that controls the pump motor. Unfortunately, if there's a small leak in any of the pipe connections, this can also trigger the motor into life. In fact, it's not unusual to hear a pump clicking in and out very briefly on account of a faulty coupling. This can be distracting during the night, so motorcaravans are fitted with an additional pump isolation switch on the 12V control panel. Indeed it becomes a habit to switch off a pump when it's bedtime. That prevents an annoying noise, but if false activation is being caused by a tiny air leak at a coupling, get this repaired promptly in case it subsequently develops into a water leak.

If pipe couplings all appear to be sound, altering the sensitivity of a pressure switch can cure false switching. Most units feature an adjuster screw to fine-tune its responses but these are often hard to locate. The panel on the previous page indicates some of the common locations.

SUBMERSIBLE PUMPS

Although a submersible pump is an example of a non-priming pump, the device achieves a state

of prime as soon as it is submersed in a water container. Water fills the casing, air is expelled, and as soon as the motor is set into motion, water is pushed into the supply pipes by an impeller.

Submersible pumps have been fitted in smaller motorcaravans (such as the Middlesex Motorcaravan's Matrix and Swift Mondial 1990s models). They are sometimes fitted in coachbuilt models, too. (Such as the Knaus Sport and Sun Ti.)

Another example of a submersible pump is the Whale Superfill 80, which is often supplied with large coachbuilts to lift water from a portable container in order to fill an onboard tank. This arrangement is described and illustrated in the earlier section *Fresh water filling*. The pump can similarly be used to fill an independent flushing reservoir of a cassette toilet, too. In both cases, a 12V connecting socket has to be mounted on an outside wall, as shown on page 134.

On van conversions that use external water containers, an input socket has to be fitted to the side of a vehicle. This has two functions. Firstly, it couples the water supply pipe into the motorcaravan system. Secondly, it connects the two cables that provide power to the submersible pump. To ensure there is good electrical safety, these cables are usually fed through a length of plastic tubing.

Submersible pumps are also used in those Thetford toilets that have a power flushing facility.

Advantages
- A well-designed submersible pump achieves a good flow rate.
- Good-quality models are sturdily built.
- A submersible pump is much cheaper than a diaphragm pump.
- Noise level is low during operation.

Disadvantages
- When the mechanism fails, a submersible pump cannot be repaired.
- If left running in an empty water container, the motor will soon get damaged.
- If the casing cracks, water will penetrate the motor compartment and cause a short in the 12V system. If this occurs, a fuse in the pump

Right: A few coachbuilt motorcaravans are fitted with submersible pumps; this 2006 Knaus Sport has a blue-capped Reich pump in the tank.

Far right: This Whale Watermaster Premium pump couples to a Truma Crystal II inlet; others have couplings to match the Truma Compact and Whale's own inlet sockets.

circuit will blow, thereby ensuring that damage isn't caused elsewhere.

Note: *1. Recent Whale submersible pumps incorporate an anti-airlock hole in the top of the casing in order to release trapped air bubbles more efficiently.*

2. In view of the throwaway nature of the less expensive submersible pumps, owners with water systems that rely on one of these units understand the wisdom of carrying a spare.

DIAPHRAGM PUMPS

These well-engineered products are widely fitted in motorcaravans. Their mechanism is elaborate and only experienced owners should attempt to carry out internal repairs. If something goes wrong, the importers or manufacturers offer an overhaul and repair service, which might include replacing all of the 'O' rings. However, there are a number of tasks an owner *should* carry out – such as cleaning the filter.

The mechanism of a diaphragm pump can be badly damaged by grit and its filter must be kept clean, as shown in the accompanying photographs. Several other faults can occur and these are described in the accompanying panel.

Advantages
- Very good output and flow rates.
- Well engineered products.
- Powerful ability to lift water – the Whale Clearstream 700, for example, is able to lift water upto 100cm (39in).

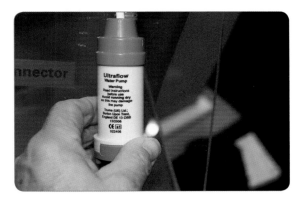

Left: When Carver ceased manufacturing motorcaravanning products, Truma introduced a range of water system accessories.

Airlocks in submersibles

If a submersible pump doesn't deliver water after it has been dropped into a water container, there are probably air bubbles caught in the casing.

- **To expel air bubbles, disconnect the feed pipe from the motorcaravan. Keep the pump under the water and swing the feed pipe so that the unit bumps several times against the side of the water container. This dislodges air bubbles, some of which may be seen rising in the water. Alternatively air is dispelled through the upper end of the hose.**
- **To reduce the likelihood of air bubbles getting caught in the pump casing, more recent products (such as the Whale 881) feature an air release hole on top of the casing.**

The Whale 881 submersible pump has an anti-airlock hole in the top of the casing.

Diaphragm pump problems

If a diaphragm pump motor fails to respond, check for an inline fuse holder near the pump. Fit a replacement fuse if you have doubts about the existing one.

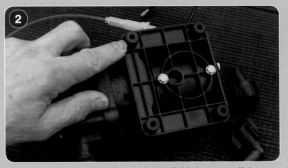

Diaphragm pumps are often noisy and this happens if the mounting screws are over-tightened. Compression of the rubber feet causes a mounting board to amplify the sounds.

An important maintenance task is to inspect the grit filter periodically, to remove it and clean out any debris. This manufacturer made sure the filter is easily accessible.

If grit gets into the mechanism, it can ruin a diaphragm pump. It is an involved job to overhaul and repair a pump, so Whale is now selling complete replacement heads.

Note: *The leading manufacturers of diaphragm pumps offer complete overhaul and repair services. Equally, an independent specialist, Leisure Accessories, has operated a mail order repair operation for many years (see Appendix D for the address).*

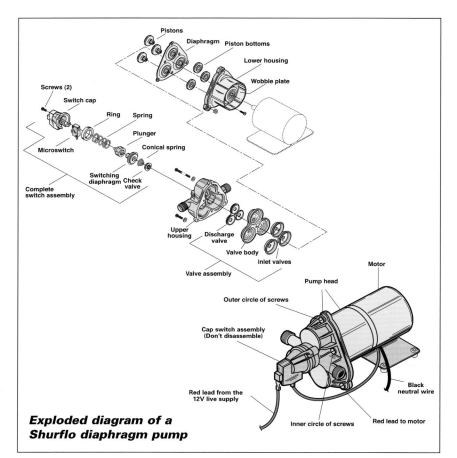

Pistons
Diaphragm   Piston bottoms
Lower housing
Screws (2)
Switch cap   Wobble plate
Ring   Spring
Plunger
Microswitch   Conical spring
Switching   Check
Complete   diaphragm   valve
switch assembly
Upper
housing   Discharge
valve
Valve body
Inlet valves
Valve assembly
Pump head   Motor
Outer circle of screws
Cap switch assembly
(Don't disassemble)
Red lead from the   Black
12V live supply   neutral wire
Inner circle of screws   Red lead to motor

**Exploded diagram of a
Shurflo diaphragm pump**

Right: The grit filter on a Clearstream 700 pump is located below a tightly fitting cap.

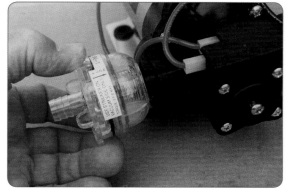

Right: On this Shurflo pump, the grit filter is screwed onto the water inlet as shown.

Far right: The gauze strainer on a Whale Evenflow filter is held within a tight-fitting enclosure.

Disadvantages

■ If the mechanism fails, a pump usually has to be sent away for repair.
■ These products are more expensive than submersible pumps.
■ Some models are inclined to be noisy.

Pump replacement

Anyone who carries out DIY repairs will find that pumps from Fiamma, Shurflo and Whale are supplied with clear installation instructions. Of course, consideration must be given to the way that the pump is going to be switched, and the options of micro-switching, or pressure-sensitive switching, have already been discussed.

If you are fitting a diaphragm pump, these usually have an inbuilt pressure switch and you merely need to couple-up live and neutral power feeds to the unit. But make sure that you fit cable of the correct gauge. For instance, Whale diaphragm pumps require $2.5mm^2$ cable (cross-sectional area), which achieves a continuous current rating of 21.5 amps. Cable selection was discussed in Chapter 5, and the manufacturer's specification must be followed to ensure efficient operation of the pump.

Also, make sure you don't screw the unit down to its mounting board too tightly. It has already been mentioned that if the rubber feet are over-compressed then the board amplifies noise from the pump.

As regards the hose coupling points, you may need to get an adaptor to suit the type of pipe fitted in the motorcaravan. And check the flow direction arrow, which is usually marked on the casing, to confirm the inlet and outlet ports.

Filter systems

There are three types of water filter:
1. A grit filter (such as those fitted on diaphragm pumps)
2. A taste filter (such as the inline Whale filter)
3. A filter that also purifies water (such as the Nature-Pure from General Ecology).

GRIT FILTERS

When a diaphragm pump is fitted, it is most important to have a grit filter installed on the in-flow

side of the unit. The photographs alongside show the filters that are fitted on three different pumps. These filters are accessible for cleaning; the Evenflow and Shurflo filters can either be dismantled or you can backwash them by directing water through their casings in a reverse direction under a running tap.

TASTE FILTERS

These products help to remove water-borne particles but their main function is to improve water palatability. Similar charcoal filters are often used in kitchens at home. While they improve the taste, they do NOT purify contaminated water.

It is usually quite easy to fit a taste filter in a motorcaravan and these are generally fitted in a pipe run as close as possible to the drinking water tap. The inline filter from Whale is especially compact and installing one of these in the supply pipe to a sink or basin is an easy task for a practically minded owner. But don't forget to replace the filter at frequent intervals. An average user could reasonably expect a filter to last a season, but some motorcaravanners leave them in place for several years, which is self-defeating. Quite apart from failing to achieve its objective, an old taste filter could become a health hazard.

WATER PURIFIERS

Few motorcaravanners drain down their fresh water tank at the end of every trip, so the wisdom of fitting a water purifier is clear. This is why many owners of motorcaravans, cabin cruisers and narrow boats fit a Nature-Pure Ultrafine water purifier. This removes tank taste, traps chemicals

such as pesticides and solvents, as well as removing disease bacteria, pathogenic cysts with disease toxins, parasites and so on. In fact, this purifier is so effective that a boat owner could even draw water from a canal and convert it into clean, clear drinking water.

This American-manufactured product is not cheap, but it is sturdily constructed and achieves its function provided a supply system has a powerful diaphragm pump. The unit isn't difficult to install and it involves taking water from the main supply pipe and directing it to the inlet on the Nature-Pure filter casing. The purified water coming from the

Above: Many types of filter can be supplied by Filtapack; this specialist helps motorcaravanners whose cartridge systems are hard to find.

Far left: An Aqua Source Clear taste filter is narrow enough to be fitted even where space is restricted.

Left: The filter used in the Nature-Pure Ultrafine water purifier from General Ecology is housed in a strong plastic casing.

Above: A dedicated fresh-water tap is supplied in an Ultrafine water purifier kit.

casing's outlet is then coupled to a purpose-made supply tap, which is provided in the kit. Alternatively you can divert it to your existing coldwater tap. A further alternative is to direct the purified water to the cold outlet of a mixer tap, although this is not the preferred arrangement. For instance, if a mixer mechanism that separates (or blends) hot and cold water is poorly engineered, the purified cold water might mix with small quantities of residual non-treated water from the hot supply. If the purifying function is critically important – for instance in an expedition vehicle travelling in under-developed countries – it's best to fit the separate Nature-Pure tap that is provided in the kit.

The Nature-Pure Ultrafine has much to commend it, but as with a taste filter product, you must change the high-specification cartridge filter at the intervals recommended by its manufacturer.

Note: 1. *New filter systems appear periodically in the leisure market and they adopt various strategies for improving water taste and quality. Some products involve adding chemicals to the water and the Truma AquaStar system uses dosage prepared sachets. In the past, Electrolux employed an electric tube housed in a plasticised container to purify water.*

2. When products come and go, it becomes increasingly difficult to trace replacement filters. One specialist often able to assist is Filtapac. Apart from manufacturing several cartridge products to suit obsolete systems, this supplier also sells rechargeable packs that are displayed at caravan and motorhome exhibitions (see the Appendix for address).

Taps and shower systems

The design of taps and showerheads has changed significantly over the last decade. Moreover, to the disenchantment of many owners, some taps have proved extremely unreliable and these are usually cheaply-built imported products.

One response by manufacturers has been to fit domestic-style mixer taps instead, and these often suit a large motorcaravan. Unfortunately, the rate of flow from a 12V pump sometimes looks rather feeble after the more familiar output from domestic taps fitted at home.

As previously explained, some taps are fitted with a micro-switch that triggers the pump into action; these need to be accessible, and it's always wise to carry a spare switch, just in case damp causes a micro-switch to fail. However, on some imported taps, the micro-switch is not accessible because it is sealed within the casing. This is a contentious sales strategy – if a tap develops a fault the entire unit has to be thrown away. What's more, replacements might no longer be available.

On Whale's recent taps like the Elegance and Modular models, changing a micro-switch is fairly easy, as the accompanying photographs show. The main problem is reaching them under a kitchen sink. It certainly helps to be a contortionist, slim of build and blessed with night vision. It is undoubtedly beneficial if you can practise the operation using a spare tap. This approach was adopted when taking the enclosed photographs in order to highlight each step with clarity. Just before you start, remember to turn off a tap completely and to switch off the 12V supply.

Changing the micro-switches on Whale taps

Feeling in the dark under your sink, locate a plastic collar clip.

Ease the clip away from the switch mounting point.

Gently pull the microswitch from its two locating pins.

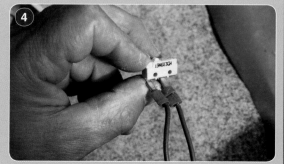

Replace the switch with a new one and reverse the operation.

If you want to fit a Whale Elite mixer tap you either need a push-fit semi-rigid pipe system, or you can get adaptors to couple-up with flexible hose.

Changing a micro-switch is undoubtedly easier if your motorcaravan is fitted with Whale's Elite mixer taps because everything is done above the sink. These models are sold in two versions – either *with* or *without* micro-switches. If there are wires coming down underneath their mounting, then they have a micro-switch inside and the procedure for changing this component is shown in the accompanying illustrations. But be warned; clasp the unit firmly so that the mechanism doesn't flick out unexpectedly when you remove the operating lever. It can be very difficult trying to work out where all the dislodged components are meant to fit!

Note: *The water inlets for Elite mixer taps are intended to accept Whale's push-fit semi-rigid pipe. If you want to fit these taps in an upgrade operation and your motorcaravan has a flexible hose supply system, buy the adaptors with a ribbed hose-coupling nozzle.*

Taps and winter precautions

When you lay-up a motorcaravan in frosty weather, you must leave all taps and shower controls OPEN. When residual water freezes it expands and this introduces pressure in the pipes which can split the couplings. Leaving all taps open provides a pressure relief facility. But take note. If you have lever-operated mixer taps, you must make sure that the lifted lever is in its CENTRAL POSITION in order to give pressure relief to both the hot AND cold supply pipes. Whale now fits warning stickers on Elite lever taps because a number of owners have experienced frost damage when a lifted lever hadn't been centralised. I was one of those owners, as the photograph here reveals. . .

Above: Whale now fits warning stickers on lever taps and shower controls to ensure that frost damage is avoided.

Left: The lever on this shower control wasn't left lifted in its central position, and the subsequent pressure build-up from freezing water completely split its casing.

Changing the micro-switches on Elite mixer taps

Working from above the tap, prise out the hot/cold plug to reveal the tap lever attachment screw.

Remove the tap lever, then lift off the switch activating plate, noting its position carefully.

Gently prise up the microswitch from its cradled location with the aid of a small screwdriver.

Pull the switch clear to disconnect the terminals; then replace it with a new microswitch.

CONTENTS

In a motorcaravan, the refrigerator makes one of the most important contributions to comfortable living. However, successful operation can only be achieved if an appliance is correctly installed and appropriately serviced.

The refrigerators installed in motorcaravans work by circulating a chemical around a network of pipes. The chemical is described as a 'refrigerant' and when it circulates, it changes state from a liquid to a gas and back again. This change of state calls for heat, which is duly supplied by drawing heat out of the food storage compartment via the silver fins inside. This is how cooling is achieved inside a fridge, and the process will be less efficient if these fins are obstructed by products stored inside. Unsurprisingly, the process is also affected in high temperatures.

In domestic cooling appliances, the refrigerant is circulated by a compressor and the motor will spring into life when a thermostat recognises the need for further cooling. The system works well and small versions of these appliances are sometimes installed in motorcaravans.

In spite of the fact that compressor fridges are used in our homes and in a few campervans, the more common type of refrigerator fitted in motorcaravans has a cooling unit whose refrigerant is circulated by the application of heat. This type of appliance is referred to as an

absorption refrigerator, and the heat that creates the circulation comes from one of three sources:

■ A 12V DC heating element
■ A 230V AC heating element
■ A gas burner.

In recognition of its alternative operating modes, this type of refrigerator is often described as a 'three-way' fridge, and an important feature is its versatility. In contrast, compressor refrigerators installed in motorcaravans can only run on 12V DC electricity. This is normally supplied by t he leisure battery, although it is also possible to buy a mains rectifier tht draws power from a 230V AC supply.

Of course, both compressor and absorption fridges have advantages and disadvantages, and their respective suitability is linked to the way a motorcaravan is used. For instance, if you park a motorcaravan for extended periods on sites that are *not* equipped with mains hook-ups, and then use a bicycle, motor scooter or support car for touring

Compressor refrigerators

Campervan manufacturers such as Bilbo's use compressor refrigerators in their conversions.

On this WAECO Coolmatic model the compressor and refrigeration components are mounted high up at the rear.

As this DIY VW converter discovered, the WAECO Coolmatic CR50 is extremely easy to install and it performs well.

locally instead of driving the motorcaravan, an absorption refrigerator is undoubtedly the preferred product. This is because it can be operated on gas, whereas a compressor refrigerator normally derives its power from a motorcaravan's 12V leisure battery, which will cease to supply electricity if it doesn't receive a periodic recharge. Furthermore, some batteries sold for leisure purposes need recharging more often than might be expected. See Chapter 5 for battery performance issues.

So let's compare these two products:

COMPRESSOR REFRIGERATORS

Advantages

- These are usually less expensive than similarly-sized absorption refrigerators.
- External ventilators are not needed and the installation task is less involved. The absence of plastic ventilators means that the appearance of a vehicle is more aesthetically pleasing.
- As a rule, there is nothing to service on a compressor fridge, although this should be checked in an appliance's operating instruction leaflet.
- Operation of a compressor refrigerator is abundantly simple. On all WAECO models there is a temperature setting wheel inside the food compartment that includes an on/off switch.
- Unlike an absorption refrigerator, a compressor fridge *does* achieve cooling when a vehicle is parked on an incline, as long as the slope doesn't exceed 30°.

Disadvantages

- Periodic noise from a compressor pump can be irritating in a confined living space.
- A significant demand is placed on the leisure battery so it will need frequent recharging. You may need to fit a battery with a greater capacity.
- If you want a spacious leisure refrigerator, compressor-driven motorcaravan models that fit under a worktop are available up to 140L, but tall models with capacities up to 190L are only available in the absorption ranges. **Note**: *Larger compressor units up to 270L are available for RVs and boats.*

ABSORPTION REFRIGERATORS

Advantages

- The operating system is silent, which is important in the compact living area of a motorcaravan.
- There is a choice of operating modes. On the road, 12V DC is used. On a site with a mains hook-up, the appliance can be run on 230V AC electricity. On other sites, or when camping in the wild, you can choose to operate it using gas.
- These types of absorption appliances are available if you want a large refrigerator with spacious cooling and freezer storage.

Disadvantages

- Ventilators have to be installed on the external sidewall of a motorcaravan (alternatively the lower one can sometimes be fitted in the floor).
- An absorption refrigerator may perform poorly if it hasn't been fitted in accordance with the fridge installation instructions. Indeed, several manufacturers have taken shorts cuts in the past – although that isn't the fault of the appliance.
- Embracing three different operating systems usually means that a three-way appliance will be more expensive than a compressor fridge.
- Manufacturers specify that an absorption refrigerator should be serviced every 12 months, and in many older motorcaravans, operations can only be completed if the appliance is transferred to a workbench.
- In keeping with the fact that there are three operating modes, operation of a leisure absorption fridge often necessitates perusal of the user's guide. Some of the older Electrolux models had a control panel that had a jumble of controls and switches. More recent Dometic and Thetford models are less confusing.
- The absorption operating system requires a refrigerator to be in a level, or near level plane in order to function. However, when a vehicle is being driven, these appliances *do* operate successfully because there will always be periods when a level position is briefly achieved.

Three-way absorption refrigerators

Several motorhome manufacturers are now installing Thetford refrigerators since their introduction in 2002.

Refrigerators from Thetford provide storage features that are similar to those included in models from Electrolux and Dometic.

This tall fridge-freezer manufactured by Dometic was installed by Mobilvetta in the 2006 Top Driver S71 coachbuilt motorcaravan.

For many years, the refrigerators fitted in leisure vehicles were manufactured by Electrolux. However, in 2001, the leisure appliance division of Electrolux became an independent company and the name Dometic was adopted. This had been a brand name used in the USA for a number of years.

In 2003, many appliances were still bearing both Dometic and Electrolux badges, which was rather confusing. However, in 2004 the licence to use the Electrolux name expired. In this chapter, both names are used because thousands of motorcaravans are fitted with products previously manufactured by Electrolux. Only post-2004 models bear just a Dometic badge, and the Company's after-sales service covers both products.

Similar issues arose with regard to Waeco which, for many years, has been a highly-regarded manufacturer of motorcaravan products, including compressor fridges. This brand of leisure accessories is still manufactured and continues to carry the Waeco badge – but it is now part of the Dometic Group.

In addition, a company called Norcold manufactures absorption refrigerators that were introduced into the UK in 2002 as part of the Thetford range of leisure appliances. In the decade that followed, Thetford's absorption refrigerators established a strong position in the leisure industry. UK caravan and motorcaravan manufacturers are fitting these products as well.

When evaluating the pros and cons of these appliances, it's essential to consider their respective features *in the light of your style of motorcaravanning*. An increasing number of campsites now have 230V hook-ups and many owners seldom stop anywhere without a mains supply. In this instance, there is scarcely any need for a fridge that runs on gas. In complete contrast, other motorcaravanners eschew these types of site and instead seek rural retreats and remote venues. That's fine, but this type of lifestyle is hardly well served by a compressor fridge and a small Ah battery with few recharging opportunities. A three-way fridge is more versatile under these circumstances.

So personal needs are important to consider. Be aware, too, that some motorcaravan manufacturers only offer models fitted with one type of fridge or the other. For example, well-respected van converters like Bilbo's normally only fit compressor fridges. However, the majority of motorcaravan manufacturers have installed three-way refrigerators from Electrolux, Dometic and Thetford. For that reason, a large part of this chapter focuses on the three-way models.

Operation

As stated earlier, operation of a compressor fridge involves little more than turning its on/off control wheel and selecting a cooling level. In complete contrast, an absorption refrigerator is considerably more involved, so let's start by considering its different cooling systems.

All operating modes on a three-way absorption refrigerator achieve efficient cooling, although the best one to choose depends on circumstances. For instance, if mains electricity is provided at a site, it is logical to use the 230V supply. Alternatively, on sites that are not equipped with mains hook-ups, you would select the gas operating mode. The 12V mode can only be used when the vehicle is being driven because it would otherwise discharge a battery very quickly.

Note: *A 12V supply on a three-way fridge doesn't drive a compressor. It operates a small heating element that is housed in a steel tube about the thickness of a pencil. This tube is mounted inside the vertical burner tube, which is fitted above the gas burner. Adjacent to the 12V element is one of a similar appearance that uses a 230V supply.*

Although a fridge has the ability to run on gas when a vehicle is being driven, this is potentially VERY dangerous. It is also strictly illegal to enter a filling station with a gas appliance in operation. Be aware that the naked flame of a fridge burner is not mounted within a sealed chamber, as it is in space heating appliances, so before taking to the road, it is extremely important to turn off a gas supply at the cylinder and to select the 12V operating mode.

Some owners are misled into thinking that 12V operation is not very efficient. This is not the case. Provided a vehicle's alternator achieves a good output, and as long as the electrical connection is made using cable of the appropriate gauge, cooling is effective. The only disadvantage with the 12V option is that the level of cooling cannot be altered; the fridge works at a steady rate, irrespective of where you set the cooling control on the control panel.

Procedures for changing the operating mode of a fridge are explained in owners' handbooks and when you use a motorcaravan frequently, the task of switching over becomes a matter of routine. However, if you haven't used your motorcaravan for a long time and it has one of the more complicated control panels, it's not unusual to forget the steps you have to follow. This is why the Electrolux Automatic Energy Selection refrigerators, first introduced in the UK during 1995, have a clear advantage: they automatically choose the most appropriate operating mode on your behalf.

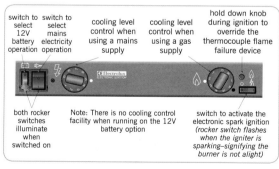

Right: Example of controls and their functions on a late 1980s and early 1990s electronic ignition fridge.

switch to select 12V battery operation / switch to select mains electricity operation / cooling level control when using a mains supply / cooling level control when using a gas supply / hold down knob during ignition to override the thermocouple flame failure device

both rocker switches illuminate when switched on / Note: There is no cooling control facility when running on the 12V battery option / switch to activate the electronic spark ignition *(rocker switch flashes when the igniter is sparking–signifying the burner is not alight)*

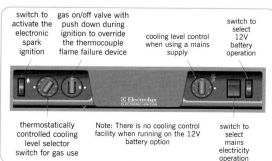

Right: Example of controls and their functions on a mid and late 1990s electronic ignition fridge.

switch to activate the electronic spark ignition / gas on/off valve with push down during ignition to override the thermocouple flame failure device / cooling level control when using a mains supply / switch to select 12V battery operation

thermostatically controlled cooling level selector switch for gas use / Note: There is no cooling control facility when running on the 12V battery option / switch to select mains electricity operation

Different control selectors fitted on post-2000 models

The simple control wheel mounted in the food compartment of a WAECO 2011 CoolMatic sets the cooling level and acts as its on/off switch.

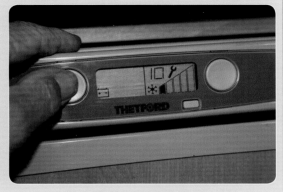

Thetford's Premium appliances, like this Smart Energy Selection model, employ an LCD panel and three buttons to access different operations.

As the drawings show, older control panels contained a multiplicity of controls; in contrast, the Dometic 2009 model is delightfully easy to operate.

The 2000 Electrolux AES refrigerator is also pleasingly simple. There is an on/off switch, a cooling level scale, and electronics to do the rest.

AUTOMATIC SOURCE SELECTION

The Dometic Automatic Energy Selection (AES) and Thetford Smart Energy Selection (SES) models employ an electronic source selector. In the case of AES products, about 12 seconds elapse once the fridge has been switched on, after which the device selects the most appropriate operating mode. The selection is made in accordance with a programmed priority system. The priority order is:

1) 230V mains
2) 12V supply
3) Gas.

Note: *On some post-2004 Dometic models there is a facility for augmenting the 12V supply using a connection taking power from solar panels.*

For instance, if an AES or SES fridge identifies the availability of a 230V supply, the unit will automatically operate on mains electricity in preference to gas or a 12V supply. However, when parked on a site without a mains hook-up, the appliance will choose its gas-operating mode – provided the cylinder contains gas and is on. Lastly, as soon as you start the engine, the refrigerator automatically chooses the 12V operating mode.

Note: *Do not start the engine when your mains*

hook-up cable is connected, as a fuse may blow.

An automatic source selection refrigerator is very convenient, although when you take to the road, you must still remember to turn off the gas supply at the cylinder for safety reasons. If you forget to turn off the gas, an automatic model will still select 12V operation when you start the engine. But what happens when you turn the engine off?

During the development of the Dometic AES products, it was realised that in the event of a motorcaravanner forgetting to turn off a gas cylinder, the fridge would automatically return to gas operation whenever the vehicle's engine was switched off. When stopping at a filling station, this would be illegal and highly dangerous. So the manufacturer programmed a 20-minute delay into the automatic selector; however, this time lapse *only* takes effect in the transition from 12V to gas operation. The switchover delay effectively resolves the filling station problem – presuming that a vehicle can be refuelled and driven away within 20 minutes. But the issue will not arise if you always turn off your gas cylinder before driving the vehicle.

Unsurprisingly, there are small differences between the Dometic AES and Thetford SES appliances, and reference should be made to their owner manuals for more detailed guidance.

Although some American RV fridges are designed to run on gas when on the move, it is strongly recommended to turn off a gas supply at the cylinder before taking to the road. On Electrolux refrigerators made prior to 1992, the burner flame is not extinguished just by turning the temperature control to its lowest setting. If your fridge is one of these earlier appliances, it will have a red ignition push button on the fascia. Only more recent Electrolux (now Dometic) fridges activate a gas shut-off valve when the temperature control is set to zero. This is why earlier models can sometimes be accidentally operated on both a 12V and gas supply simultaneously. The user wrongly presumes the gas option will not work because the control has been set to zero, and also hasn't remembered to turn off the gas at the cylinder before starting the engine. Apart from the danger of having a naked flame when driving, the use of two supplies at once is bad for the fridge.

Merely turning the gas control knob to its lowest setting does *not* extinguish the gas flame on early Electrolux models which are fitted with a red ignition button.

Right: A refrigerator can hold many items, but avoid packing the food so tightly that air is not able to circulate inside.

GETTING THE BEST FROM A REFRIGERATOR

There are several ways for you to get the best results from your motorcaravan's fridge.

Prior to departure

Before leaving home, it helps to pre-cool a refrigerator's storage compartment. Do this by adding non-perishable items, such as bottles of mineral water and cans of drink, then operate the appliance for at least three to four hours. If you can hook up to a mains supply you'll save gas, but an adaptor is needed to connect a motorcaravan's industrial-style hook-up plug into a household 13-Amp socket. You should also fit a portable RCD device in the socket to offer protection to anyone working near the trailing lead. These components were discussed and illustrated in Chapter 5.

Far right: Some refrigerators are fitted with a false door front which unfortunately hides the control panel.

Also note the following points:
- Only transfer perishable items like butter, meat and milk when the temperature has dropped.
- Avoid packing food so tightly that air cannot circulate around the storage area.
- Freshly washed lettuce or other damp vegetables should always be packed in a bag.
- Never completely cover the silver cooling fins inside the food storage area. Cooling efficiency is often impaired when an owner stows a shrink-wrapped pack of beer cans hard against the fins at the rear of the food compartment.

- Before taking to the road, always remember to secure the door's travel catch.

On-site use
Ignition problems

If initial attempts to ignite the burner are not successful, it is often because air is in the gas line. Repeated attempts will usually purge the air. Should the problem continue, it is probably time to have the appliance serviced, which includes cleaning the ignition electrode and checking its alignment. This will be checked during a refrigerator service.

Ventilators obscured

Ensure that its ventilators on the outside are not obscured. For instance, in hot weather, refrigerator cooling is impaired if a motorcaravan's door completely covers the vents when left fully open. **Note:** *Compressor fridges don't have external wall ventilators and do not need servicing.*

Voltage loss

On crowded sites, particularly abroad where electrical standards might not be as strict, power from a 230V hook-up is often reduced. It can fall as low as 190V and cooling is seriously affected as a result. Under these circumstances, you should switch back to gas operation to achieve better cooling. If your motorcaravan is fitted with an AES fridge, this switches to gas automatically whenever its power module detects low voltage.

Cooling loss

Open the fridge door as briefly as possible. Regrettably, some refrigerators are fitted with a false door front that completely hides the fascia controls. Admittedly, this cosmetic addition allows the fridge to match adjacent furniture, but it also means that a refrigerator has to be opened simply to alter the cooling control or energy selection

Technical Tip

Leave some of the cooling fins at the rear of the food compartment exposed, as they are the means by which the operating system at the rear of the casing draws heat from the food compartment. Also, be careful not to dislodge the thermostat capillary tube, which is sometimes clipped to these fins. This would cause the thermostat to make false readings and the appliance would then over-cool food in the storage compartment.

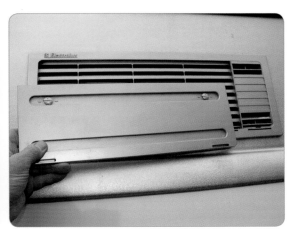

Far left: On Dometic absorption refrigerators, users are advised to add a winter cover when outside temperatures fall below 10°C (50°F); this one is made so that it doesn't obscure the separate flue outlet.

Left: On this Electrolux refrigerator, the travel catch failed to hold the door ajar to ventilate the food compartment during storage periods.

switches. This inevitably causes a loss of cooled air from the food compartment.

Over-cooling

If you use your motorcaravan in the winter, low outside temperatures may bring the reverse problem – over-cooling. It's not unusual to find that milk, cucumbers, and yoghurt are frozen solid. In reality, this is only likely on older Electrolux models fitted with a gas valve such as the RM212, RM4206, RM4230 and RM4200. It doesn't occur on refrigerators fitted with a gas thermostat like the RM2260, RM4237, RM4271 and later models.

Winter covers

If a refrigerator over-cools in low temperatures, Dometic, Electrolux and Thetford manufacture 'winter covers' that clip onto the ventilators. These plastic shields reduce the flow of air across the rear of the appliance. Dometic and Electrolux recommend that their purpose-made winter covers are fitted when outside temperatures fall below 10°C (50°F). Thetford recommends that covers are fitted when temperatures fall below 8°C (46°F)
Note: *Winter covers are not designed to exclude draughts, although they might achieve this up to a point. If wind blows into a motorcaravan through the outside vents, the refrigerator has been incorrectly installed. (See the later section on Ventilation.) Also, be aware that a cover must NOT block a discharge of exhaust fumes coming*

from the gas burner. Since there are different arrangements for the removal of exhaust fumes, check advice in your owner's manual regarding the use of winter covers on your particular appliance.

On returning home

On completion of every trip, remove foodstuffs from the fridge and leave the door partially open – fridges usually incorporate a catch to hold the door slightly ajar so that air can circulate and prevent mould from forming inside. On a few models, such as early examples of the Electrolux Powerfridge and some early models with AES controls, the manufacturer apparently overlooked this feature.

No less pleasing are the actions of some motorcaravan manufacturers who remove perfectly good refrigerator catches before fitting a false wooden door front. Although these additions can look attractive, the conventional furniture catch doesn't provide a fridge ventilation position for storage situations.
Note: *The doors of most leisure fridges are finally pulled shut by a strong magnet, but you need to augment this with a travel catch to prevent the door flying open when you are driving. In addition, there needs to be a mechanism to override the magnetic closing device when an empty fridge is in 'storage mode'. Somewhat surprisingly, creating a two-position security door catch has proved to be one of the toughest challenges facing refrigerator manufacturers. Many examples will be found, some of which are fragile; others move out of place.*

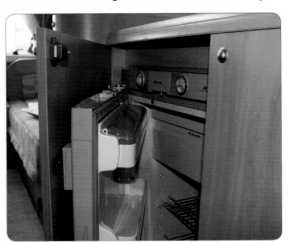

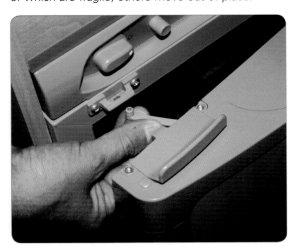

Far left: This wooden door improved appearances in a Swift Kon Tiki Vogue, but the manufacturer didn't fit a replacement catch that would secure the fridge door in a part-open storage position.

Left: The simple but effective strut fitted on some Thetford models ensures that a door remains slightly ajar, thereby ventilating the storage compartment.

Right: Electrolux recommends cleaning the interior of a fridge using a mixture that you make up by stirring a teaspoonful of bicarbonate of soda into half a litre of water. Other cleaners are NOT recommended as some types cause cracks in the cabinet lining several weeks after the cleaning operation.

Right: Thetford initially recommended cleaning-out a fridge using mild domestic detergents; now you are advised to use the company's 'Bathroom Cleaner'

At the end of a season, clean the inside of your refrigerator. Electrolux recommended using a weak solution of bicarbonate of soda, by mixing a teaspoonful into half a litre of warm water.

Thetford initially recommended the use of a 'soft cloth and mild detergent', but some owners used products that were too aggressive. At the time of writing, the company now advises the use of Thetford 'Bathroom Cleaner', which is formulated to clean the similar plastic surfaces used in its toilet products.

If you lay-up your motorcaravan for an extended period after your return home, it is wise to consider having the refrigerator serviced by a specialist before the annual rush at the start of the following season.

Stain removal

Sometimes the interior of a refrigerator can become stained. A broken egg, for example, will leave discoloration from the yolk. Equally, the movement of drink cans during a journey can leave metal marks on the plastic lining. To remove a stubborn mark in a Dometic or Electrolux refrigerator, the technical staff advise owners to use a very fine wire wool pad liberally lubricated with water to reduce its abrasive effect. If used carefully, this will remove stubborn stains without damaging the plastic lining material.

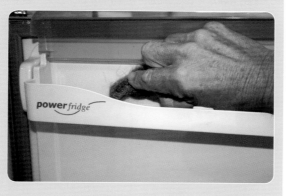

Installation

The following information provides guidance for anyone engaged in motorcaravan self-build or renovation work. Bear in mind that any DIY installation must be checked by a qualified technical specialist before being put into use. This section also provides a point of reference for anyone buying a motorcaravan or for existing owners whose fridge performance is disappointing. Regrettably, a few motorcaravan manufacturers have disregarded some of the requirements laid down in fridge manufacturers' installation literature.

It is also clear that many requirements relating to the installation of three-way absorption refrigerators are markedly different from those applicable to compressor appliances. Apart from the following section on fridge location, the differences are sufficient to justify two separate descriptions.

CHOOSING A LOCATION

A refrigerator is a heavy appliance, especially when fully loaded, so its position may have an effect on the suspension, particularly if it is situated at the extreme rear of a vehicle. And whereas a tall fridge-freezer or a conventional fridge installed at chest-height is particularly convenient to use, a higher centre of gravity inevitably contributes to body roll when a vehicle is cornering. Finally, if a three-way fridge is positioned where its ventilators are obstructed when the main entrance door is secured in an open position, its cooling efficiency could be impaired.

Note: *A fridge should not be fitted where an enclosed awning is often used.*

INSTALLATION ISSUES RELATING TO COMPRESSOR REFRIGERATORS

Taking the WAECO Coolmatic CR50 as an example (gross capacity 48 litres including its 5-litre freezing compartment), the first job is to prepare a location within the kitchen cabinets. Before commencing work, check the installation manual because some Coolmatic products, *eg* the MDC models, should have a small gap between the casing and the aperture in which it is fitted. There should be a narrow gap, for example, at the back between the appliance and the wall of the motorcaravan.

A compressor fridge also needs to be secured with care, and WAECO models often have four installation points inside the food compartment for fixing screws. As an optional accessory, there are two types of fitting frames to secure the front of the fridge. One allows the front of a refrigerator to project outwards of the kitchen cabinet; the other provides flush face fitting, as shown alongside.

Note: *For technical data for WAECO cooling products visit www.my-caravanning.com or www.waeco.com*

Finally, it is important that the 12V cables supplying power to a compressor fridge are of the correct gauge. There have been cases of fridges performing poorly because the cable has been too thin. Inadequate cables lead to a voltage drop, so check the installation information carefully and use PVC-sheathed, flexible automotive cable. If the total length

Installing a compressor fridge in a self-build campervan

A VW Transporter is a popular vehicle for DIY conversions and fitting a compressor fridge eliminates the need to cut holes in its side for ventilation.

The WAECO Coolmatic CR50 offers either a standard or flush-mounted frame as optional accessories for securing the appliance around its door.

Having built a suitable enclosure, and fitted location battens to the floor at the sides and rear, the appliance is offered-up to check it fits.

Six screws secure the flush-mount-frame and the stainless steel decor door panel was retained rather than adding a veneered plywood panel.

of both the live and neutral cables running between the appliance and the battery doesn't exceed 3m, you can use cable of 4–5 mm². However, if the total length *does* exceed 3m, a thicker gauge of cable is needed. (See Chapter 5 for cable gauge and performance, as well as fridge installation instructions.)

INSTALLATION ISSUES CONCERNING ABSORPTION REFRIGERATORS

Since circulation of the refrigerant in an absorption fridge is hindered if the appliance isn't level, an installer should first park the motorcaravan on level ground. A spirit level should be used to confirm that the vehicle is level, and should be used continuously throughout installation work.

LEVELLING REFERENCE POINTS

On Electrolux refrigerators, the traditional reference point for verifying that an appliance is level was the shelf in the freezer compartment. Of course, a short spirit level is needed to take a reading here. However, this isn't possible on the RM123 models, which have a sloping shelf: on this model the spirit level should be placed on the base of the food storage cabinet. For reference points of other products, check their installation manuals.

Note: *1) All Electrolux refrigerators manufactured before 1986 had to be level to operate, and cooling will not occur if there's a tilt in excess of 2–3°. Since 1989, all higher specification Electrolux models have been described as 'tilt tolerant'. Some models will operate at an angle of 3° (eg RM122 and RM4206), while others operate at 6° from a level plane, (eg RM4217, RM4237, RM4271 and RM6271). But check the information given in an applicance's installation manual.*

2) On the road, a fridge will seldom be level, particularly when driving along a carriageway with a pronounced camber. However, as long as a level position is achieved periodically – which is the case on most roads – chemical circulation will take place and cooling duly occurs.

STRUCTURAL FIXING

When a motorcaravan is being driven, its appliances receive a considerable shake-up, especially on bumpy country lanes. To resist this, a refrigerator needs to be carefully secured. It is prudent, for example, to fit a wood batten or block on the floor at the rear of the unit. Normally, blocks are not needed at the sides as long as robust support is afforded by the adjacent kitchen units.

Side anchorage used to be achieved by driving screws through furniture panels on either side and directly into the metal casing of the appliance. As long as they penetrated no further than 12mm (½in), the interior plastic lining wouldn't be damaged. In truth, this was a crude system, and

Right: More recent
Electrolux refrigerators
have side mounting points –
plastic caps hide the heads
of the screws.

SEALED VENTILATION PATH

In both the heat of summer and the cold winds of winter, an owner whose motorcaravan is fitted with an absorption refrigerator will experience problems if the installation doesn't meet the ventilation requirements specified by the manufacturer.

To ensure efficient operation, the refrigeration unit fitted on the back of the casing must be kept cool. When this is achieved, a well-maintained absorption refrigerator operates effectively in air temperatures as high as 38°C (100°F). However, if a motorcaravan is parked in a non-shaded spot on a hot, sunny day, temperatures inside the vehicle can rise to considerably higher levels. This is why the rear of the casing must be completely sealed off from the living space; in direct sunshine, the temperature indoors can rise well above 38°C.

To achieve its cooling potential, a three-way fridge requires a ventilation facility in which air gets drawn from the outside, passes over the cooling unit fixed to the rear of the casing by convection and then discharges outside via an upper ventilator. To facilitate the release of warmed air, a tilting metal deflector must be fitted on top of the casing as shown in the accompanying diagram.

models like the Electrolux RM2260 and RM2262 were later manufactured with a projecting flange around the front to provide alternative fixing points.

In addition, Dometic refrigerators and Electrolux models made since 1994 also incorporate holes in the sides of the food compartment. This means that long screws can be driven from the *inside* outwards, thereby achieving anchorage from adjacent structures – usually kitchen cupboards. The heads of the screws are then concealed by a white plastic cap, which matches the food compartment lining.

Whichever method is adopted, three objectives must be achieved:

- ▓ The fridge should be in a level position when the vehicle is parked on level ground.
- ▓ It must not shake loose when driving on rough roads.
- ▓ The appliance should be easy to remove for servicing.

In order to help installers create a sealed ventilation path, Electrolux manufactured an aluminium shield, complete with a tilting deflector, for mounting between the appliance and the sidewall of the vehicle. This was referred to as the IK1 Kit. Alternatively, a custom-made shield can be formed using aluminium sheet and this is often preferred when an enclosure has to be shaped to fit closely against the curving profile of a side wall in a van conversion. As mentioned earlier, forming a ventilation facility that is sealed off from the living area is important.

Creating a sealed ventilation facility is often quite involved and, regrettably, there have been some motorcaravan manufacturers who have disregarded this requirement. There is no excuse for this because the procedures have been clearly laid down in refrigerator installation manuals. Although an absorption fridge is likely to provide *some* cooling, if the ventilation pathway at the rear of the appliance is not kept entirely separate from the living space, two problems arise:

Below: Correct installation
is important and the need to
fit a metal shield deflector
at the rear is emphasised by
the manufacturer.

Below: In this DIY installation, an aluminium deflector is screwed down to wooden strips bonded to the refrigerator.

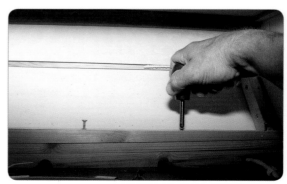

Typical installation requirements

This drawing highlights features applicable to Electrolux three-way fridges.

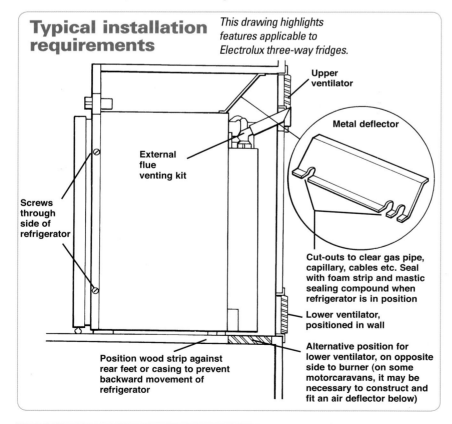

Upper ventilator

Metal deflector

External flue venting kit

Screws through side of refrigerator

Cut-outs to clear gas pipe, capillary, cables etc. Seal with foam strip and mastic sealing compound when refrigerator is in position

Lower ventilator, positioned in wall

Position wood strip against rear feet or casing to prevent backward movement of refrigerator

Alternative position for lower ventilator, on opposite side to burner (on some motorcaravans, it may be necessary to construct and fit an air deflector below)

If a worktop over a refrigerator gets hot, this is a certain sign that the ventilation facility has not been properly sealed.

When this upper ventilator was removed, it was clear that the installation had a deflector shield as specified by the manufacturer.

This motorhome had a useful chopping board, but when withdrawn, you could see light coming through the upper fridge ventilator. The installer had disregarded the fridge manufacturer's instructions.

1) A refrigerator does not operate to its maximum potential in hot temperatures.
2) In cold weather, draughts blowing through the wall vents will penetrate the interior.

Note: *It is wrong to resolve the draught issue by applying adhesive sealant around an installed fridge – a practice seen in some German and Italian-built motorcaravans. This makes it extremely difficult to remove the appliance for routine servicing work. The use of adhesive-backed draught-excluding strips is a better strategy as long as the strips do not interfere with the exhaust system or the flame guard. They must also be made with a fire-retardant, closed cell form.*

If your refrigerator doesn't cool as well as you think it should, feel the worktop, draining board, or shelf directly above the appliance, and if these feel hot, warm air from the rear of the cooling unit isn't being correctly deflected outside via its upper ventilator. Another way to ascertain if an installation meets an appliance manufacturer's specification is to remove the upper ventilator on the outside wall and to peer inside. If you can see into the living space, the installation does not fulfil the requirements. Equally, if, when you remove the kitchen drawers and open some cupboard doors, you can see directly through the upper ventilator, the installer has most definitely disregarded the fridge manufacturer's instructions. Not only will the appliance fail to work at its best, it will certainly be draughty when you stand in the kitchen. **Note**: *Also check the Safety Panel on page 147.*

VENTILATION COMPONENTS

If a sealed ventilation path has been constructed correctly, there is no need for an electric fan to accelerate air movement over the rear of an appliance (except on large fridge-freezers). Nevertheless, motorcaravanners who frequently visit hot regions often fit a compact 12V-operated fan. These can be obtained from dealers. The Dometic fan is both thermostatically controlled and easy to fit.

The size of the ventilators also contributes to performance. For example, on Dometic models with a storage capacity of less than 60 litres

(approximately 2cu ft), the ventilators should provide at least 240cm^2 of free air space. Models offering more than 60 litres storage need ventilators achieving a minimum of 300cm^2 free air space. Unfortunately the effective area is significantly reduced if a vent is fitted with an insect mesh.

The A1609 and A1620 ventilators formerly made by Electrolux meet these requirements but are quite expensive. This is why a few manufacturers fitted cheaper products, some of which were not rainproof, as Electrolux units were. Furthermore, some of the less-expensive ventilators cannot accept winter covers – just like some of the early Electrolux ventilators.

If an owner decides to upgrade the ventilators, the Electrolux A1620 version incorporates the flue outlet as part of the ventilation unit, whereas on older models, the flue had a separate fitting. To suit more recent appliances, Dometic offers the LS 100, which has its own dedicated flue outlet, as well as 200, and 300 ventilators. In the case of Thetford's

Left: Some owners fit a fridge fan to the upper ventilator to enhance air flow in hot weather conditions.

Left: Later products from Electrolux incorporated the flue outlet in the upper ventilator as shown here.

Above: The fridge freezers from Dometic do not have a separate flue outlet; all the combustion waste is discharged through the upper ventilator.

Below: The 12V connection and cable specifications applicable to three-way fridges must follow an appliance manufacturer's instructions. This drawing is based on instructions applicable to Electrolux models.

upper ventilator, fumes from the flue have to discharge through the ventilation grilles rather than via a separate outlet.

The position of ventilators relative to the appliance is also important. Dometic specifies that the top vent should be located so that its lower edge aligns with the top of the appliance. This ensures that the upper edge will be at least 55mm above the refrigerator.

In many of the Electrolux installations, the lower vent could be fitted in either the sidewall or in the floor. If the latter option has been adopted the vent should be situated as far away from the burner as possible so that the flame is not extinguished by draughts. A deflector shield should also be fitted under the floor so that road dirt doesn't get into the enclosure when you're driving.

THE REFRIGERATOR FLUE

The provision of a flue is necessary in order to disperse the products of combustion when an appliance is operating on gas. This is nothing to do with the ventilation requirement; the fact that the flue outlet is accommodated in the latest ventilators is purely for tidiness. On older installations the outlets were entirely separate.

The assembly of the flue pipe supplied with a refrigerator is straightforward and clearly explained in the fitting instructions, which an installer should meticulously follow. The tubing supplied must not be lengthened, since this could lead to an imbalance in the gas/air mixture at the burner. On Electrolux and Dometic products, the flue pipe that couples to the burner tube has a junction connector referred to as a 'lazy T'. On a Thetford refrigerator there is a curving deflector instead, which steers the products of combustion towards the central area of a ventilation grille. This is shown in the later sequence on servicing operations.

Similar to Thetford fridges, the large fridge-freezers from Dometic don't have a separate flue outlet. Instead, the entire area offered by the upper ventilator is used to discharge combustion fumes to the outside. For this reason, it is critically important that the ventilation facility at the rear of the unit is effectively sealed from the living space. If the continuity of the sealant deteriorates, there is a risk that fumes from the gas burner could seep into the living area.

Note: *A double-door Dometic fridge must be served by the 300 type ventilation grill and NOT one fitted with a separate 'pepper pot' flue outlet. Always follow instructions on vent requirements given in the installation manual.*

MAINS CONNECTION

Like most home appliances, motorcaravan refrigerators are now supplied with a moulded 13-Amp plug that needs to be connected to a mains supply socket. Typically there is a dedicated socket for the fridge, which will be protected by a miniature circuit breaker on the mains consumer unit, as described in Chapter 5. The mains plug for a fridge should be fitted with a 3-Amp fuse.

LOW VOLTAGE CONNECTION

One problem with 12V operation is that there will be a voltage loss if the connecting cables are too long and of insufficient gauge (thickness).

In most refrigerators the operating supply is taken from the base vehicle's starter battery, albeit via a relay that prevents the supply being available until the engine is running. A second supply for operating the electronic spark igniter is usually taken from the leisure battery – as shown in the diagram.

However, in the case of an AES refrigerator, both the operating supply *and* the electronic igniter supply are taken from the leisure battery rather than the base vehicle's battery. There is a reason

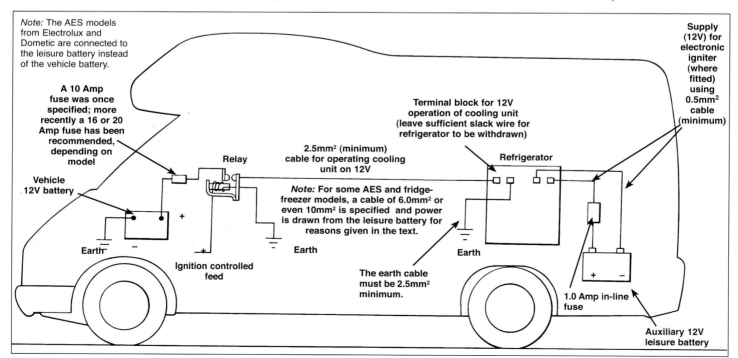

Note: The AES models from Electrolux and Dometic are connected to the leisure battery instead of the vehicle battery.

A 10 Amp fuse was once specified; more recently a 16 or 20 Amp fuse has been recommended, depending on model

Vehicle 12V battery

Earth

Relay

Ignition controlled feed

2.5mm² (minimum) cable for operating cooling unit on 12V

Note: For some AES and fridge-freezer models, a cable of 6.0mm² or even 10mm² is specified and power is drawn from the leisure battery for reasons given in the text.

Earth

The earth cable must be 2.5mm² minimum.

Terminal block for 12V operation of cooling unit (leave sufficient slack wire for refrigerator to be withdrawn)

Refrigerator

Earth

Supply (12V) for electronic igniter (where fitted) using 0.5mm² cable (minimum)

1.0 Amp in-line fuse

Auxiliary 12V leisure battery

for this. On Electrolux AES models available in 2001, the refrigerator can completely discharge the supplying battery if the user omits to switch off the appliance using its on/off fascia control when the vehicle is stationary. Even if you've turned off the gas supply, disconnected a mains supply and the engine isn't running, the 'computer' responsible for automatically selecting the operating mode continues to draw electricity if the fascia switch remains on. The current drain is small, but over a long lay-up period it can completely discharge a battery – and discharging a leisure battery as opposed to a starter battery is the lesser of two evils. Even though the cooling system is no longer in operation, always switch off the AES circuitry as well, via the control button on the fascia.

Key elements in a 12V supply:

■ A 16- or 20-Amp fuse, depending on the model, which must be fitted close to the positive terminal on the supply battery. **Note:** *At one time a 10-Amp fuse was specified, but this recommendation has since been revised due to greater power demand.*

■ A relay – this is an electric switch to ensure that a refrigerator will only run on a 12V supply when the engine is running and the battery is receiving a charge from the alternator. This is because the drain on a battery is considerable – a fridge draws at least 8 Amps when running on 12V. Suitable relays are available from motorcaravan dealers, towbar installers and auto electricians.

■ Cable of the correct gauge as specified by the fridge manufacturer. For example, to prevent current loss, Electrolux, and now Dometic, specify; a) connecting cable of at least 2.5mm² gauge where a total cable run (live and neutral) does not exceed 10.5 metres; b) connecting cable of at least 4.0mm² gauge where the total cable run (live and neutral) does not exceed 17 metres; and c) connecting cable of 6.0mm² or 10mm² gauge for some AES and fridge-freezer models.

■ Connection to the appliance. The live and neutral feeds are coupled to a terminal block on top of the refrigerator casing, just behind the control fascia. The polarity *is* important on the AES models, but seldom on other absorption models. (Confirm the requirement in your model's installation instructions.)

■ A 12V feed to the electronic igniter for the gas burner (where this form of ignition is fitted). This is a separate supply needing 0.5mm² (minimum) cable and a 1-Amp fuse; it is normally taken from the leisure battery.

GAS OPERATION

Requirements for the gas supply:

■ An independent gas control tap in the supply to the fridge – usually situated in a kitchen cupboard.

■ Copper feed pipes usually of 8mm (³⁄₈in) outside diameter (OD) – the final connection to the

Above: Connection to a 12V supply often uses a block that is fastened behind the fascia control panel.

appliance must never be made with flexible gas hose.

■ A flue arrangement – this is *entirely different* from the ventilation system described earlier. On the outside of the vehicle, the flue cover plate used to be separate from the ventilator grilles. Then in 1994, Electrolux introduced the A1620 grilles, which incorporated both the flue and upper ventilation outlets. These have since been replaced by the LS 100 grills. However, Dometic fridge-freezer and Thetford's fridges use the entire upper vent for both the discharge of combustion fumes and the ventilation facility.

■ An ignition system – in the 1960s and early 1970s, the gas burner on refrigerators from manufacturers like Morphy Richards had to be lit with a match. Later, push-button igniters that use a piezo crystal to generate a spark were fitted. Then, in the mid-1980s, electronic ignition was introduced, and this is now much more common. In order to create a spark at the burner, the gap must be set to the manufacturer's specification. On a Dometic appliance, for example, it has to be set to 3mm and the components must be clean and free of soot.

■ Where an older A1609 wall ventilator has been fitted, a low level 'drop out' hole of 40mm (1⅝in) has to be formed in the floor to allow escaping gas to discharge to the exterior. The A1609 vent cannot act as an alternative escape route because it would be completely obstructed when a 'winter cover' is fitted. However, more recent Dometic ventilators *can* afford an accepted gas escape facility as long as the lowest louvre is below floor level. This portion of these later vents remains unobstructed even when a 'winter cover' has been attached.

■ For many years, the connection point to couple-up with the vehicle's gas supply was often situated just behind the control fascia. On more recent models, however, it is more conveniently fitted at the rear where it can be easily reached, merely by removing a wall vent.

Note: *The DIY enthusiast can tackle many aspects of refrigerator installation. However, making the final connection to a gas supply should be entrusted to a competent gas installer. The connection used to employ a threaded coupling but all recent models use a compression fitting with an 'olive'. A jointing compound is not recommended by Dometic. A generous length of copper pipe should be left on top of an appliance so that it can be drawn slightly forward from its housing when a fridge has to be removed for repairs or servicing.*

Safety

Whenever a refrigerator is repositioned, or withdrawn and later reinstated, a gas pressure check must be carried out immediately afterwards.

Checks carried out by a service technician

1 This 2006 Dometic refrigerator has been removed and transferred to a workbench. The burner is behind a shield at the bottom right, the insulated vertical burner tube is above it, and the two heating elements (12V and 230V) have grey and red cables.

2 To access the burner assembly, the protective shield is removed from the casing. Provided the lower ventilators are positioned in the correct place in an external wall of a motorcaravan, which isn't always the case, this could be accessed by removing the grille.

3 The burner assembly on this Dometic refrigerator is screwed to the foot of the burner tube. The thin copper connection linked to the burner is part of the flame failure device and the black and white sheathed cable takes power to the spark igniter.

4 On this 2009 Thetford fridge, the burner assembly is different in several ways. However, it is still fastened at the foot of a burner tube. You also get a clearer view of the angular end of the spark igniter and its white collar. It's the burner itself that is different.

5 The burner tube will be coated with carbon deposits and flakes of rust so this will later be cleaned. To prevent any of this debris landing on the burner, the assembly is detached and eased to one side. Here you can see the end of the FFD, which also needs cleaning.

6 Inside an Electrolux and Dometic burner assembly there is a replaceable gas jet that needs changing at every service. The tiny hole in the helmet-like fitting is made to a critical dimension. It must never be wiped; nor must anything be put in the hole.

7 There are four different types of burner on a Thetford fridge, none of which look like the Dometic components. The flame emerges from the upper left side of this tube and there is an air inlet low on the right. There is *not* a replaceable jet in a Thetford burner.

8 At the upper end of the insulated burner tube, Electrolux and Dometic fridges have a detachable connecter piece that looks like a letter 'T', albeit with a sloping top. Named as a 'lazy T', this couples the outlet at the top of the burner tube to a flue outlet on the sidewall.

9 On a Thetford fridge, the top of the burner tube is connected to the component shown here, which discharges the flue emissions towards the louvres on the upper-wall ventilator. Whether this component or a lazy T is fitted, a screw allows these items to be removed.

10 When a service specialist has detached the flue couplings from the burner tube, this baffle has to be removed. It will be coated with carbon and needs cleaning. The wire suspends it at the right height to retain heat in the lower part of the burner tube.

11 Now the narrow pipe inside the burner tube can be thoroughly cleaned. Service technicians use a purpose-made wire brush with a long handle. This job can be difficult unless the appliance has been moved to a bench.

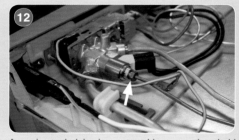

12 A service technician inspects cable connections behind the fascia panel. The large bronze assembly in the centre houses the gas control valve, and the copper pipe connected to it with a bolt must be checked for tightness. This conducts current from the FFD.

Servicing

As with any gas appliance, periodic servicing is important. Not only does this ensure efficient operation, it is a safety requirement, too. Despite this, some motorcaravanners *never* have their fridge serviced and it seems to run well season after season. But nothing is more annoying than a fridge failing on holiday, especially in hot weather.

Note: *A full refrigerator service is not carried out within a standard habitation operation schedule. As stated in the service guidance section later in this manual, a standard service operation confirms whether an appliance is cooling sufficiently, and a cursory check is made to see that an installation is safe and sound. It does not include the dismantling work, cleaning, and setting operations described here. A full refrigerator service is a separate operation that should always be carried out by a qualified service technician.*

Appliance manufacturers recognise that owners use their motorcaravans with varying frequency, but they recommend that servicing work should be carried out every 12 to 18 months. The servicing operation takes around an hour to complete, but it can be time-consuming to remove an appliance from the motorcaravan and reinstate it afterwards. This can take around 20 minutes on some models, but in extreme cases it occasionally takes a whole day. This was allegedly the case on a Laika coachbuilt model with a refrigerator intricately built into an unusual kitchen layout.

It is sometimes claimed that some of the latest refrigerators can be left in situ for servicing. This is based on the premise that many components requiring cleaning and adjustment can be reached by removing the wall ventilators and reaching through the apertures. However, many service specialists assert that removing loose rust and carbon deposits from a burner tube flue is extremely difficult to carry out if a refrigerator isn't removed and transferred to a work bench.

Servicing tasks must be carried out by a competent, experienced and trained refrigerator specialist and the job should not be tackled by a DIY enthusiast. On the other hand, a labour charge might be reduced if a competent owner were able to remove the fridge from its housing. Reinstatement could also be considered, but only a qualified gas service specialist should reconnect a gas supply and carry out a leak test.

The charges for servicing a refrigerator are usually divided into three separate elements by Dometic:

- The workshop's labour rate for the removal and reinstatement of the appliance.
- The workshop's hourly rate for the service, which normally takes about an hour.
- The cost of new parts fitted. In practice, the overall cost of parts is usually modest.

The accompanying panel shows the scope of a servicing operation and highlights a few of the tasks involved. In broad terms, the servicing operations on Dometic, Electrolux, and Thetford absorption appliances are similar. These photographs were taken during service training courses conducted by Dometic, Electrolux and Thetford.

OTHER TYPES OF REFRIGERATOR

In very small motorcaravans, there may not be sufficient space to accommodate a fixed refrigerator so semi-portable cool boxes are often fitted instead. However, some cool boxes employ a different method of cooling, and examples built with an electric fan employ what is known as the Peltier effect. Others employ the full functions referred to in this chapter. Some use a three-way cooling facility; others are compressor-driven products. Cool boxes from WAECO have been available for many years.

Portability is certainly an asset, and some motorcaravanners who already have a fixed fridge purchase a cool box to keep in an awning or to take to the beach. As stated at the beginning of this chapter, 'in a motorcaravan, the refrigerator makes one of the most important contributions to comfortable living...'

Problem solving

If a refrigerator doesn't work on gas, check the following:
- the fridge's selection switch is set to gas operation
- the supply cylinder contains gas and its control is switched on
- the gas control valve near the appliance is switched on
- the refrigerator has been serviced in the last 18 months.

If a refrigerator doesn't work on 12V:
- ensure the fridge's selection switch is set to 12V operation
- remember that this option only works when the engine is running
- check all fuses that protect the 12V supply
- get an electrician to check that a 12V supply is reaching the fridge's connector block.

Note: *See panel alongside 'Drops in voltage'.*

Drops in voltage

Poor cooling is not just a result from a poorly constructed ventilation facility at the rear of an absorption fridge. Its 12V operation is also affected if there is a drop in the supply voltage. This usually arises when the feed cables are of insufficient gauge, which often becomes apparent at the time of a service. Tests with a voltmeter at the fridge terminals will soon indicate whether a 12V supply is reaching the appliance.

If a refrigerator fails to work on 230V check that:
- the fridge's selection switch is set to 230V operation
- the mains is connected and the consumer unit's RCD and MCBs are switched on
- the refrigerator 230V plug is in the socket and the switch is on
- the fuse is intact if a 13-Amp plug is fitted.

Flame failure device (FFD)

As explained in Chapter 6, gas only flows to a burner when the tip of its thermocouple has warmed up. The metals in this device then create a small electric current that operates an electro-magnetic valve situated in the main gas control assembly behind the fascia panel. If the flame blows out, the probe cools, current fails, and a spring on the electro-magnetic valve closes the passage gas. This is a very useful safety element.

However, during the initial warm-up period, a reduced level of heat is not enough to create the amount of current needed to activate the electro-magnetic valve. On older types of fridge (including pre-2004 models) you must therefore hold the valve open manually by keeping the gas control knob on the fascia depressed for a few seconds. If a flame fails to stay alight when the control knob is released, this may be caused by excessive soot on the thermo-couple probe. Or perhaps the probe isn't pointing into the heart of the flame. Another problem occurs during the pitch and toss of driving. The connecting nut (shown in the final photo of the servicing sequence) can sometimes become loose, thereby causing a poor electrical connection. This is why it is checked for tightness during a service.

The interior design of a motorcaravan is important to the owner. It is not just a matter of layout or the number of beds; the styling is important, too. In fact, the design of the furniture and the choice of fabrics is one of the first things you notice when entering the living area.

When it comes to interior design, none of our tastes are the same. We also have different reasons for owning a motorcaravan. Some owners, for example, enjoy passive leisure activities and prefer traditionally styled motorcaravans with comfortable carpet, good quality curtains and plush fabrics. However, 'carpet-slipper' comforts do not suit everyone, especially motorcaravanners who participate in active outdoor adventures, or those who share their van with dogs.

In the past, surprisingly few UK manufacturers have recognised that motorcaravanners often enjoy cycling, fishing, walking, or taking children to play on the beach. This has now changed, and fewer models are being built with ornate florid fabrics, fixed carpets, costly curtains, and illuminated cocktail cabinets embellished with 'plastic glass' doors.

Of course, tastes and interests vary, but the realities of rain and the nature of campsites raise issues that must be addressed. For instance, a smart fitted carpet looks fine in a showroom but is much too 'precious' when it's raining; shoes will be muddy and campsite grass cuttings will appear indoors. A vinyl floor covered with removable sections of carpet provides an alternative way of dealing with these conditions.

This is only one example of change, and the radical move away from 'cottage comfort' is clearly evident when you compare the interior of an Auto-Sleeper model built in 1994 with an Auto-Sleeper model built in 2004. Anyone planning to buy a pre-owned model should keep these points in mind.

Given the fact that we all have different lifestyles, the rest of this chapter is concerned with the realities of ownership. For example, in order to keep upholstery clean, many owners purchase protective covers. This is often adopted by motorcaravanners who own dogs, or parents with youngsters at a 'sticky-finger' age. Of course there can be accidents when drinks get spilt, or something gets trodden into the carpet. So let's start with cleaning operations and then consider some upgrading projects.

Below: The Auto-Trail Grand Frontier, with a drop-down bed over the cab, offers a notably attractive and well-appointed interior without the frills and florid fabrics typical of the 1990s.

Below right: Motorcaravans like this Knaus Sport were being equipped with practical vinyl floor coverings and shaped carpet overlays before the idea became generally adopted by UK manufacturers.

Far left: This 1994 Auto Sleepers model with its ornate styling, fitted carpet and florid fabrics might be fine for passive leisure but is hardly suitable for outdoor sports enthusiasts.

Left: In complete contrast, this 2004 Auto-Sleepers Trident has clean lines, easy-clean surfaces and a vinyl floor covering – just what active owners need.

Interior cleaning

Apart from routine 'house' maintenance, you will need to periodically undertake more thorough cleaning work. When that time comes, it's often easier to transfer seats and seat backs to a workbench outside. You can then use proprietary products, and it's surprising how dirty a cloth can get when you're wiping away the cleaning fluids.

Many domestic cleaning shampoos are suitable for motorcaravan furnishings but vehicle upholstery cleaners are also available. Products such as Auto Glym Car Interior Shampoo are suitable for use on most motorcaravan fabrics, including velour covers. With this product, the cleaning process entails:

- Spraying Auto Glym cleaner directly on to the fabric
- Stippling the surface gently with a soft brush to agitate its fibres
- Wiping the material with a clean cloth.

Note: *If you do this work outdoors, cleaning fumes disperse easily and you avoid the problem of condensation forming inside the vehicle. It is often wise to wait until the weather is warm – but don't delay a cleaning operation if it involves removing stains.*

Another product in this range is Hi-Foam Interior Shampoo, which is sold in aerosol cans. Used by many motorcaravan valeting specialists, Hi-Foam is not only effective for cleaning fabrics, it is also formulated to clean carpets, vinyl and plastics, as shown here.

Using Car Interior Shampoo

Left: First spray the shampoo onto selected areas of the fabric that needs to be cleaned.

Left: Then agitate the fibres to work in the shampoo by stippling the fabric with a soft brush.

Below: Finally, wipe the material with a clean cloth, which in turn lifts off the dirt.

Using Hi-Foam Interior Shampoo

Left: The fabric panel on the driver's seat is sprayed with Hi-Foam.

Left: A synthetic chamois cloth is used to lift dirt when the foam is removed.

Left: This foam also cleans faced plywood table tops and cupboard fronts.

Right: Many loose covers are machine washable, and if this is the case it should be indicated on the label.

Far right: Specialist upholsterers that manufacture zipped covers for motorcaravans are often able to supply these in high-quality fabrics and the covers can be removed in seconds for washing.

Handy Tip

If cushion covers have a label indicating that they can be machine washed at home, bear in mind that they might start to shrink as they dry, which can make them a struggle to fit. The tip is to slip them over their foam filling and zip or stitch-up the cover while it's still slightly damp. If the cover shrinks as it dries, it will grip the foam with pleasing results.

REMOVABLE COVERS

Everyone has the occasional accident, but if there is a regular risk of stain damage – perhaps from pets or young children – it might be wise to have protective covers made for selected seats. These are usually machine-washable, as their labels confirm. Incidentally, the older types of budget nylon 'stretch-covers' are hugely different from modern removable covers made from high specification fabrics.

DEALING WITH STAINS

It's useful to keep a small container of general-purpose stain remover as a permanent item in your motorcaravan, but bear in mind that a 'do-everything' product is seldom as successful as a cleaner made specifically to deal with a particular blemish.

Alternatively, there are a number of kitchen products that can be used for removing stains, and a useful cleaning kit can be created using the following:

- Absorbent white cloth
- Nylon scouring pad
- Spray mist 'atomising' bottle
- Blunt, round-bladed table knife
- Nail brush
- Salt
- Lemon juice
- White methylated spirits
- White vinegar
- Household ammonia
- Biological washing powder
- Glycerine
- Borax

General guidance
Keep these points in mind:
- Keep an emergency cleaning kit in your motorcaravan so you are ready to deal with problems.
- Deal with damage immediately and apply a stain remover without delay. If a stain-specific treatment is available rather than a general purpose cleaner, so much the better.
- If you have doubts about the way a fabric might react with a cleaning chemical, use the product on a small corner first to check compatibility.
- Always remove individual stains before washing an entire item.
- Always apply a treatment with a clean white cloth, such as a piece from an old bed sheet. If you use a coloured or patterned cloth, dye can run into the fabric you're cleaning.
- Scrape away any surface deposit with a blunt knife before applying the cleaning compound.
- When removing a mark from a velour fabric, always work in the direction of the pile to avoid surface damage.
- Be gentle in your approach, using a dabbing action where possible. Fabric fibres can be damaged if a rough, rubbing action is employed.
- Be sparing when using fluids, and periodically blot the area to lift marks and to avoid deep penetration into the material.
- After treatment, remove as much of the cleaning material as possible. Some chemicals leave a mark of their own.
- If a trace of water is needed on an area of damage, a mist spray bottle is ideal. This type of atomiser bottle is sold in garden centres.
- For safety reasons, wear surgical gloves, open windows to release fumes, extinguish flames (some chemicals are flammable), keep cleaning chemicals in labelled containers, and never mix chemicals together – the result could be explosive.

Below: A very effective stain removal kit can be made up using products taken from the kitchen.

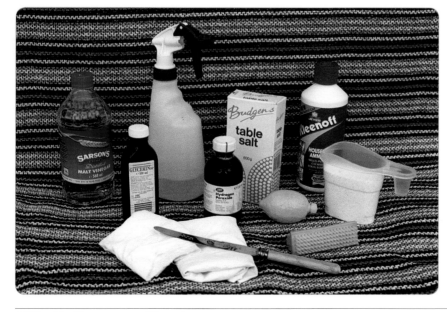

Far left: If you apply or remove treatments with a cloth, it should be clean and white. If you make the mistake shown here, colour from the cloth can be released into the fabric.

Left: If something gets dropped on to a cushion, remove it immediately using an old blunt house knife, then apply the stain remover or cleaning compound.

TACKLING SOME COMMON STAINS

Beer
Using a solution of one part white vinegar to five parts cold water, gently sponge the area. Blot well before repeating with cold water. Allow to dry naturally; don't apply heat.

Blood
Sponge with salt water solution followed by a mild household ammonia and water mix. Blot at every stage, finish with clean water, and allow it to dry without applying heat.

Chewing gum
Freeze using ice cubes packed in a polythene bag, then tap away the brittle gum with a knife handle. Alternatively, use Scotch 3M Clean Art – this comes from stationery specialists and removes deposits left on book covers by gummed-back price tickets. It can be similarly used to dissolve chewing gum.

Chocolate
Gently scrape away any residue. The remaining blemish should respond to washing powder mixed into a paste with water. Apply with the knife in your cleaning kit, leave for 30 minutes, and then carefully scrape it all away.

Coffee stains
Soften using glycerine and leave for 25 minutes. Sponge away with clean water.

Egg
Scrape off any dried residue, apply a paste of biological powder and water, and leave for 30 minutes. Brush this off before thoroughly sponging with clean water and blotting frequently. Avoid using external heat because this can set the stain permanently.

Grass stains
Remove using a mixture of two parts white methylated spirits with one part water. Spray with water mist and then dry.

Grease
The remedy for this stain can cause colour problems. As a rule it's best to use a recognised grease solvent first, such as Mangers De-Solve It or Homesure Carpet and Upholstery Remover, before shampooing the area. Be prepared to repeat the treatment at a later date – grease spots have a habit of reappearing.

Ink
Gently dab the area with either clear methylated spirits or a proprietary ink remover. Blot frequently throughout the treatment to avoid spreading the mark, and take care in case fabric colours run. Finally, use a suitable fabric shampoo.

Jam and marmalade
If the jam has only recently been dropped on a cushion, remove it with a blunt knife. Then use a proprietary cleaning product. If it has hardened, soften using glycerine and leave for up to 30 minutes. Sponge away with clean water and follow up with a solution of one part white vinegar to five parts water. Blot well throughout.

Sauces and ketchup
If hardened, soften with glycerine; remove excess then sponge with a 50–50 mixture of white vinegar and water. Biological washing powder and water may help to remove any remaining dye marks but be prepared for problems – some sauce stains are exceptionally hard to remove.

Tar
Where possible, remove any surface deposits before applying glycerine to soften the remaining mark. Leave for about an hour before blotting and then apply a proprietary product, such as Mangers De-Solve It. Be careful not to drive tar further into the fabric fibres; use a gentle lifting action instead. Incidentally, a product traditionally used for removing tar is lighter fluid, but this is highly flammable.

Tea stains
Treatment for coffee often works for tea as well. Alternatively, sponge the area with a mixture of 1.5ml of Borax added to half a litre of cool water.

Urine
This is a difficult mark to remove successfully and professional help may be needed for any lingering odours. To loosen the stain, soda water can be applied and then blotted thoroughly. Follow this by using a proprietary product. Work even harder on the potty training.

Vomit
Add a few drops of household ammonia to water and gently but thoroughly sponge the area. Apply a paste of washing powder and water, leaving this for 30 minutes. Brush off the paste, then rinse and blot the area with fresh water.

Wine
Remove as much colour as possible using a white vinegar and water solution. Alternatively, if you have no white vinegar, substitute this with a mixture of lemon juice and salt. Then apply a paste of washing powder and water and leave for around 30 minutes. Brush this away before continuing to dab with clean water.

Worktop stains
Lemon juice often successfully removes discolouration.

Refrigerator staining
See Chapter 8 for dealing with food stains inside a fridge.

Note: *Professional advice is available from customer help lines operated by the manufacturers of proprietary stain removers. Check the brand labels for contact details.*

Above: When the driver of this 2006 Swift Sundance turned onto a motorway slip road, the child seat depressed the cushion, tipped, toppled, and swung into the aisle in an inverted position. *(A doll was used here to re-enact the incident).*

Improving the soft furnishings

Being able to sit and recline in comfort is important, but everyone has different preferences when it comes to cushion resilience. Moreover, being seated during a journey is different from being seated when parked on a site. To address this issue, some motorcaravans have dual-purpose seats that are equipped with safety belts. However, these can be too soft to support a child seat or booster base. When matched with inertia reel belts, a base cushion will often depress, the belt deploys its strap and a child's seat then topples over. Seats designed for children are considerably more stable when used in the cab. Alternatively, a child seat should be positioned next to the sidewall while an adult is seated alongside; this reduces the likelihood of it tipping over. Unfortunately this advice is often omitted from owner's manuals.

FOAM FAILURE

In some motorcaravans, seat foam loses its resilience surprisingly quickly. This is usually because a cheap product was used so the foam soon 'bottomed out'. This means you abruptly hit the under-base when sitting down firmly. Fortunately, many cures are available from upholstery specialists. These include:

Right: Bunk beds sometimes use 'split-folder' units with cover fabric joined to form a hinge. Foam depth in a split folder is typically 50-75mm (2-3in).

TOP-UP FOAM

When the original foam has slightly compressed there is often room within its cover to add a thin layer (typically 25mm/1in) of high-resilience foam. The cover will need to be opened for the top-up layer to be inserted, and then re-stitched. This is done with factory machinery and the cost is usually quite reasonable.

FOAM REPLACEMENT

Replacing the foam with a high-resilience product is obviously the best solution, and several specialists provide this service. However, good quality foam is costly, and if you're purchasing by mail order, request some samples first to check their characteristics.

There are also different classifications used for foam. In most instances, this is a synthetic product manufactured to various specifications. High-density foam is guaranteed to retain its shape and comfort for a long period. Synthetic foams are available in soft, medium or firm grades, which relate to the amount of support they provide. As a guide:

- **Soft** is suitable for backrests but is not advised for use as a seat or bed base.
- **Medium** is sometimes specified for backrests or, possibly, as a mattress for a child. It is unlikely to provide sufficient comfort or support for an adult.
- **Firm** is usually too hard for back or arm rests, but is the best choice for a seat that will also be used as a mattress. Foam of this designation is both comfortable and durable. It is also possible to combine any of the above grades to meet individual preferences. A good specialist is able to produce a 'sandwich mix' – for example, a bonded three-layer cushion with a hard centre section and layers of softer foam on either side.
- **Dunlopillo** uses latex, which is the sap from rubber trees. It is naturally fire-retardant and non-allergenic. Though costly, Dunlopillo is a superior foam offering excellent support, long life, durability and good ventilation properties. It is commonly used in domestic furniture but is seldom fitted as standard in motorcaravans.

As regards the thickness of foam, this varies considerably and anything from 50mm (2in) to 150mm (6in) is used. Foam for a sleeping base intended for adults usually has a depth of 100mm (4in), although some manufacturers are using a depth of 150mm (6in) for a permanent 'master bed'. On bunk beds that are made up using 'split folding' units, the foam is generally 50–75mm (2–3in).

If you are refurbishing a motorcaravan it is pleasing to know that specialist upholsterers are able to cut foam to any size you want. It is also straightforward to bond additional sections to create special shapes. For example, making a 'knee roll' (the raised front portion of a bench seat that gives support behind the knee) is also a routine task for a professional upholsterer. Also be aware that it is usual to add a stockinette cover material, as this greatly reduces the friction against the inner face of the cover fabric.

Replacement foam

Suppliers can cut upholstery foam to any size or shape and angled cuts are achievable too.

If extra sections are needed, these can easily be bonded together using special adhesives.

The forward edge of a seat can be fitted with a 'knee roll' for added comfort if required.

Foam offering different levels of resilience can be bonded together where needed.

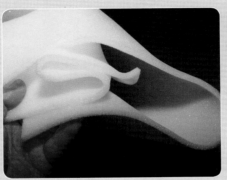

Fibre-wrap or a layer of thin, resilient foams helps to round off sharp corners on a cushion.

To reduce friction against the foam when fitting a cover, a stockinette fabric is usually added.

Safety

The *Furniture (Fire Safety) Regulations 1988* have focussed attention on foams as well as fabrics. The ability of products to meet ignitability tests is confirmed on their labelling. Bear in mind that this is strictly a UK matter and models manufactured abroad do not have to comply with these regulations. However, as the DTI publication, *A Guide to the Furniture and Furnishings (Fire Safety) Regulations, May 1995* pointed out, the regulations apply to upholstered furniture supplied with new touring caravans manufactured in the UK and sold from 1 March 1990. In response to this, UK manufacturers use a fire-resistant product described as 'combustion modified' foam.

Curiously, motorcaravans are *not* covered by these regulations because they are classified as motor vehicles and therefore fall within different legislation. In practice, some motorcaravan manufacturers voluntarily decide to fit the same products in their vehicles' living areas that are mandatory in touring caravans. Cab seats, however, are not altered.

The position regarding imported models is another issue. Normally, a UK importer selling motorcaravans manufactured abroad will substitute any products that do not comply with UK legislation with compliant alternatives. This would include things like the upholstery and soft furnishings. However, private importers are less likely to make these changes.

Fumes emitted from burning upholstery foam can cause severe respiratory problems, regardless of what standards and directives are drawn up, so an owner's decision to discard non-fire-resistant foam and replace it with a combustion-modified product makes good sense. However, foam fillings are not the only issue.

In addition, cushion covers must be resistant to cigarette or match ignition, too, and new UK models carry a label verifying their compliance

Sometimes this resistance can be lost after dry-cleaning, although it is possible to reapply and reinstate these qualities using certain products. In summary, it is fair to presume that this complex area with its curious anomalies will eventually become the subject of a European-wide directive.

RESISTANT

Filling material(s) and covering fabric(s) meet the requirements for resistance to cigarette and match ignition in the 1988 safety regulations

CARELESSNESS CAUSES FIRE

CARELESSNESS CAUSES FIRE
BATCH I.D.No. CH4S
TO COMPLY WITH THE FURNITURE AND FURNISHINGS (FIRE)(SAFETY) REGULATIONS 1988:
THIS ITEM DOES NOT INCLUDE A SCHEDULE 3 INTERLINER. ALL FOAMS, FILLINGS & COMPOSITES HAVE BEEN TESTED BY OUR SUPPLIER(S) TO ENSURE COMPLIANCE WITH THE RELEVANT IGNITABILITY TEST. COVERS & FILLINGS ARE CIGARETTE RESISTANT. COVERS ARE MATCH RESISTANT.
FURTHER DETAILS ARE AVAILABLE FROM YOUR RETAILER

Right: Replacement foam can be bought by mail order, but a template helps to ensure the size is correct.

Far right: Diagrams showing unusually-shaped sections of foam are helpful when ordering by post.

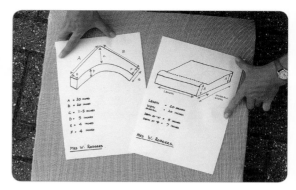

CREATING A MULTIPLE-LAYERED FOAM

It was mentioned earlier that a number of specialists are able to bond two or three layers together to produce a composite foam; for example, a harder foam is often preferred as an under layer, with a softer product bonded on the top. Specialists such as the Caravan Seat Cover Centre of Bristol can even create a 'his 'n' hers' mattress in which the two halves of a double bed are made using bonded foams of different resilience to suit individual preference.

If you decide to have new foam fillings in all your cushions, the finished job is even smarter if a final 'fibre wrap' is added. This is a white fibrous synthetic material often used as padding in quilted jackets and it has the effect of rounding off the angular corners of block foam. Alternatively, a thin layer of softer foam is sometimes used to achieve this effect.

Most owners prefer to have refill operations completed professionally; however, mail order services are available for owners wishing to pick open a cover and later stitch it up again. If you order foam by mail order, it is wise to provide both clear drawings and paper templates of cushion shapes.

SPRING INTERIORS

Spring interiors have been used for several years in more expensive motorcaravans and can often be specifically requested if you're having reupholstery work done.

Regarding the mattress on a bed, a spring interior is the preferred choice of some motorcaravanners. However, on a bench seat used while you're travelling, a spring interior cushion can produce a bouncy ride. Equally there are instances where the forward edge of this type of seat is inclined to collapse, thus reducing leg support. Good support on a travel seat, together with safety belt security, is especially important. So the case for specifying this kind of core isn't straightforward.

CURES FOR UNDER-MATTRESS DAMP

If you use your motorcaravan in cold weather, it is not unusual to find damp patches developing on the underside of mattresses. This is especially prevalent if a mattress is supported by a table top or solid ply base; it is far less frequent when a bed has a slatted base as described later in this chapter.

To facilitate the movement of air under a mattress – which helps to prevent the build-up of condensation – several underlay materials are available. A 15mm non-slip, rubberised coir pad is available from The Natural Mat Company, Vent Air Mat is sold by Hawke House Marine and DRY Mat is available from Ship Shape Bedding. Many marine specialists sell these types of products, too, because the problem is particularly prevalent in boats.

Right: In some situations a spring interior product is needed and these can be supplied by upholstery specialists.

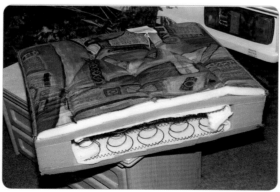

Right: This rubber material prevents mattress slippage on the ply bed base but a lack of ventilation will lead to damp patches caused by condensation.

Far right: The use of a ventilation underlay is important when using a plywood base. Various products are sold by marine specialists.

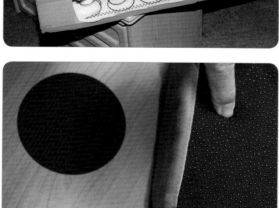

COVER FABRICS

Moving on to cover fabrics, a cost-effective way of improving appearance is to fit loose covers. These are sometimes made with stretch fabric, and a zipped version is undoubtedly better than one with tie tapes. Some loose covers are machine washable and these are a great help to parents with young children. However, a problem with loose covers is that they can slip around the cushions. This is often solved by fitting removable upholstery buttons.

Alternatively, if you are refurbishing an elderly model but don't want to spend large sums of money, specialists such as Magnum Caravan Surplus sell cushions they have purchased from leading manufacturers when a model is coming to an end. You will also see surplus products on sale at outdoor motorcaravan shows.

Motorcaravan exhibitions held around the country are also attended by upholstery specialists, and their stands display items such as fabrics, carpets, cushions and cab seating. The accompanying panel shows products from several suppliers.

If you're renovating a motorcaravan and are prepared to spend a reasonable sum on the upholstery, having new covers made professionally will achieve a stunning transformation. Caravan, motorhome and boat upholstery specialists are equipped to make unusually-shaped cushions, including split folders.

Left: One way to hide stitched junctions in a cushion is to add piping.

Provided you prearrange your visit, several motorcaravan upholstery specialists can make and fit covers while you wait at their factory. However, with a large coachbuilt model, this is likely to be more than a full day's work.

Send for fabric samples prior to booking an appointment; the range of suitable materials is remarkable. Not only are there hundreds of patterns, there are also tweeds, velours and printed cottons to consider. In addition, you need to choose the edging trims. These include:

- *Taped edges* – usually a budget alternative, often used on a cushion base where the backing fabric is stitched to the main material.
- *Piping* – either made in matching material or in a contrasting colour.

Only a few samples of fabrics are taken to exhibitions but it enables visitors to compare a variety of different materials.

Several stand holders take examples of completed seating units to illustrate the quality of the work they produce.

High quality leather products can look impressive but you need to sit on the seats to evaluate their level of comfort.

Some specialists also manufacture loose-fit carpets with taped or stitched edging. Plenty of colours and grades are on offer.

This manufacturer is displaying cab floor coverings that have been made for a variety of popular base vehicles.

The business of covering cab seats calls for different skills and several exhibitors at outdoor shows carry out this work.

Right: Here, decorative ruche is stitched around the edges, but there are various alternative products to consider including piping, cord and tape.

- *Ruche* – decorative woven tape that gives a smart appearance. (*Pronounced 'roosh'.*)
- *Cord* – used in a number of recent models, often with spiralling striped colours in the lay of the cord.
- *Cut ruche* – a fluffy edging that suits more ornate interiors.

These trims are sometimes applied on a rotating table top linked to a sewing machine that stitches the main fabric to the edging trim and encapsulates the foam in a single operation. On the other hand, you may prefer the covers to be made with a zip,

The Caravan Seat Cover Centre: case history

When this self-build VW conversion neared completion, its builder drove it to the owner of an upholstery company in Bristol for an estimate.

Comfort is important and the Caravan Seat Cover Centre has dozens of samples of fabric-covered foam to help customers choose the right product.

Foam sections are tested on a hard seat in the showroom using contrasting densities side-by-side. It can take longer than expected to make a final decision.

A rack in the showroom displays around 30 different completed cushions in a wide variety of fabrics, thicknesses, and edging trims.

The showroom includes many fabric samples, some of which are held in stock inside the factory so it's easy to get a clear idea of appearances.

Measuring and cutting is carried out by experienced staff who have served The Caravan Seat Cover Centre since the company was formed.

Some self-builders try to make their own cushion covers, but without training and an industrial machine, it is hard to achieve comparable results.

In addition to examples of ruche, there are decisions to make about upholstery buttons. These will need refitting whenever a cover is removed.

With one of the company's kits, owners can fit buttons themselves. The plastic plates that are attached on the underside are easier to disconnect and reattach than 'T' pieces.

which makes dry-cleaning a feasible proposition at a later date.

Some determined owners tackle this kind of refurbishment themselves, but if they don't own an industrial sewing machine, the results won't always be successful. A specialist will also make matching upholstery buttons to prevent a cover from slipping around the foam. These are pulled through both the fabric and its foam core using an industrial needle. Careful and patient use of an opened metal coat hanger and some insulation tape achieves the same result. Tags like the letter 'T' on the back secure each button, but if you want to remove the cover for laundering, the securing tape has to be cut. In consequence, some upholsterers now fit the removable plastic plates shown alongside.

CAB SEATING

Nearly all motorcaravans built in Britain are based on light commercial vehicles (LCVs). Compared with commercial vehicles manufactured 25 years ago or more, current models have refinements like power steering and efficient heaters, but they are still principally designed for commercial use. In a few areas they lack the level of refinement appropriate for leisure accommodation vehicles; cab seating is a case in point.

SWIVELLING SEATS

It undoubtedly makes sense to use the cab to augment space available in a living area.

In some vehicles, this can be achieved retrospectively by fitting swivels to the seat mechanisms. This idea has become sufficiently popular for the manufacturers of several recent base vehicles to include swivelling seats in the original cab option list.

To enhance personal comfort, there are also replacement seats with padded head restraints and arm rests on both sides. Then, to make the cab even more 'homely', the original plastic lining material used on the inside of commercial cab doors can be easily covered using a fabric that matches the rest of the living space.

The retrospective installation of seat swivels was a straightforward job on this 1999 Fiat Ducato coachbuilt – as the accompanying photographs show. However, there are two points to keep in mind. Firstly, the addition of a swivel mechanism normally raises the height of a seat, and for taller drivers, this means that their line of vision is lifted inconveniently close to the top of the windscreen. That was overcome in this project by fitting lower seat bases. TEK Seating is able to supply low profile bases for older Fiat Ducato, Peugeot Boxer, and Citroën Relay models and can often supply

Installing a low-level seat base and swivels

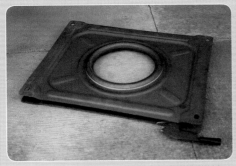
Crash-tested approved turntables are supplied by many automotive seat specialists.

The original Fiat seats were removed first and then the high base was unbolted from the floor.

The lower bases from TEK are made to fit the shape of a cab floor; cross brackets are also supplied.

The safety belt buckle was originally fitted to a lug on the sliders. This had to be sawn off and the buckle was then fitted to the swivel assembly.

The sliders are bolted to the swivel, though it's slightly different on the driver's side because there's a rise and fall mechanism on this seat.

The finished Fiat cab. Now it's possible to swivel the front seats round once parked and bring them into use as part of the living area.

Right: Slip-over covers for cab seats can be disappointing; this cover fitted poorly around the tilt controls and after only four months was badly chafing around the seat squab.

bases for other vehicles too. However, if your motorcaravan's leisure battery is stowed under a cab seat, you need to check its dimensions to confirm whether it can still be accommodated.

A second potential problem is the fact that a steering wheel sometimes limits clearance and prevents a driver's seat from swivelling through 180º. On older vehicles that were not equipped with airbag protection, fitting a removable steering wheel can sometimes solve this. This also acts as an anti-theft strategy. In fact, Auto-Trail included removable wheels as an option several years ago. However, the proliferation of regulations means that removable steering wheels are less frequently fitted today. In consequence, the feasibility of retrospectively fitting seat swivels is something to discuss with a specialist like TEK Seating. In some instances, it might only be possible to rotate the passenger seat.

UPGRADING THE SEATS

Many motorcaravans are now sold with matching fabric covers which merely fit over the standard commercial seats. This is a pity because these can sometimes pucker, slip and get damaged.

Where possible, it's better to have an original seat professionally re-upholstered. This is a job for a fabric trimmer. The addresses of A Baldassarre and TEK are given in the Appendix.

Alternatively, if you prefer to replace the original cab seats, TEK carries stocks of new products, some of which you can try for comfort at the factory. High-quality versions such as Aguti seats

– fitted to top-of-the-range motorhomes – are also imported by TEK.

For many years, TEK has supplied upholstered cab seats to motorcaravan manufacturers and today it plays a major part in the truck industry, too. Needless to say, when the company is contracted to supply seating in heavy commercial vehicles, one-off jobs for private motorcaravanners may involve a wait of several weeks. However, this will be the case with any upholstery specialist working in industries with seasonal peaks.

This situation was recognised when the author wanted to achieve a noteworthy finish in a self-build motorhome; securing the services of TEK meant making a booking but this was well worth the wait. In the project shown alongside, four Aguti high-back seats with arm rests were chosen. Two were replacements for the original Fiat seats; the additional seats had special swivelling plinths and built-in crash-tested safety belts to offer seating for two more adults. These secondary seats are also easily removable from their purpose-made floor mountings because the vehicle is principally used by only two adults.

The four Aguti seats were trimmed in light grey leather with navy blue piping and contrasting panels using heavy-duty automotive fabric. Sufficient fabric had also been purchased to create matching bench seating in the lounge together with scatter cushions. Finally, the plastic door liners were similarly trimmed with this fabric to disguise the commercial origins of the Fiat base vehicle. Not surprisingly, these improvements are costly, but if you wish to replicate the finishes in professionally built motorcaravans, good trimming and upholstery work is an important element.

Anyone refurbishing an older model will want to consider improvements like these. As regards recent vehicles, many are already fitted with swivelling seats as standard. In addition, new legislation and safety issues have reduced the opportunities to have major alterations carried out where seat bases, seatbelt attachment points and air bag installations are involved. Alteration to cab trimming in general, however, is still in demand and TEK's workmanship is shown here.

Below: If you want to change your style of seat, specialists like TEK can supply new products.

Below right: When you visit the TEK factory, you'll often see fabrics that you recognise from the latest motorcaravans.

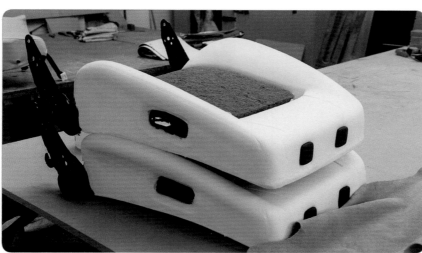

Conversion to Aguti seating

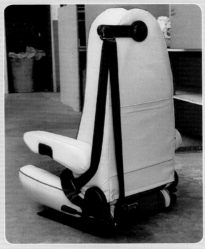

The Aguti seats which are fitted to high-quality motorcaravans can be supplied with an integral swivel system.

Aguti seats can be specified with arm rests whose height is adjusted with a knurled wheel.

In this project, two additional 'occasional' removable seats were needed, and these featured integral crash-tested safety belts.

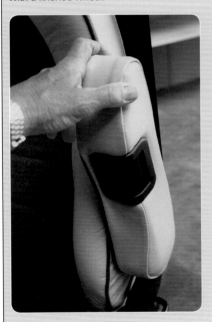

The high backs, leather edging, dark piping and contrasting fabric panels of these specially trimmed Aguti seats are a notable improvement.

Below left: The original plastic-covered door panels of this Fiat Ducato betrayed the commercial origins of the vehicle.

Below: At TEK, door panels can be covered with upholstery fabric which is bonded to the original plastic and stapled around the perimeter.

Furniture construction and repair

Considerable skill is shown by cabinet makers who construct and fit furniture in motorcaravans. Three objectives have to be met:

1) Structures have to be strong enough to withstand the rigours imposed by bumpy roads and uneven surfaces.
2) The entire structure has to be light.
3) The finished product should look attractive.

PRODUCTS, SUPPLIERS AND BUILDING TECHNIQUES

There is no doubt that many amateur converters with joinery experience are successful in producing smart, strong furniture, but some fail to keep the structures light. Even if you just want an extra shelf, it is appropriate to use weight-saving strategies. For that reason, both decorative veneered chipboard and Medium Density Fibreboard (MDF) – commonly used in our homes – is considered too heavy for leisure vehicle applications.

Unfortunately, many of the light but sturdy timber products, accessories and fittings used in

Faced 15mm ply, like Vohringer's products, is often used for structural assembly.

Magnum carries many patterns of 3mm wall, ceiling and furniture cladding plywood.

Surplus hollow tables, worktops and large doors are bought-up from manufacturers.

To add a solid appearance to light, ply panels, Magnum sells hardwood edging.

A popular weight-saving strategy is to fit thin matching ply within a hardwood frame

Magnum stocks attractive curved hollow doors recently used in well-known models.

All manner of flexible trims like this are available in various colours from Woolies.

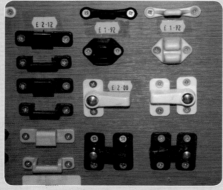
Hinges, stays, catches, brackets and similar items are listed in the CAK catalogue.

Wire baskets and storage shelves are part of the many items supplied by Woodfit.

motorcaravan construction are not usually available from DIY stores, builders' merchants or other local suppliers. This means it can be tantalisingly difficult to trace items needed for repair and improvement projects.

Sometimes materials are obtainable from caravan and motorhome breakers, but these items often show the marks of prolonged use. However, there are other sources to consider; in the accompanying book from Haynes, *Build Your Own Motorcaravan, a* complete chapter is devoted to tracking down parts, and reference is made to specialists who purchase surplus items from motorcaravan manufacturers when their models are no longer produced. This occurs whenever a new range of models is launched.

One specialist of surplus parts is Magnum Mobiles & Caravan Surplus in Grimsby. Other suppliers of trims and edging strips include Woolies, whose mail order service and catalogue is used by many Kit Car enthusiasts. Similarly there's Woodfit which, for many years, has similarly supplied DIY constructors with hinges, catches, self-assembly drawers, wire storage baskets and myriad other items. As regards CAK, this supplier has been mentioned in the earlier chapter on water systems. To highlight some of these components, the accompanying panel illustrates a selection of their products.

As stated earlier, conventional particle boards and traditional plywoods are heavy, so for major structural work, motorcaravan manufacturers use Vohringer 15mm (⁹⁄₁₆in) lightweight plywood, which is normally faced with a plastic veneer. Within its multi-layer structure, balsa wood laminates help to achieve a reduction in weight. Many dealer workshops use this product and there are suppliers around the country.

In addition to Vohringer's panels for structural work, thin, decoratively faced plywood is also used for ceilings, wall cladding, furniture and shelving. This type of ply is only 3mm thick and is remarkably light. To obtain decorative ply to match your motorcaravan, it might be necessary to place an order for products like this with the manufacturers after-sales department. However, dozens of patterned boards are held in stock at the premises of Magnum Mobiles and Caravan Surplus in Grimsby. Moreover, if you are renovating an Avondale motorcaravan, it is Magnum that bought-up all the spares when this company ceased manufacturing touring caravans and motorhomes.

Ceiling, wall and mock-woodgrain boards for cabinets can be inspected at Magnum's storage facility. Bear in mind, however, that their wood effect is generally achieved using a mock veneer printed on paper and stuck onto light grade plywood. The result looks convincing, but on no account should it be rubbed down with abrasive paper, as the paper veneer would simply rub off.

To achieve a smart finish on faced-plywood carcasses, hardwood trim is often used as a surround moulding. This is the only concession in the weight-watching battle. In addition to supplying

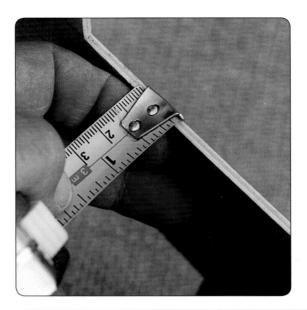

Left: The print-faced decorative ply used in motorcaravans is only 3mm thick.

Below: To get a clean edge, 3mm lightweight ply is best cut to shape using a woodworking knife and a large rule.

decorative plywood, Magnum also stocks hardwood trims and countless items of furniture, including lightweight cupboard doors. Many of the doors are hollow, of course, and are assembled using two pieces of faced 3mm ply held apart by spacer blocks or a honeycomb of corrugated paper. Hardwood lipping around the edges adds the finishing touch and makes the unit look heavy and strong. It is only when an unhinged door is lifted up that you suddenly appreciate these weight-saving strategies.

Having obtained a supply of faced 3mm plywood, a skilled DIY woodworker can undoubtedly copy the techniques used by manufacturers. Using a steel edge and a sharp woodworking knife, it is easy to cut this thin ply with several passes of the blade to achieve a clean edge.

The fixings used by motorcaravan self-builders will usually be rust-resistant woodscrews with an appropriate adhesive, instead of staples, which are often used by a converter for speed of construction. However, if you buy an electric staple gun, you will find that its abrupt impact often causes less damage when assembling a structure than repeated blows with a hammer.

Woodworking techniques

When a hollow door is cut down to reduce its dimensions, a spacer has to be glued into the void.

A 'G' cramp holds the assembly temporarily in place while the woodworking adhesive is setting.

A slender veneer pin is used in a hand-drill to prepare pilot holes in the edging strip.

In this task, a grooved lipping piece is used to give strength to the edges of a 3mm plywood shelf.

Another point to remember is that the overall size of a hollow door bought from surplus stock will probably need altering. The photographs here show how a hollow drawer front was reduced in size and an insert slipped into the core to act as a spacer. A wood adhesive (Evo-Stik Resin W) was applied before introducing the spacer piece to create a good bond. A 'G' cramp held the assembly temporarily in place for 24 hours, using scrap timber to protect the surface of the workpiece from direct pressure and to extend the zone of compression.

An exposed edge is finally covered with a thin lipping cut on a circular saw table. Veneer strip is an acceptable alternative but it is less resistant to bumps because it's so thin. Although a thin lipping can be held in place with an impact

adhesive, additional strength is achieved by using veneer pins as well. Panel pins are too thick and a thin veneer pin is less conspicuous. However, you will need to drill pilot holes to prevent the lipping from splitting and the pin from bending. Some woodworkers nip off the pointed head of veneer pins, which helps to overcome the splitting problem, but it's better to drill a pilot hole first.

If you don't possess slender twist drill bits, use one of the pins themselves. Cut off the head with pliers so that the pin seats well in a hand-drill chuck, then offer up the pointed end and keep the drill turning quite fast. It gets hot as it penetrates the lipping, but it does its drilling job surprisingly well.

Another recommendation, if you want to strengthen a small shelf made from 3mm ply, is to cut 8mm (or thicker) hardwood lipping and prepare a groove in it using a circular saw table. Alternatively use a grooving plane or a combination plane. As the accompanying photograph shows, this is glued and slid onto the edge of the ply to add surprising strength to an otherwise flexible, lightweight sheet. However, if you need a hollow worktop, surplus specialists often sell these (as shown in the panel on page 172).

As regards furniture catches, hinges and handles, specialists like CAK and Woodfit supply a whole range of items. Woodfit also sells self-assembly drawer kits with roller rails similar to those fitted on office filing cabinet drawers. Both CAK and Woodfit catalogues are worth obtaining and both specialists offer mail order services.

IMPROVING BEDS

It is surprising that so many bed bases are constructed using solid plywood to support the mattress or seat cushions. It was mentioned earlier that if there is no free-flow of air under a mattress, damp patches from condensation soon appear, especially during cold weather.

Flat softwood slats help to prevent this, but they lack resilience, and contribute very little to comfort. Slats made with a camber from solid beech or with a laminated construction are much better. As long as the ends of each slat are retained within a sleeve to permit movement, these products add to the resilience provided by a mattress.

However, flexibility can be further improved if each slat is mounted within a *cushioned* end cap as shown alongside. This arrangement permits even greater resilience and bed kits of this type are

Right: This table top used Vohringer ply, and its edge was grooved to accept a plastic trim strip that has a barbed flange; glue helped to hold it firmly in place.

Far right: To disguise the bare edges of plywood and to mask irregular junctions where panels abut, flexible edging strips like this piping are often used.

obtainable from The Natural Mat Company. Having created a double bed using two of these kits, the author is able to report that the arrangement provides pleasing comfort, even with a mattress as shallow as 100mm (4in).

Taking the idea further, a German manufacturer is now offering the Calypso system, where slats are supplied to suit the length of a double bed. Slats of this length have always flexed too much at the mid-point, but the Calypso product includes intermediate plastic supports to overcome this problem.

In both systems, the ends of all the slats need to be supported on a rail, but they are free fitting and not fixed in place. In consequence, it is possible to lift out the assembly of cross members if they need to be removed. Anyone wishing to upgrade a motorcaravan bed could certainly have one of these products installed. The length of each slat will need to be cut to suit its location, but the result is well worth the effort involved.

In Germany the developments in bed systems have proceeded even further. Whereas a slatted system works well, an assembly of wooden struts and fittings can be fairly heavy. This has led to the development of the Froli and Lattoflex systems, which have been used in motorcaravans manufactured by la strada and Knaus.

The Froli components that provide support for a mattress look rather like the heads of flowers. They can either be mounted individually on a baseboard, or clipped to flat strips of interlocking plastic. They also include a clever feature whereby coloured inserts can be added in the centre of selected units to limit the spread of the 'petals', thus creating a firmer support. It means that individual zones can be firmed-up for anyone wanting to create extra support in particular places.

Today, there are six or more variations on the basic design, and it's fairly easy to construct a bed base using Froli components. They can be purchased from Froli Kunstoffwerke Fromme GmbH and further information appears on the website www.froli.com in English. A similar system is sold under the Calypso brand name, and there's also a further variation on the theme. A hybrid system of springing comprises sprung wooden slats to which the builder adds Calypso plastic units to create even more flexion.

The CarWinx system from Lattoflex uses other flexible plastic components, and the accompanying photograph shows its plastic cross bars and their circular plastic supports. Resilience is derived from both the flexion of the bars as well as the supports, and this system is notably light. The photograph here was taken of a fixed rear bed fitted on a 2001 la strada Nova, and CarWinx products are also used on Knaus Traveller models of the same year. Provided there is a suitable base, a CarWinx system can also be fitted retrospectively. Further information on the product is available from Thomas GmbH & Co Sitz und Liegemöbel KG, or the website www.lattoflex.com.

Beds in many motorcaravans are not always as comfortable as their owners would like and the introduction of new systems like the ones described here are certainly welcome.

Cambered wood slats from The Natural Mat Company are mounted in end caps which offer additional springing.

The extra-long slats in a Calypso double bed kit include flexible supports which are fitted at the mid-point.

Different bed systems

The Froli system has removable units which also accept coloured inserts to firm-up selected parts of the bed.

The CarWinx system from Lattoflex is now being used in a number of German-built motorcaravans.

10 Accessories and projects

Drawing on the technical descriptions given earlier, here are some popular products with guidance on installation, operation and maintenance. Advice on self-building is also given.

Taking account of the weight constraints discussed in Chapter 2, it would be misguided to install new components if you have no idea what your motorcaravan currently weighs. Every vehicle has a weight limit, and some laden motorcaravans get so close to their permitted maximum, there simply isn't the scope to add more accessories. Exceeding a specified weight limit is not just illegal; it could render a vehicle unsafe on the road.

Of course, the addition of a TV support arm is hardly a major claim on the available payload, but it is a sound principle to take a vehicle periodically to a weighbridge to know exactly where you stand. Other items, such as glass-fronted solar panels, are certainly heavier than many people expect.

None of the pictorial descriptions which follow tell the entire story about the installation of this or that. There simply isn't the space. Come to that, the instructions which accompany products are usually pretty good. Suffice it to say, the reviews here give you an idea what a job involves, whether you tackle it yourself, or decide to get it done at a motorcaravan workshop. In the case of the under-floor 'Beeny' storage boxes, these are not available for DIY installations because every made-to-measure box is different.

Finally, existing owners might disagree with some of the comments which precede these projects. For example, products like solar panels are certainly useful, but some sales staff seem to imply that a couple of panels could light up the beaches at Blackpool. With regard to all the accessories mentioned here, seek further advice from existing owners. Then you can decide which products to buy.

Flat screen TV support arms

Comments: Many of the latest flat screen portable televisions designed for mobile leisure users are supplied with VESA fixings on the back of the casing. These fittings are normally found on free-standing 15in models and larger. Two versions of VESA threaded couplings are currently fitted. One has its four threaded sockets at 75mm (3in) centres: on the other they are fitted at 100mm (4in) centres.

A variety of VESA mounting brackets is available, some of which fix a TV set directly to a wall or panel. Others have articulating single or double-length arms. These can also be used in conjunction with quick release plates which allow a TV set to be quickly removed from a motorcaravan and re-mounted on a second bracket in your house.

Provided you purchase a flat screen set with VESA mountings, support brackets are available from many electrical specialists. Versions with or without a quick-release plate are easy to attach to a TV but the length of the screws is critically important. If they are too long, they might intrude into the casing itself and cause internal damage. Apart from that, the coupling is easy to make; a less straightforward attachment is at the other end of the bracket.

Motorcaravan shelves cupboards and furniture are often built using 3mm decorative ply and this needs strengthening by bonding-on some additional, thicker plywood to provide a sounder fixing for the mounting bracket.

When being driven, a motorcaravan encounters undulating road surfaces which could pose a challenge to a bracket's mounting point. Not only does the fixing have to bear the dynamic weight of a deflecting TV set: extending arms also act as levers and therefore add to the load. If there is any uncertainty concerning the integrity of a fixing point, it is wise to disconnect and stow a television set before every trip.

Grade UK supplies motorcaravan dealers with the B Tech BT 7513 articulating arm unit shown here. This can support a maximum weight of 15kg (33lb), presuming, of course, that its fixing is sound. The manufacturer is certainly anxious to encourage careful workmanship and states in the instruction sheet that failure 'to mount this bracket correctly may lead to serious injury and/or death.' You must ensure that it's safe.

Time taken: Bracket assembly 20 minutes; wall mounting time will vary.

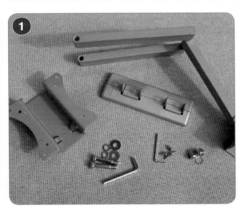

Several types of bracket are available. This one features a double arm and tilting facility which allows a screen to be angled as needed.

On this television the four VESA couplings are used to attach a carrying handle/support base which has to be removed.

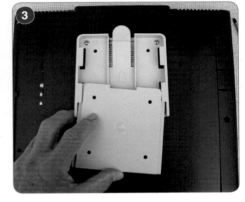

With the rear handle removed, a quick-release assembly can be fitted to the TV using its VESA threaded coupling sockets.

Good kits include well-illustrated assembly instructions; this one also included two hexagonal spanners to tighten the assembly bolts.

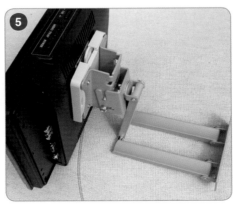

The brackets can also be assembled so that a television is able to be adjusted by rotation on a pivot fitted to the outer end of the arm.

There is no need to fit the quick-release clamp shown here but it permits tool-free removal of a TV set when a motorcaravan is not in use.

Installing a Grade UK Status 530 directional aerial

Comments: Although a directional aerial usually achieves better reception than an omni-directional model, it has to be orientated in accordance with the location of the nearest transmitter. It also has to be inclined correctly because the signals from a transmitter are either horizontally or vertically polarised. Equally a TV usually has to be retuned whenever you move to a new location.

Orientating an external aerial to achieve a good signal is made more difficult when a TV set is located indoors and isn't visible through a window. Communication between two people doesn't always achieve a good result quickly and the task is certainly less pleasant when it's raining. The difficulties prompted the development of aerials which are installed and adjusted indoors even though the antenna itself is mounted outside.

Of course the mast has to be lowered before a motorcaravan is driven on the road and the longer the pole, the greater its intrusion indoors. For this reason Grade UK developed the Status 530/5 so that its short 485mm mast, when lowered, could be accommodated in a typical ceiling locker: alternatively the 530/10 has a 920mm mast which is usually fitted where the tubular mast can be lowered into either a wardrobe or a purpose-made locker.

These two models both include an FM Radio Antenna and a Power pack which can either amplify or reduce a signal as required.

Before fitting a roof-mounted product, the structure of a motorcaravan roof must be carefully checked, bearing in mind that coachbuilt models have a surprising variety of structures. Moreover, when a motorcaravan is still within its warranty, it is likely that the installation of a product that necessitates cutting holes in its structure might invalidate the terms of cover. Owners of vans under warranty should check the position most carefully.

When the author was invited to fit one of the first prototype 530/10 models on behalf of Grade UK, the issue of roof strengthening and weatherproofing was given special attention. Consequent to this operation, the product was slightly modified by the manufacturer prior to going on general sale. Now, after ten years in use, the 530/10 has performed without fault and there is no evidence of either roof fatigue or water ingress.

As regards the installation shown here, this shows the short mast 530-5 version which is less intrusive when lowered indoors. Although there are times when the higher an aerial, the better it performs, a long pole has a greater need for roof reinforcement especially in gusting winds. This can be achieved by bonding a wooden block in the roof void, bearing in mind that the removal/reinstatement of a small section of ceiling ply is less conspicuous when it falls within a wardrobe or locker. Note that this aerial was being fitted on an imported motorcaravan which had a roof rack. However, the rack's cross members did not limit clearance when the aerial was lowered.

Time taken: Approximately a full day depending on how much roof strengthening is needed.

As this earlier project shows, the mast supplied with a Status 530-10 provides good elevation but intrudes more when it's lowered.

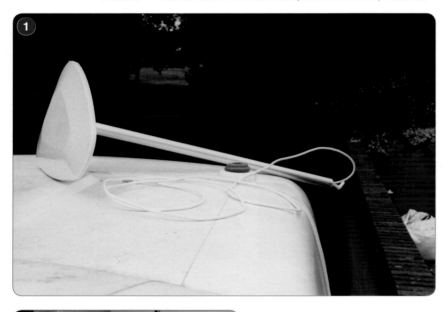

A tall, narrow cupboard was constructed to accommodate the mast of a Status 530-10 aerial. The enclosure also accommodates its amplifying power pack.

INSTALLING A 530-5 AERIAL

Using a flue pipe as a reference point, measurements were taken inside a wardrobe to check where pole brackets might be fitted.

On the roof, measurements were now taken from the flue outlet cover to establish that there were no obstructions outside.

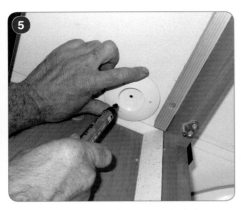

Cutting and drilling templates are included, although in this instance the position of a pilot hole was marked with the ceiling collar itself.

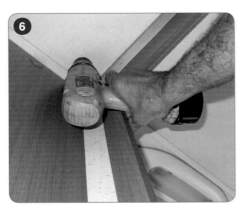

Using a cordless drill, a pilot hole was drilled from inside. This was then enlarged using a 45mm hole saw from outside.

The external mounting plate is supplied with a foam seal and is fixed in place using the three 16mm screws supplied in the kit.

The mounting foot with its central sleeve and weatherproofing gaiter is fitted next and secured with three 32mm screws.

The pre-connected coaxial cable and mast now project inside the wardrobe and both the locking plate and collar are fitted.

The antenna, which is pre-fitted to its mast, is now fitted from outside. When the van is parked level the mast must be vertical.

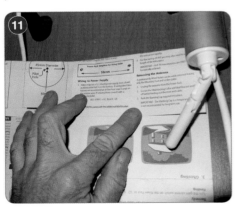

A convenient location was chosen for the power pack inside the wardrobe, and the template providing its fixing holes is offered up next.

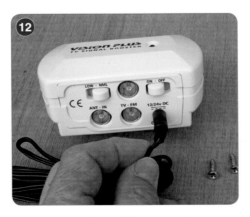

The markings on Grade UK's power packs are very clear and a plug with a length of wire is supplied for connecting to a 12V supply.

The cables are shortened, coaxial plugs are fitted as described in the detailed instructions and a warning label is affixed to the wall.

Satellite TV installations and equipment

Comments: With good satellite TV equipment and favourable conditions, a picture is usually of very good quality. Digitally created, satellite-transmitted pictures are not spoilt by crackling, interference or fringing. It is only in extreme weather when a picture is less than perfect. Moreover, the benefits can be enjoyed on the same recent types of TV set that are used for terrestrial TV. There is also an opportunity to receive over 100 free stations on the FREESAT system. Also be aware that a satellite system offers dozens of radio stations including those from the BBC. Inevitably, satellite TV for motorcaravanners is developing at a fast pace and new equipment is always being introduced. Several suppliers publish guidance booklets and instructions to help new users. Two sources of information worth noting are: 'DIGITAL SATELLITE & TERRESTRIAL TV ON THE MOVE' from Maxview; and TECH TIPS TV Reception on the Move in the catalogue from RoadPro.

Three key items are needed to receive Satellite TV: A television with appropriate connections, a receiver, and a satellite dish. There are also supporting accessories such as a satfinder, a spirit level to confirm that a dish is level, and a good quality tripod if it is decided use a standalone portable dish.

It is important to recognise that you can receive TV from a satellite without having to subscribe to providers such as SKY. Thanks to BBC and ITV, approximately 150 TV and radio stations can be received free of charge through the Freesat service. These include popular channels from BBC, ITV, Channel 4 and Channel 5. Information on topics like this is given in the literature produced by distributors of satellite equipment.

From a practical point of view, motorcaravanners have to assume the role of a professional satellite dish installer whenever arriving at a new venue. Although a picture from a satellite is usually superb, trees and buildings can block alignment with a satellite and that prevents a signal from being received. Incidentally, although TV satellites move at great speed, this speed matches the rotation of our planet so they appear to remain in a fixed position in the sky. Then you have to align with the one that you want.

The illustrations here show different types of equipment. Be aware that satellite TV channels can be received for under £200 using a portable dish whereas if you want everything to be carried out automatically, devices incorporating satellite-locating systems run into four-figure sums. And each product has its merits. For instance roof-mounted, permanent installations are virtually, fit-and-forget appliances – but don't forget to lower a dish before driving off. In contrast, a dish on a tripod has to be erected and manually set up at every destination; later, it will have to be dismantled and stored. On the other hand, not every motorcaravan owner wants a heavy and often clumsy dish arrangement permanently fixed to their vehicle's roof. You might prefer to purchase a mini-dish to put on a table indoors where it can be pointed through a window. And portable dishes *can* work ... until rain starts running down the window pane. So here is an overview of products. To find out more, contact specialist suppliers, but also speak to other motorcaravanners who use satellite TV systems. Their experiences will help to shape your views concerning the numerous products on sale.

Time taken to install roof-mounted dishes: This is likely to take a full day depending on the structure of the roof and the task of discreetly hiding the cables.

A folding satellite dish fixed permanently on the roof allows a setting-up operation to be carried out without needing to leave your van, apart from coupling the mains supply cable.

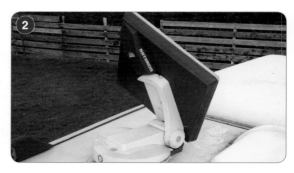

The Kathrein range is manufactured in Germany and includes compact automatic 'planar-type' dishes. This 50 x 50cm model performs like a circular 60 x 60cm dish.

An Omnisat 'crank-up' model from Maxview is permanently fitted to the roof. It is raised to the elevation angle from indoors and then rotated by turning a bezel to find the satellite.

The Camos sat-domes have a 10-satellite search capability and are available in both static and 'in-motion' versions. Their remote operation is easily activated from indoors.

Portable dishes like the Maxview Omnisat 66 are far less expensive than roof-mounted products and weigh under 9kg. In a wind they just need pegging-down carefully.

The Wineguard tripod has a built-in compass and spirit level. Moreover, its central mast can be rotated when the feet have been anchored. A ground spike is included.

Depending on where a motorcaravan is parked, there are brackets which allow a dish like the Multimo compact 40cm product to be clamped directly to part of the vehicle.

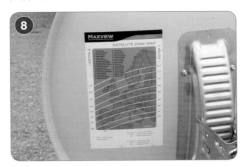

Portable products have to be set-up correctly and Maxview zone maps are often mounted on the rear of a dish to help when starting the alignment operation.

The elevation angle has to be set manually on a portable product using a graduated scale. At a campsite 60 miles north of London, this dish was set to 23.5°.

Many dishes have a low noise block (LNB) on a long arm which receives the satellite signals. It can be twisted for fine-tuning eg when near the edge of a reception zone.

Signals from the LNB go by coaxial cable via a satfinder to the receiver inside the vehicle. To avoid draping cable through a window, a weatherproof socket is easily fitted.

The satfinder is prepared so that its six lights are off; then the dish is moved until a squealing sound reaches a high pitch and as many lights come on as possible.

Once the system logs on to a satellite, it is possible to use a receiver and TV to select a 'Systems Set-up Menu'. This will confirm the signal strength and signal quality level.

Once a satisfactory signal is registered, the satfinder is then unplugged from the connecting coaxial cable whereupon you can now choose your entertainment.

Purpose-made underfloor storage for coachbuilts

Comments: Many motorcaravan owners wish they had got more storage space. A popular response is to have a roof box fitted together with an access ladder installed on the vehicle's rear wall. However, this solution isn't without its problems. Firstly, it is tempting to fill a large plastic container with clumsy, and often heavy, equipment. And when you're driving, the last place to carry heavy gear is on the roof. Secondly, roof-mounted storage boxes affect the aerodynamics of a vehicle and poorer fuel economy is an inevitable result.

Another strategy is to fit a large storage box on the rear wall. Several manufacturers supply these plastic containers and they're mounted using the fixing methods employed for attaching cycle racks. On the plus side, these products place the weight closer to the ground but carrying gear right at the back introduces the same risk as carrying heavy bikes. It's all-too-easy to exceed the maximum loading limit of a vehicle's back axle, especially on motorcaravans built with a prominent rear overhang.

Underfloor, slide-out boxes are clearly much better and 'Beeny Boxes' are the best-known examples.

Constructing and installing an underfloor box is not easy. Every model of coachbuilt motorcaravan is different and there is always something under the floor that gets in the way. Anything from an exhaust pipe to a waste water tank presents the designer with problems. Not that Beeny Boxes are always fitted in the side skirts of motorcaravans: some are mounted under their rear walls instead. Either way, they are neat and robust – and even strong enough to carry an extra leisure battery or two.

Ever since Paul Stimpson purchased the rights to build Beeny boxes from its eponymous inventor, hundreds of one-off designs have been made in his Camborne workshop in Cornwall. It starts when a client places a booking for as long as it takes to create and install one or more boxes. It's a labour intensive operation but two things are abundantly clear. The appearance of a vehicle is cleverly maintained and each box is hand-built with painstaking care. Examples are shown here and sequence photos reveal how they're made.

Time taken: Every job is different but to make these two boxes took three days. The motorcaravan was used for overnight stops on the workshop forecourt.

EXAMPLES OF BEENY BOX PROJECTS

Right: This box was constructed in a space rearwards of the wheel and by careful cutting, the original panel was grafted on to the front of the box to preserve the vehicle's styling.

Below: The side skirts on this Swift Capri are made in moulded aluminium. That still didn't present a problem to the builder who used a section to cover the matt black box.

Below: The box on this Auto-Sleepers coachbuilt still has its green protective sheet on the aluminium panels. Note how the section of the original side skirt was remodelled.

Below: Stainless steel sliders show the working operation of a Beeny Box and this owner uses the container for typical motorcaravan items that you wouldn't want to stow indoors.

The above photograph supplied by Paul Stimpson, BEENY BOX.

1. After a thorough under-floor inspection and a box needed on each side, part of the GRP skirt was cut away.

2. Prior planning had ensured that there would be no major obstructions in the area intended for each box.

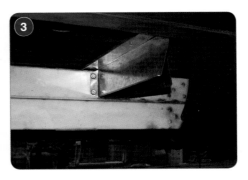

3. Apart from drawer runners, all metal components like these side supports are made in the Camborne workshop.

4. When the exact measurements for each box have been established, the material is cut and folded into shape.

5. It is an exacting task to form the ends of each box, with folded flanges to connect up with the main structure.

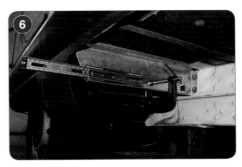

6. Another critical operation is to mount the runners in complete alignment so that they fit squarely in the aperture.

7. When both end sections have been riveted into place, part of each runner then has to be fixed to the box itself.

8. The box is now offered-up to check its accuracy and operation. Later it is sprayed matt black on the outside.

9. Another painstaking operation is to attach a tidied-up piece of the GRP side skirt so that it aligns perfectly.

10. The only joins in the aluminium sheet are at the ends but to ensure a box is water-tight, sealant is applied.

11. The lockable turn handles have now been fitted leaving Paul Stimpson the final tidy-up with touch-up paint.

12. Six years later and with oil added on the runners periodically, the boxes work as well as they did when completed.

Choosing and fitting a solar panel

Comments: It is wrong to regard the purchase of a solar panel simply as a money-saving strategy. When a 70-Watt panel and regulator can cost around £450 and an 85Ahr battery can be purchased for around £65, it would take several years to recuperate the cost of a solar system. Buying a new battery every two years might work out less-expensive. So why are solar panels popular at the moment?

In essence, solar systems are 'convenience' products because they provide a useful trickle charge for a leisure battery. This is particularly beneficial when stopping on sites with no mains hook-ups and during storage periods, too.

Motorcaravanners opt for several types of solar panels. As the accompanying photographs show, some are content to have a portable product rather than one which is permanently installed on their van. Many panels are also heavy and look unattractive on some types of roof. For instance, products which comprise an aluminium frame and have a protective panel of heavy duty glass need a sturdy support system when fitted to a motorcaravan. Fortunately, installation brackets are now available which make the task easier.

Slightly more expensive are semi-flexible lightweight, frameless panels which are protected by an Ethylene Vinyl Acetate plasticised surface. These are often bonded to the decks of boats and don't get damaged when members of the crew walk across them. They also weigh a fraction of panels that are covered with heavy glass protection.

A flexible panel, together with an all-important solar regulator is shown in the illustrations here. As usual, the hardest task is hiding the runs of cable which link the panel to a leisure battery via a regulator.

GB-SOL, based in South Wales, manufactures flexible panels in 35 Watt and 70 Watt options; these weigh 2.0 and 3.0kg respectively. The larger version is shown here and this was installed using adhesive sealant and no further fixings. Only one hole has to be drilled in the roof and that is for the cable. Although inexpensive solar regulators work well in protecting a battery from over-charging, a Steca product was installed here on account of its useful monitoring facilities. For instance the chosen model can keep an ongoing total of all the Amp hours produced and information is displayed in both a numerical and diagrammatic form. It is also features a built-in resetting electronic fuse.

Once you have worked out how to gain safe access to your motorcaravan's roof, and how to hide the cable, this is an easy product to fit. However, removing it to transfer to another motorcaravan might not be an easy operation.

Time taken: approximately 8 hours.

Framed panels with glass protection can be quite heavy so many motorcaravan owners use portable panels rather than roof-mounted ones.

To double-up the output, some manufacturers sell hinged solar panels that open and close like a book. Use a lockable cable to prevent theft.

Mounting a heavy panel on the roof of a motorcaravan can be difficult but these brackets help installers.

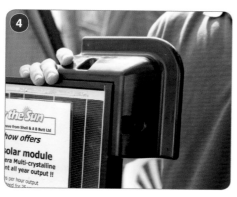
Another useful type of moulded plastic bracket is designed to support the corners of a solar panel.

The semi-flexible encapsulated panels from GB-SOL are available in 35 and 70 Watt versions and will bond direct to a roof.

On a bright day a panel often produces around 20V which would ruin a 12V battery; this is one of the reasons for fitting a regulator.

A connection block complete with a generous length of cable to suit customer needs is mounted on the front of GB-SOL panels.

Removing some interior lights helped confirm if any obstructions were in the roof void and revealed where the cable could be fitted.

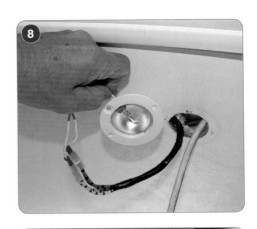

Plastic strips covering joints in the plywood ceiling panels were unclipped; this also revealed other potential cable routeways.

The panel was temporarily laid in position and a hole was drilled through the roof material to take the pre-coupled cable.

The aluminium backing of a GB-SOL panel can flex provided its curvature gains no more than 40mm over a one-metre length.

Having thoroughly cleaned the roof surface, the panel was put in its intended position and masking tape used to define its perimeter.

A generous application of white Sikaflex-512 Caravan was placed around the perimeter; remnants of black 512 were used too.

Weight discs held the panel down in its curving profile; 24 hours later a further beading of sealant was added at the edges.

The cable from the panel was taken through into a wardrobe. The Steca PR1010 regulator's connection block is at the bottom edge.

A small strengthening panel of 9mm ply was stuck inside the wardrobe to give a secure mounting point for the fixing screws.

Additional 2.5mm² automotive cable was then taken from the solar controller to the leisure battery, with in-line fuses fitted at both ends of the run. On a clear day and in direct line with a strong sun, the Steca PR1010 records a little over 3A.

Cassette toilet maintenance and repairs

Some motorcaravans built in 2008 had this new cassette which provided far better access to the internal fittings.

Comments: Since Thetford first introduced fixed cassette toilets in the 1980s, numerous variations on this basic theme have appeared. The first flushing and cassette toilets were portable and these are still used today in small van conversions. A portable appliance is usually stowed in a locker because there simply isn't room to create a separate toilet compartment.

Then bench-style products were introduced which are mounted permanently, and many examples are found in coachbuilt motorcaravans. These were followed by a swivel bowl version which offers more versatility when a small toilet compartment is designed. Many motorcaravans, including large van conversions, now have swivel bowl units. Throughout these developments, the cassettes were broadly similar and the accompanying servicing photographs show older cassettes. Then, in 2008, a cassette was designed with a large removable circular panel that gives greatly improved access to the components inside.

Differences also occur in respect of flushing systems. In some motor caravans, flushing water is taken from its fresh water supply tank. However, some bench and swivel bowl models incorporate their own flush water reservoir in the casing itself. They have a refill point mounted externally above the cassette retrieval hatch. This arrangement permits the use of flush water additives but the supply mustn't be overlooked when water needs draining down at the onset of frosty weather.

Since there are several dissimilar designs of fixed cassette toilet in a range of around ten models, it is impossible to present detailed descriptions of all the repair operations. Furthermore, the repairs that have to be undertaken out of sight, within the waste tank itself, are not really feasible projects for an untrained person to tackle. As shown here, service technicians learn to carry out these (sometimes) unpleasant tasks using a dummy training top. Since owners seldom have access to this training aid, the selected repair jobs shown alongside are among the easier ones to carry out.

Time taken: Variable, but the task of replacing a 'Lip Seal' valve can be completed, first time, in around 30 minutes.

Useful tips

If an electric flush isn't working, some models draw 12V from the leisure battery; others use small batteries that might need changing.

Service technicians learn how to replace components in a waste tank by practising procedures with one of these dummy training tops.

A float which signals when the tank is nearly full has a magnet to activate the gauge. Floats break if you swirl water around too forcibly.

If you check closure blade operation when the tank is removed, reset the knob parallel to the side before reinstating the tank.

General points

In 2006 Thetford changed the name of 'Plastic Cleaner' to 'Bathroom Cleaner'. The foam is easy to use and leaves a shine.

Check an appliance's instruction leaflet on how to drain down the flushing water. The bung here is only for removing the final drops.

The swivelling drainage outlet on a cassette can be pulled from the main body of the container when turned to a release position.

Like several of the moving components fitted to a cassette, the swivel outlet has an 'O' ring; these need replacing if leaks appear.

Replacing a lip seal

Note: *To confirm the date when your toilet was manufactured, the code number printed on a sticker affixed to the underside of the waste tank is its completion date printed backwards (year/month/day).*

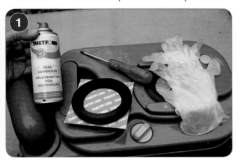

Basic equipment, but get the right lip seal. Toilets manufactured up to 15 June 2000 had a different pattern from the later ones.

There were changes to the lip seal assembly and earlier models lacked a slider plate. But removal of screws is easy.

Prise off the two side flanges with a small screwdriver. This reveals six more crosshead screws to remove.

Put the screws in a safe place before lifting off the plastic frame that holds the lip seal in its recess.

Look most carefully at the lip seal when you remove it because there's a right and wrong way to fit it.

Liberally spray the new lip seal with Thetford's 'Seal Lubricant'. Perhaps protective gloves should have been worn from the start.

An old towel is handy for cleaning the seating flange on which the lip seal is mounted. Clean the closure blade too.

Apply more seal lubricant to the blade, and the seating flange. Fit the new lip seal the correct way up and reinstate the whole assembly.

Replacing an 'O' ring on the blade control knob

This is one of the items which has to be removed using touch alone by placing your hand into the tank with the blade fully open.

This photograph of the dummy training top shows how you use a screwdriver to depress the spring lugs which keep a knob in place.

When the knob has been pulled out of its housing, you can see the spring lugs on either side that you depressed with the screwdriver.

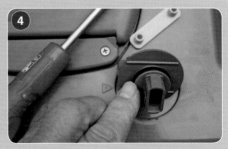

Like most of the components attached to a waste tank, the blade control knob has an 'O' ring that needs replacing if liquid seeps out.

Bicycle and motorcycle racks

Right: Provided a towbar's downforce limit is sufficient, motorbike racks made by PWS are designed to attach to the flange plate made for bolt-on towballs.

Below: Thule products now form part of Dometic Group's range of accessories. This cycle rack is made for direct coupling to a towball.

1 The rear overhang on this Swift Lifestyle coachbuilt might be too long to carry a heavy motorcycle; it was decided to fit a rack for a lightweight pedal cycle.

2 Bolts need to be driven through the rear wall to achieve strong mounting points and this tubing was cut to length and inserted into the wall to provide four spacers.

3 This is one example from Fiamma's Carry-Bike range which includes around 40 models. Each rack's weight and Max. load is given in the Fiamma catalogue.

4 Although this rack is designed to carry two bicycles, whether the van's rear axle could cope would only be established after making checks on a weighbridge.

*Comments: Many motorcaravanners take pedal bikes, battery-driven bikes and motorcycles on their trips and the most common way to transport them is on a rack fitted at the back. This can place a significant load on the rear axle, particularly on coachbuilt motorcaravans which have a long overhang. Before getting a rack fitted, it is essential to check the initial loading on your rear axle and to get weight information about the new rack and its bikes. On some motorcaravans, proposed additions are simply too heavy. Carrying a motorcycle, for example, often necessitates having major revisions to the rear suspension and weight-bearing components. A new weight plate would also be needed to verify revised loading data. Be mindful that carrying a heavy weight at the rear of a vehicle can affect road-holding and a rack's fixing points **must** be fit for purpose. It has also been reported by owners that some dealers selling racks are not giving any advice about vehicle weight limits or the implications of overloading a motorcaravan's back axle.*

Some motorcaravans are manufactured with factory-fitted mountings as standard. Others, including models in the Laika range, have a modified chassis which incorporates a slide-out motorcycle rack complete with a number plate/lighting board. Also noteworthy are motorcycle racks from AL-KO Kober which are designed for motorcaravans built on an AL-KO chassis (as described in Chapter 4.) Cycle racks in the Thule range and purpose-made motorcycle racks made by PWS are designed for attachment to a towbar assembly. In this instance, a motorcaravan owner must establish if the permitted weight carrying capacity of his or her towbar would permit the addition of a rack and its proposed load.

Time taken: Products coupled to a tow bar or to an AL-KO chassis might be accomplished in 1–2 hours. Mounting a rack securely to a coachbuilt depends on the motorcaravan. In some models it might even take 4–5 hours to fasten the bolted attachments and to reinstate furniture that is fixed against the rear wall.

Self-build projects

Comments: When a recent count was made of professionally-built motorcaravans currently on sale, it was found that there's a grand total of more than 750 models. On further analysis, it was revealed that around 260 of these models were from UK manufacturers, around 420 were European imported models and around 85 in the total were American RVs. Frankly, the choice is enormous, and that doesn't take into account earlier models now being sold as pre-owned motorcaravans.

Since a huge choice of models is presently available, why do so many prospective owners ignore what is on offer and embark on a self-build project? There is no easy answer to questions like this and everyone's reasons are different.

Having built two coachbuilt motorcaravans and part of a van conversion, the author can offer some comments. Project Number One was claimed to be a 'kit' and a Starcraft motorcaravan was completed when money was short. A new touring caravan was providing pleasurable holidays at the time, and the idea of building a motorcaravan, seemed a strange thing to do. However, two years were spent on the project and there were moments of pleasure and pain. A great deal was learnt in the process and the vehicle was in use for ten years before it was reluctantly sold.

The next one was different. A major difference was the fact that it was constructed on a brand new Fiat Ducato Maxi chassis cab and used a GRP shell that was being sold as scrap. The author's aim on this occasion was to produce a personalised vehicle that was unlike anything else on the market. For instance it had to provide accommodation to support family interests in outdoor pursuits. It had

to tow a boat or a support car, it needed an internal system for transporting kayaks and storage for climbing, skiing and walking gear. Comfort and a hot shower were important as well. Not many of these features are found in professionally-built models and 12 years since the chassis was first delivered, it continues to perform as intended.

A third recent project involved fitting out a pre-owned 2006 VW T5 Transporter. Compared to the earlier self-build projects, and working with a colleague, this conversion was really quite easy. But there's a mantra I firmly believe: good self-builders don't try to do *everything* themselves. We all have different skills and there are times when professional help is needed. In this instance, a rising roof was professionally installed on the VW van.

It is undoubtedly important that every self

Above: After periodic weighbridge checks throughout its construction, this motorcaravan was finally checked when the work was complete.

Left: Self-build projects meet their owners' requirements. Few models offer hatchback storage or a high level bed that drops down at the rear.

builder recognises his or her personal limitations and enlists the assistance of others. For example, all the kit cars and motorcaravans that I've constructed have looked magnificent in the driving area; thanks to the skills of professional trimmers and upholsterers. Neither my skills nor the quality of the household sewing machine could produce the finish that's needed.

Needless to say, there is so much to be written about self building motorcaravans, that this topic could easily fill a book. And it has: *Build Your Own Motorcaravan* was first published in 2006 and has been updated successively in four subsequent reprints. And, as stated earlier in *The Motorcaravan Manual*, some self-build enthusiasts even went further and became highly respected professional manufacturers. The origins of Auto-Sleepers, Elddis, and dozens of small-scale manufacturers began when a keen self-builder constructed a caravan or motorhome. The spirit of self-builders is a force to be noted.

Above: Comfort was important in this unusual project and it was designed to carry two, three or four in belted seats, each of which was professionally covered.

Right: Modern replicas of VW vehicles are manufactured in Brazil and this self-builder wanted to fit-out one of these imports to recall the days of his youth.

Right: This Optare bus was purchased at a peppercorn price by a member of the Self-Build Motor Caravanners' Club. Check the website for similar projects.

Left: Externally, the features of a bus are hard to disguise, but when this determined couple converted its interior, the results were truly impressive.

Left: Not many self builders tackle dismountable pods but this one was painstakingly fitted-out; its DIY owner created a noteworthy finish.

Far left: Cutting apertures in the side of a nearly-new panel van is daunting at first, but Seitz framed windows are easy to fit and their instructions are clear.

Left: Woodworking skills learnt in the construction industry were used in this conversion to good effect. An inner panel for a window was built with care.

Servicing the living area

All motorcaravan owners recognise the need to service a road-going vehicle, whereas servicing conversion elements often get overlooked. To avoid confusion, work on the conversion and living area is referred to as 'habitation servicing', as opposed to 'vehicle servicing'. Vehicle service specialists normally leave this to motorcaravan dealers, although there are exceptions. A few motorcaravan service centres have qualified staff and equipment to tackle *both* operations.

To ignore conversion inspections and the servicing of appliances in your living area would be very unwise; personal safety might be at risk. For example, it is important that a qualified technician carries out routine integrity tests of your gas supply system. If leaks are detected during a habitation service, faulty couplings should immediately be repaired by a qualified person. Even a small gas leak could lead to a fire. Similarly, a gas appliance that isn't working properly can emit carbon monoxide; although fatalities are rare, they *have* occurred. Without doubt, incidents like these are far less likely to happen if servicing work is routinely carried out in accordance with the instructions given by manufacturers of appliances.

HANDBOOK ADVICE

A motorcaravan handbook, normally referred to as the owner's manual, should provide detailed advice about which items need to be inspected and serviced, but this information is variable – both in quality and detail. In some instances, motorcaravans from smaller companies are not even supplied with an owner's manual. Instead, purchasers are merely given a handful of leaflets from the manufacturers of its appliances. This is *most* unsatisfactory, and several years ago the Society of Motor Manufacturers and Traders (SMMT) and the National Caravan Council (NCC) decided to look into the whole subject of habitation inspection and servicing work.

THE SMMT/NCC ANNUAL HABITATION CHECK

The collaborative efforts of the SMMT and the NCC led to the publication of a booklet entitled the *Recommended Annual Habitation Service Check*. Its objective was to identify areas of attention in relation to conversion elements and associated supply systems that should be included in a motorcaravan habitation service. The booklet endeavoured to promote a greater level of consistency in the work carried out at all UK dealer service centres.

The guide points to 11 areas requiring attention:

- The integrity of body-mounting points
- Windows
- Doors
- Attachments to the chassis
- Attachments to the body exterior
- Internal components
- Rising roof mechanisms (if fitted)
- Gas system
- Water system
- Electrical system
- Ventilation provision

Above: Some motorcaravan centres are able to provide both vehicle and habitation servicing.

Right: Ventilator outlets must not be obscured, particularly when they function as escape points for leaking gas.

SERVICE SCHEDULES

Although the SMMT and NCC booklet pinpointed areas of attention, many workshops continued to adopt their own servicing practices using job lists they had compiled themselves. There were also instances where owners went to collect their serviced motorcaravan but were not issued with documentation stating what work had been carried out. Uncertainties about the entire operation caused some owners to stop bothering with a habitation service at all.

ANNUAL SERVICE SCHEDULE

Motorcaravans

Make: .... Model: .... Year: ....

Type:
    a) Fixed roof van   e) Coachbuilt
    b) Elevating roof   f) A-Class
    c) High-top   g) American
    d) Dismountable   h) Other
Circle the type above.

Chassis: i) Original chassis   ii) AL-KO conversion
Circle the type above.

Registration number: ....

Vehicle Identification Number: ....

THE SCHEDULE

Note: ■ Under Comments, write n/a alongside any element which is not applicable to the model undergoing the service

Note: ■ Report under Comments any defect, signs of wear, etc. Report depth of tread on the tyres, including the spare.

Section 1: Undergear
Comments

1. Visually inspect body-mounting fixings ☐ ....
2. Visually inspect cab-to-body junction ☐ ....
3. Check mounting of underfloor tanks ☐ ....
4. Check spare wheel cradle operation and tyre ☐ ....
5. Examine wheel boxes for corrosion/damage ☐ ....
6. Check and lubricate corner steadies (if fitted) ☐ ....
7. Check step operation (if fitted) and lubricate ☐ ....
8. Lubricate axle tube on AL-KO chassis ☐ ....
9. Inspect non-original suspension additions ☐ ....
General comments on undergear including tyres: ....

Section 2:
External Bodywork & General Condition
Comments

1. Inspect sealant; check potential leak points ☐ ....
2. Check/oil door locks; oil hinges ☐ ....
3. Check body attachments, vents, roof lights, racks ☐ ....
4. Confirm window operation, lubricate hinges/stays ☐ ....
5. Inspect rising roof mechanism (where fitted) ☐ ....
Comments on bodywork/general condition: ....

Section 3: Internal elements
Comments

1. Carry out a damp test; mark on diagram ☐ ....
2. Verify cab seat operation ☐ ....
3. Check furniture; lubricate catches & hinges ☐ ....
4. Confirm blind and curtain operation ☐ ....
5. Check vents (high and low) & drop-out holes ☐ ....
6. Check floor and wall for delamination ☐ ....
Other comments: ....

Section 4: Fire warning systems
Comments

1. Smoke alarm – check operation and battery ☐ ....
2. Check expiry date on extinguisher and notices ☐ ....
3. Check operation and safety of DIY additions ☐ ....
Other comments: ....

Section 5: Gas/gas appliances
Comments

1. Carry out pressure test on system ☐ ....
2. Replace washer on butane cylinder regulator ☐ ....
3. Replace flexible hose; use new hoseclips ☐ ....
4. Fridge: light and test for cooling ☐ ....
5. Light and verify operation of cooking appliances ☐ ....
6. Check space heater operation, clean burners ☐ ....
7. Check water heater operation, clean burners ☐ ....
8. Check LP gas and carbon monoxide alarms ☐ ....
9. Check refillable gas tank mountings ☐ ....
General comments on gas appliances: ....

Section 6: Electrical
Comments

1. Check RCD and MCBs on central unit ☐ ....
2. Test 13 Amp mains sockets ☐ ....
3. Test 12V sockets ☐ ....
4. Check integrity of all wiring and fuses ☐ ....
5. Check operation of all interior lights ☐ ....
6. Check awning lamp/outside pump socket ☐ ....
7. Check auxiliary battery ☐ ....
Other comments: ....

Section 7: Water systems
Comments

1. Check operation of water pump, clean grit filter ☐ ....
2. Check waste & fresh water system for leaks ☐ ....
3. Flush through with purifying cleaner ☐ ....
4. Inspect tanks/emptying system ☐ ....
5. Change charcoal water filter, if fitted ☐ ....
6. Check toilet flush and blade operation ☐ ....
Other comments: ....

Work completed on: ....

Work completed by: ....

These elements relate to a standard service; further items might be added (with a separate charge). These could include:

☐ Full service of refrigerator in accordance with Dometic/ Electrolux/ Thetford instructions.

☐ Full service of space and water heaters in accordance with their manufacturer's instructions.

☐ Check operation/mounting of all seat belts (acknowledging that some are fitted retrospectively by the motorhome manufacturer rather than the base vehicle manufacturer).

☐ if fitted, check built-in generator for safety.

Anxious to improve this situation, the author attended training courses run by industry experts, including chassis manufacturers, body repair specialists, and manufacturers of appliances such as refrigerators, cookers, water heaters, and space heaters. Additional investigative work included visits to water system manufacturers (including Carver, Optimus and Whale), nationally recognised repair specialists (including Crossley Coachcraft), and to several 'service workshops'. Drawing on information gained during these courses and visits, service schedules were compiled and subsequently published in the caravan and motorcaravan manuals produced by Haynes Publishing in the 1990s.

The publication of these recommended service schedules provoked widespread interest and technical staff based at the NCC office enquired if they could be used as discussion documents. In addition, the author was invited to join a small working party with the aim of creating formally approved habitation service schedules that could be used nationwide. Constructive meetings took place and service schedules appropriate for touring caravans and motorcaravans were subsequently produced. The motorcaravan schedule is given on the previous page.

DAMP TESTS

Although a damp test forms part of a habitation service, it is often possible to get one of these carried out as a separate operation. A disappointing number of coachbuilt motorcaravans fail prematurely on account of water damage and any points of weakness in a body shell need to be identified at the earliest opportunity. If you suspect a leak at any time, act at once; don't wait for the next servicing operation.

Information on damp testing operations and the interpretation of meter readings was given in Chapter 3, and the certificate showing the 50 or so points where readings are taken was also mentioned.

GAS APPLIANCE SERVICING

The shape of a gas flame and its colour were discussed in Chapter 6. If there's an incorrect mix of gas and air, there could be an emission of carbon monoxide. This is why expert attention is extremely important.

A 'three-way' refrigerator is one of the gas-operated appliances needing routine attention. For instance, Dometic (formerly trading as Electrolux) has stated that a refrigerator should be serviced annually. Information on this was given in Chapter 9.

Although manufacturers state that their fridges need servicing once a year, a standard habitation service will usually only check that the appliance achieves cooling. This is described as an 'operational check'. Dealers treat a full 'fridge service' as an entirely separate job, which incurs an additional charge. So don't be misled into thinking that the operational check carried out during a habitation service constitutes 'refrigerator servicing'. Unfortunately, many owners are unaware of this and if their refrigerator fails shortly after a habitation service, they often complain bitterly that 'it was only serviced about a month ago.' However, when complaints are followed up, it usually turns out that the motorcaravan was only booked-in for a three hour habitation service and no extra services were requested for its appliances. So the fridge didn't get serviced as its owner had claimed. Perhaps this matter needs to be made clearer at service reception desks.

The situation is similar with heating appliances. Operational checks during a standard habitation service confirm whether an appliance is 'firing-up' correctly and producing heat. Whether the burners are cleaned depends on their accessibility.

Unfortunately, when left unused for an extended period, gas heating appliances sometimes perform poorly. As explained in Chapter 6, the accumulation of dust is one contributor to inefficient operation; spiders and insects can also create problems. In consequence, a gas specialist periodically needs to clean most types of heating appliance. Also, spark ignition components might need realigning.

However, if an appliance needs a significant amount of dismantling work in order to yield access to its burner assembly, this work is *not* normally undertaken during a standard habitation service. As explained above in the context of refrigerators, some gas appliances may need to be removed and transferred to a bench. Substantial dismantling work may also be necessary in order to carry out more involved jobs. This normally incurs an additional fee, depending on the time it takes to carry out a manufacturer's recommended schedule.

Right: A trained service specialist knows how to use a professional damp meter and is able to interpret the results in the context of motorcaravan constructional methods.

Far right: Burners may need cleaning and igniter spark gaps readjusting, but these tasks are not always completed in a habitation service.

Far left: One of the ways to test that a gas supply system is free from leaks is to use a purpose-made air pump.

Left: This Approved Workshop exclusively offers servicing facilities for motorcaravans; it is also an AL-KO Approved Service Centre.

DIY SERVICING

When a recently purchased motorcaravan is still within its warranty period, habitation servicing work has to be carried out by an authorised workshop at the prescribed intervals. (Check with the dealer who sold the motorcaravan, what is deemed an 'authorised workshop'.) Once the motorcaravan falls outside its warranty, some owners prefer to do the servicing work themselves.

There's no doubt that motorcaravanners with practical experience, technical knowledge and an appropriate level of competency would be able to carry out some of the tasks listed in the accompanying service schedule. Checking window catches, lubricating door hinges and tightening the spring mechanism on a roller blind is not taxing.

At the same time, there are other operations – like pressure-testing a gas system – that should *only* be undertaken by a qualified gas specialist.

Similarly, safety tests on a 230V mains supply system need to be carried out by a qualified electrician familiar with installation practices in motorcaravans. Sometimes these items can be carried out as 'stand-alone' inspections by qualified persons, after which a dated and signed certificate is issued. A written certificate on the company's headed paper is important, of course. Being able to pass on service records and dated safety certificates is always helpful when selling a motorcaravan.

APPROVED WORKSHOP SCHEME

In addition to creating habitation service schedules, The National Caravan Council launched a

complementary initiative in conjunction with The Camping and Caravanning Club and The Caravan Club. The aim was to create a nation-wide chain of '**Approved Caravan Workshops**' with a level of service and standard of workmanship that would 'meet high standards of competency and comply with a Code of Practice.' Approved caravan workshops that fulfilled the scheme's assessment criteria began operations in 1999. It was soon decided that a parallel initiative would be introduced to focus on motorcaravan habitation servicing as well. This was implemented in 2003, at which point participating dealers' servicing departments were then renamed '**Approved Workshops**'.

As regards acceptance into the scheme, a leaflet published by the NCC states that: 'workshops must pass an annual inspection by a team of independent assessors and comply with the Scheme's rigorous standards.' To obtain assurance that the assessment mechanism was conducted with the rigour implied in the scheme's documentation, the author shadowed one of these inspections.

This in-depth assessment was not only informative; it was remarkably thorough and took four hours to complete. Even racks in the spare parts department were carefully examined in order to confirm that servicing components were of the approved type and quality. Accreditation certainly isn't easy to achieve.

When a servicing centre achieves Approved Workshop status it must:

■ Display a menu of pricing, specifying labour rates

Far left: An independent assessor checks the service records during a visit to a dealer who has applied for Approved Workshop status.

Left: All members of the Approved Workshop scheme are required to display prices for service work. *Note: These were the charges in 2007.*

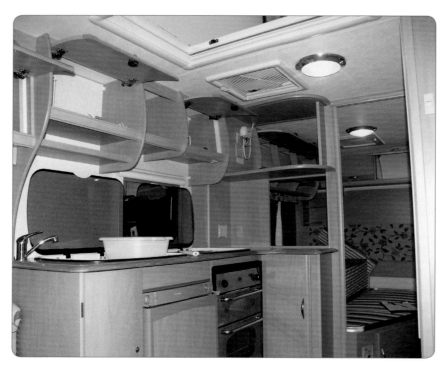

Above: The CITO Handbook states that all lockers must be empty and their doors left open to stabilise inside temperatures *before* damp test readings are taken.

Below: In the City & Guilds practical examination, candidates are shadowed by a examiner who ensures that good practices are adopted during a service operation.

■ Provide an estimate for additional servicing or repair work over £150
■ Give an estimated time for completion and collection
■ Use genuine parts where available
■ Ensure all work is carried out using skill, care and professional judgement
■ Always provide customers with a checklist of work completed
■ Not begin work without the express authority of the customer
■ Contact the customer for authority to continue if additional work is identified
■ Notify a customer in writing of faults that have not been rectified, with an honest assessment of the urgency of the repairs.

Every workshop in the scheme operates a straightforward complaints procedure, and if this does not achieve satisfactory results, complaints are then independently investigated.

The latest information about the scheme is available on www.approvedworkshops.co.uk and there's a search facility so you can locate your nearest workshop. Leaflets are also available from the NCC, call 01252 318251, or visit www.thecaravan.net

CITY AND GUILDS EXAMINATION

Apart from the existence of qualifications related to areas of attention like gas installations and mains electricity supplies, there is also a national qualification entitled 'The City and Guilds Examination in Caravan Engineering (Touring Caravans and Motorhomes)'. In the practical work of this multi-section test, candidates have to perform a full service in front of an examiner using a detailed service schedule. Prior to this, participants undergo a substantial training programme using the *Caravan Industry Training Organisation Engineers' Handbook*. The organisation, normally referred to as CITO, has worked with the NCC to compile this comprehensive sourcebook, which explains service operations in precise detail.

The document also states that whereas a caravan service will take four hours to complete, a motorcaravan habitation service normally takes three hours. In the case of a touring caravan, road lighting, brake system, suspension, coupling mechanisms and tyres have to be included under the 'umbrella' of a habitation service. In contrast, these elements are covered in a motorcaravan's base vehicle service and (where necessary) MoTs – hence the allocation of only three hours to complete its habitation service.

Without doubt, the work by CITO has played a further part in raising the standard of servicing operations. It is also pleasing that the City and Guilds examination embraces both a test of experience/knowledge as well as a challenging practical assessment of 'real life' servicing at an Approved Workshop.

ISSUES AND CONSTRAINTS

In many cases, work on a motorcaravan's chassis and running gear is undertaken by a commercial vehicle specialist. Of course, owners of a Fiat base vehicle, for example, may be more inclined to use a Fiat specialist. However, that is only possible if the workshop is large enough to accommodate a motorcaravan. Some franchise dealers have neither large enough ramps nor sufficient access to accommodate large motorcaravans. There is also another issue that owners need to recognise.

If a motorcaravan is constructed using its base vehicle's original chassis and suspension, automotive technicians undertaking a service at a franchise dealer will carry out the appropriate work on these elements. However, some motorcaravans are constructed on a replacement

Above: The owner of this large motorcaravan found that work on the base vehicle had to be carried out at a commercial truck centre that was fitted with heavy duty lifting gear.

ALKO AMC structure and suspension instead. As pointed out in Chapter 4, there are important greasing points on an AL-KO rear axle tube that keep its torsion bar suspension system lubricated. It stands to reason that a Fiat (or other vehicle) trained service specialist that hasn't encountered the AL-KO AMC product could overlook an important operation like greasing a torsion bar suspension. Whether this work is undertaken during the vehicle servicing operation, or as part of the habitation service, it needs checking by the owner.

Today, the whole system of motorcaravan servicing is greatly improved and owners are recommended to have both base vehicle and habitation work carried out at the appropriate intervals. Procedures are constantly under review and improvements are frequently being made. For the latest information on this topic, both the major clubs and the National Caravan Council can provide you with ongoing information.

Service Workshops

■ The number of Approved Workshops is ever-increasing, although it should be noted that some participating companies specialise in either touring or motorcaravans. There are also a few mobile service specialists who have gained Approved Workshop status.

■ There is no implicit suggestion that a service workshop that is not an accredited member of the Approved Workshop scheme is unable to provide owners with a professional and high standard of service. Some definitely do offer good service and workmanship; conversely, there are others who don't.

■ Similarly, it would be entirely unrealistic to suggest that Approved Workshops are never at fault in one way or another. The scheme is very sound, but the NCC staff are continually looking for ways to improve it.

■ If arranging a habitation service at a workshop outside of the scheme, enquire what procedures are in place if something is found to be faulty during the inspection. For example, in some workshops, minor tasks like repairing an inoperative interior light are done within the time allotted for the service. Spare parts, of course, will be charged separately.

■ Check the workshop procedure if an expensive replacement part needs fitting. Although it often makes sense for a repair to be carried out there and then, insist that you are consulted before any major work commences, and leave full contact details.

■ Service charges partly depend on a dealer's hourly rate for labour. Parts will be charged separately, of course. Whereas members of the Approved Workshop scheme are required to display prices and labour rates in their service reception, this procedure is not always followed elsewhere.

APPENDIX B

Standards and regulations

Supplied by Martin Spencer, Technical Manager for The Caravan Club

Let's face it, it's hard to get excited about standards and regulations. Don't they just concern manufacturers, and not motorcaravan owners? There is some truth to that, at least as far as the finer details are concerned, but whether you're buying a new or used vehicle, or planning to modify the one you already have, there are some things worth bearing in mind. Please note that this section is intended to provide only an overview of what is a very complex topic.

LEGALITY FOR ROAD USE

Your vehicle must meet the technical requirements for use on UK roads. For many years, this meant mainly the Road Vehicles (Construction & Use) Regulations (C&U), which defines amongst other things, dimensions, braking requirements and safety matters. Lights and reflectors are covered separately in the Road Vehicle Lighting Regulations (RVLR). These regulations have been steadily updated and gradually harmonised with similar European Directives, but from 2009 a process called Type Approval began to supersede these for new vehicles. Type Approval confirms the design meets a raft of European Directives or international Regulations, and can be achieved at one of three levels:

1 European Community Whole Vehicle Type Approval (ECWVTA) is the most comprehensive assessment of the vehicle, requiring it to meet relevant environmental, safety and security standards. This then allows the manufacturer to sell unlimited quantities anywhere in Europe, but the downside is that this is a complex and expensive process. As an owner, you can rely on any motorcaravan approved to this level being safely designed, and also built to a consistent standard, as 'Conformity of Production' (CoP) is a key element of the requirements. This is the same process that the overwhelming majority of cars go through.

2 National Small Series Type Approval (NSSTA) is a UK national scheme for low volume manufacturers who intend to sell only in the UK. The technical requirements are somewhat relaxed, and there's a simpler CoP requirement, making the administration and testing costs less.

3 Individual Vehicle Approval (IVA) is a UK national scheme for those manufacturing or importing single vehicles, or building very small numbers, where Type Approval is impractical to achieve. Every vehicle built is inspected in a form of 'super-MoT' by the Vehicle and Operator Services Agency (VOSA) in Great Britain or the Driver and Vehicle Agency (DVA) in Northern Ireland.

All these options result in a safe, legal vehicle. More areas are included under ECWVTA, however, and further practical tests are required at this level. This proves that the motorcaravan meets the highest possible standards for both design and construction. Vehicles approved to other levels *may* be as good, but are not *proven* to be.

Approval became optional for motorcaravans on 29 April 2009, and some manufacturers rapidly started selling approved models. Approval is mandatory for all motorcaravans first registered from 29 April 2012. Vehicles complying with ECWVTA or NSSTA should come with a 'Certificate of Conformity' (which might be included in the handbook, rather than being a separate document), while vehicles tested to IVA should come with an inspection certificate.

Vehicles that don't comply with one of these schemes will not be capable of being registered and brought into service for road use after 29 April 2012.

A key issue with vehicles having Type Approval (even those made before the mandatory date) is that any towbar you subsequently fit to them also has to be a Type Approved model (to Directive 94/20EC). This is also the case with NSSTA motorcaravans, and with those going through IVA. For non-Type Approved vehicles, it's still worth choosing a Type Approved towbar if one is available, as the test standard for these is very stringent. Alternatively, look for one that has reached the requirements of British Standard BS AU 114b, or the similar International Standard ISO 3853.

While self-build conversions are really outside the scope of this book, it's worth noting that you

Definition of a motorcaravan

The following definition is used in various Directives, Regulations and other documents:

'A motorcaravan is a Special Purpose M1 Category Vehicle constructed to include at least the following equipment: seats and table, sleeping accommodation which may be converted from the seats, cooking facilities, storage facilities. The equipment shall be rigidly fixed to the living compartment; however, the table may be designed to be easily removable.'

can still do your own conversion on a pre-registered base vehicle (new or second-hand) without having to re-Type Approve the vehicle if it is already approved, or Type Approve it if it isn't. If you self-build on a new (unregistered) vehicle, it will need an IVA inspection.

With vehicles which pre-date Type Approval, problems sometimes occur if the motorcaravan is imported, usually for those models imported in very low numbers. The importer or retailer has to ensure the vehicle meets the requirements of C&U and RVLR. For instance, on European-sourced vehicles, that means the kph speedo needs to be changed to a mph one, and the headlights changed to right-hand drive deflection. For North American vehicles, lighting will need to be modified to European standards, and in a few cases, vehicles may be too wide. For vehicles imported individually or in very small numbers, a predecessor to the IVA scheme mentioned above, the Single Vehicle Approval (SVA) scheme, was optionally available for motorcaravans until 29 April 2012, and the presence of an SVA 'Minister's Approval Certificate' with the vehicle is useful proof of its legality.

Your motorcaravan should have a weight plate fixed to it. Usually, this will have four figures – from top to bottom these are:

- Gross Vehicle Weight – the maximum weight your vehicle can be when fully loaded.
- Gross Train Weight – the combined maximum weight of your motorcaravan and anything it's towing.
- Front Axle Weight – the maximum load on the front axle.
- Rear Axle Weight – the maximum load on the rear axle.

These figures must not be exceeded. To do so makes the vehicle unroadworthy, may well invalidate your insurance, and gives the Police grounds to prevent you carrying on your journey if they stop you. It's strongly recommended that you take your motorcaravan to a weighbridge, loaded as you usually use it, and carefully check that there is enough payload capacity for your needs.

Note that you may find two, or even three, weight plates on the vehicle if it is built in stages where the maximum allowed weight changes, perhaps as a result of a chassis extension. On motorcaravans with three axles, there will be an extra weight figure for the third axle. For some drivers, their driving licence restricts them to vehicles of no more then 3,500kg Gross Vehicle Weight, thus giving another important reason to check the weight plate carefully.

Since October 1994, motorcaravan engines have been rated for their emissions against a series of European Directive requirements (Euro 1, Euro 2 etc). Unlike passenger cars, this is not yet used to determine the rate of Vehicle Excise Duty (road tax). However, it is relevant if travelling into a low emission zone, such as London and many

Changes in standards and regulations

While this summary was correct when printed, changes occur with surprising regularity. Please check the latest legislation, bearing in mind that many administrative bodies like the DVLA have websites giving up-to-date guidance.

European cities. Most such zones require at least Euro 3 (January 2001 onwards), and some demand Euro 4 (January 2006 onwards) – undoubtedly more will demand this over time. If your vehicle fails to meet the right level, you may be banned from the zone, or fined if you enter it. When buying a second-hand motorcaravan, check carefully which emissions standard it meets.

HABITATION AREA

There remain relatively few legal controls on this area of a motorcaravan. For instance, the legal requirements that apply to gas installations in houses and other buildings do not apply to privately used motorcaravans, and because they are motor vehicles, the furniture in motorcaravans does *not* need to comply with the legislation relating to the fire safety of domestic furnishings, unlike it does in towed caravans. Some areas *are* legally controlled; for instance, the installation of mains electrics must comply with BS 7671 'Regulations for Electrical Installations (IEE Wiring Regulations 17th Edition)'. Some aspects of Type Approval creep into the habitation area too, including seatbelt system performance, and restrictions against having sharp edges and corners around the area that travelling passengers sit.

Key sources of information

While not an exhaustive list, the following may help those wishing to find out more about this topic:

Construction & Use Regs*: www.legislation.gov.uk/uksi/1986/1078/contents/made

Road Vehicle Lighting Regs*:
    www.legislation.gov.uk/uksi/1989/1796/contents/made

Vehicle Type Approval from (DfT)
    www.dft.gov.uk/topics/vehicles/ecwvta/

Vehicle Type Approval (from VCA):
    www.dft.gov.uk/vca/vehicletype/index.asp

And for those with real stamina for heavy-going documents, here's the full Type Approval documentation from the EU:
ec.europa.eu/enterprise/sectors/automotive/documents/directives/directive-2007-46-ec_en.htm

British Standards are not freely available, but can be purchased from BSi via shop.bsigroup.com/ and some public and university libraries hold sets for reference; www.bsieducation.org/Education/resources/libraries.shtml

*These are the original (unamended) versions of these regulations – both have been subject to many subsequent amendments, which are listed on the legislation.gov.uk website separately.

Seatbelts

Motorcaravans first used since October 1988 must have seatbelts for the driver and for the row of seats next to the driver. Until relatively recently, belts were not legally required for the seats in the habitation area, but are clearly desirable, and must be used if fitted and 'available' – *ie* not already occupied. From October 2007, however, new vehicles have had to be fitted with seatbelts for all seats intended for use while travelling. Strangely, it isn't currently a requirement to fit as many seatbelts as there are berths – an anomaly that some manufacturers use to save money. Check there are enough for your needs.

From 1989, though, the Society of Motor Society of Motor Manufacturers and Traders (SMMT) introduced 'The Motor Caravan Code of Practice', which was then updated from September 1992 in a joint SMMT/National Caravan Council (NCC) 'Code of Practice 201'. This specifies various requirements relating to the health and safety of the habitation area, but is not a legal requirement. NCC member companies have to comply with it, but others may well choose not to – this includes many smaller converters and many importers. If a motorcaravan displays the SMMT/NCC 'CoP 201' badge, or from 1998, the updated equivalent 'Approved Motor Caravan EN 1646' badge, its design will have been inspected and approved by NCC Certification Engineers. Designs without this approval may still be safe and extremely well-produced – it's just much harder to be certain that this is the case.

Things changed again from September 1998, when many new European Standards were adopted as British Standards in the UK:

BS EN 1646-1 'Habitation Requirements Relating to Health and Safety'. Covers amongst other issues entrance step design, door dimensions, bunk strength and safety, drinking and waste water system designs, heating requirements, fire precautions and handbook requirements. This is perhaps the most crucial habitation standard. It sets safety requirements that prevent children from falling out of bunks, and grades the heating system to indicate whether you'll be comfortable using the vehicle all year around.

BS EN 1646-2 'User Payload'. Definitions of vehicle weight and payload terminology, and minimum user payload requirement.

BS EN 1648-2 '12V Direct Current Extra Low Voltage Electrical Installations'. Installation, performance and safety requirements.

Tachographs and speed limiters

These are not required on motorcaravans unless the vehicle is being used for commercial purposes, and generally only then if it is being used to transport goods. However, some base vehicles may have them fitted at build, meaning they need to be de-specified when the base vehicle is ordered by the converter, or removed as part of the conversion process.

BS EN 721 'Safety Ventilation Requirements'. Requirements and evaluation methods to check that there is enough fresh air ventilation, and sufficient gas drop out holes to protect in the event of a gas leak. This is one of the most common areas in which non-certified motorcaravans fall short.

In 2002, an additional European Standard was added, covering the gas system:

BS EN 1949 'Specification for the Installation of LPG Systems for Habitation Purposes in Leisure Accommodation Vehicles and in Other Road Vehicles'. Safety, performance and installation requirements for cylinder storage, pipework, appliances and flues etc.

These replace and enhance the requirements previously covered in CoP 201. Again, they are not legally binding, but their European relevance means that more manufacturers adopt them. Vehicles checked for compliance by the NCC carry a revised badge of approval stating 'EN 1646', which indicates the main habitation standard, although the certification checks carried out by the NCC cover a wider range of topics as well as those detailed in the standards. As European Standards, these should have been adopted by countries throughout Europe (although not at the same time in each country), meaning that imported motorcaravans are more likely to comply with them as well. The NCC does inspect and certify some imported motorcaravans, but other overseas manufacturers may simply claim compliance with the standards, without going through the certification process.

Where regulations and standards do not cover important topics, the NCC has developed additional Codes of Practice to fill in the gaps, and these are requirements for motorcaravans that pass their Certification Scheme. Examples include requirements for carbon monoxide alarms and a specification for user-refillable fixed LPG tanks.

SUMMARY

When buying a new or used motorcaravan, check the following issues:

- Is the motorcaravan Type Approved? If not, is there evidence of its road legality (*eg* an SVA certificate)? In the absence of other evidence, a valid MoT certificate helps, but consider an independent inspection if in any doubt prior to purchase.
- Is the Gross Vehicle Weight enough to give you sufficient payload capacity, and within any driving licence restrictions that apply to you?
- Are the engine emissions good enough to let you travel into London and many European cities without problems?
- Does the vehicle have an NCC Certification Scheme approval badge? If not, does the manufacturer claim compliance with the EN 1646 standard at least?
- Are there enough seatbelts provided for the number of passengers you will carry?

APPENDIX C
Pre-storage tasks

If you are not going to use your motorcaravan for several months, a number of pre-storage jobs have to be carried out. This is especially true when laying-up a vehicle for the winter.

OUTDOOR TASKS

Select a parking place where there's no likelihood of damage from trees, falling branches or roof tiles. Remember too, that trees leave a green algae deposit during long storage periods.

■ Storing a free-standing awning

Make absolutely certain that your awning is dry before packing it away. Brush off bird lime and clean the plastic skirts if necessary. If an awning is dirty or has been used under trees that exude sticky substances, attention is needed. It is usually best to re-erect it for cleaning. Products are available like Awning Cleaner from Camco.

■ Checking a roller blind

Set up a wall-mounted blind and make sure that it is absolutely dry before rolling it back into its cassette.

■ Consider chocking the wheels

As long as a vehicle is well chocked and parked on a sound, level pitch, leave off the handbrake – especially if your last trip was in wet weather. This prevents it seizing up during an extended storage period.

■ Mechanical security devices

To discourage thieves, consider the wisdom of fitting a robust wheel clamp. Products that achieve Sold Secure Gold Standard accreditation are strongly recommended.

■ Remove gas cylinders

Transfer gas cylinders to a secure, well-ventilated, covered, outdoor store. If you leave cylinders in a motorcaravan locker, they may get stolen and could be a fire risk. Never store cylinders in a cellar or a location where leaks of this heavier-than-air gas would be unable to escape. Ensure the cylinders are kept upright.

■ Keep batteries in a good state of charge

A battery will be ruined if left in a discharged condition. Transfer a leisure battery to a garage or work-shed where you can monitor its condition and recharge when necessary. Trickle chargers are sold for keeping both leisure and vehicle batteries

in sound condition, many of which can be left coupled-up.

■ Ensure that both fresh and waste water tanks are empty

Drain down the tanks, leave the taps open, but fit a breathable insert to act as a stopper. This is because spiders and other insects often crawl inside an open pipe to make a nest.

■ Preparation before fitting a cover

Ensure your motorcaravan is clean, free of dirt and surface dust. This is particularly important for acrylic windows, but never cover them with clingfilm; this practice might cause crazing cracks to appear later. Position protection pieces over sharp corners so that friction holes don't develop in a fabric during windy weather. Use a breathable cover and carefully check it's secure.

INDOOR TASKS

■ Drain down a water heater

Repairing a frost-damaged water heater is costly, so follow the all-important draining-down procedures given in the appliance's owner's manual.

■ Fresh water pipes

Consider removing the residual water from supply pipes, recognising that many water systems have a non-return valve near the point of entry. Note the earlier advice in Chapter 7 about residual water in downturns of pipe that can freeze and cause damage.

■ Taps and shower controls

As described in Chapter 7, leaving taps open releases any build-up of pressure if residual water in pipe-runs starts to freeze. To achieve this with a lever mixer tap and shower control, ensure that its lever is lifted and left in a central position.

■ Replacing a water 'taste' filter

Residual water in a cassette filter can freeze and split its casing. Remove it and buy a replacement. Arguably, this could be left until spring, but doing the job in late autumn means you can get off the mark quicker when active again. What's more, the price of a filter might be higher next season.

■ Plugging waste water outlets

Put plugs in the sink, basin and shower tray to prevent smells from the waste tank creeping into the living compartment. Reasons for drain smells were explained in Chapter 7.

■ Shower heads and submersible pumps

Make sure no residual water is left in the shower head. Handsets are often unhooked from their bracket and laid down in the shower tray. If you have a portable submersible pump, similarly check that no water remains in its casing.

■ Refrigerator care

Leave the fridge door ajar using its second catch position. If you shut the door completely, the interior might start to smell. See earlier cleaning advice in Chapter 8.

■ Clean cooking appliances

Degrease the oven and hob with a proprietary cleaner. Remove dust from the burners using a stiff bristle brush. Some service specialists use an accessory extension linked to a vacuum cleaner.

■ Work on a cassette toilet

If your cassette toilet has its own separate flush water tank, drain this down. Clean the cassette interior using a product recommended by its manufacturer. Leave the release flap on your cassette wide open during the storage period. Apply a treatment lubricant to the rubber seal following the manufacturer's recommendations.

Procedures are shown in the toilet project section in Chapter 10.

■ Upholstery care

Stains should always be removed as soon as possible. If left too long, they become permanent. See guidance in Chapter 9 regarding stain removal and cleaning. Ideally, transfer mattresses indoors so they don't get damp inside your motorcaravan. This is also a good security strategy; thieves are less likely to steal a motorcaravan that has no soft furnishings inside.

■ Window blinds

There is a dilemma here. Many owners lower all the window blinds to hide the interior and to protect upholstery from the effects of the sun. This makes sense but cassette blind manufacturers point out that a spring mechanism in a roller then gets fatigued and its recoil action subsequently becomes sluggish. Of course, weak springs can be tightened, and this doesn't arise if an external cover is fitted.

■ Make a reminder list of repairs needed

If you need any parts, order them at the end of a season. Delivery is quicker in winter.

Pre-season tasks

After a long lay-up period – especially during the winter – a motorcaravan usually needs some preparatory work before it is ready for use. Here is a selection of general pre-season reminders:

■ Check the tyres

Check the tyre pressures, including the spare; and carry out a visual check of their sidewalls; look carefully at both sides to confirm there's no sign of cracking or premature failure. Make a further tyre check after your first trip.

■ Check the handbrake

Make sure the brake operates freely by pulling/releasing the lever several times.

■ Reinstate the soft furnishings

Replace the cushions and any other soft furnishings that were previously transferred to a warm storage base.

■ Services

Carry out a run of all the services. Couple-up a gas cylinder and make sure the gas appliances are working. Note that it may take several moments for air to be purged from the supply pipes. Reinstate the leisure battery – take a reading with a voltmeter if you own one to ensure it achieves

12.7V or more. Chapters 5 and 6 provide more detailed advice.

■ Water filter

If the system has a cartridge fitted and you didn't replace it at the end of the previous season, fit a new one.

■ Sterilising a water system

Some owners start a new season by running a sterilising solution through the water pipes. A product like Milton is often used, which is available from any good chemists. Milton is the product widely used for sterilising babies' feeding bottles.

■ Clean the motorcaravan

Use a brush to remove webs, insects, and dust from around the doors and locker lids. Green algae may have formed on the roof, especially when a vehicle is parked near trees. Cleaning advice is given in Chapter 3.

■ Servicing

If you didn't finish the previous season by arranging a habitation service, arrange this in good time. Workshops are heavily booked in springtime and early summer. Also check the base vehicle's service records. Then enjoy the season ahead in comfort and safety!

Contact addresses

Please note: This address list was correct at the time of going to press. It includes specialist suppliers and manufacturers whose products and services have been mentioned in the text. Several of the firms have websites that can be easily found using search engines.

The motorcaravan manufacturers listed here include specialists offering bespoke building services and individual fitting operations such as the installation of high top roofs. To obtain a more complete list of motorcaravan manufacturers and importers, consult the monthly buyers' guides published in magazines such as

1. *Motorcaravan, Motorhome Monthly*
2. *Practical Motorhome*
3. *Which Motorhome*

ABP Accessories,
27 Nether End,
Great Dalby,
Leicestershire, LE14 2EY
Tel: 08700 115111
(American RV Accessories including Camco products)

Adrian Bailey Classics,
Unit 1-1A Thornton Grove Works,
Thornton Grove,
Whingate, Leeds, LS12 3JB
Tel: 0113 263 4288
(Supplier of obsolete and used spares for Bedford CF vans)

Alan H. Schofield Classic Volkswagen,
Unit 14, Dinting Lane,
Glossop, Derbyshire, SK13 7NU
Tel: 01457 854267
(Fabrication and supply of VW panels and parts)

Albert Jagger Ltd,
Centaur Works,
Green Lane, Walsall,
West Midlands, WS2 8HG
Tel: 01922 471000
(Manufacturers/suppliers commercial vehicle fittings)

Alde International (UK) Ltd,
14 Regent Park,
Booth Drive,
Park Farm South,
Wellingborough,
Northamptonshire, NN8 6GR
Tel: 01933 677765
(Central heating systems, SMEV cooking equipment, gas leak detector)

Al-Ko Kober Ltd,
South Warwickshire Business Park,
Kineton Road,
Southam,
Warwickshire, CV47 0AL
Tel: 01926 818500
(AMC conversions)

Amber Plastics Ltd,
Broombank Road,
Chesterfield Industrial Estate,
Sheepbridge,
Chesterfield, S41 9QJ
Tel: 01246 456525
(Rotational mouldings including inboard fixed tanks)

Anglian Developments Ltd,
The Granary,
School Road,
Neatishead,
Norfolk, NR12 8BU
Tel: 01692 630808
(GRP specialist building monocoque commercial body shells)

Apollo Chemicals Ltd,
Sandy Way,
Amington Industrial Estate,
Tamworth,
Staffordshire, B77 4DS
Tel: 01827 54281
(Manufacturers of adhesives for repairing delaminated composite panels)

Arc Systems,
13 Far Street,
Bradmore,
Nottingham, NG11 6PF
Tel: 0115 921 3175
(Service, repair and parts for Carver heating products)

Autocraft Motor Caravans,
Fan Road Industrial Estate,
Fan Road,
Staveley,
Chesterfield,
Derbyshire, S43 3PT
Tel: 01246 471199
(Van conversion accessories)

Autogas 2000 Ltd,
Carlton Miniott, Thirsk,
North Yorkshire, YO7 4NJ
Tel: 01845 523213
(Caratank LPG bulk storage tanks)

Auto Glym,
Works Road,
Letchworth,
Hertfordshire, SG6 1LU
Tel: 01462 677766
(Extensive range of automotive cleaning products)

Autovan Services Ltd,
32 Canford Bottom,
Wimborne,
Dorset, BH21 2HD
Tel: 01202 848414
(Major body repair and rebuilding work; inspection service)

A. Baldassarre,
Upholsterer and Coachtrimmer,
103, Coventry Road,
Queens Park,
Bedford, MK40 4ES
Tel: 01234 359277
(Upholstery work, foam supply and soft furnishings)

Banner Batteries (GB) Ltd,
Units 5-8,
Canal View Business Park,
Wheelhouse Road, Rugeley,
Staffordshire, WS15 1UY
Tel: 01889 571100
(Vehicle and Leisure batteries, AGM batteries)

Bantam Trailers,
Units 5 & 6,
Wollaston Industrial Estate,
Raymond Close, Wollaston,
Northamptonshire, NN29 7RG
(Trailers for small cars including Smart for two)

BCA Leisure Ltd,
Unit H9, Premier Way,
Lowfields Business Park,
Elland,
West Yorkshire, HX5 9HF
Tel: 01422-376977
(Manufacturers of Powerpart mains kits)

BeenyBox.co.uk,
Station Garage,
Trevu Road,
Camborne,
Cornwall, TR14 7AE
Tel: 01209 711093
(Underfloor sliding storage locker system)

Beetles UK Ltd,
– See Danbury Motorcaravans

Belling Appliances
– See Glen Dimplex

Bilbo's Design,
Eastbourne Road, (A22)
South Godstone,
Surrey, RH9 8JQ
Tel: 01342 892499

British Car Auctions Ltd,
Sales & Marketing Department,
Expedier House,
Portsmouth Road,
Hindhead,
Surrey, GU26 6TJ
Tel: 01428 607440
(Motorcaravan auctions)

British Rubber Manufacturers'
Association Ltd,
6 Bath Place, Rivington Street,
London, EC2A 3JE
Tel: 020 7457 5040
(Trade Association advising on tyres)

C.A.K. – See Caravan Accessories

Calor Gas Ltd,
Athena Drive,
Tachbrook Park,
Warwick, CV34 6RL
Tel: 0800 626626
(Supplier of butane, propane and LPG products)

CAMCO products – See ABP Accessories

The Camping & Caravanning Club,
Greenfields House,
Westwood Way,
Coventry, CV4 8JH
Tel: 024 7647 5448

Campingaz
Coleman UK Inc.,
Gordano Gate,
Portishead,
Bristol, BS20 7GG
Tel: 01275 845024
(Supplier of Campingaz butane and LPG appliances)

Carafax Ltd,
Rotterdam Road,
Sutton Fields Industrial Estate,
Hull, HU7 0XD
Tel: 01482 825941
(Caraseal ribbon and cartridge sealants)

Car-A-Tow – See Pro-Tow

Caravan Accessories (C.A.K. Tanks) Ltd,
10 Princes Drive Industrial Estate,
Kenilworth,
Warwickshire,
CV8 2FD
Tel: 0870 757 2324
(Water tanks, accessories and components)

The Caravan Club
East Grinstead House,
East Grinstead,
West Sussex, RH19 1UA
Tel: 01342 326944

The Caravan Centre,
Unit 3A,
Gilchrist Thomas Industrial Estate,
Blaenavon, NP4 9RL
Tel: 01495 792700
(Specialist breakers supplying caravan/motorhome products)

The Caravan Panel Shop
Unit 7, Willacy Yard,
Bay Horse Lane,
Catforth, Preston,
Lancashire, PR4 0JD
Tel: 01772 691929
(Copy GRP mouldings made from damaged body parts)

The Caravan Seat Cover Centre,
Cater Business Park,
Bishopsworth,
Bristol,
BS13 7TW
Tel: 0117 941 0222
(Seat covers, new foam, new upholstery, made-to-measure curtains)

Carver products – See Arc Systems and Truma

Concept Multi-Car,
Unit 1, Pennypot Industrial Estate,
Hythe,
Kent, CT21 6PE
Tel: 01303 261062
(High top roof installation, Reimo products, van conversions)

The Council for Registered Gas Installers (CORGI) - see Gas Safe Register™,
Former holder of gas registration scheme rights. See Gas Safe Register.

Cramer UK – See Dometic

Country Campers,
The Grove,
Three Gates Road,
Fawkham,
Kent, DA3 7NZ
Tel: 01474 707929
(High top roof installation, van conversions to order)

Crossleys,
Unit 33A, Comet Road,
Moss Side Industrial Estate,
Leyland,
Lancashire, PR26 7QN
Tel: 01772 623423
(Major body repair and rebuilding work)

Customer Enquiries (Vehicles), DVLA,
Swansea,
SA99 1BL
Tel: 0870 2400010
(Guidance on vehicle registration)

Danbury Motorcaravans,
Armstrong Way,
Great Western Business Park,
Yate,
Bristol, BS37 5NG
Tel: 01454 310000
(VW Type 2 Campervans with modern conversions, Type 2 VW Brazilian imports, supply of retrofit interiors)

Davids Isopon – Through auto accessory stores (Polyester fillers and reinforcing compounds)

Design Developments,
24 Carbis Close,
Port Solent,
Portsmouth,
Hampshire,
PO6 4TW
(Barry Stimson design consultant and motorcaravan manufacturer)

Devon Conversions,
Mainsforth Road,
Ferryhill, Co Durham, DL17 9DE
Tel: 01740 655700
(Van conversion specialist)

DLS Plastics,
Occupation Lane,
Gonerby Moor,
Grantham,
Lincolnshire, NG32 2BP
Tel: 01476 564549
(Plastic components, plumbing items for motorcaravans)

Dometic Group,
Dometic House,
The Brewery,
Blandford St Mary,
Dorset, DT11 9LS
Tel: 0844 626 0133
(Formerly Electrolux Leisure; amalgamated with WAECO in 2007: Air conditioners, refrigerators, Seitz windows, Cramer cookers)

Draper Tools, Ltd,
Hursley Road,
Chandlers Ford,
Hampshire,
S053 1YF
Tel: 023 8026 6355
(Tools of all types)

Driftgate 2000 Ltd,
27 Little End Road,
Eaton Socon,
St Neots,
Cambridgeshire, PE19 8JH
Tel: 01480 470400
(Manufacturers of XCell Mains inverters; X-Calibre stage chargers)

Drinkwater Engineering
– see VB Air Suspension
(Air suspension systems, chassis work and motorhome levelling)

Driverite Air Assistance Systems
(Available through dealers - air assistance units;
NOT full air suspension)

Eberspächer (UK) Ltd,
10 Headlands Business Park,
Salisbury Road,
Ringwood,
Hampshire, BH24 3PB
Tel: 01425 480151
(Petrol and diesel-fuelled space and water heaters)

E.E. Calver Ltd,
Woodlands Park,
Bedford Road,
Clapham,
Bedford, MK41 6EJ
Tel: 01234 359584
(Indoor motorcaravan storage)

Electrolux Leisure Appliances –
See Dometic

Essanjay Motohomes,
Unit 2,
Sovereign Business Park,
48 Willis Way,
Poole,
Dorset, BH15 3TB
Tel: 01202 683608
(Motorhome and habitation servicing, components)

Europa Specialist Spares,
Fauld Industrial Estate,
Tutbury,
Burton upon Trent,
Staffordshire, DE13 9HR
Tel: 01283 815609
(Vehicle trims, light clusters, and all specialist vehicle parts)

Exhaust Ejector Co,
Wade House Road,
Shelf,
Nr. Halifax,
West Yorkshire,
HX3 7PE
Tel: 01274 679524
(Replacement acrylic windows made to order)

Exide Leisure Batteries,
Customer Services (Until 2012)
Unit 2,
Pisces,
Moseley Road,
Trafford Industrial Estate,
Manchester,
M17 1PF
Tel: 0845 4502400
(Exide base vehicle and leisure batteries)

Elddis Motorhomes,
Explorer House,
Delves Lane,
Consett,
Co Durham,
DH8 7PE
Tel: 01207 699000
(Motorcaravan manufacturer; formerly Explorer Group)

Farécla Products Ltd,
Broadmeads, Ware,
Hertfordshire, SG12 9HS
Tel: 01920 465041
(Caravan Pride G3 acrylic window scratch remover, GRP surface renovator, Mer cleaning products)

The Farnborough VW Centre,
10 Farnborough Road,
Farnborough,
Hampshire, GU14 6AY
Tel: 01252 521152
(High quality VW Campervan restorations)

Fiamma accessories – Contact your motorcaravan dealer

Fiat Auto (UK) Ltd,
Fiat House,
266 Bath Road,
Slough, SL1 4HJ
Tel: 01753 511431
(Book 'Commercial Vehicles; Manual for conversions/special outfits')

Fifth Wheel Co,
Holywell Road,
Rhuallt,
Denbighshire, LL17 0AW
Tel: 01745 583000
(Fifth Wheel leisure vehicles)

Filtapac,
2, Highcliffe, Wellingore,
Lincoln, LN5 0HG
Tel: 01522 810340
(Water filters, refills and purification products)

Foam for Comfort,
Unit 2,
Wyther Lane Trading Estate,
Wyther Lane, Kirkstall,
Leeds, LS5 3BT
Tel: 0113-274 8100
(Synthetic foam, latex, composite bonded foam)

Footman James & Co,
Waterfall Lane,
Cradley Heath,
West Midlands, B64 6PU
Tel: 0845 330 1662
(Quotations on self-built motorcaravan insurance)

Froli Kunststoffwerk Fromme GmbH,
Liemker Strasse 27,
D-33758 Schloss Holte-Stukenbrock,
Germany.
Tel: 49 (0) 52 07 - 95 00 0
(Froli bed support systems)

Gaslow International,
Castle Business Park,
Pavilion Way,
Loughborough,
Leicestershire, LE11 5GW
Tel: 0845 4000 600
(Refillable gas systems, Gaslow gauges, regulators, and components)

Gas Safe Register™,
PO BOX 6804,
Basingstoke, RG24 4NB
Tel: 0800 408 5500
(Information about Gas Safety Checks - formerly conducted by CORGI)

GB-Sol,
Unit 2,
Glan-y-Llyn Industrial Estate,
Cardiff Road,
Taff's Well,
Cardiff, CF15 7JD
Tel: 02920 820910
(Semi-Flexible lightweight solar panels)

General Ecology Europe Ltd,
St. Andrews House,
26 Brighton Road,
Crawley, RH10 6AA
Tel: 01293 400644
(Nature Pure Ultrafine water purifier)

Glen Dimplex Home Appliances,
Stoney Lane,
Prestcot,
Merseyside, L35 2XW
Tel: 0871 22 22 503
(Belling, New World, Stoves, Vanette appliances)

Grade UK Ltd,
3 Central Court,
Finch Close,
Lenton Lane Industrial Estate,
Nottingham, NG7 2NN
Tel: 0115 986 7151
(Status TV aerials and accessories)

Häfele UK Ltd,
Swift Valley Industrial Estate,
Rugby,
Warwickshire, CV21 1RD
Tel: 01788 542020
(Furniture components and hardware)

Hawke House Marine Ltd,
Unit E1,
Heritage Business Park,
Gosport,
Hampshire, PO12 4BG
Tel: 02392 588588
(Cut-from-roll Vent Air-Mat anti-condensation underlay)

HBC International A/S,
Fabriksparken 4,
DK9230 Svenstrup,
Denmark
Tel: +45 70227070
(Professional system for repairing aluminium body panels)

Hella Ltd,
Wildmere Industrial Estate,
Banbury,
Oxfordshire,
OX16 3JU Tel: 01295 272233
(Hella Towing electrical Equipment)

Hodgson Sealants,
Belprin Road, (Off Swinemoor Lane),
Beverley,
East Yorkshire, HU17 0LN
Tel: 01482 868321
(Sealants used in the caravan industry)

IMP,
RO24 3-4 Jarman Way,
Royston,
Hertfordshire, SG8 5FE
Tel: 01763 241300
(Zwaardvis high stability table pillars and sliding mechanisms)

International Tool Co,
Interlink Way South,
Bardon Hill, Coalville,
Leicestershire, LE67 1PH
Tel: 08449 395910
(Mail Order precision tyre gauges.)

JC Leisure,
Strand Garage,
Winchelsea,
East Sussex, TN36 4JT
Tel: 01797 227337
(Van conversions on various base vehicles)

John Guest Speedfit Ltd,
Horton Road,
West Drayton,
Middlesex, UB7 8JL
Tel: 01895 449233
(Push-fit plumbing couplings and pipe)

Johnnie Longden Ltd,
Unit 24, Dawkins Road
Industrial Estate, Poole,
Dorset, BH15 4JD
Tel: 01202 679121
(Accessory wholesaler supplying Henry
GE water heater to dealers)

Just Kampers,
Unit 1, Stapeley Manor,
Long Lane, Odiham,
Hampshire, RG29 1JE
Tel: 01256 862288
(VW Camper and Transporter parts
1968–2004; accessories)

Kingdom Industrial Supplies,
610, Bancrofts Road,
Eastern Industrial Estate,
Chelmsford,
Essex, CM3 5UQ
Tel: 01245 322177
(Gramos kits for repairing ABS plastic
mouldings)

Labcraft Ltd,
Sunderley Barns,
Thaxted Road,
Wimbish
Nr. Saffron Walden,
Essex, CB10 2UT
Tel: 01799 513434
(Lighting and 12V products)

Lattoflex Bed Systems,
Thomas GmbH + Co.
Sitz- und Liegemöbel KG
Walkmühlenstrasse 93
27432 Bremervörde, Germany
Tel: 0049 4761 979138
(CaraWinx mattress support systems)

Leisure Accessories,
Britannia Works,
Hurricane Way,
Airport Industrial Estate,
Norwich, NR6 6EY
Tel: 01603 414551
Diapragm pump repairs and sales.

Leisure Plus,
Unit 5, New Road Industrial Estate,
New Road, Hixon,
Staffordshire, ST18 0PJ
Tel: 01889 271692
(Wholesaler of adhesives, delamination
repair products, sealants)

Leisure-Serve UK,
8 The Buntings,
Bicester,
Oxfordshire, OX26 6WE
Tel: 01869 247936
(Supplier of refrigerator components
and accessories)

**Magnum Mobiles and Caravan
Surplus,**
Unit 9A, Cosalt Industrial Estate,
Convamore Road,
Grimsby, DN32 9JL
Tel: 01472 353520
(Caravan/Motorcaravan Surplus Stock;
bespoke building services)

Marlec Engineering,
Rutland House, Trevithick Road,
Corby,
Northamptonshire, NN17 5XY
Tel: 01536 201588
(Wind and Solar systems)

Maxview,
Common Lane,
Setchey,
King's Lynn,
Norfolk, PE33 0AT
Tel: 01553 813300
(TV aerials, satellite TV products, free
guidebooks)

Merlin Equipment,
Unit 1, Hithercroft Court,
Lupton Road,
Wallingford,
Oxfordshire,
OX10 9BT
Tel: 01491 824333
(PROwatt inverters)

Mer Products, See Farécla

Metrol Springs,
75 Tenter Road,
Moulton Park,
Northampton, NN3 6AX
Tel: (01604 499332)
(Gas struts with pressure-release bleed
valve for fine-tuning)

Middlesex Motorcaravans,
22 Station Parade.
Whitchurch Lane,
Edgware,
Middlesex,
HA8 6RW
Tel: 020 8952 4045
(Complete and part-build panel van
conversions)

Miriad Products,
Park Lane,
Dove Valley Park,
Foston,
South Derbyshire, DE65 5BG
Tel: 01283 586060
(UK Distributor of Truma parts)

Morco Products Ltd,
59 Beverley Road,
Hull, HU3 1XW
Tel: 01482 325456
(Water Heaters, accessories)

The Motor Caravanners' Club,
Wood Farm Estate,
Marlbank Road,
Welland,
Malvern, WR13 6NA
Tel: 01684 311677

Munster Simms
Engineering Ltd,
Old Belfast Road,
Bangor,
Co. Down,
Northern Ireland,
BT19 1LT
Tel: 02891 270531
(Whale heaters, semi-rigid pipework,
pumps, taps and water accessories)

Murvi,
4 East Way,
Lee Mill Industrial Estate,
Ivybridge,
Devon, PL21 9GE
Tel: 01752 892200
(Van conversion specialist)

**The National
Caravan Council,**
Catherine House,
Victoria Road,
Aldershot,
Hampshire,
GU11 1SS
Tel: 01252 318251
(Trade association for caravans and
motorhomes)

**National Inspection Council for
Electrical Installation Contracting,
(NICEIC)**
Warwick House,
Houghton Hall Park,
Houghton Regis,
Dunstable,LU5 5ZX
Tel: 01582 539000
(Certification to confirm a motorcaravan
is correctly wired for mains electricity)

The Natural Mat Company,
99 Talbot Road,
London, W11 2AT
Tel: 0207 9850474
(Slatted sprung beech bed systems,
anti-condensation underlay)

**National Trailer and Towing
Association,**
1, Alveston Place,
Leamington Spa,
Warwickshire, CV32 4SN
Tel: 01926 335445
(Trade association for all aspects of
towing equipment)

Noise Killer Acoustics (UK) Ltd,
103 Denbydale Way,
Royton,
Oldham, OL2 5UH
Tel: 0161 643 8070
(Noise reduction systems for
motorcaravans)

North East Truck+Van,
Cowpen Bewley Road,
Haverton Hill,
Billingham,
Cleveland, TS23 4EX
Tel: 01642 370555
(Major chassis alterations: Air
suspension installations)

Nu Venture Campers,
Unit 7, Actons Walk,
Wood Street,
Wigan,
Lancashire, WN3 4HN
Tel: 01942 238560
(Motorcaravans built to customer
specification)

Nu Venture Motor Homes,
Unit 2,
Seven Stars Road,
Wallgate,
Wigan,
Lancashire, WN3 5AT
Tel: 01942 494090
(Motorcaravans built to customer
specification)

O'Leary Spares and Accessories,
314 Plaxton Bridge Road,
Woodmansey,
Nr Beverley,
East Yorkshire, HU17 0RS
Tel: 01482 868632
(Caravan/Motorcaravan surplus stock)

Osma rainwater products
– Sold through Builders' Merchants
(Osma weld adhesive used for waste
pipes and tank connections)

Parma Industries,
34-36 Carlton Park Industrial Estate,
Saxmundham,
Suffolk, IP17 2NL
Tel: 01728 745700
(Wheel trims, dashboard plastic veneer,
general accessories)

Pennine Leisure Supplies,
Unit G9,
Lock View,
Elland,
West Yorkshire, HX5 9HD
Tel: 01422 313455
(Wholesaler of accessories and BCA
Powerpart products)

Pleitner's PS Wohnmobil GmbH,
Laerstrasse 16,
33775 Versmold,
Deutschland.
Tel: 0049 054 23 20 40 0
www.pleitner.de
(Dealer linked with VW based Athano
self build A Class)

Plug-In-Systems – Contact your
motorcaravan dealer (12V control
components, water level sensors,
gauges)

Powerpart 230v accessories – See
Pennine Leisure

Propex Heat Source Ltd.,
Unit 5,
Second Avenue Business Park,
Millbrook,
Southampton, SO15 0LP
Tel: 023 8052 8555
www.propexheatsource.co.uk
(Propex compact blown air gas heaters;
Malaga Mk II water heater)

Pro-Tow
Unit 1, 565 Blandford Road,
Hamworthy, Poole,
Dorset, BH16 5BW
Tel: 01202 632488
(Car-a-Tow towing frames; Solar
Solutions solar panels)

PWS,
Unit 5,
Chalwyn Industrial Estate,
Old Wareham Road,
Parkstone, Dorset, BH12 4PE
Tel: 01202 746851
(Racks, protector bars, custom-made
tow bars)

Rainbow Conversions,
Unit 1 Algores Way,
Wisbech,
Cambridgeshire, PE13 2TQ
Tel: 01945 585931
(Van conversions built to order;
Vöhringer ply & accessories)

Regal Furnishings,
Unit 4,
Merlin Way,
Quarry Hill Industrial Estate,
Ilkeston,
Derbyshire, DE7 4RA
Tel: 01159 329988
(Upholstery, foam, bespoke curtains)

Remis UK, – Through accessory
dealers (Remis blinds, flyscreens, roof
windows)

RoadPro Ltd,
Stephenson Close,
Drayton Fields,
Daventry,
Northamptonshire, NN11 5RF
Tel: 01327 312233
(Accessories, chargers, reversing aids,
TVs)

Russek Publications,
Unit 6, 29a Ardler Road,
Caversham,
Reading,
Berkshire, RG4 5AE
Tel: 0845 0942130
(Vehicle repair manuals including Talbot
Express models)

Ryder Towing Equipment Ltd,
Alvanley House,
Alvanley Industrial Estate,
Stockport Road East,
Bredbury,
Stockport, SK6 2DJ
Tel: 0161 430 1120
(Electrical towing equipment)

Sargent Electrical Services, Ltd,
Unit 39,
Tokenspire Business Park,
Woodmansey,
Beverley, HU17 0TB
Tel: 01452 678987
(12V controls and panels)

Seitz Windows – See Dometic Group

The Self Build Motorcaravanners Club,
PO BOX 3345,
Littlehampton,BN16 9FU
www.sbmcc.co.uk

SF Detection,
Hatch Pond House,
4 Stinsford Road,
Poole,
Dorset, BH17 0RZ
Tel: 01202 645577
(Carbon monoxide detectors, LP Gas alarms)

Shield Total Insurance,
Floor 9,
Market Square House,
St James's Street,
Nottingham, NG1 6FG
Freephone 0800 39 30 33
(Motorcaravan insurance including Self-builds)

Ship Shape Bedding,
Turners Farm,
Crowgate Street,
Tunstead,
Norfolk, NR12 8RD
Tel: 08704 464233
(Cut-from-roll DRY Mat™ Anti-condensation mattress underlay)

SHURflo Ltd,
Unit 5, Sterling Park,
Gatwick Road,
Crawley, RH10 9QT
Tel: 01293 424000
(Water pumps)

Sika Ltd,
Watchmead,
Welwyn Garden City,
Hertfordshire, AL7 1BQ
Tel: 01707 394444
(Sikaflex cartridge sealants and adhesive sealants)

Silver Screens,
P.O. Box 9, Cleckheaton,
West Yorkshire, BD19 5YR
Tel: 01274-872151
(Insulated window covers)

Single Vehicle Approval Scheme (SVA) – See Appendix B.

The Society of Motor Manufacturers and Traders,
71 Great Peter Street,
London, SW1P 2BN
Tel: 020 7235 7000

Sold Secure Trust,
5c Great Central Way,
Woodford Halse,
Daventry,
Northamptonshire, NN11 3PZ
Tel: 01327 264687
(Test House conducting security device testing)

Spinflo – See Thetford (UK)

Sterling Power Products,
Unit 8, Wassage Way,
Droitwich, WR9 0NX
Tel: 01905 277771
(Chargers, inverters and related products)

Stoves plc,
Company name changed to:
Glen Dimplex Cooking Ltd,
Stoney Lane, Prescot,
Merseyside, L35 2XW
Tel: 0151 426 6551
(Grills, Hobs, Ovens)

SvTech,
Chandler House,
Talbot Road, Leyland,
Lancashire, PR25 2ZF
(Specialist consultants on weight up-grades and official weight plate alterations)

Symonspeed Ltd,
Cleveland Garage,
1 Cleveland Road,
Torquay,
Devon, TQ2 5BD
Tel: 01803 214620
(SOG toilet system)

TEK Seating Ltd,
Unit 32, Pate Road,
Leicester Road Industrial Estate,
Melton Mowbray,
Leicestershire, LE13 0RG
Tel: 01664 480689
(Cab seating, seat swivels, seat bases and upholstery)

Thetford (UK) Spinflo,
4-10 Welland Close,
Parkwood Industrial Estate,
Rutland Road,
Sheffield, S3 9QY
Tel: 01142 738157
(Norcold refrigerators, toilets and treatments, Spinflo cooking appliances)

TOWtal,
Grove Road,
Stoke-on-Trent, ST4 4LN
Tel: 01782 333422
('A' Frames, electric brake actuators, trailers, scooter racks, tow bars)

Trade Grade Products,
Unit 2, Thorne Way,
Wimborne,
Dorset, BH21 6FB
Tel: 01202 820177
(Injection adhesive kits for repairing delaminating floors)

Truma UK,
Truma House, Beeches Park,
Eastern Avenue,
Burton-upon-Trent,
Staffordshire, DE13 0BB
Tel: 01283 511092
(Space and water heating systems, gas components, Carver spares)

Trylon Ltd,
Unit J, Higham Business Park,
Bury Close,
Higham Ferrers,
Northamptonshire, NN10 8HQ
Tel: 01933 411724
(Resins, glass and guidance on glass reinforced plastics)

The 12Volt Shop,
9 Lostwood Road,
St Austell,
Cornwall, PL25 4 JN
Tel: 01726 69102
(Mail Order of 12V electrical components)

Tyron Safety Bands,
Castle Business Park,
Pavilion Way,
Loughborough,
Leicestershire, LE11 5GW
Tel: 0845 4000 600
(Safety bands for filling wheel wells)

Van Bitz,
Cornish Farm, Shoreditch,
Taunton,
Somerset, TA3 7BS
Tel: 01823-321992
(Strikeback T Thatcham-Approved security, gas alarm, Battery Master)

Van Window Specialists,
Unit 4, Riverside Works,
Methley Road,
Castleford,
West Yorkshire, WF10 1PW
Tel: 01977 552929
(Made-to-measure windows, supply and fit, VW van conversions)

Varta Automotive Batteries,
Broadwater Park,
North Orbital Road,
Denham,
Uxbridge,
Middlesex, UB9 5HR
Tel: 01895 838989
(Leisure batteries, including Gel batteries)

VB Air Suspension,
Unit 13, Elder Court,
Lions Drive,
Shadsworth Business Park,
Blackburn,
Lancashire, BB1 2EQ
Tel: 01254 848010
(Full air suspension systems, air assistance and jacking products)

Vehicle & Marine Window Co.,
Victoria Street,
Birmingham, B9 5AA
Tel: 0121 772 6307
(Window manufacturers, fitters and suppliers)

The Vehicle & Operator Service Agency,
91/92 The Strand,
Swansea, SA1 2DH
Tel: 0870 60 60 440
www.vosa.gov.uk/
(Vehicle legislation and general enquiries)

V & G Caravans,
107 Benwick Road,
Whittlesey, Peterborough,
Cambridgeshire, PE7 2HD
Tel: 01733 350580
(Replacement replica panels in GRP)

WAECO UK products
– See Dometic Group

Watling Engineers Ltd,
88 Park Street Village,
nr. St. Albans,
Hertfordshire, AL2 2LR
Tel: 01727 873661
(Specially designed towing brackets)

Webasto Products UK Ltd,
Webasto House,
White Rose Way, Doncaster Carr,
South Yorkshire, DN4 5JH
Tel: 01302 322232
(Diesel-fuelled heaters, water evaporative air conditioners)

Whale – see Munster Simms
(Water accessories)

Wheelhome,
Tip's Cross,
Blackmore Road, Hook End,
Brentwood,
Essex, CM 15 0DX
Tel: 01277 822208
(Specialist building compact motorcaravans from MPVs)

Witter Towbars,
Drome Road,
Deeside Industrial Park,
Deeside,
Chester, CH5 2NY
Tel: 01244 284500
(Towbars and cycle carriers)

Woodfit Ltd,
Kem Mill,
Whittle-le-Woods,
Chorley,
Lancashire, PR6 7EA
Tel: 01257 266421
(Hinges, fittings, hardware, wire storage baskets and catches)

Woolies,
off Blenheim Way,
Northfields Industrial Estate,
Market Deeping,
Peterborough, PE6 8LD
Tel: 01778 347347
(Trim, accessories and window rubbers)

W4 Ltd,
Unit B,
Ford Lane Industrial Estate,
Arundel,
West Sussex, BN18 0DF
Tel: 01243 553355
(Mains 230V kits, socket testers, ribbon sealants)

Young Conversions,
Unit 47, Barton Road,
Water Eaton,
Bletchley,
Milton Keynes,
Buckinghamshire, MK2 3BD
Tel: 01908 639 936
(Full or part conversions on any base vehicle, stage payment conversion, one-off designs)

ZIG Electronics, Ltd,
Saxon Business Park,
Hanbury Road,
Stoke Prior,
Bromsgrove,
Worcestershire, B60 4AD
Tel: 01527 556715
(12V controls, chargers, water level sensors and gauges)

Zippo UK,
Unit 27,
Grand Union Centre,
336B Ladbroke Grove,
London W10 5AS
Tel: 020 8964 0666
(General purpose large-size gas lighters)

Zwaardvis – See IMP
(High quality table support systems and accessories)

3M Co,
(Minnesota Mining and Manufacturing Co.)
To find local supplier
Tel: 0161 237 6130 or
(Manufacturer of Thinsulate thermal insulation)

Index

Author Acknowledgements

The Motorcaravan Manual embraces many technical topics and I am indebted to the experts whose advice, encouragement and photographs have helped me to write and illustrate this book. I would particularly like to thank:

Sophie Blackman:	Editorial Assistant, Haynes Publishing
Colin George:	Antenna installation photographs
Nick Howard:	Permission to watch crash testing and cold chamber research
Simon Howard:	Front cover main photograph
Jeremy Harris:	Senior Technical Manager, Dometic Group – proofreading
John Harvey:	Technical Support Manager, Dometic Group – proofreading
Lorraine Houghton:	Motorcaravan photography
Paul Jones:	Marketing Manager, AL-KO Kober UK – proofreading
Gordon King:	Commercial Director, BCA Leisure – technical advice
Louise McIntyre:	Project Manager, Haynes Publishing
Middlesex Motorcaravans:	Photographs of installation work
Jon Redish:	Director, Caravan Seat Cover Centre – Factory photography
David Sellick:	VW Project Van photography
Martin Spencer:	Technical Manager of The Caravan Club – Appendix